CATHOLIC HIGHER EDUCATION
IN PROTESTANT AMERICA

THE JOHNS HOPKINS UNIVERSITY PRESS

CATHOLIC HIGHER EDUCATION IN PROTESTANT AMERICA

*The Jesuits and Harvard
in the Age of the University*

KATHLEEN A. MAHONEY

THE JOHNS HOPKINS UNIVERSITY PRESS
Baltimore and London

© 2003 The Johns Hopkins University Press
All rights reserved. Published 2003
Printed in the United States of America on acid-free paper
9 8 7 6 5 4 3 2 1

The Johns Hopkins University Press
2715 North Charles Street
Baltimore, Maryland 21218-4363

www.press.jhu.edu

Library of Congress Cataloging-in-Publication Data
Mahoney, Kathleen A.
    Catholic higher education in Protestant America : the Jesuits and Harvard
in the age of the university / Kathleen A. Mahoney.
        p. cm.
    Includes bibliographical references (p.   ) and index.
    ISBN 0-8018-7340-1 (alk. paper)
    1. Church and college—United States—History.   2. Catholics—
Education (Higher)—United States—History.   3. Catholic universities and
colleges—United States.   4. Jesuits—Education (Higher)—United States.
5. Protestant churches—United States—Relations—Catholic Church—
History.   6. Harvard University—Administration—History.   I. Title.
    LC383.M325 2003
    378'.0088'22—dc21   2002013624

A catalog record for this book is available from the British Library.

For my parents, Neil and Dorothy

CONTENTS

ACKNOWLEDGMENTS

I wish to thank the many people who have helped me write this book. They have been generous in their support and insightful in their feedback. This book is better for their assistance.

This study began to take shape, first as a seminar paper, then as a doctoral dissertation, while I was a student at the University of Rochester. I am grateful to members of the faculty—Mary Young, Harold Wechsler, Lynn Gordon, and especially to my advisor, Bruce Kimball—for stoking my interest in history and introducing me to the historical craft.

My debts to those who helped me locate source material are numerous. The archivists and librarians from the following institutions were particularly helpful: Boston College, Georgetown University, the Catholic University of America, the University of Notre Dame, Harvard University, the University of Rochester, and the Jesuit archives in Rome. I am also indebted to Jesuit friends and colleagues: Joseph Appleyard, Howard Gray, Anthony Kuzniewski, R. Emmett Curran, and the late

Charles Donovan, who graciously shared materials with me and, more importantly, helped me sharpen my understanding of Jesuit history and culture. I also wish to thank those who helped me translate documents from Latin; George Pepe of Washington University in St. Louis deserves special mention, as do members of the classics department of Boston College.

The Spencer Foundation furnished generous assistance on three occasions. A dissertation fellowship, followed by a postdoctoral fellowship through the National Academy of Education, made sustained periods of writing possible. The foundation's support also enabled me to use the Jesuit archives in Rome.

I am especially grateful for those who read and commented on drafts of this work. George Marsden, John Schmalzbauer, Howard Gray, Dennis Shirley, Julie Reuben, and an anonymous reviewer each made valuable suggestions. Philip Gleason and Caroline Winterer read the manuscript in its entirety more than once; I deeply appreciate their attention to detail and, even more, many enjoyable conversations. I would also like to thank those who provided encouragement: Bill Durbin, Peter Robinson, Hugh Hawkins, Jim Youniss, and my amiable colleagues in the higher education program of the Lynch School of Education at Boston College, Philip Altbach, Karen Arnold, Diana Pullin, Ted Youn, and Ana Martinez Aleman. My research assistants—Andrew Simmons, Lisabeth Timothy, Krisitn Hunt, Kate McKee, Sara Luddy, and Mandy Savitz—also have my thanks. I would be remiss not to mention my editor, Jackie Wehmueller, whose encouragement and advice have meant a great deal to me.

For many years my friends and family have listened with unflagging patience as I have described the ins and outs of writing this book. Without a doubt, they now know more about the history of Jesuit higher education than they ever wanted to know. What I really want them to know is how very much I appreciate them and their support.

CATHOLIC HIGHER EDUCATION IN
PROTESTANT AMERICA

Introduction

The year 1893 will be the turning
point in educational life.

—Rev. P. J. Muldoon on the
Catholic educational exhibit at the
Chicago World's Fair, 1893

American higher education, from its colonial beginnings through the
second half of the twentieth century, was profoundly shaped by Protestantism. This holds true not only for Protestant higher education but also
Catholic. Established to serve the religious and educational needs of
American Catholics and their church, Catholic higher education was ineluctably affected by the fact that it developed in a "nation with the soul
of a church," whose social, cultural, and intellectual life drew deeply
from the Protestant tradition. From its inception, Protestantism in the
United States assumed a profound sense of mission rooted in the widely
held and powerful belief that God intended America to stand as a light to
the nations of the world, to be a city upon the hill, rendering visible the
designs of a providential creator. Toward such impressive ends, the religious majority pressed its churches and voluntary associations, cultural
institutions and presses, schools and colleges into the cause of a Protestant America. Absent an appreciation of this Protestant agenda, the

history of education in the United States, whether Protestant or Catholic, is largely incomprehensible.[1]

Thus for the Roman Catholic minority, the project of higher education has entailed the complex task of contending with Protestantism, wrestling not only with anti-Catholic sentiment but Protestantism's profound influence in society and culture exercised through its educational institutions. Defining the boundaries of engagement with American Protestantism and Protestant America has shaped Catholic higher education, determining in large measure the degree to which it has been able to achieve academic respectability and social relevance in the American context while maintaining its Catholic character.

This book explores the vital relationship between religion and higher education in the nineteenth and early-twentieth centuries and how an academic revolution in the postbellum era, signaled by the emergence of the modern university and its ascent to the apex of a reconstituted academic order, affected Catholic participation in American higher education. More precisely, it delineates the challenges faced by Catholics in the closing decades of the nineteenth century as the age of the university opened: how liberal Protestant leaders of the university movement linked the newly created modern university with the cause of a Protestant America, and how Catholic students and educators variously resisted, accommodated, or embraced Protestant-inspired educational reforms during this revolutionary era in higher education. It was a formative and critical period: a new academic order was coming to fruition, and Catholic responses were not inconsequential. Postbellum changes in America's academic landscape endured. The ramifications of decisions made by Catholics in the midst and wake of this academic upheaval persisted. They are still felt today as Catholic colleges and universities struggle to come to terms with what it means to be a Catholic institution of higher learning in modern America.[2]

This academic revolution in higher education, wherein the age of the college gave way to the age of the university, was keenly felt by those associated with the denominational colleges that had dominated the academic landscape for most of the nineteenth century. Their disparate religious loyalties notwithstanding, hundreds of Catholic and Protestant institutions founded in that century bore notable similarities: clergymen presidents, largely if not entirely prescribed curricula with heavy emphases on the classics, small student bodies drawn primarily from local youth, and discipline saturated with piety.[3] Then, rather suddenly, hundreds of years of relative stability and homogeneity, owing much to Eng-

lish and Continental collegiate traditions and that of Christian humanism, gave way in a burst of academic reforms and changes in student
demographics during the last three decades of the nineteenth century.
Recently come of age, modern science triggered a prodigious expansion
of knowledge; under the weight of this new burden, the relatively staid
liberal arts curriculum fragmented—into disciplinary specialties for the
faculty, and majors, elective courses, and new degrees for the students.
The colleges themselves became more complex institutions, and a variety of new academic institutions, such as normal schools, business institutes, and university-based professional schools, carved out niches in
the educational landscape. The number and percentage of persons seeking advanced education increased significantly, and the student population became more diverse. Unknown just a few decades earlier, by the
end of the nineteenth century the modern American university was well
established.[4]

It was in the midst of this academic tumult that the modern research
university displaced the denominational college and moved to the head
of an increasingly regularized and systematized academic order. Indeed,
it can be argued that this academic coup d'état can be dated precisely.
The universities gained from the colleges the lion's share of student enrollment during the 1890s, and sharp, even exponential growth in the
number of colleges at midcentury decelerated and then ended in 1893.
In 1892, the Columbia University president, Seth Low, noted the displacement: "Time was when the college was the top of the educational
system in the United States," but "it is so no longer, and it never can become so again."[5]

The historical segue between the age of the college and the age of the
university signaled a basic reconceptualization and shift in emphases in
the aims of higher education driven largely by the success of industrial
capitalism. Usually offering little more than what we would now understand as high-school-level instruction, nineteenth-century denominationally affiliated colleges provided the nation's villages, towns, and cities with important cultural and intellectual resources. They trained the
clergy, educated citizens, engendered civic pride, fostered piety, offered
intellectual entrée into the worlds of classical antiquity, and through
public lectures, concerts, plays, and recitations added a patina of culture
to frontier towns.[6] Proponents of academic reform and the modern university deemed this type of education inadequate. "Should not a university," asked the president of the Johns Hopkins University, answer the
"wants of today?"[7] Many were convinced that the educational wants of

the day differed significantly from those of past generations. Fueled by the belief that the social and technological changes that Americans had witnessed in their lifetimes constituted a vast improvement in the human condition, forward-looking citizens' enthusiasm for "modern progress" grew; as it did, classical liberal arts colleges appeared moribund. The study of the "dead" languages of Greece and Rome and ancient European civilizations, the heart of the collegiate curriculum for centuries, seemed useless and irrelevant.[8] And thus a chorus of educational reformers arose, praising the utilitarian: the United States needed modern, innovative institutions that allowed collegians to master useful, practical, relevant subjects, especially the sciences, which fueled the engines of national progress.[9]

The persons most responsible for this academic revolution constituted a remarkable band of university presidents who "seized the initiative in American higher education after the war in the way that John D. Rockefeller seized it in oil, Andrew Carnegie in steel, Washington Duke in tobacco."[10] Charles W. Eliot, the renowned president of Harvard University (1869–1909), stood foremost in an august group that included, among others, Daniel Coit Gilman of the Johns Hopkins University (1876–1901), Andrew Dickson White of Cornell University (1867–85), James B. Angell of the University of Michigan (1871–1909), David Starr Jordan of Stanford University (1891–1913), and William Rainey Harper of the University of Chicago (1891–1906). Drawing their religious inspiration from liberal Protestantism and invoking the cause of Protestant America, the university builders' most immediate objective was the creation of an academic institution responsive to the needs of a modern nation.[11] Their broader but no less vital mission was the improvement of education at large, which, they claimed, suffered from a deplorable lack of standards, organization, and oversight. Bringing the colleges under the beneficent, constructive influence of the more enlightened, progressive universities would, in their view, substantially contribute to the improvement of higher education and, by extension, the good of the nation. Harper, the president of the University of Chicago, who considered prospects for the colleges in the age of the university rather dim, took big business as his model. "Why should not this university erected at Chicago," queried President Harper of benefactor Rockefeller, act as an "educational trust" for a "score of colleges with a large degree of uniformity in their management?"[12]

The great university builders of the late-nineteenth century deserve much of the credit for the system of higher education we have today, but

certainly not all of it. Students drove the transformation of higher education in a number of critical ways. They "grew" the colleges and universities, with the national rate of attendance roughly doubling between 1870
and 1900.[13] And students insisted that their education be useful. Just as
previous generations of students mastered Latin and Greek in preparation for careers in ministry or statecraft, those in the second half of the
nineteenth century sought advanced education to prepare themselves for
a world of work reshaped by the industrial revolution. But this generation
understood something more clearly: they went to college in pursuit of
valuable academic credentials and desirable social networks that would
help them to get ahead in their future professional endeavors. While
university builders reformed higher education institutionally and organizationally, students transformed it socially, bequeathing to future generations now-familiar patterns and structures of popular student life. Athletics staked an immense claim on the academy, and club life came of
age as students insisted, vigorously and successfully, that the four years
spent in college be fun—as much social as intellectual in nature.[14]

A tenacious mainstay of American higher education, the nation's denominationally affiliated colleges thus faced two critical challenges in
the decades following the Civil War. Organizationally, changes realized
during the course of the academic revolution mirror the broad movement
outlined in Robert Wiebe's exploration of Americans' turn-of-the-century "search for order": during the century's final two decades, colleges
that in the antebellum period operated as "island communities" were ineluctably drawn into the "distended society" of modern higher education.[15] Though never subject to the degree of oversight envisioned by
Harper, the universities came to exercise considerable influence over
the colleges. They did so through major educational associations, nascent accreditation programs, early standardization efforts, and the development of admission standards. Just as significantly, the universities
seriously competed with the colleges for students, who increasingly bypassed the smaller institutions, favoring the new, larger ones. Only in
the 1910s, after decades of anxiety and experimentation, did the colleges secure a firm niche in the new academic order, emerging as the
quintessential embodiment of the undergraduate experience, the traditional home of the liberal arts, and as feeder institutions for the universities' new graduate and professional schools.[16]

This book focuses on the vicissitudes of Jesuit higher education
during this revolutionary era, looking closely at the role of religion—
Protestant and Catholic—in shaping social and institutional patterns of

Catholic participation in higher education. By 1900 there were approximately five dozen Roman Catholic colleges sponsored by various religious orders, with the Jesuits (formally known as the Society of Jesus) holding primacy of place with almost half of these institutions under their direction. Like Protestant colleges, through most of the nineteenth century Catholic institutions enjoyed a significant degree of autonomy, subject only to the pressures of the market and some oversight from their sponsoring religious bodies. Institutional autonomy notwithstanding, in curriculum, discipline, and scale of operations, homogeneity marked much of Catholic higher education (as it did, too, in Protestant circles). Yet the status of Catholic colleges as a subset within higher education was not merely a case of distinction without difference: their identification with Roman Catholicism set them apart as a subculture within the broader ecology of Protestant-dominated American higher education. The sponsorship of Catholic colleges by religious orders largely explains their distinctiveness. Members of religious orders led relatively circumscribed lives. They taught, lived, studied, worshipped, and socialized in relatively small groups in or in close proximity to the colleges they staffed.[17] Rather than looking to the proceedings of the National Educational Association, the pages of the *Educational Review*, or other contemporary sources for their educational ideals and strategies, they turned to one another and their European predecessors.[18] Moreover, they and their students were part of a religious minority, and they often belonged to ethnic cohorts close to the experience of immigration—realities that often complicated and sometimes strained their relationship with Protestant society. Furthermore, their affiliation with the Roman Catholic Church made it nearly impossible for Jesuit and other Catholic educators to weave their colleges into the broader story about the United States, the great Protestant nation.

Unbidden, the storm and stress of the academic revolution arrived belatedly and unequivocally in the late 1890s, when two interrelated crises forced the Jesuits and other Catholic educators to reckon with the rise of a new academic order. In the Catholic educational community, where three decades of intellectual and academic ferment had gone largely ignored, Harvard Law School's refusal to recognize the diplomas of Jesuit colleges in its newly adopted admission process shook Catholics out of their complacency. As tensions between Harvard officials and Jesuit college presidents erupted in 1900 into a full-blown, nationally publicized controversy, the growing influence of the universities, as well as the limitations and vulnerabilities of Catholic higher education, became strikingly and undeniably apparent. The second crisis involved Catholic students' enrollment patterns. A survey published in 1898 revealed that most Catholic collegians were enrolled in non-Catholic institutions—a finding that rattled Catholic educators, whose colleges were often undersubscribed. Thus the power of the universities emerged not only as an institutional force but as a social reality, with the major nonsectarian universities, including Harvard, drawing numerous Catholics into their halls. As the age of the university opened, the Jesuits quickly lost their equanimity. Publicly criticized by officials from Harvard and ignored by a significant portion of their own constituency, the Jesuits were plunged into a state of crisis and deep concern for the fate of their colleges.

Beset by formidable challenges, the Jesuits took up the pressing academic issues of the day with a sudden urgency at the turn of the century, seeking ways to respond to the new academic order without abandoning their educational ideals or sacrificing the religious identity of their schools. They wrestled with the implications of the Protestant-inspired university movement and fretted over enrollments. In pursuit of sound learning, curricular coherence, appropriate discipline, and more students, they vigorously debated what constituted worthwhile innovation or made for academic faddishness. But unlike their Protestant counterparts, the Jesuits and other Catholic educators took on this critical project as members of a religious minority who had established schools and colleges as a means of communicating the faith to Catholic students in a Protestant-dominated country. Protestants, both conservatives and the reform-minded, were able to invoke the cause of a Protestant America, either to support or resist reform, but Catholics' status as members of a religious minority complicated the ways in which they could respond to the reforms that remade much of higher education. More broadly, they were part of a complex, international church struggling intensely to come to terms with the modern world and, with it, some of the very forces that had given rise to the American university and a new academic order.

Religion shaped and reshaped American higher education throughout its first three centuries. In 1636, just six years after arriving in the New World, the Puritans of the Massachusetts Bay Company established Harvard College to help train a ministerial class. To the nine successful colleges established in the colonial era, hundreds more were added in the antebellum period as the evangelical fervor of the Second Great Awakening deepened the young country's self-identification with Protestantism. As local centers of piety and learning, gospel and culture, colleges in the reformed tradition sat squarely in the civic-religious matrix of Protestant nationalism. Pushing westward across the frontier, the Protestant majority peppered the landscape with colleges in the hope that students and graduates, pious and lettered, would civilize and Christianize the West. Such colleges, proponents argued, were essential for America to realize its providential destiny as a Protestant nation.[19]

As Protestants founded colleges to advance their religious agenda for America, Catholics launched college-building efforts on behalf of "our holy religion" and "our youth." Like educators associated with Protestant colleges, Catholic educators held fast to the ideal of producing Christian gentlemen who were versed in the classics and faithful to their religion. They, too, claimed to be educating youth to be good citizens. But civic rhetoric among Catholics belies complex social realities. One hears in Catholics' efforts to build colleges for "our youth" in the service of "our religion" the ever-present "theirs" of the Protestant majority. Although Protestant and Catholic colleges were in practice similar, they assumed different socioreligious functions: while Protestants aspired to build a Christian empire, Catholics sought to develop and sustain a religious subculture. Eager to prove to an often deeply skeptical Protestant populace that they were good citizens, it behooved Catholics to stress Catholic education's contribution to the civic commonweal. Yet Catholic educators needed to highlight the fundamental difference between Protestant and Catholic colleges; namely, the latter's affiliation with the "one true religion." Catholic colleges were mechanisms for building a Catholic subculture, ensuring that the most highly educated members of the Roman Catholic Church would hold fast to Catholicism and resist the sway of Protestantism. Herein lay the fundamental rationale for a separate educational system.[20]

During the age of the college, religion shaped higher education along confessional lines; during the academic revolution, religion helped reshape higher education, with liberal Protestantism playing patron to the modern, nonsectarian university. George M. Marsden, Julie A. Reuben, and other historians have documented the modern university's deep debts to liberal Protestantism.[21] Drawn from the liberal end of the religious continuum, the men at the forefront of the university movement harnessed religious liberalism's growing vitality within nineteenth-century American Protestantism in the service of educational reform. Wearied by decades of fractious denominational rivalry and horrified by the carnage of the Civil War, many Americans moved toward a more liberal version of Christianity. In the name of "true Christianity" they abandoned the pessimism of their Calvinist ancestors in favor of a more optimistic view of human nature, setting aside contentious dogmas and creeds in favor of a Christian life construed in ethical terms. Finding fullest expression in the development of Unitarianism, this flexible, less dogmatic approach to religion seeped into mainline Protestantism, setting the stage religiously for the rise of explicitly nonsectarian universities that welcomed students of all religious persuasions—including Catholics. To many, the new, nonsectarian universities appeared more enlightened and socially beneficial than "narrow" denominational colleges still tied to their respective denominations and a lamentable history of religious rivalry and dissension.

Theological modernism, the conviction that the ancient faith should adapt to the modern world,[22] helped religious liberalism underwrite the academic revolution. The university reformers shook off the encumbrances of sectarian affiliation not merely to affect social harmony. As legatees of the Reformation and the Enlightenment, leaders and proponents of the university movement believed that sectarianism shackled men's minds to an outdated past and intellectually suspect creedal formulations. In an era of marvelous scientific vitality and wondrous technological progress (a certain sign of God's favor), the leaders of the academic revolution were adamant about the necessity of free inquiry, both as a condition of scientific inquiry and national progress and as a means to higher moral ends and more enlightened religious understanding. Freeing higher education from "dogmatism," an undesirable vestige of its medieval past, was an important step toward a progressively better and Christian future for Protestant America.[23]

In Catholic circles, liberalism and modernism (the latter to a far lesser degree) also encouraged participation in the university movement and engagement with modern intellectual life. Though the Catholic Church expended considerable energies challenging modernity in the nineteenth and early twentieth centuries, the Catholic community was not entirely free from liberalism and modernism. Compared with Europe, there were few bona fide modernists in the United States, but there was a well-known cadre of high-ranking, liberal clergymen. These men reached the peak of their influence in the 1890s and played important roles in the founding and leadership of the Catholic University of America during its early years.[24] As historian Philip Gleason points out, the university's establishment, a landmark in U.S. Catholic higher education, signaled support in some quarters for the university ideal and a desire to contribute to modern intellectual life. But the Catholic University and its liberal supporters led an increasingly troubled existence, with the latter running afoul of the church's increasingly strident campaign against modernity.[25] Hardly enamored with the modern world, the papacy of the nineteenth century issued numerous condemnations of liberalism and the modern heresies it spawned. Orchestrated in large measure by the European-based leadership of the Society of Jesus, the campaign culminated in 1907 with the promulgation of *Pascendi Dominici Gregis,* wherein Pius X condemned "modernism" as the "synthesis of all heresies" and the misbegotten legacy of Luther's reforming spirit.

Catholics, therefore, entered the fray of the academic revolution largely deprived of the theological resources that served liberal Protestants so well. With a broad, flexible theology, these Protestants had stretched a sacred canopy over the modern academy, simply sanctifying the whole project of reform.[26] Lacking such theological resources and operating as a religious minority in a Protestant-dominated country, Catholics were ill-prepared to join forces with the academic revolution. As Gleason ably described it, they were contending with modernity and the forces reshaping the academy, but doing so without the resources of religious liberalism and theological modernism.

As scholars have recognized, the papacy's hostile judgment on Protestant-inspired modernism largely foreclosed Catholic engagement with the intellectual mainstream for most of the twentieth century.[27] More broadly, this oppositional, defensive posture vis-à-vis the modern world filtered through the Society of Jesus, an order internationally renowned for its work in the field of education. Its effects left many Jesuits more disposed to resist the exigencies of a new academic order than to adapt to it, for a number of them, especially those in leadership positions in Rome, could see in modern American higher education little but the disordered effects of its Protestant patrimony.

As the largest and most influential group of Catholic educators, the Jesuits have functioned as a bellwether for much of Catholic higher education; thus their responses to the academic revolution reveal a great deal about the broader state of American Catholic higher education.[28] Founded in 1540 by Ignatius of Loyola, the Jesuits garnered immense fame over the centuries for their remarkable exploits in the remotest corners of the globe as explorers, missionaries, pastors, political operatives, and educators. In the field of education their achievements were unparalleled. By 1773 their educational institutions numbered eight hundred, forming a vast network of schools—one that, according to historian John W. O'Malley, the "world had never seen before nor has it seen since."[29]

In 1900, Jesuit institutions of advanced education could be found in Europe, the Middle East, the Far East, and throughout the United States, where the Jesuits' ventures in higher education began in 1789 with the establishment of Georgetown Academy, which evolved into the nation's first Catholic college. With colleges subsequently established on the East and West coasts, in the Pacific Northwest, Midwest, and the deep South, the Jesuits came to dominate Catholic higher education in the nineteenth and early twentieth centuries, with approximately two dozen colleges under their direction by 1900. Currently there are approximately 230 Catholic colleges and universities in the United States; twenty-eight, including some of the larger and more notable, are sponsored by the Jesuits.[30] No other religious order has come close to this number.

Revered by their supporters and reviled by their foes, the Jesuits brought to their legendary labors in education two critical, complementary resources that go far in explaining their striking success. The first was the *Ratio Atque Institutio Studiorum Societatis Iesu*. A plan of studies formalized in 1599 after decades of trial-and-error experimentation, the influential and widely emulated *Ratio Studiorum* set forth the aims, principles, methods, and pedagogical strategies that came to define Jesuit education. The second resource the Jesuits brought to their work in education was less tangible but no less important: in the section devoted to education, the *Constitutions* of the Society directed Jesuits to adapt their educational practices as necessary to suit the "places, times, and persons" they encountered. The balance struck between the structure of the *Ratio Studiorum* and the flexibility encouraged by the *Constitutions* served the peripatetic Jesuits immensely well, whether in the courts of China, the jungles of Latin America, or frontier outposts along the Mississippi.[31]

The directive in the Society's *Constitutions* to adapt their educational practices to the places, times, and persons they encountered marks an openness to the world and cultures that was recognized by contemporaries and historians as quintessentially Jesuit and essential to their resounding success as a religious order. Ignatius and the men who bound themselves together in the work of "helping souls" envisioned a religious order deeply engaged with the world, not in flight from it. Abjuring monastic ideals and traditions that still shaped much of sixteenth-century clerical life, members of the Society of Jesus saw and sought God in the everyday experiences of the world. Their openness to other cultures, even those radically different from their own, made them tremendously effective missionaries. Their willingness to draw from the pedagogical storehouses of others made them excellent educators. Their propensity to see the hand of God in the workings of the world fostered intellectual curiosity and scholarly devotion, the fruits of which won for them a notable reputation in humanistic studies and early modern science in Renaissance Europe.[32]

Three centuries after the *Ratio Studiorum* was developed and the *Constitutions* were written, the rise of a new academic order in American higher education critically tested the Jesuits' ability and willingness to adapt to new circumstances. Reform and innovation swept through the academy; traditional forms of education associated with the collegiate tradition suddenly seemed out of date. Students flocked to the new universities with their professional schools, graduate programs, elective courses, looser discipline, and vital student life. At the 1893 International Congress of Education at the Chicago World's Fair, congress organizer Charles G. Bonney announced unequivocally that the "educational systems of the past have been outgrown."[33] But what of the *Ratio Studiorum*? Had it been outgrown in the throes of the academic revolution? If so, how should the Jesuits respond? Should they adapt, conforming their colleges to the standards of the modern academy and propensities of collegians? Or should they resist? These were the issues that riveted the Jesuits and many other Catholic educators as the ramifications of the academic revolution became clear at the turn of the century.

For the Jesuits, the implications of this new academic order came quickly and sharply into focus in 1893 when they were forced to defend the caliber of their colleges in a high-profile dispute with Harvard University President Charles W. Eliot, the nation's leading educator and one of its better-known citizens.[34] A vote by the faculty of the Law School to adopt a more selective admissions policy sparked what became a seven-year-long controversy; in effect, the new policy barred graduates of Jesuit (and other) colleges deemed inferior from regular admission to the Law School. At the forefront of the university movement and the height of his influence, Eliot responded to Jesuit allegations of unfair treatment and discrimination by defending the Law School's admissions process and denigrating Jesuit education. His disparaging, inaccurate comments about Jesuit education published in an 1899 issue of the *Atlantic Monthly* only exacerbated tensions.[35] A pamphlet war ensued. Alumni from Jesuit-run Boston College and the College of the Holy Cross rallied. The religious and secular press ran front-page articles. Speakers and editorialists debated the caliber of Jesuit education or, more often, excoriated Eliot with charges of bigotry. Culminating in 1900, the Law School controversy proved a defining moment in American Catholic higher education: it illuminated on whose terms and on what bases Catholics and Catholic colleges would participate in American higher education in the age of the university.[36]

Although ultimately unsuccessful in reversing the standing of Jesuit colleges at the Law School, the controversy with Eliot and other Harvard officials might have become a satisfying vindication of Jesuit education and a minor triumph for the Catholic academic subculture, for the Jesuits responded with a compelling defense of Jesuit education, a damning critique of Eliot's Harvard, and substantial evidence of incongruities in the Law School's admissions policy. But Catholic collegians proved the Jesuits' undoing. If an admissions policy was cause for serious indignation, enrollment patterns were cause for outright alarm. It was at the very height of their troubles with Harvard that the Jesuits discovered that most Catholic students, seeking professional education, academic credentials, and social opportunities, had bypassed Catholic colleges in favor of non-Catholic higher education. In fact, while the Jesuits were wrangling with Eliot over an admissions policy that they considered nothing less than overtly discriminatory, there were more than three hundred Catholic collegians enrolled at Harvard—the largest number at any institution in the country, Catholic or non-Catholic.

In these interrelated crises, the Jesuits faced new challenges in the trinity of time, person, and place. Each challenge was substantive in its own right; in concert, they were daunting. The first challenge for the Jesuits had to do with popular conceptions of *time*. Americans had come to understand the era in which they lived as an age of modern progress, a powerful temporal construct making formidable claims on both Christianity and higher education. Being timely, modern, and up-to-date became cultural imperatives in many quarters and a driving force in the university movement. Committed to a system of education devised in sixteenth-century Europe, in late-nineteenth-century America the Jesuits suddenly found themselves hounded by the issue of timeliness. Still firmly planted on the wrong side of the great religious divide in Protestant America as the age of the university opened, the Jesuits found themselves slipping down the slopes of ascendant modernity toward irrelevance.

The second challenge encountered by the Jesuits was that of *persons* in the form of a nascent Catholic middle class that took many of its social and cultural cues from the Protestant middle class. Catholic recourse to

Protestant-sponsored and Protestant-inspired higher education—to academic institutions outside the Catholic subculture—signaled tensions within the Catholic community about the social, economic, and religious functions of higher education. Was higher education a mechanism for development of a religious subculture? Or was it a platform for greater engagement with and success in the world? Could it be both at once? The question resonated deeply among Catholics of Irish descent who were making substantial inroads into the middle class and attending college at rates that by 1900 were nearing the national average. Like their Protestant counterparts, they had come to appreciate the socioeconomic value of higher education and they sought academic opportunities that accorded with their middle-class aspirations and sensibilities. During a period when professional education migrated from community-based practitioners to university-based schools and professional work became the sine qua non of middle-class life, Harvard's refusal to recognize the degrees of Jesuit colleges made it all the more difficult for the Jesuits to attract and retain students.

The third challenge encountered by the Jesuits was that of *place* in the form of Protestant America. How should Catholics as individuals and the church as an institution relate to the Protestant majority and a society infused with Protestant values? Through a series of disputes in the 1890s that together became known as the "Americanism controversy," Catholic liberals argued for greater Catholic engagement with and adaptation of Catholicism to American society in order to widen the church's beneficent influence, while conservatives argued for vigilance and a strategy of separatism in order to protect Catholics and their church from Protestantism's taint. By virtue of its timing, newly gained cognizance of the extent of Catholic patronage of non-Catholic higher education was destined to become another flash point in the highly polarized Americanism controversy, with liberals applauding and conservatives decrying Catholic students' recourse to non-Catholic institutions. Among the Jesuits, who were on the whole more sympathetic to the conservative position, an analogous fault line appeared relative to their colleges, with a more liberal element arguing for adaptation of their colleges to American circumstances and mores in order to attract more students and a larger conservative faction arguing for resistance to Protestant-inspired educational reforms.

Embedded within the compact drama of the Law School controversy and concurrent conversations about Catholic participation in American higher education was the fundamental dilemma of the new academic order for the Jesuits. In holding fast to tradition and resisting reform, the Jesuits rendered themselves vulnerable to criticism from influential Protestant educators for being too Catholic and antiquated for modern, Protestant America. In considering and implementing changes, reform-minded Jesuits opened themselves to charges from conservative members of the Society and their European superiors of becoming too Protestant and modern in their approach to education. In staying the course, the Jesuits risked implicit criticism from their traditional constituency, who were flocking to Protestant colleges and the new nonsectarian universities. Resolving this conundrum, I argue, constituted the central project for Jesuit (and by extension most of Catholic) higher education during the tumultuous years spanning the turn of the century. The basic task was to make Jesuit colleges academically respectable to other educators and socially and professionally attractive to students without abandoning the wisdom of the *Ratio Studiorum* or the religious identity of their colleges in favor of Protestant-inspired, modern education. Could they adapt without losing the soul of Jesuit education? It was no small feat. The Jesuits took up this critical task not only lacking the religious and theological resources of Protestant educators, but at a moment when the historic Jesuit willingness and capacity to adapt to circumstances was in short supply—especially among the Jesuits of the Maryland–New York Province, where the force of the controversy with Harvard hit hardest.

The controversy between Harvard and the Jesuits runs through the following chapters both as the focus of this study and a lens through which to examine broader forces shaping Catholic participation in higher education, socially and institutionally. It provides historical entrée into the turbulent turn-of-the-century world of Jesuit higher education and the social, cultural, religious, and theological factors that shaped the Jesuits' responses to the rise of a new academic order. As the controversy with Harvard unfolded and the extent of Catholic patronage of non-Catholic colleges became clear, the exigencies of a new academic order finally registered with the Society of Jesus. Of course, the significance of the academic revolution would have become patently clear to the Jesuits had they not become ensnarled in controversy with Eliot and Harvard; the development of pace-setting universities, the trend toward standardization and accreditation, and Catholic enrollment patterns could hardly be ignored. But no single event captured the attention of the Catholic educational community more powerfully than the Law School controversy; no other event illuminated the academic challenges of the era more clearly. For almost a decade, the Jesuits' troubles with Harvard were widely discussed, publicly and privately, nationally and internationally, among Catholics and non-Catholics.

It is also true that this critical event cannot be understood apart from Catholic enrollment patterns. For no single trend proved more effective in driving reform and modernization in early twentieth-century Catholic higher education than widespread recourse among Catholics to non-Catholic higher education. At the very least, if Catholic students had crowded Jesuit colleges instead of non-Catholic institutions, the Jesuits could have ignored Harvard's rebuff and continued offering a traditional course of study in line with their *Ratio Studiorum.*

Examination of Catholic patterns of participation in higher education also sharpens our understanding of the academic revolution and religion's role in it by bringing to bear the experience and perspectives of historic outsiders. While the Jesuits' troubles with Harvard reveal much about Catholic higher education, the converse—Harvard's troubles with the Jesuits—sheds light on the successes, limitations, and the ambiguities inherent in the new academic order. They provide further evidence of the universities' newly accrued power in setting standards for the academy at large and the resounding success of the concept of non-sectarian education. Yet Eliot's relations with Catholics and his contretemps with the Jesuits demarcate important boundaries, including the limits of liberal Protestantism when faced with Catholics and their church.[37] Moreover, the Jesuits' defense of the *Ratio Studiorum* and critique of Eliot's Harvard foreshadows future criticism of the modern academy, hinting at the toll that Protestant-inspired individualism would exact on the curriculum and the extracurriculum in the twentieth century.

The conversations spurred by and surrounding the Law School controversy were usually complex, sometimes contradictory, occasionally cacophonous, their timbre profoundly affected by their social location. Only through careful attention to what historian Thomas Bender described as the "interplay of private talk and public talk, private talk and public silence, public talk and private silence"[38] does the significance and complexity of the Law School controversy emerge, for conversations carried on between Protestant and Catholic educators, among Catholics, and within the Jesuit community differed significantly. In those differences lay great and telling ironies: how Charles Eliot, a well-known Unitarian and avid proponent of religious toleration, found himself accused of bigotry; how Catholics could claim discrimination when there were hundreds of Catholics studying at Harvard; and how the Jesuits could si-

CHAPTER ONE

The Descendants of Luther and the Sons of Loyola

No place can be so dangerous to
the young as a Jesuit college.

—Noah Porter, Yale professor,
1851

There is a fight for supremacy on
between two great systems of
teaching. One is under the banner of Catholicism, the other
wears the colors of Protestantism.

—A commentator on the Harvard
Law School controversy, ca. 1900

The university was born, in the words of Pope John Paul II, *ex corde ecclesiae*—from the heart of the church. An enduring and valuable legacy of the Middle Ages, the university began to take shape in the late-eleventh and twelfth centuries in the great urban centers of Paris, Bologna, Salerno, and Oxford, where students gathered near the learned men of the day. As were other formal educational institutions, the university was inextricably linked to the Catholic Church, with its charters bestowed by Rome, its summae created by scholarly monks for the glory of God, its students admitted to clerical orders, its discipline regulated by not only the methods and rigors of scholasticism but the diurnal and seasonal rhythms of the liturgy.[1]

Born from the heart of the medieval church, the university in turn played midwife to the Reformation. Religious abuses troubled the great reformer Martin Luther (1483–1546); so, too, did theological quandaries raised by his studies.[2] The challenge Luther issued from the heart of the university—to reform the church—ultimately fractured Christendom, and as it did so it pressed institutions of higher education into the service of opposing religious camps. Henceforth, higher education in the West operated in the context of a divided Christendom, its subsequent history formed and reformed as the reverberations of the Protestant Reformation and the Roman Catholic Counter Reformation traveled through time and space.

In the middle of the nineteenth century, Yale professor Noah Porter (1811–92) heard the reverberations of the Reformation and Counter Reformation echoing across America's academic landscape. In 1851, Porter penned a ninety-five-page tract, *The Educational Systems of the Puritans and Jesuits Compared,* as part of an evangelical Protestant effort to garner support for college-building efforts in America's West. For Porter, who served as Yale's president from 1871 to 1886, the Puritan epitomized the quintessential American Protestant; the Jesuit embodied the essence of the despicable "romish church." Using the two as archetypes for the Protestant and Catholic in education, Porter distilled the history of higher education in the United States into a long academic battle for the nation's soul, in which the Puritan principles of education as practiced in Protestant colleges produced the most agreeable political, social, and religious ends, while Jesuit colleges imperiled the commonweal religiously and politically. According to Porter, Jesuit colleges on American soil threatened the very future of the United States as a Protestant nation.[3]

Portraying Protestant colleges in the western states as frontier citadels of piety, virtue, and learning established in the cause of a Protestant America, Porter penned his tendentious tract on Puritan and Jesuit education in the heyday of the American college and during a period of pronounced anti-Catholic sentiment. Waves of Catholic immigrants from Germany and famine-depleted Ireland fanned the flames of nativism and bigotry among many alarmed Protestants.[4] Looking to build support for Protestant college-building efforts along the yet-to-be-tamed frontier, Porter played upon growing anti-Catholic sentiment. Voicing an age-old conviction, Porter depicted the Jesuits as powerful, dangerous men whose schools differed radically from those sponsored by Protestants. As bastions of religious tyranny and outposts of the Romish church, he claimed their schools had no place in a Protestant republic.

Porter was a man of his age, but it was an age that was at its peak and about to fade: the age of the college was giving way to the age of the university, and the nation was shifting its academic energies from founding denominational colleges to building nonsectarian universities. An ordained Congregational minister, Porter served as tutor, professor of classics, and then president of Yale, his alma mater. Intellectually robust, he joined with leading intellectuals in the New Haven area active in professionalizing the work of scholars: how they defined their fields, marshaled their evidence, and shared their research with other scholars and broader audiences. But in many ways, Porter's religious and academic framework was more rooted in the past than shaped by an evolving present. With time, Porter's attention tellingly turned from building Protestant colleges to defending collegiate ways. As the winds of reform blew through the postbellum academy and the modern American university began to take shape, Porter emerged as a conservative voice. Though Yale accrued professional schools during his presidential tenure, he resisted many other changes associated with the university movement. While the reform-minded at other institutions embraced innovations that reshaped the academic landscape, including modern sciences, curricular electivism, voluntary chapel, and even, on occasion, coeducation, Porter held fast to traditional discipline and classics-based education for male undergraduates. The increasingly popular concept of nonsectarian higher education concerned him; an institution that opened its doors to all points of view, thought Porter, might do so at the expense of its own particular denominational identity and religious commitments.[5]

In the second half of the nineteenth century, Porter, like other Americans, had witnessed an academic revolution that gave birth to the modern American university. Blending the English collegiate tradition with new German research ideals, the modern university differed significantly from its medieval progenitor and that progenitor's American descendant, the college, with its classical liberal arts curriculum, denominational allegiance, and traditional religious discipline. The modern university was research oriented. Men of science replaced men of the cloth. In an act of curricular egalitarianism, theology and philosophy, once queen and handmaiden of the curriculum, were demoted to the level of other subjects. Having taxed young minds for centuries, Latin and Greek were set to the side in favor of the vernacular and modern languages.[6] The curriculum itself mushroomed with new disciplines, and students were allowed to elect their own courses of study. Religious discipline was relaxed. Professional schools, once largely independent and few in number, were reaffixed to the new universities, where they then proliferated. The ideal of nonsectarian education supplanted denominationalism as an organizing principle.[7]

While Porter sided with tradition, Harvard President Charles William Eliot (1834–1926) emerged as an effective reformer and national academic leader. Like Porter, Eliot served as president of his alma mater, but unlike Porter, he came to the position as a scientist, not as a clergyman. As did Porter, he wanted to extend Christianity's influence through higher education, but unlike Porter he took as his task the reformation of higher education itself, rather than the westward expansion of the collegiate system. In this, Eliot was immensely successful. Assuming the presidency in 1869 with a vision of "The New Education,"[8] during his forty-year tenure he transformed Harvard from a local, parochial college into a cosmopolitan university that stood foremost among the nation's institutions of advanced education.

But Eliot's efforts were not confined to Cambridge; by the 1890s, he had become a key figure in American education at large. "President Eliot," wrote Western Reserve President Charles F. Thwing, "has a full and clear conception of what education from the primary school to the university ought to be" and approached his reform efforts with a "confidence . . . worthy of Luther." For his efforts, Eliot won wide attention and notoriety. According to one contemporary, "for twelve years past no public addresses, save those of the Presidents of the United States themselves, have been so widely read throughout the country as have those of President Eliot." When he retired in 1909, he was a well-known, national figure, dubbed the "First Citizen of the Republic" by Theodore Roosevelt.[9]

The postbellum revolution in American higher education that gave rise to the modern, nonsectarian university and Porter's defensive posturing drew its religious inspiration from liberal Protestantism. Evangelical Protestantism, a potent animating force in America's college-building efforts, was loosening its hold on American society as a more liberal strain of Christianity, one that put greater stock in ethical behavior and religious toleration than denominational differences, gained ground.[10] Inspired by the social vision of liberal Protestantism, the leaders of the university movement—Eliot, Andrew Dickson White (Cornell University), and Daniel Coit Gilman (Johns Hopkins University), among others—dismissed Porter's concern for the college as a site for asserting denominational *identity* in favor of the university as a site for advancing a broader religious *mission*—namely, fostering religious toleration. No less than the college men of Porter's era, the university men who came of age in the wake of the Civil War considered their educational endeavors a service rendered on behalf of a Protestant America; they were merely employing nonsectarian means to (liberal) Christian ends.[11]

The gains that religious liberalism realized in American Protestantism during the nineteenth century were not obtained at the expense of the concept of the United States as a Protestant nation. Few among the religious majority would have disagreed with an 1877 contributor to the *Princeton Review* who informed readers that "a government of the people, by the people, and for the people, is . . . as our own republic for a hundred years has been—a *Protestant* republic."[12] Nonetheless, the inroads liberalism made in religious circles affected Protestant-Catholic relations and did so significantly in the area of higher education. The success of liberal Protestantism vis-à-vis the emergence of the nonsectarian university deeply complicated Catholic participation in American higher education. On the one hand, it created opportunities for Catholics hardly imaginable in 1850, when the age of the college was at its peak and anti-Catholicism was rampant. Even so, anti-Catholicism endured in the more liberal age of the university. Born in the Old World and carried to the New by the Puritans, anti-Jesuit sentiment proved a particularly resilient strain.

In 1893, the fruits of religious liberalism and legacy of religious antipathy found concurrent expression at Harvard University. In that year, Eliot, already a well-known religious liberal, won kudos and laudatory press coverage for Harvard's high-profile overtures to Catholics. Liberals rejoiced at what appeared to signal the advent of a new era of religious harmony. But Eliot's Harvard also garnered less flattering attention and press coverage over a newly announced admissions policy at Harvard Law School that seemed to discriminate against graduates of Jesuit colleges. In the contradiction lay fundamental tensions and potent forces shaping Catholic participation in higher education. Between the Congregationalist Porter and the Unitarian Eliot—men who respectively embodied the soul of the denominational college and the spirit of the nonsectarian university—existed substantive differences, yet they were of one mind regarding the Jesuits, the leading educators of the Roman Catholic Church. Liberal to the bone, Eliot had inherited from his Puritan ancestors a deep and abiding faith in the religious and social efficacy of education. He also inherited and shared with Noah Porter a deep disdain for the Jesuits and their schools. Religious liberalism had helped transform American higher education in the postbellum era, but anti-Jesuit attitudes endured, even at Harvard, the most liberal of institutions.

The comings and goings of Catholics at Harvard in 1893 and Eliot's defense of the Law School's admissions policy to the Jesuit president of Georgetown provide occasion to examine Protestants' disparate views about Catholic participation in higher education. Religious liberalism helped open important doors in higher education to Catholics, but anti-Catholicism proved tenacious, particularly as directed toward the Jesuits. The first act of what would become known as the Harvard Law School controversy illuminates the powerful and persistent claim of anti-Jesuitism on the American Protestant imagination. Religious liberalism muted but had hardly silenced the reverberations of the Reformation and Counter Reformation in the age of the university.

On July 1, 1893, two articles, "Bishop Keane and Harvard" and "Harvard and Catholic Colleges," appeared in adjacent columns of the *Pilot,* a Boston-based publication. Privately run from its establishment in 1829 until becoming the official newspaper of the archdiocese of Boston in 1908, the *Pilot* catered to the growing Irish Catholic population in and around Boston throughout the nineteenth century.[13] On that day, readers of the first article learned that Harvard University had awarded an honorary doctorate to a Catholic bishop, John J. Keane (1838–1918). A popular figure in Catholic and non-Catholic circles, Irish-born Keane was first rector of the Catholic University of America (1889–96). Modeled after the Johns Hopkins University in nearby Baltimore, the Catholic University of America in Washington, D.C., represented the Catholic community's corporate response to the university movement. Emphasizing research and focusing on graduate and professional education, its founders intended it to function as a capstone institution in the world of American Catholic higher education.[14]

This June 1893 visit was Keane's third public appearance at Harvard. A well-known liberal and an accomplished speaker, in 1890 Keane had delivered one of Harvard's Dudleian Lectures. Bedecked in his episcopal garments, Keane spoke on "The Evidences of Christianity" and joined his audience in singing "Nearer, My God, to Thee" and "Rock of Ages" before dismissing them with an apostolic blessing. It was, according to a Dublin newspaper, an "unusual sight to see a bishop clad in purple standing in a pulpit where only Protestants and a Jew had spoken before." The conservative *L'Universe* of Paris hinted at the possibility of impropriety in Keane's decision to "speak to an audience of heretics" clad in "episcopal garments." "Such strange scenes can be seen only in America, sometimes in England."[15] Indeed, Keane himself almost declined the invitation to speak. For at the direction of benefactor Judge Paul Dudley, who established the quadrennial lecture series in 1750, the third of the lectures was to be devoted to "detecting, and convicting, and exposing the Idolatry of the Romish church, their tyranny, usurpations, damnable heresies, fatal errors, abominable superstitions, and other crying wickednesses in their high places; and finally, that the Church of Rome is that mystical Babylon, that man of sin, that apostate church, spoken of in the New Testament." Given the topic of the third lecture, Keane initially considered the invitation to deliver the second on the "great articles of the Christian Religion" a "little ludicrous," but Keane's liberalism got the better of him: "I have no intention of being made narrow by the narrowness of other people and . . . I am entirely willing to show my friendliness towards Harvard by lecturing under its auspices."[16] He demonstrated that friendliness again in February 1893, when he delivered another lecture, "The Wisdom of the Ages," before "Representatives of Educational Life and Fashionable Society," as the local headline read.[17]

Keane's host in Boston was Harvard president Charles Eliot. A quintessential Boston Brahmin, Eliot's genealogical lines were impeccable, traceable to an early round of Puritan migration to New England. In the two centuries that followed, his family amassed a great fortune and, until a financial crisis struck in 1857, Eliot counted himself a member of what was probably the wealthiest family in Boston. Like many of their class, the Eliots were involved in civic affairs; his father, Samuel Atkin Eliot, was the mayor of Boston from 1837 to 1839. The Eliots had ties with Boston's great cultural institutions, and the connections to Harvard were particularly strong.[18] His male relatives routinely attended Harvard, and his female relatives married its graduates. With some regularity, his relations assumed positions at their alma mater as overseers, professors, fellows, tutors, and librarians. Eliot's father served as Harvard's treasurer, and his grandfather endowed a professorship in Greek. After his training at Boston Latin School, Charles predictably entered Harvard, but unpredictably took up chemistry, studying in the laboratory of Josiah Parsons Cooke, while other students limited themselves to the more traditional liberal arts course. In 1853 he graduated second in his class. Sixteen years later, at the age of thirty-five, Eliot was named president of his alma mater, a position that he held for four decades, spanning the most revolutionary period in U.S. educational history.[19]

Eliot's Boston Brahmin world was also a Unitarian world. Unitarianism, the most liberal of denominations, germinated in the soil of New England in the eighteenth century and blossomed in the nineteenth. Rejecting the concept of revealed religion and embracing ethical behavior and religious toleration as the heart of true religion, Unitarianism garnered strong support within the Eliot family. In Boston circles, his uncle, Andrews Norton, an author and Harvard divinity professor, was known as the Unitarian pope. His father, who studied for divinity but decided against ordination, served as warden and choirmaster at King's Chapel, home of one of Boston's leading Unitarian congregations. One biographer identified Eliot's own "ardent spiritual faith" as the "central secret of his life," casting him as one of the four pillars of Unitarianism, alongside William Ellery Channing, Ralph Waldo Emerson, and Theodore Parker. Eliot surely would have declined the ascription; his religiosity was far too understated. Yet his faith was central to his life and work; it was described by his son as "simple but profound and sufficient . . . the mainspring of his private life and of his public endeavors."[20] Given a "belief in God so simple and so deep that few suspected its existence" (as Harvard historian Samuel Eliot Morison described it), he was pleased in 1894 when his colleague George Palmer commented on his "reliance on the Eternal for personal strength." Eliot responded:

> I belong to the barest of the religious communions, and I am by nature reserved except with intimates, and even with some of them. I feel glad that what has been, I believe, a fact in my inner life these thirty years past has been visible to a close observer of my official career.
>
> I should not like to have it said by the next generation, as has often been said by my contemporaries, that I was a man without ideals and without piety. . . . It has been hard to have people suppose— even some of my friends—that my interest in the religious policy of the university was a matter of expediency and not of conviction. I am glad that you have inferred from my habitual conduct an underlying principle.[21]

Among the men at the forefront of the university movement, Eliot was not alone in his religious sympathies. Though the particularities of their religious histories, commitments, and beliefs varied, the university leaders were religious men of decidedly liberal tendencies who linked their efforts to reform higher education to the cause of Protestantism. Daniel Coit Gilman, first president of the Johns Hopkins University (1875–1901), was licensed to preach in the Congregational Church but set aside his ministerial aspirations and turned to academics as a way to "influence New England minds." As president, he assumed the traditional responsibility of preaching to the undergraduates and, after his retirement, served as the vice president and president of the American Bible Society.[22] Raised in a devout Episcopalian family, Cornell President Andrew Dickson White (1867–1885) maintained the loosest of ties with the Episcopal Church in his adulthood, preferring to describe himself as a Christian who defined his own beliefs. His magnum opus was devoted to explicating the relationship between science and religion; the final sixty pages of his autobiography described his own religious affairs, closing with his hope for the "cultivating, each for himself, obedience to 'the first and great commandment, and the second which is like unto it,' as given by the Blessed Founder of Christianity."[23]

The first president of the University of Chicago, William Rainey Harper (1891–1906), was a devout Baptist and Hebrew scholar for whom the university figured as a linchpin in his multifaceted, expansive plans for religious education.[24] Clark University President G. Stanley Hall (1889–1919) was deeply religious; Columbia University President Seth Low (1889–1902) was an active Episcopalian; Cornell University President Jacob Gould Shurman (1892–1920) was a Unitarian; Princeton University President Francis L. Patton (1888–1902) was a Presbyterian minister. Woodrow Wilson, Patton's successor (1902–10), who was raised Presbyterian, embraced a liberal Protestant faith in adulthood; while president of the United States (1913–21), he informed a friend, "My life would not be worth living if it were not for the driving power of religion, for *faith*, pure and simple."[25]

As liberals, leaders of the university movement held religious toleration in high regard. Fractious denominational rivalry was, according to liberals, antithetical to the spirit of true Christianity and thus, by extension, the good of the nation. As such, sectarianism was a social bane that had no place in the modern university. In assuming office they repeatedly rejected sectarian claims on modern higher education. In his 1869 inaugural address, Eliot declared, "A university is built, not by a sect, but by a nation." In putting on the mantle of the presidency of Johns Hopkins, Gilman embraced the founders' vision of an institution free from "sectarian . . . control." In speaking of his aspirations for Cornell, White asserted, "We will labor to make this a Christian institution—a sectarian institution may it never be." Even Princeton, with its historic ties to Presbyterianism, shook off the encumbrances of sectarianism. Its soon-to-be inaugurated President Patton told the New York Alumni Club, "I shall not shrink from saying . . . that we must keep Princeton a Christian College," though it was "too big to be sectarian."[26]

Protestant leaders of the university movement were at the helms of public institutions with diverse constituencies or private institutions with increasingly national aspirations, and thus the development of nonsectarian education was, in part, making virtue of necessity. In common-sense fashion, Eliot asserted that the "unsectarian college is the most useful type in a country where there is no established church, and no single denomination [is] numerically, socially, or morally dominant."[27] But nonsectarianism meant more than that to the university men. Nonsectarian universities were part of the project of Protestant America. Fostering religious toleration was "one of the most wholesome functions of great universities . . . in a great Protestant democracy like our own," according to Eliot. They prepared men for the religiously pluralistic world they would encounter after their college years. In such universities, the "differences between the various religious denominations are softened, and mutual respect . . . is cultivated,"[28] and students, purported Eliot, obtained a "precious knowledge that the doctrines upon which all denominations agree in the main have vastly more practical importance than those about which they differ." The university men conceded that parents had a right to send their children to denominational colleges, but regretted that such colleges sent young men and women "out into the world knowing well, perhaps, the doctrines and practices of that denomination, but presumably ignorant of all other modes of religious thought and religious life."[29] Eliot made a special note regarding Catholics. An "educated Roman Catholic . . . is much better for all American uses than an uneducated Roman Catholic," but his "influence" in a Protestant nation was "diminished, not increased, if his education has deprived him of all knowledge of his Protestant contemporaries and of the Protestant mode of thought and feeling."[30]

If Eliot's comments on the benefits of religious diversity in higher education carried the unmistakable strains of Protestant entitlement cast in national terms, Keane's ecumenical efforts evinced traditional strains of classic apologetics cast in liberal terms. Bishop Keane was one of an influential group of liberal prelates, known as the "Americanists," that included James Cardinal Gibbons (1834–1921) of Baltimore, Bishop John Lancaster Spalding (1840–1916) of Peoria, Archbishop John Ireland (1838–1918) of Saint Paul, and Bishop Denis O'Connell (1849–1927), who served as third rector of the Catholic University (1903–8).[31] Like their liberal Protestant counterparts, they were convinced of the religious value of improved Protestant-Catholic relations; but they also sought to strengthen relations between Protestants and Catholics as a means of strengthening the Catholic Church and spreading its salubrious influence among the nation's Protestant citizenry. Busy on the lecture circuit, Keane understood the numerous speeches he delivered before non-Catholic and religiously diverse audiences in ambassadorial terms; he hoped that, in word and action, his efforts would help ameliorate bigotry by presenting Catholicism in ways that would appeal to American Protestants.

Keane's visits to Harvard University occasioned hearty liberal rejoicing. In a region where anti-Catholic sentiment ran deep, Keane's presence at Harvard, the academic jewel of Protestant Boston, was an important symbolic event for Protestants and Catholics alike. During his 1893 visit to address those gathered in Union Hall on the "Wisdom of the Ages," Keane responded to a warm welcome from Eliot with effusive thanks. "Surely, dear friends," said Keane, "we can feel that the wisdom of the ages is bringing forth good fruit when, at the close of the nineteenth century, men who seemed to stand so far apart in religious convictions can meet and grasp hands so warmly, so friendly, in a great all-embracing Christian charity." At the alumni dinner held in conjunction with commencement, Keane announced that the "old period of hostility and suspicion" had passed; a "new era of trustfulness and love has taken its place."[32]

A year later, on the occasion of Eliot's twenty-fifth year in office, the long-time president was honored for his contribution to bringing about this new era of friendly religious relations. Alumnus Joseph Choate (A.B. 1852, LL.B. 1854) praised Eliot, noting that Harvard had become "absolutely and forever free and open to all on equal terms," a place where "the Christian and the Jew, the Papist and the Protestant" could "study side by side with equal right and learn alike whatever is worth learning." With biblical resonance, Choate heaped generous honors on Eliot's Harvard: "No form of religion, or belief or of unbelief, now bars the doors of Harvard: to whosoever knocketh they shall be opened."[33]

But were those papists actually welcome at Harvard? Had a new era of religious harmony really dawned in Cambridge? The article in the *Pilot* that ran adjacent to that reporting on Keane's honorary doctorate suggested that Catholics might not be welcome at Harvard, raising the unpleasant specter of bigotry. In "Harvard and Catholic Colleges," readers learned that Harvard Law School had recently announced a change in its admissions policy. After the 1895–96 academic year, only those men who held a bachelor's degree from a select list of colleges would be admitted to the Law School as regular students; others would be eligible to enroll only as "special students." No Catholic college or university appeared on the initial list of sixty-nine institutions, a fact that did not escape the notice of the *Pilot* staff.[34]

Was the absence of Catholic institutions from the Law School's list of colleges evidence of discrimination on the part of Harvard University? The *Pilot* raised the question of bigotry, but then quickly and roundly dismissed it. In 1893, Catholics in New England laid claim with some vigor to a full share of American life, including its historic cultural and academic riches. Though seventeenth-century Protestants had founded the venerable institution, the *Pilot* expanded proprietorship of Harvard to all citizens of the Commonwealth: "Puritan-born Harvard has no nineteenth century honor in which we Massachusetts Catholics do not glory as well as the descendants of the straightest Puritans." The *Pilot* attributed this liberal turn of events to Eliot, who had earned a solid reputation in Catholic circles over the years as a "broad-minded man" who had "done much to eliminate narrow sectarianism from the great University" that he headed. If readers entertained doubts, if they needed "further proof," the *Pilot* directed their attention to the "fact that Harvard has just conferred the honor of LL.D. on a Catholic Bishop whom all Catholics love and honor, Rt. Rev. John J. Keane, Rector of the Catholic University."[35]

In 1893, the news of Keane's honors at Harvard overshadowed the *Pilot*'s story about the Law School's more restrictive and potentially troubling admissions policy. Pleased to witness the arrival of a "new era" of Protestant-Catholic relations, the *Pilot* was willing to give Eliot and Harvard Law School the benefit of the doubt. But the darker of the two stories ultimately proved more tenacious and newsworthy. Out of journalistic view for several years, the Law School story took on a life of its own before erupting, in 1900, into a full-blown public controversy between Eliot and the Jesuits. The new era of religious harmony at Harvard was complex and fragile. Even as universities became sites to foster and celebrate friendly religious relations, old antipathies endured.

Charles Eliot's fall from grace with many members of the Catholic community began with a decision made a few weeks before the bestowing of doctoral honors on Keane. On the evening of April 18, 1893, the faculty of Harvard Law School—Professors Langdell, Smith, Gray, Ames, Wambaugh, Beale, and Williston—met at the home of President Eliot. It was not customary to hold the faculty meetings of Harvard Law School in the president's home, but it was customary for Eliot to attend such meetings, a practice distinguishing him from his predecessors, who interfered little in the affairs of the Law School.[36] Long committed to the reform and improvement of legal education, in the twenty-four years since Eliot had become president and the twenty-three years since he had appointed Christopher Columbus Langdell as dean, Harvard's law faculty had introduced substantive reforms that eventually became standard practice in legal education, including teaching the law through the case method (a pedagogical innovation developed at the Law School), extending student residency from eighteen months to three years, using examinations (instead of attendance) as gateways to annual promotion and graduation, and requiring a bachelor's degree for admission to the program leading to the LL.B.—the law degree.[37] The minutes from the meeting of April 18 suggest that Eliot and the faculty of the Law School devoted almost all of their attention that evening to the issue of admissions requirements, one of their long-standing concerns. They certainly could not have foreseen that the decision they reached that evening—to limit admission to the LL.B. program to graduates from a select list of colleges—would sully Eliot's and Harvard's liberal reputations and precipitate a crisis in Catholic higher education.

Eliot was no stranger to reform or to controversy. Two articles in the *Atlantic Monthly* in 1869 on "The New Education," where he argued for sweeping reforms, propelled the young alumnus into candidacy for the venerable position of president of the nation's oldest university. At the end of the thirty-five-year-old president's famous inaugural address, faculty member John Fiske concluded, "We are going to have new times here at Harvard"—and they did. Reform became the hallmark of Eliot's tenure as president. In the course of four decades marked by regular skirmishes and hard-fought battles, he ultimately realized the goals set forth in his inaugural—raising academic standards, enlarging the curriculum, expanding the elective system, improving instruction, and diversifying the student body. By the end of his distinguished tenure, he had transformed Harvard into the nation's preeminent institution of advanced learning; Harvard now exercised immense influence in academic and cultural life.[38]

On the eve of his retirement, Eliot wrote a retrospective in which he counted the "re-making of the Law School under Langdell" and the "requiring of a previous degree" for admission to the university's professional schools among the most significant accomplishments of his presidency.[39] It was no small accomplishment. When Eliot appointed Langdell to the deanship in 1870, requirements for students at Harvard and other law schools were, by twentieth-century standards, remarkably low. Men were admitted solely on the basis of some testimonial of good character and with varying degrees of secondary and postsecondary education. In the mid-1870s, Harvard took the unusual step of introducing an academic criterion—namely, a bachelor's degree—for which it would be subject to criticism of elitism. Men holding a bachelor's degree were admitted automatically; men without degrees were categorized as special students.[40] In 1893 the faculty gathered at Eliot's home decided to restrict regular admission further to those men who held diplomas from a select list of colleges. The minutes from the meeting tersely report: "Voted, that, after Commencement day 1896, the following persons will be admitted as candidates for a degree without examination." Those persons fell into two categories: "Persons qualified to enter the senior class of Harvard College" (i.e., those Harvard students who had successfully completed their junior year) or holders of degrees from one of sixty-nine colleges. The faculty did not consider the list "exhaustive," noting that it would need to be "enlarged from time to time." Those who met neither criterion were to be admitted as special students and required to take exams not required of regular students. The new rules for admission coupled with more stringent requirements for special students led a writer for the *Harvard Law Review* to conclude that the effect "was virtually to legislate special students out of the catalogue."[41]

On June 19, 1893, James Jeffrey Roche (1847–1908), the editor of the *Pilot,* wrote Eliot about the Law School's new admissions policy and the list of colleges whose graduates were automatically eligible for regular admission. Well connected with the Irish Catholic literary establishment and friendly with Boston's Protestant elite, the Irish-born Roche contributed frequently to periodicals such as the *Atlantic Monthly, Harper's,* and *Century.*[42] Roche was curious: the list "does not contain a single name of the many excellent Catholic universities and colleges in the United States and Canada." This was, Roche thought, a "strange" omission, so strange that he wrote Eliot to inquire "whether or not the list" was "authentic." He found it "hard to believe that Harvard University would discriminate against Catholic institutions of learning."[43]

Eliot replied the following day. "I beg to assure you that there was not the slightest intention on the part of the Faculty of the Law School to discriminate against Catholic institutions of learning." He insisted that the absence of Catholic colleges from the list was "very far from being intentional," explaining that the list was a compilation of "colleges from which young men have actually entered the Law School in recent years."[44]

Had Eliot left it at that, his future troubles with the Jesuits and the Catholic educational community might have been averted. Unfortunately, as historian Samuel Eliot Morison noted, "Eliot's personality enabled him to get things done, but there was nothing in that personality to make his way easier, and much to make it harder." In particular, he was forthright to a fault and felt little if any reluctance about expressing his views. Friends and critics alike acknowledged a lack of tact and propensity to "woo opposition." Ralph Barton Perry put it this way: "I think we may assume that the specific organ of tact was lacking in Eliot's congenital anatomy."[45] Case in point: Eliot gratuitously expounded on the Law School's list in his reply to Roche. "There is doubtless," Eliot explained, "some reason for the failure to include a single Catholic college in this preliminary list." Eliot then offered his own reason: "The programme of studies in Catholic colleges is so different from that pursued in the leading Protestant or undenominational colleges, that, when a young graduate of a Catholic college desires to enter a Protestant or undenominational college with advanced standing, he finds that his studies have, to a considerable extent, not been equivalent to those pursued in the college which he wishes to enter."[46]

Eliot was not the first to claim that students from Jesuit colleges lagged behind students in Protestant colleges, although his prominence and Harvard's growing influence rendered his reproof more critical. In 1870, President G. W. Samson of Columbian College, told an audience at the Baptist National Convention that the "American boy" who spent "two or three years in such a college," upon transferring to an "ordinary American college" found himself "behind pupils in the first year of actual mastery of Latin."[47] Twenty-five years earlier, in 1845, the Reverend William S. Potts informed those gathered at the Second Presbyterian Church in Saint Louis that graduates of Jesuit institutions (which would include the Jesuit-run Saint Louis University) were "not qualified to enter the junior class at Princeton, Yale, or any of the more respectable Protestant colleges of our land." Potts's disparagement of the Jesuit colleges drew a sharp rejoinder from journalist and Catholic convert Orestes Brownson. "The regular course of studies in our Jesuits' colleges is as thorough, as extensive, and of as high an order, as that of the best Protestant colleges," wrote Brownson, "and those who take the regular and full course will have, on graduating, no occasion to regard themselves as inferior to the graduates of Protestant universities."[48]

In his letter to Roche, Eliot both asserted differences between Protestant and Catholic colleges and proposed reasons for them. The lack of equivalence between the two, Eliot explained, derived from two sources: the "different historical development of the Catholic colleges, which inherit a great deal directly from the Jesuit schools of the past four centuries" and the fact that the "directors of Catholic colleges have generally received only or chiefly the education of priests."[49]

Roche thanked Eliot for his reply, but noted that graduates of Catholic colleges would still wonder whether discrimination was at play. They had occasion to do so because Roche published Eliot's letter in the *Pilot* as part of "Harvard and Catholic Colleges." J. Havens Richards, S.J., the president of Jesuit-run Georgetown College (1888–98), harbored those exact suspicions, as did, Richards claimed, a "number of Catholic educators."[50] As a Jesuit, Richards had had, as Eliot put it, the education of a priest, but not solely. Having demonstrated a promising interest in science, his religious superior sent him to study at Harvard in the summers of 1879 and 1880. The time in Cambridge was time spent close to home. Richards, whose ancestral line linked him to the seventeenth-century Plymouth Bay Colony, had moved from Columbus, Ohio, to Boston with his family in 1869. The son of a convert, Richards took up studies at the recently opened, Jesuit-run Boston College and entered the Jesuit order in 1872.[51]

Richards wrote Eliot about the absence of Catholic colleges from the Law School's list two weeks after Eliot's letter to Roche appeared in the *Pilot*. Richards pointed out that the "omission would have been explained, if not satisfactorily, at least without offence," if Eliot had merely stated that "no Catholic College had presented at your Law School a sufficient number of graduates to enable the committee to judge of the value of its degree."[52] To Richards, Eliot's explanation seemed a "public attack on the standing of all Catholic colleges," for a "want of equivalence which causes the degrees of all Catholic colleges to be refused, while those of obscure Protestant or undenominational institutions are accepted, can be construed only as inferiority." In fact, argued Richards, "other things being equal" (such as "associations of home life, and other precedent or collateral educational influences"), those who graduated from "reputable Catholic colleges are better prepared for a course of Law, than any other class of students." He forwarded materials by which to acquaint Eliot with the work of Georgetown. If Eliot were "satisfied . . . by a fair inquiry" that Georgetown warranted inclusion on the list, he hoped Eliot would make a "public retraction" to undo what he could not "help considering a public, though doubtless unintentional, injury" to Catholic higher education.[53]

In his response to Richards, Eliot gave Richards what he wanted, but only in part and not without further offense. Eliot reported that his review of materials sent by Richards convinced him that Georgetown "should be included in the list of colleges." The faculty of the Law School, Eliot added, had come to the same conclusion independently. As a result, Georgetown and the "names of the two Catholic colleges in Massachusetts"—Boston College and the College of the Holy Cross in Worcester—would appear on the official list to be published in the Harvard University *Catalogue*. This would be, Eliot felt, the "most effective way of repairing such injury as may have been done by the publication of the preliminary list." Yet Eliot did not find anything that he could "retract." A "lack of equivalence" was "brought out very clearly in the catalogue and examination papers of Georgetown College." Eliot then reiterated, almost verbatim: the "very marked difference between all the Catholic colleges and all the Protestant colleges" stemmed from the "strong inheritance from the famous Jesuit schools, and in the fact that the directors of Catholic colleges are generally priests." Nonetheless, the "graduates of these Catholic colleges may well be admitted . . . [T]hat is the practical point; and that Harvard University will do."[54]

At the direction of his religious superior, who chided him for looking out for the interests of Georgetown alone, Richards pressed Eliot further, initially for a retraction, later for the inclusion of the other American Jesuit colleges, twenty-four in number in 1893 (see table 1). He argued that all Jesuit colleges used the same curriculum, therefore all deserved inclusion on the list. His efforts came to naught. Only Georgetown, Boston College, and Holy Cross secured places on the list—three among forty-four colleges and degree programs added to the original list of sixty-nine prior to its first official publication in the *Catalogue* of 1893 (see appendix A). In following years, the list was regularly augmented, but after the addition of the University of Notre Dame in 1894 and Manhattan College in 1900, no other Catholic colleges were added to it (see appendix B).[55]

The "famous Jesuit schools" that Eliot none too subtly criticized were indeed famous (or infamous, depending upon one's viewpoint), as were their sponsors. For more than three centuries, the Jesuits loomed large in the Protestant imagination, where they were variously subjects of awe and vitriol. Founded by one-time soldier Ignatius of Loyola (1491–1556), the Jesuits' adventures and achievements across the globe won them large measures of fame and notoriety, celebrity and animus, renown and hostility. "Of all the religious orders," noted a Protestant essayist in 1855, "the Jesuits have been the most slandered and the most praised, the most studied, and yet the most difficult to be understood.

Table 1
Jesuit Colleges in the United States in 1893

Institution	Location	Jesuit Province or Mission	Established
Boston College	Boston, Mass.	Maryland-New York	1863
Canisius College	Buffalo, N.Y.	German Mission	1870
College of the Holy Cross	Worcester, Mass.	Maryland-New York	1843
Creighton College (now Creighton University)	Omaha, Neb.	Missouri	1878
Detroit College (now University of Detroit-Mercy)	Detroit, Mich.	Missouri	1877
Georgetown College (now Georgetown University)	Washington, D.C.	Maryland-New York	1789
Gonzaga College (now Gonzaga University)	Spokane, Wash.	Turin Mission	1887
Gonzaga College (now Gonzaga College High School)	Washington, D.C.	Maryland-New York	1821
Immaculate Conception (now Loyola University New Orleans)	New Orleans, La.	New Orleans Mission	1849
Loyola College	Baltimore, Md.	Maryland-New York	1852
Marquette College (now Marquette University)	Milwaukee, Wisc.	Missouri	1881
Sacred Heart College* (now Regis College)	Denver, Colo.	Naples Mission	1877
St. Francis Xavier College (now Xavier High School)	New York, N.Y.	Maryland-New York	1847
St. Ignatius College (now University of San Fransisco)	San Fransisco, Calif.	Turin Mission	1855
St. Ignatius College (now Loyola University Chicago)	Chicago, Ill.	Missouri	1870
St. Ignatius College (now John Carroll University)	Cleveland, Ohio	German Mission	1886
St. John's College (now Fordham University)	Fordham, N.Y.	Maryland-New York	1841

(continued)

Table 1

(Continued)

Institution	Location	Jesuit Province or Mission	Established
St. Joseph's College (now St. Joseph's University)	Philadelphia, Pa.	Maryland-New York	1851
St. Louis University	St. Louis, Mo.	Missouri	1818
St. Mary's University**	Galveston, Tex.	New Orleans Mission	—
St. Peter's College	Jersey City, N.J.	Maryland-New York	1872
St. Xavier College (now Xavier University)	Cincinnati, Ohio	German Mission	1831
Santa Clara College (now Santa Clara University)	San José, Calif.	Turin Mission	1851
Spring Hill College	Spring Hill, Ala.	New Orleans Mission	1830

Source: WL 23 (1894): 470.
*Originally located in Las Vegas and called "Las Vegas College," Sacred Heart College moved to Denver in 1887 after a brief stint in Morrison, Colorado.
**St. Mary's College was destroyed in September 1900 by a storm. Founding date unknown.

They have ever had the most enthusiastic admirers and the most implacable enemies." He summed up politely: "We love them, or we hate them, cordially and decidedly."[56] Ironically, Ignatius had no intention of founding an order devoted to teaching. In fact, little in Ignatius's early life suggested that his would be a life spent in Christian service to others. Raised in the Basque region of northern Spain, his privileged life as a courtier included its share of brawling and womanizing. Having entered the military, his life took a radical turn when a cannonball shattered his leg. He emerged from a long, painful recuperation at the Castle of Loyola transformed by a profound religious experience. He cast about for some years thereafter, traveling as far as the Holy Land, increasingly convinced that his vocation in life was to "help souls."[57]

Ignatius also became convinced of a pressing need to further his own formal education. Lacking in the rudiments, he began his formal studies with students less than half his age, declining verbs and parsing sentences in Latin. After two years of preliminary study, he entered the University of Alcalá, although his time there was short. Running afoul of the local Inquisition, Ignatius moved on to the more prestigious University of Salamanca, only to tangle with the forces of orthodoxy once again. Though again found innocent of the charges leveled against him, the experiences propelled him toward the University of Paris, where he studied grammar, philosophy, and theology, primarily at the College of Sainte Barbe. He departed Paris in 1535 with a master of arts degree. More importantly, he left the university with nine companions committed to one another in the work of helping souls *ad majorem Dei gloriam*—for the greater glory of God. They formed the nucleus of what became the Society of Jesus, recognized five years later as an official order of the Church of Rome.[58]

Their initial plan to go to the Holy Land scuttled by the vicissitudes of weather and politics, Ignatius and his companions eventually ended up in Rome, where, with the blessing of the pope, they devoted themselves to the work of helping souls by preaching in the streets, caring for the needy, teaching the catechism, and offering spiritual guidance. Two of their number took up lecturing at the University of Rome. In the meantime, their numbers grew significantly, as did the geographic scope of the Society. With their headquarters settled in Rome, by 1550 the Jesuits were ministering in Italy, Spain, Portugal, Germany, France, Japan, and India; by 1556, they had moved into Brazil and Ethiopia. The Jesuits reached Mexico by 1572 and established an initial base in the north, in eastern Canada, in the 1610s. By the 1620s they were established in Quebec.[59]

The global expansion of the Society was completely consonant with Ignatius's vision of an itinerant ministry; the unusual decision to operate schools was not. Quickly convinced of the need to educate new members of the Society, in the 1540s the Jesuits established residential (i.e., noninstructional) colleges near universities. In 1548 they made a momentous decision that dramatically affected the Society and, in a substantive way, the history of formal education: they admitted and offered instruction to lay students at their college at Messina. In that moment, they grasped schooling as an additional means of helping souls, embracing education as one of their principal ministries. "There are two ways of helping our neighbors," wrote Juan Alphonso de Polonca in 1560: "one in the colleges through the education of youth in letters, learning, and Christian life," the other "in every place to help every kind of person through sermons, confessions, and other means that accord with our customary way of proceeding." There was nothing customary whatsoever in the decision to adopt education as a primary focus of the work of the Society. In time, the education of youth became a hallmark endeavor, but in the mid-sixteenth century it was not part of the typical, formal repertoire of ministerial and apostolic activities for men and women in religious orders. For well over a millennium, religious men and women lived out their vocations in cloistered lives of prayer, in selfless lives of service to the needy, or as ministers of word and sacrament; religious orders had yet to embrace education as a ministry in itself.[60]

What factors contributed to this unusual departure? The fact that Ignatius and his earliest companions were educated at one of the leading universities of the day certainly created sympathy for the academic and the intellectual. Linking learning with piety, the Jesuits came to understand scholarly endeavors as a "path to God." To the traditional means of sanctification, such as sacraments and devotional practices, the Jesuits added intellectual activity. "Let everybody know that the Society has two means by which it strives for this end," wrote Jerónimo Nadal, an influential early Jesuit. The "one is a certain force, spiritual and divine, which is acquired through the sacraments, prayer, and the religious exercise of all virtues," while "the other force is placed in the faculty which is ordinarily found through studies."[61]

In an age in which learning and scholarship flourished, the Jesuits' intellectual road to God was no narrow path hemmed in by scholasticism but a scholarly pilgrimage enriched by the vitality of Renaissance humanism with its enthusiasm for ancient texts and humane letters. This openness to humanism derived from a distinctive feature of the Society of Jesus that also supported their turn toward scholarship and schools: a worldliness and ease with culture rooted in the conviction that it was possible to find God in all things. Moreover, one of the fundamental tenets of humanist educational theory—that study and mastery of the literary texts of antiquity fostered individual virtue and the development of upright character—dovetailed neatly with the Jesuits' commitment to "help souls." Thus, in their colleges, the Jesuits expended their energies molding their students into virtuous, lettered, Christian gentlemen who would contribute to the good of society as leading citizens and well-educated Catholics. For example, in opening their school in Tivoli, they explained that their endeavors were rendered *ad civitatis utilitatem*—for the sake of the city.[62]

The Jesuits' decision to establish schools was not merely a foray into the intellectual ferment of humanism but, just as importantly, a commitment to the pastoral care of students placed in their charge. In the *Constitutions*, members of the Society learned that the schools were meant to help members of the Society and "their fellow men to attain the ultimate end for which they were created"—that is, salvation.[63] The operation of schools not only advanced students' learning; it gave the Jesuits opportunities to tend to their students' souls through moral exhortation, spiritual direction, religious teaching, and Catholic devotional life.

Although often portrayed in such a manner in popular and scholarly literature, and even by some of the earliest Jesuits, the Society was not founded to battle Protestantism, nor did the Jesuits adopt education as a ministry as part of a grand plan to squelch the gains realized by the heretical followers of Luther. The earliest records related to the establishment of the Society and its schools reveal little interest in the reform movement sweeping across northern Europe.[64] Yet given the ecclesial tumult of the mid-sixteenth century, the Jesuits inevitably found themselves contending with Protestantism in their educational work. In the closing years of Ignatius's life, the Society assumed an anti-Protestant stance and mission, with the schools (especially in northern Europe) aiming to inoculate students, religiously and academically, against the incursions of Protestantism. Thus it was only after his death that Ignatius was cast in the perdurable image as the "great David raised up by God to put down Luther, the Goliath," as historian John O'Malley described it.[65]

Having taken the momentous turn toward education, the Jesuits then sought an effective means of educating their students, their efforts resulting in the famous *Ratio Studiorum*. Ignatius's insistence that the Society develop a clearly articulated pedagogical modus operandi stemmed from his own experiences as a student. Stymied intellectually by his inchoate, disorganized course of studies at the University of Alcalá, he recommenced studies at the University of Paris and, there, following a more orderly, coherent academic regime, he succeeded academically. Thus Ignatius insisted that the Jesuits develop a plan for studies along the lines of the *modus et ordo Parisiensis*—the systematic fashion by which he was instructed in Paris. Given this mandate, years of collaborative trial and error with many popular educational strategies of the day culminated in the 1599 *Ratio Atque Institutio Studiorum Societatis Iesu*. More commonly known as the *Ratio Studiorum*, it was less a treatise on educational theory than a well-developed pedagogical guide outlining the aim, matter, and methods of Jesuit education for members of the Society who found themselves teaching youth in the remotest corners of the globe.[66]

The *Ratio Studiorum* set forth pedagogical principles applied to a curriculum that mixed elements of Renaissance humanism with aspects of medieval scholasticism; put another way, it mixed the science of man with the science of God. The Jesuits considered curricular gradation essential: subjects should be taught one at a time in order of increasing complexity, beginning with the rudiments of grammar, followed by the humanities, rhetoric, philosophy, and then, for clerical students, theology. The Jesuits also adopted the complementary principles of coordination and subordination. Coordination meant that various subjects were brought together at a given point in the course of studies under a particular disciplinary umbrella, such that they reinforced and complemented one another; for example, in the development of "perfect eloquence" befitting Christian gentlemen, those in the rhetoric class studied Roman and Greek oratory, some vernacular, as well as history, mythology, and archeology. Subordination meant that subjects that did not contribute to the immediate educational objectives were relegated to accessory status. Further, the *Ratio Studiorum* not only defined what subjects were to be taught, and when, it also explained how to teach. The Jesuit system of education became known for a distinctive cluster of pedagogical practices that included personal interest in the student, repetition, pupil activity, classroom competition, and promotion based on achievement.[67]

The strengths of the Jesuit educational system lay in the counterbalance affected between the methodicalness of the *Ratio Studiorum* and the flexibility encouraged by the *Constitutions*. The *Ratio* provided Jesuits scattered across the globe with common goals, methods, and a curriculum. It contained strategies for educating new members of the Society, including supervision and training for their work as educators. On the other hand, the *Constitutions* directed the Jesuits to adapt their program of studies as necessary to "times, places, and persons." Methodicalness and flexibility, coupled with a theologically rooted openness to culture, proved immensely effective in the work of education. Once committed to education as a means of helping souls, "they did not falter."[68] Swept up in the spirit of the Age of Discovery, by the time of Ignatius's death in 1556 the Society was operating more than thirty-five schools. When the *Ratio* was published in 1599, there were more than two hundred educational institutions under their direction. By 1625 the number reached 372, and by 1773 the Jesuits were operating, worldwide, more than eight hundred educational institutions.[69]

The Jesuits' willingness to adapt to times, places, and persons that contributed to their success in education served them well in their manifold missionary endeavors, including their North American missions. From their base in Quebec, the Jesuits launched their legendary seventeenth-century missions among the Iroquois, the Hurons, and other tribes in the northeast, the Great Lakes Region, and the Mississippi Valley. Their far-flung adventures and relative proximity were cause for great consternation among Eliot's ancestors, the Puritans of New England, who arrived in the New World in 1630 with a profound sense of religious mission and a deep faith in education. They also brought with them an intense loathing for the Jesuits, a disdain that proved perdurable from one generation to the next, even into the late-nineteenth century. The roots of the controversy between Eliot and the Jesuits stretched deep into the soil of colonial New England.[70]

Fleeing religious persecution in the Old World and seeking financial gain in the New, the Puritans of the Massachusetts Bay Company arrived in New England in 1630 with a remarkable set of theological resources at their disposal. Armed with a theology that made much of the idea of covenant and a prodigious religious imagination, they conceived of an idea as bold as any: that they were on an errand from God to reform the European church through their example of godly living. Appropriating a truly epic role unto themselves, they cast their community, as Perry Miller put it, as an "organized task force of Christians, executing a flank attack on the corruptions of Christendom," framing their Exodus-like sojourn from the Old World to the New as an "essential maneuver in the drama of Christendom." They would start quite literally from the ground up to build a reformed community of "visible saints" absolutely free from the accretions of Romanism and the corruptions bedeviling the European churches. Their "Citty upon a Hill," this "hyper-Protestant society," in the words of historian George Marsden, would, through its example, reinvigorate the languishing Reformation, bringing it to fruition.[71]

A truly reformed society consisted of people who based their lives, individually and communally, on the Word of God found in the Scriptures; education and literacy were, therefore, paramount concerns among the visible saints of New England. Having already passed a law holding parents and masters responsible for their children's and apprentices' ability to read, in 1647 the General Court of Massachusetts, hoping to protect themselves from the "ould deluder, Satan," passed a law mandating schools. Those towns that the "Lord hath increased . . . to the number of fifty householders" were directed to employ a teacher for their children, while those of "one hundred families or householders" were to establish a grammar school and secure a master "able to instruct youth so far as they may be fitted for the university."[72]

There was no university as such in New England, but there was a college for which young men might be fitted. In 1636, just six years after arriving in the New World, members of the General Court, acting upon colonists' concerns, voted to establish a "schoale or colledge" that they and later generations would know as Harvard. *New England's First Fruits* (1643) recounts the institution's origins: "After God had carried us safe to *New England,* and wee had builded our houses, provided necessaries for our liveli-hood, rear'd convenient places for Gods worship, and setled the Civill Government: One of the next things we longed for, and looked after was to advance *Learning* and perpetuate it to Posterity; . . . the Colledge was, by common consent, appointed to be at *Cambridge,* (a place very pleasant and accommodate) and is called (according to the name of the first founder) *Harvard Colledge.*"[73]

Religious concerns had an important role in establishing Harvard, for "dreading to leave an illiterate Ministry to the Churches, when our present Ministers shall lie in the Dust," the Puritans built the college to train clergy for their wilderness Zion.[74] It was not Harvard's sole purpose; according to John Eliot, missionary to the native population, "Youth at the college are brought up for the holy service of the Lord either in magistracy or ministry especially," and only 40 to 50 percent of early graduates pursued ecclesial careers.[75] Yet a deeply felt need for a learned clergy clearly fueled the move toward a college. This concern for a learned clergy stemmed from the Reformation, which, having stripped the clergy of much of its mediational role, recast it primarily in terms of preaching. Some within the broad folds of Protestantism, particularly those given to a more enthusiastic style, deemed advanced education for the clergy unnecessary,[76] but most considered it essential if the Scriptures were to be fully and properly understood and preached effectively. So central was the idea of a learned clergy to Protestantism that holding the bachelor's degree became common among clergymen during the seventeenth century, and wearing an academically styled robe became customary attire for preaching. The importance of a learned clergy within Protestantism was rhetorically underscored by references to the ignorance of Roman Catholic priests and an often-invoked argument that a learned Protestant clergy would keep Catholicism at bay.[77]

Modeling their institution after the Puritan-run Emmanuel College at Cambridge (alma mater of many early New Englanders), the earliest Harvardians took religion seriously.[78] The laws of Harvard College stipulated that students were to be instructed such that they would come to "*know God and Iesus Christ* . . . and therefore to lay *Christ* in the bottome, as the only foundation of all sound knowledge and Learning."[79] Despite the Christocentric orientation, the curriculum bore, like the *Ratio Studiorum,* the imprint of humanism; supported in part by Calvin's theology of common grace, Harvardians studied classical languages and pagan authors in pursuit of oratorical skills that would enhance the preaching of the Scriptures.[80] The rest of the curriculum was more clearly religious in orientation, with biblical and theological studies filling out a student's course of studies. Students were exhorted to pray twice daily, directing their spiritual attention to the Hebrew Scriptures in the morning and the Christian Scriptures in the evening. Communal prayer complemented the private; the college community gathered for prayer twice daily, worshipped with the local community on Sundays, and held sessions for prophesying. Tutors were responsible for the academic and the spiritual progress of their students, while students were expected to recite to their tutors sermons they had heard. Expulsion awaited those students who transgressed the easily conflated laws of God and the laws of the college; the latter included missing religious services or blaspheming on the Sabbath. Along those lines, President Henry Dunster was removed from office in 1654 when he questioned the orthodox practice of baptizing infants.[81]

The intensity and purposefulness with which the Puritans and the earliest Harvardians approached their ecclesial, civil, and academic affairs reflected the very nature of their mission—the further reformation and concomitant revitalization of Christendom. The daunting task that they assumed, their errand into the wilderness, was bound to produce anxiety. The threat of declension from within their ranks clearly provoked it; each wayward saint rendered visible the tenuousness of the entire venture and undermined the vitality of their mission.[82] Threats from without bedeviled the community as well. In fact, the Puritans' efforts to create and maintain a thoroughly religious "Citty upon a Hill," including the establishment of Harvard College, can be fully understood only in light of what James Axtell has described as a contest of cultures, one pitting the Puritans of New England against enemies old and new. Though Puritan divine Cotton Mather deemed New England "Immanuel's Land," in the seventeenth and much of the eighteenth centuries it was still contested terrain. As such, the drama of the Reformation was to be worked out over and against other communities: Native Americans, French Catholics, and their Jesuit consorts.[83]

The presence of Native Americans deeply complicated the Puritan project of establishing a wilderness Zion. On the one hand, Native Americans were perceived as targets for missionary work—thus, the seal of the Massachusetts Bay Company depicting a solitary native mouthing the words "COME OVER AND HELP US." To replace superstition and barbarism with the gospel of Christ and civilized ways, missionaries such as John Eliot preached the Christian faith and founded praying towns for the natives, while Harvard established the soon-to-fail Indian College and a press for printing the Bible and other tracts in native languages.[84] On the other hand, the Puritans perceived the natives as threats to a way of life, their religious mission—indeed, to life itself. The imaginary native's plea for help on the company's seal makes all the more poignant the quite real pleas that eventually uttered forth from the Puritans: pleas to God to protect their communities from the natives, and pleas to the natives for food, safe passage, mercy, and for kinfolk and neighbors taken into captivity. The fears provoked by the natives were exacerbated by political alliances between various tribes and the French on their northern border. The French and their native allies represented a certain political danger, but they signaled spiritual and religious dangers as well, in no small part because the Jesuits lived with the French and among the natives.[85]

In 1647, the Massachusetts General Court felt compelled to legislate on the matter of dangerous religious interlopers, revealing deeply ingrained fears of the Jesuits among the earliest European settlers in Massachusetts. Laying primary blame for the "great warrs & combustions which are this day in Europe" on the "secrit practises of those of the Jesuiticall order," the court banned any "Jesuit or ecclesiasticall pson ordayned by yᵉ authoritie of the pope" from Massachusetts "for the prevention of like euills amongst oʳselues." First-time offenders were to be banished; second-time offenders could be put to death, with the exception of "any such Jesuit as shalbe cast vppon oʳ shores by shippwrack or other accydent." In 1700, the court passed another law on this topic, directing "every Jesuit, seminary priest, missionary, or other spiritual or ecclesiastical person" whose authority derived from Rome to leave Massachusetts. Those who persisted would be "deemed and accounted an incendiary and disturber of the publick peace and safety, and an enemy to the true Christian religion" and made to "suffer perpetual imprisonment." Death awaited any recaptured escapee, while those who did "wittingly and willingly receive, relieve, harbour, conceal, aid or succour any Jesuit, priest, missionary or other ecclesiastical person of the Romish clergy" faced stiff fines and several days in the pillory. And fearing that they might encounter crafty, glib-tongued Jesuits determined to disabuse them of their Protestant convictions, citizens of Massachusetts fortified themselves with texts such as *A Protestant's Resolution, Shewing his Reason why he will not be a PAPIST: Digested Into so plain a Method of Ques-*

tion and Answer, that an ordinary Capacity may be able to defend the Protestant Religion against the most cunning Jesuit, or Popish Priest, a tract that went through at least twenty-eight editions.[86]

Early Harvardians did their part to stem the Roman tide. The Jesuits fell victim to public excoriation at commencement exercises, where new bachelors and masters demonstrated their rhetorical skills and acumen. In 1697, Adam Winthrop took up the question "An Jesuitæ possint esse Boni Subdit?"—Is it possible for a Jesuit to be a good citizen?—and argued that it was not. In 1704, Thomas Tufts responded in the negative to the question "An Æquivocatio Jesuitica sit licita?"—Should Jesuit dissembling be permitted?[87]

Pervasive disdain for the Jesuits surfaced in contemporaries' reactions to the debacle surrounding Harvard's first president, Nathaniel Eaton. The colonists' noble efforts to establish an institution of higher learning were tempered by the ignoble tenure of Eaton, who was accused of starving his charges, whipping the students, and beating an assistant master. (He probably embezzled college funds as well.) Appropriately enough, Eaton was dismissed from his post in 1639, and the college closed for a year. His actions earned him the opprobrium of Nathaniel Rogers, who in a 1652 commencement address derided him as a *"Iesuitæ versipellis"*—a turncoat Jesuit.[88] It was a certain insult. As early as the 1500s, the Jesuits found themselves described as "assassins, ferocious wild boars, thieves, traitors, serpents, vipers," and the devil's very agents. So intense and negative were reactions to the Jesuits that the words *Jesuit* and *Jesuitical* assumed opprobrious meanings as they entered the French, German, Portuguese, Italian, and Dutch languages and dictionaries; a "Jesuit" or "Jesuitical" person could be taken for not only a member of the Society of Jesus but a "cunning zealot," a "hypocritical person," or a "perfidious person." As early as the 1640s, an English-speaker might use the word *Jesuit* to indicate a "dissembling person; a prevaricator."[89]

In considering the Eaton affair, Governor John Winthrop wrote in his journal, "And, being thus gone, the church proceeded and cast him out"—the only fitting recourse for a community of saints. Winthrop mused further that, prior to his emigration to the New World, Eaton "had been sometimes initiated among the Jesuits," though "his friends drew him from them"; but now exiled from New England, "it was very probable, he now intended to return to them again, being at this time about thirty years of age, and upwards." Actually, after a less-than-godly stint in Virginia, matriculation at the University of Padua, and a rectorship in

England (where he persecuted dissenters), Eaton died a debtor in King's Bench prison.[90]

By 1763, the contest of cultures had resolved in favor of the English. As Axtell put it, the "English had all but won the palm, France had been expelled from the continent, and the Indians faced a bleak future." Political and military triumph did not, however, mean spiritual or religious success. The Puritans' errand into the wilderness, their efforts to create a "Citty upon a Hill," failed in large part because the second generation lacked the religious fervor of the first. Even with such fervor, it is difficult to believe that they would have been able to "rivet the eyes of the world upon their city on the hill" and thereby realize a thorough reformation of the European church.[91] But the Puritans of New England were far from ineffectual. They left their successors in America a most remarkable legacy. Having conflated sacred history with secular, their journey with God's will, future generations of Americans would understand their lives and history in providential terms, claiming their country for Protestantism. And they would continue, like their Puritan ancestors, to disdain Roman Catholicism and the Jesuits, particularly as the Jesuits established colleges in Protestant America.

The American Revolution was a remarkable victory whereby thirteen colonies severed their political ties with England. It was, however, in the words of contemporary Benjamin Rush, merely the "first act of the great drama." Subsequent acts, wherein the nascent country would succeed or fail, entailed establishing an entire system of government and creating rules of law. Here again, the colonists-turned-citizens made a revolutionary move by disestablishing religion. There would be no national or state church, nor would the government interfere with the free exercise of religion by its citizens. Enlightenment thought provided the theoretical framework for the separation of church and state; religious demographics created the social context for the development of this uniquely American construct. America was at high tide politically, but low tide religiously, with religious adherents only making up approximately 17 percent of the population in 1776. The principle of separation of church and state found in the First Amendment was not, then, solely a case of political liberalism or religious largesse on the part of more powerful denominations. Quite simply, no denomination or block of denominations had sufficient membership or power to lay claim to or maintain a legally privileged position in a largely unchurched nation. In effect, the First Amendment thrust Catholic and Protestant churches alike out onto the free market of religion.[92] Absent the constraints of religious establishment, Protestant denominations and Catholic religious orders were at liberty to establish colleges and compete for students, which they did with vigor in the antebellum years, a period aptly described in the history of American education as the age of the college.

As the nineteenth century opened, evangelical fervor swept through the cities, countryside, and colleges as America's languishing spiritual pulse quickened. The intensity of the Second Great Awakening eventually diminished, but its effects persisted. Notably, it contributed to a doubling in the rate of religious adherence, which reached 35 percent by the Civil War, and a complementary intensification of America's self-identification with Protestantism.[93] Though largely unchurched, many early republicans were deistic and could, therefore, conceive of their new nation as one under God. The next generation defined the United States more narrowly as a Protestant nation. Here the Puritan legacy—the conflation of the sacred and the secular, the religious and the civic—bore fruit again. America was not just one Protestant nation among many. To many nineteenth-century Americans, God providentially selected their country, and as such it was to stand foremost among all nations. Its emergence as a leading industrial nation, coupled with its survival and concomitant sanctification in the purifying crucible of the Civil War, only confirmed and strengthened the conviction that the United States was a Protestant nation with a unique and critical role to play in salvation history. Thus could Methodist Bishop Matthew Simpson of Chicago unabashedly inform British listeners, in rhetoric resoundingly Puritan, "God is making our land a kind of central spot for the whole earth. The eyes of the world are upon us."[94]

The United States had rejected a national church, but soon thereafter it embraced a national religion, and thus a "*de facto* establishment grew where the old legal one had fallen," according to historian Martin E. Marty. "A national Church is one thing, a national Religion is quite another thing," announced an editor in *Harper's New Monthly Magazine* in 1858. The Protestant nature of that national religion was taken as a given. "We are," asserted a contributor to an 1859 issue of the *Princeton Review*, "eminently a Protestant nation." This identification with Protestantism was realized largely through voluntary organizations and popular institutions, especially schools that were, as Brown University President Francis Wayland (1827–55) put it, "inseparably connected with Protestant Christianity."[95] Recognizing the inherent political value of schools, many early republicans argued for the importance of universal education; considered a fragile political entity, the very success of their fledgling republic depended upon the widest possible diffusion of knowledge in order to make citizens more virtuous and knowledgeable. But the generation of men who built the wall between church and state were conflicted about the relationship between religion and education. Some deemed religious training essential and denominational sponsorship of schools prudent; others considered religion divisive and antithetical to one of the central aims of education—namely, building a sense of national identity by fostering unity. Over the course of a few decades, as America's sense of its Protestant identity and providential destiny matured, divergent views gave way to a fairly widespread consensus that the nation's common schools were Protestant institutions.[96]

Higher education figured prominently in the religious majority's efforts to make of the United States a civilized Protestant nation. The drive for colleges was fueled in part by boosterism; town after town considered itself, at least potentially, an "Athens of the West" and thus welcomed the requisite institution of high culture and advanced learning.[97] Just as importantly, denominationally sponsored colleges were seen as essential building blocks in extending the infrastructure of Protestantism westward. Spreading the beneficent influence of Christianity and civilization westward through college building required resources. Financial resources flowed from the eastern states to the West through organizations such as the Society for the Promotion of Collegiate and Theological Education at the West (SPCTEW, established in 1843), while human resources in the form of evangelical Christians, such as seven theological students known as the Yale Band, went west to open and staff new colleges, preaching the New England way as they did so.[98]

During the nineteenth century, colleges proliferated, especially in the West. By one count, more than two hundred colleges operated in the period between 1800 and 1860; in the next thirty years, the number topped four hundred.[99] The increase provoked concern among some, with one commentator wondering "how England, with a population of twenty-three million, managed with four degree-granting institutions, while the State of Ohio, with a population of only three million, supported thirty-seven."[100] Less skeptical souls saw in it a phenomenon uniquely American and Protestant as well. In response to a proposal (that surfaced with some regularity) for the development of a national university, a SPCTEW essayist rejoined, "It was never intelligently proposed to concentrate these advantages in a single University, 'cum privilegio,' nor to confine them to a few Colleges, at great distances from each other." To the contrary. "The wide extent of the country, the prospective increase of population, the form of government, the independence of the States, and above all the Protestant principle of universal education," this writer claimed, "have forbidden such a design . . . our country . . . is to be a land of Colleges."[101]

The extraordinary multiplication of colleges during the antebellum years illuminates the growing vitality and dynamism of American Protestantism, including denominational rivalry, which many blamed for what they considered to be an overproliferation of colleges. It also sheds light on some of the complexities and ironies of the American Protestant experience. Despite a tiny Catholic population (especially through the 1830s), Roman Catholicism and "Jesuitism" became large-scale concerns. Unabashed claims that the United States was a Protestant nation did not mean that Protestants could rest on their religious laurels. America, the country, was still being made: the West, "rushing up to a giant manhood," in the words of Lyman Beecher,[102] served as a constant reminder of both the promise and the perils inherent in the task of creating and sustaining a Protestant nation that would serve as a light to the nations of the world. For many, every Catholic steeple, every Catholic immigrant—every Jesuit and his school—was cause for concern, providing incontrovertible evidence that the Protestant Kingdom of God was still in the making, its very existence tenuous.

If early republicans believed that the success of the fledgling republic lay in the widest possible diffusion of knowledge, antebellum Protestant leaders were convinced that the success of the United States as a Protestant nation lay in large measure in wide diffusion of information about the threats posed by Roman Catholicism. Protestant preachers mounted the pulpit and public speakers took to their lecterns spelling out the dangers of romanism, while publishers papered the country with pamphlets and tracts stoking the flames of anti-Catholicism with hyperbolic rhetoric, conspiratorial theories, and salacious accounts of clerical debauchery (what historian Richard Hofstadter dubbed the "pornography of the Puritan").[103] So voluminous was anti-Catholic literature that larger cities could support bookstores trading solely in anti-Catholic works, stocking their shelves with monographs that regaled readers with the progress, errors, and dangers of romanism. The titles themselves were inflammatory: *Popery an Enemy to Civil and Religious Liberty, and Dangers to Our Republic* (1836); *A Letter from Rome, Showing the Exact Conformity of Popery and Paganism* (1835); *Priests' Prisons for Women* (1854); and *Female Convents: Secrets of Nunneries Disclosed* (1834).[104]

The descendants of Luther were regularly exhorted to be particularly wary of the sons of Loyola. At midcentury, anti-Jesuit literature was flourishing in America and in its golden age in Europe.[105] Sensational titles attracted large readerships: *Intrigues of Jesuitism in the United States of America* (seventh edition, 1846); *Americans Warned of Jesuitism; or, the Jesuits Unveiled* (1851); *Jesuit Juggling: Forty Popish Frauds Detected and Disclosed* (1835); *Secret Instructions to the Jesuits; Faithfully Translated from the Latin of an Old Genuine London Copy* (1841); *The Jesuit; a National Melodrama in Three Acts* (1850); and *A Book of Tracts, Containing the Origin and Progress, Cruelties, Frauds, Superstitions, Miracles, Ceremonies, Idolatrous Customs of the Church of Rome: with a Succinct Account of the Rise and Progress of the Jesuits* (1856). Feature articles about the history and current activities of the Jesuits appeared in popular and scholarly journals, including the *Princeton Review*, the *Journal of Sacred Literature*, the *Southern Quarterly Review*, the *American Monthly Magazine*, *De Bow's Review*, and the *Ladies' Repository*.[106] More temperate in tone than the fictional works, they were often just as derogatory.

Antebellum lexicographers sharpened Americans' understanding of the Jesuit. Those consulting Noah Webster's 1850 *American Dictionary of the English Language* learned that a Jesuit was a member of the Society of Jesus, a "society remarkable for their cunning in propagating their principles; Hence . . . [a] crafty person; an intriguer," and that Jesuitism meant "cunning deceit, hypocrisy, prevarication, deceptive practices to effect a purpose." Webster's 1864 *Dictionary* adopted a more moderate tone, noting that Jesuits "have displayed in their enterprises a high degree of zeal, learning, policy, and skill." Nonetheless, "their opponents" have claimed that they used "art and intrigue in promoting or accomplishing their purposes, whence the words *Jesuit, Jesuitical,* and the like, have acquired an odious and offensive sense." An earlier dictionary (1839) was apparently written by one of those opponents, who explained that the Jesuits " 'pretend to follow exactly the footsteps of our blessed Saviour, whose name they have usurpt. At first they gained to themselves the people's esteem by their tolerable carriage: but now they are generally hated and feared, because of their devilish maxims, their bold enterprises, and secret intrigues.' A *Jesuit* is, in English usage, an intriguer; a crafty, subtle designer or plotter."[107]

It was during the nineteenth century that Americans began to write their first national histories, forging national narratives of the origins, the fight to establish, and the subsequent life of the new nation. Scholars such as George Bancroft (1800–1891) and Francis Parkman (1823–93) and contributors to popular journals crafted historical works reaching large audiences. As legatees of the Puritan myth of America, these historians afforded religion a large explanatory role in the history of America, with Protestantism predictably assuming the role of protagonist over its perennial antagonist, Roman Catholicism. But unlike seventeenth-century Puritans, who roundly feared and loathed the Jesuits, nineteenth-century Protestants writing American history evinced some awe, even respect, for the Jesuits of yesteryear and their daring exploits and adventures. So it was with the Harvard-educated Parkman, author of more than a half-dozen books on French-English relations in colonial North America. (An essayist in the *Catholic World* wrote that Parkman "does prosaic justice to our glorious missionaries and the Catholic heroes who opened up this vast region to Christianity and civilization.")[108] He would write in the preface of *The Jesuits in North America in the Seventeenth Century* that there were "Few passages of history . . . more striking than those which record the efforts of the earlier French Jesuits to convert the Indians." Influenced by romanticism, Parkman found the stories of the Jesuits full of "dramatic and philosophic interest." Philosophically, the Jesuits' experience in North America surfaced critical issues about religion and liberty, useful for understanding the American experience, particularly how Protestantism was conducive and Catholicism antithetical to liberty. Dramatically, the history of the Jesuits burgeoned with courageous, almost superhuman exploits.[109] Thus in the hands of nineteenth-century historians, the once-despised Jesuit missionary became a heroic character who, to quote a contributor to the *Southern Quarterly Review*, "with his breviary under his arm, his beads at his girdle, and his crucifix in his hand, went forth without fear to encounter the most dreaded dangers—martyrdom was nothing to him. He knew that the altar which might stream with his blood, and the mound which might be raised over his remains, would become a most cherished object of his fame and an expressive emblem of the power of his religion."[110]

But the more salutary image of the Jesuit as heroic missionary evaporated when the historical lens foreshortened time and the Jesuit mutated from missionary to educator. Jesuit missionaries were safely entombed in the historical annals of time; Jesuit educators were not. Some would admit, begrudgingly, that the Jesuits were "skillful teachers" who realized remarkable success in academics akin to their achievements in the missions. "With whatever duty these men were charged, spiritual, educational, or merely secular," wrote a Reverend Floy, for the *Ladies' Repository*, "they performed it with consummate ability, and almost uniformly with success." Recognized as the "best teachers of youth . . . [s]chools, academies, colleges, were placed under their supervision."[111] Unfortunately, they achieved academic success through ignoble means.[112] These were men, their Protestant critics claimed, who conspired to insinuate themselves among the elite and powerful, using despotic, manipulative methods to gain their students' trust and loyalty.

For some, the college-building efforts of the United States stood in the grand sweep of history commenced in the late-fifteenth and early-sixteenth centuries. "There was certainly never an age," wrote an 1843 contributor to the *Christian Review*, "which has exerted so powerful an influence on our own times." Nor were there "two men on earth better fitted to become the leaders of the powerful parties, that rallied under their separate and opposing standards, than were Luther and Loyola." Indeed, in the nineteenth century these two "master-spirits of the age"[113] emerged as symbolic personifications of the battle for the soul of America waged during the age of the college. Though American Protestant higher education intellectually owed more to Calvin than to Luther, nineteenth-century American Protestants understood their work in the field of higher education as a continuation of an epic battle between Luther and Loyola. The two, historiographically shackled in the minds of nineteenth-century American Protestants, were juxtaposed with great regularity. It was Luther who "asserted the power of the Word of God" over and against a corrupt Rome, and Loyola, in the "hour of Rome's despair," who "arose as a champion against her vigorous adversaries." It was a common theme: "The arch-heretic Luther was troubling the peace of the Church, and the Vatican trembled. Loyola deemed himself destined to turn back the tide."[114]

For a number of nineteenth-century Protestants, it was time once again to turn back the Jesuit tide. Loyola had already stymied Luther; his efforts "effectually checked the progress of the Reformation and gave stability to the tottering throne of the Pontiff," complained one essayist in 1860. "No Protestant can be expected to look with favor upon the schools of an Order whose vigorous efforts stayed the progress of the Reformation," wrote Henry Barnard, a well-known educator.[115] Now the sons of Loyola threatened to thwart America's providential destiny as a Protestant nation by establishing Jesuit colleges, those dens of religious despotism. Professor William Wells recognized that "religious liberty" gave the Jesuits a "capital field to pursue their march unmolested," but the effects deeply concerned him. "As a nation, and as Protestants, we are clearly taking the matter too coolly," he wrote, adding that "unless we bestir ourselves, we shall wake up to learn that, while we have slept, the enemy has been sowing tares."[116]

To "bestir" the Protestant public on behalf of the cause, the Reverend Lyman Beecher, author of "A Plea for Western Colleges" (an essay that first appeared in the *New York Observer* and subsequently as an appendix to *The First Report of the Society for the Promotion of Collegiate and Theological Education at the West* in 1844), informed readers that "Rome is at this time making unprecedented efforts to garrison this valley with her seminaries of education," with many under the direction of the Jesuits.[117] His son Edward was of like mind. Before an audience gathered at the Park Street Church in Boston in 1845, Edward spoke passionately of the need for Protestant colleges in the West lest the Jesuits capture the field and undermine the cause of a Protestant America. The Jesuits "needed no urging to go into this work; if you would let them, they would educate the whole world." He challenged his fellow Protestants: "Ought Puritans, whose very religion is based on thought and reasoning—Puritans, the authors of the system of popular education—Puritans, the great antagonists of the church of Rome, to be less zealous in the great work of education than the Jesuits, those supple and crafty instruments of Rome—those enslavers of the human race?" One of Beecher's colleagues followed with another diatribe against the Jesuits and their work in the United States: "The Jesuits are willing, nay, longing, nay, plotting and toiling, to become the educators of America. Let them have the privilege of possessing the seats of education in the west, and of moulding the leading minds of the millions that are to inhabit there, and we may give up all our efforts to produce in the west what Puritanism has produced here."[118]

The remedy proposed by Protestant educators was the Protestant college: "Place efficient Protestant colleges in the proximity of the Catholic, and the latter will wither."[119] In that vein, a Boston clergyman, E. N. Kirk, expounding on "our great battle with the Jesuit, on western soil," exhorted his listeners: "We must build College against College. If the musty atmosphere of a Jesuit School suits the freeborn western youth; if the repetition of scholastic modes of discipline can captivate the child of the prairies, then we may fail in the contest. But all experience has confirmed our anticipation, that America is a field on which the open, manly, Christian discipline of a Protestant College must annihilate the rival system of Jesuitical instruction."[120]

It was under the auspices of SPCTEW that Professor Porter published

The Educational Systems of the Puritans and Jesuits Compared (1851), notable if for no other reason than its predictability. Porter's essay developed two themes commonly found among Protestant commentators: that Jesuit education was inherently dangerous and fundamentally different from Protestant education. He lauded the "college and school systems of the United States," where the "glory and strength of the Protestant interest, have been expounded and defended," making "Protestant civilization, Protestant freedom, and Protestant piety, to be what they are." In Protestant schools, wrote Porter, students approached their studies with a spirit of freedom beneficently affecting their character and learning. Conversely, the Jesuit college was a "thorough despotism . . . far more dreadful than any civil or ecclesiastical system; for it takes into its iron grasp the intellect and soul of a living man." There the Jesuit strangled free inquiry and denied the student "right training of his character" by refusing him the "freedom and separate responsibility which are necessary to make a character possible." In this country, "no man . . . would think of sending a son to a Jesuit college," asserted Porter, "if he wished to fit him to take an honorable position as an American and a free citizen."[121]

American Protestants' concerns for the presence of the Jesuits and their colleges were not limited to the American West. Waves of immigration from famine-starved Ireland constituted nothing less than a "roman tide" swelling the Catholic population in cities along the East coast, including Boston. Who could have imagined, queried Harvard's 1853 Dudleian lecturer on the "Errors and Superstitions of Rome," that a "Catholic population would throng the streets . . . that a convent would rise within sight of the spires of Harvard, and a Catholic College"—referring to Holy Cross—would "be established in the very heart of Massachusetts!"[122] Another author contended that this Catholic college perched on a hill overlooking the city would undoubtedly provoke "amazement" among the "fathers of New England if they could revisit these scenes." As for their successors, "it is almost too much for the children of the Puritans to bear. Out from the heart of our beloved Commonwealth are now to graduate, from year to year, Jesuit priests,—the O'Briens, the O'Flahertys, and the McNamaras. Ireland and Rome together make a combination of a not very attractive character to the sons of New England sires."[123]

Given the degree and intensity of anti-Catholic and anti-Jesuit sentiment among Protestants at midcentury, Harvard's 1893 decision to grant

Bishop John J. Keane an honorary doctorate understandably felt like the dawn of a "new era" of religious relations to some observers. This sea change in Protestant-Catholic relations was not lost on Charles Eliot. Near the end of his lengthy presidency, he had occasion to comment on the presence of Catholics at Harvard. "Harvard University was founded by the Puritans," wrote Eliot in 1907, "but their doctrine has been so far evolved as to become very catholic and comprehensive." The presence of Catholics at Harvard would be "rather startling to the Puritan founders," admitted Eliot, "although it is their descendants that have brought it about."[124]

Those Puritan ancestors would have been far less startled by Eliot's critical remarks about the Jesuits and their "famous schools." Anti-Jesuit sentiment was deeply rooted in the Protestant consciousness. The Jesuits, as missionaries and educators, laid claim to the Protestant imagination, summoning up a plethora of disparate reactions, from awe to disdain, respect to fear. While the growing influence of religious liberalism softened Protestant-Catholic relations, anti-Jesuit sentiment persisted. Even as Eliot the Unitarian extended the hand of religious friendship to Bishop Keane, even as he won praise from local Catholics for his support of a school bill, even as Harvard opened its doors to "papists," the Jesuits remained beyond the religious pale in Eliot's liberal world.

Through the centuries, the Jesuits seemed particularly astute at living beyond the pale of Protestant acceptability, turning their position as religious outsiders into mythic status. "Where they met with hostility," wrote one insightful Protestant observer, "they seemed to triumph in exact ratio with the virulence of their enemies."[125] There were, of course, immense costs. Jesuit missionaries sacrificed their lives, their famous schools faced challenges and violence, and the Society itself was expelled from numerous countries during the eighteenth and nineteenth centuries. Nonetheless, the Jesuits seemed to thrive on opposition. Though the Society itself was not founded to battle Protestantism, Ignatius of Loyola, the one-time soldier, came to understand the value of the adversarial; opposition became an ironic measure of success.

For three centuries, the Jesuits thrived on tensions created by the Reformation, their stature derived in large measure from the role they played in the machinations of the Counter Reformation. But changes were in the making, and the Harvard Law School controversy would make them apparent to the Jesuits working in colleges in the United States. The controversy between Eliot and the Jesuits was not simply another skirmish between the descendants of Luther and the sons of

Loyola. As is sometimes the case when the earth shakes, more than one fault line was at play. Modernity—in large part a mindset that privileged the new over the old—created a new divide in an academic system already cleaved by the Reformation: the traditional and the modern. Such profound change, felt throughout Christian higher education, created opportunities for some and exigencies for others. The Jesuits fell into the latter camp. As old antipathies endured, new academic and social realities emerged. A potent critique of Jesuit education developed: that it was not modern. Jesuit education, its new critics claimed, was rooted in the past and thus irrelevant to the wants of the day in modern, Protestant America. Directed in their *Constitutions* to adapt to the times, as the Law School controversy evolved into a public controversy the Jesuits found themselves on the defensive, forced to demonstrate that traditional forms of education were indeed relevant in modern America. But the challenge to adapt to the times, to prove themselves and their colleges timely in the age of the university, would prove far more daunting and taxing than grappling with familiar Protestant antipathies that flourished during the age of the college. The Jesuits' ongoing, unresolved troubles with Harvard over the Law School's admissions policy would make the challenge of time, in the form of the modern mindset, quite clear.

CHAPTER TWO

Time: The Harvard Law School Controversy and the Modern Imperative

The universities need a sound and
thorough reformation. I must say
so no matter who takes offense.

—Martin Luther

The story is told that one of President Eliot's predecessors was accustomed to conclude his chapel
prayers by asking the Lord to
"bless Harvard College and all inferior institutions." Whether there
is any documentary evidence for
the anecdote I do not know, but
this is unnecessary, because its
authenticity is sufficiently proved
by the fact that the prayer has
been answered.

—Edwin Slosson, *Great American
Universities*, 1910

In 1850, the peak of the age of the college, America stood on the eve of
great changes. In a decade's time, the more perfect union for which the
Revolutionary generation fought would hang precariously in the balance
as the Civil War threatened to dissolve the union of states into a political
mess. In the aftermath of this national crucible, industrialization, urban-
ization, and immigration increased apace, transforming the United States
socially, demographically, economically, and technologically. For the
celebrated Henry Adams, whose ancestral lines anchored him to the
Revolutionary generation, the sense of change was acute at the 1893
Chicago World's Fair, that great celebration of American technological
prowess. Awe-inspiring exhibits and evidences of incredible technologi-

cal advances housed in grandiose buildings left the classically educated Harvard man discombobulated and brooding. "Education ran riot" for those who had "never talked through a telephone, and had not the shadow of a notion what amount of force was meant by a *watt* or an *ampère* or an *erg*," according to Adams. He later wrote of his experiences at the fair in his inimitable, stuffy third-person style: "Chicago asked in 1893 for the first time the question whether the American people knew where they were driving. Adams answered, for one, that he did not know, but would try to find out."[1]

Many Americans shared Adams's views of the times in which they lived: America was changing quickly and profoundly. So much seemed new on so many fronts that Victorians readily concluded that their era was significantly different from those of previous generations. But modern times were not merely different—they were substantially better, filled with myriad evidences of social, spiritual, and material improvement. In their struggles to come to terms with immense changes, Victorians set aside earlier conceptions of time as an Edenic fall from grace or time as a cycle, enthusiastically embracing and reifying an emergent concept of time-as-progress, or improvement in the human condition realized temporally. They cast this beneficent temporal flow as a divinely ordained, immutable law of nature and, in celebratory fashion, christened their era the age of modern progress. Adams may not have known where America was driving, but others certainly did. Here again, Americans' propensity to collapse the sacred and secular, the religious and civic, came into play. The world was headed toward a progressively better future, with America in lead position, its social improvements and immense materials gains providentially marking the path forward.[2]

But what of the past in an era of modern progress? The past fascinated many Victorians,[3] but on the whole it led an increasingly troubled existence. In the United States, the new nation freed from the entrapments of antiquated Europe, the issue of relevance vigorously dogged the past. "What is to us the experience of past ages?" asked one commentator in 1872.[4] According to author Herman Melville, for those destined to "break a new path in the New World that is ours" the value of the past was negligible. "The Past is dead, and has no resurrection," wrote Melville, "but the Future is endowed with such a life, that it lives to us even in anticipation. The Past is, in many things, the foe of mankind; the Future is, in all things, our friend."[5]

The ramifications of Americans' waning regard for the past and waxing enthusiasm for progress were immense, registering across the spectrum of Victorian life. As progress was considered divinely ordained and nothing less than a law of nature, to be timely and progressive became cultural imperatives of modern life in many circles. Within liberal Protestantism, where the perceived boundaries between the natural and the supernatural were weak, even religion was expected to set aside the past in favor of the march of progress. If religion did not adapt to the age, if it refused to march forward with the times, if it clung too tightly to the past, it would become irrelevant.[6] To Protestant proponents of progress, Catholicism was the great case in point. In his 1853 Dudleian Lecture at Harvard on the errors and superstitions of the "romish church," the Reverend George Burnap railed against the church that, having "cast in her lot with the past," behaved "as if the world remained where it was six centuries ago." Refusing to adapt to modern conditions, the Roman Catholic Church in America had become little more than a "disintegrating relic of the Middle Ages, floated down among the things of modern times."[7]

The great university builders of the postbellum era cast their lots with the cause of progress. To reform education such that it addressed the oft-invoked "wants of the day" was holy work for the men who built the modern American university. As liberal Protestants with a flexible, adaptive theology and expansive religious worldview at their disposal, the university reformers simply "sacralize[d] . . . the entire enterprise of higher education," according to historian George Marsden, doing so in the name of national progress and the cause of Christianity.[8] To the institutions they were creating, they appropriated the vital work of Christianity as they understood it: leading men and women to a knowledge of God, fostering personal development, promoting religious toleration, and advancing national progress. Of course, representatives of the colleges claimed identical goals for their institutions. But the university men understood their work as furthering these Christian goals by freeing higher education from the tyranny of tradition and the vestiges of its medieval (read Catholic and European) past that bedeviled the colleges and limited their effectiveness. In this, the universities superseded not only the colleges but the churches themselves. While Christians had historically argued for the importance of the schoolhouse *and* the church, for the university men the schoolhouse *became* the church. The "university has succeeded to the place once held by the cathedral as the best embodiment of the uplifting forces of the modern time," claimed Columbia University President Nicholas Murray Butler.[9]

The triumph of the concept of progress created both a powerful impetus for academic reform and a potent critique of traditional forms of collegiate education. "In education, as in all else," wrote an 1880 contributor to the *Princeton Review*, "our age is one of transition from the *old* to the *new*."[10] Forms of education that served previous generations for centuries suddenly seemed inappropriate and irrelevant. "Everywhere prevails the conviction that the world has outgrown old methods and the ancient curriculum," according to an 1885 contributor to *Overland Monthly*.[11] In an era of modern progress and the age of the university, the Jesuits and other Catholic educators suddenly became vulnerable to charges that their colleges were superannuated cogs stymieing national progress; they were, critics claimed, stuck in a medieval past, an era yet to see the redeeming light of the Protestant Reformation. And though the era had given birth to university education, the medieval university was a product of and fitted for the Middle Ages of Catholic Europe, not modern times in Protestant America. The "American university has nothing to learn from medieval universities, nor yet from those still in the medieval period," announced Harvard's President Charles Eliot.[12]

This chapter explores the development of Jesuit higher education in the United States and the challenges it faced as a revolution in American higher education gave rise to the modern university and a new academic order. It focuses on the three Jesuit colleges at the center of the Law School controversy—namely, Georgetown, Boston College, and the College of the Holy Cross. Although regional differences and particular institutional histories created variance, the homogenizing effect of the *Ratio Studiorum* created more similarities than dissimilarities among Jesuit colleges; thus, the history of these three institutions reveals much about Jesuit education writ large. Through their historical trajectories, we return to the Harvard Law School controversy, to the second and third acts wherein Boston College and Holy Cross lost their places on the Law School's select list of colleges and Eliot's disparaging comments about Jesuit education sparked public controversy and protest. As seen in chapter 1, the Jesuits were used to criticism, but a new criticism was in the making. Even as the reverberations of the Reformation and the Counter Reformation echoed, modernity was creating another great divide in the academy, between those who held fast to tradition and those who spurned the past in the name of progress and a better future. During the course of the Law School controversy, the Jesuits encountered a formidable criticism: that the *Ratio Studiorum* was ill-suited to modern times in Protestant America. Directed in their *Constitutions* to adapt their educational practices to the times, as the age of the college gave way to the age of the university, the Jesuits were devolving from dangerous to dated; they were suddenly perched on the cusp of irrelevance. The challenge for the Jesuits was to convince their critics that the *Ratio Studiorum* was both sound and timely in Protestant America.

Anti-Jesuit sentiment arrived in what would become the United States in the early seventeenth century with the first settlers; the Jesuits themselves arrived in 1634, establishing their first North American English-speaking mission in Maryland. Protestants and Catholics alike settled in Maryland, a colony originally known for religious tolerance, although a network of Anglo-Catholic families dominated politically and economically during the colony's early years. Separated by the vastness of plantations and the watery tentacles of the Chesapeake, the Catholic community was remarkably vital. The Jesuits themselves ran a plantation, named Saint Inigoe's, after their founder, a base from which they evangelized Native Americans and ministered to Catholic families in the region. A high mortality rate kept the number of Jesuits in residence low, rarely more than a handful at any given time, and thus the Catholic families in Maryland saw the Jesuits and celebrated the sacraments of mass and confession only sporadically. As historians have noted, lacking regular access to the clergy and carrying forward a legacy of manor-based devotionalism from England proved conducive to the development of a vital lay piety. But such conditions—a widely dispersed population and a paucity of priests—did not lend themselves to the establishment of schools and colleges, although the Jesuits in Maryland were connected with some early, short-lived ventures. Those families who wanted advanced education for their sons frequently employed a tutor or turned to the Jesuits for private, home-based instruction. If they desired a college education, Catholics in Maryland did what Catholics in Britain did and sent their sons to a Jesuit college on the Continent.[13]

In the United States, the Jesuits' and other Catholic educators' work in higher education began in earnest in the nineteenth century. Although Protestants regularly claimed universal education as a Protestant-inspired phenomenon, Catholics made a noteworthy contribution to the academic landscape during the age of the college, opening more than three dozen institutions by 1850. Of thirty Catholic colleges in operation at midcentury, nine were sponsored by dioceses, with seven others run by religious orders, one apiece for the Sulpicians, Lazarists, Holy Cross Fathers, Augustinians, Benedictines, Franciscan Brothers, and the Brothers of Mary. The Jesuits, with fourteen, or nearly half of all the Catholic colleges in the country, clearly carried the day. Though the field expanded, the Jesuits retained this dominance through the nineteenth century.[14]

As the Jesuits were building colleges they were also rebuilding the Society. Their success as educators, their famous "intriguing" in the courts of eighteenth-century Europe, and their notable global exploits proved costly. It won them legendary, almost mythic status, and with it, powerful enemies. To assuage politically formidable critics, Pope Clement XIV suppressed the Society of Jesus in 1773. Only Catherine II of Russia defied the papal order, harboring a remnant group from which the Jesuits rebuilt when the Society of Jesus was restored in 1814 by Pope Pius VII. In restoring the Society, Pius directed the Jesuits to return to their work in the field of education, but they had to start over, almost from scratch. Between the suppression of the Society and its restoration forty-one years later, the Jesuits' massive educational empire dwindled from eight hundred institutions spanning the globe to a handful, with five in White Russia, four in the Kingdom of the Sicilies, a few in France, and one in the United States—Georgetown. Established in 1789, Georgetown was the nation's first Catholic college and acted as the parent institution for the subsequent development of Jesuit higher education in the United States.[15]

John Carroll, S.J. (1735–1815), the nation's first bishop,[16] secured a foothold for Catholic higher education in the United States through his concerted efforts to establish a college. True to his Jesuit roots and training, this well-known Marylander appreciated the Society's historic commitment to education: "To diffuse knowledge, promote virtue & serve Religion . . . we conceive this end alone well worth our most earnest concurrence."[17] Cognizant of pressing pastoral needs, he envisioned a college "for the education of youth, which might at the same time be a seminary for future clergymen." Despite pressing duties as spiritual leader for a flock scattered along the vast Atlantic seaboard, Carroll persisted in the cause of the proposed college, upon which, he wrote, "is built all my hope of permanency and success to our H. Religion in the United States." In 1789 a deed was secured for the land upon which to build the college, and in 1791 Georgetown Academy admitted its first student. Thus the project Carroll described as the "object nearest my heart" was realized.[18]

Though the Society of Jesus was still suppressed when Georgetown opened, the style and character of Jesuit education suffused the newly opened academy on the banks of the Potomac. Its first president, Robert

Plunkett, and several of the early faculty members were, like Carroll, originally ordained as Jesuits. Intended to "unite the Means of communicating Science with an effectual Provision for guarding and improving the Morals of Youth,"[19] Georgetown's curriculum, pedagogy, and discipline bore the unmistakable marks of the *Ratio Studiorum*. And Carroll gave evidence of the Jesuit propensity for adaptation in staffing the new institution. Lacking suitable candidates in the New World for the presidency, Carroll looked to Europe for a man "capable of abstracting his mind from the methods used in the colleges, where he has lived, so as to adopt only as much of them, as is suited to the circumstances of this country, and of substituting such others as are better adapted to the views and inclinations of those with whom he has to deal."[20]

Georgetown started quite humbly. Classes commenced in 1792 with two students in residence. By 1815, the year Carroll died, Georgetown had matured into a college with 107 students. Carroll also lived to see the process of the restoration of the Society begun in 1804 reach fruition in 1814, with cries of "Te Deum laudamus" rising from the once-suppressed Jesuits and their supporters. With that restoration, Georgetown became officially what it already was by nature and in practice: a Jesuit college.[21]

Pope Pius VII's 1814 pronouncement restoring the Society, with its directive to return to their work of educating youth, meant that the Jesuits were back in good graces ecclesiastically, a status they valued and cultivated during the nineteenth and early-twentieth centuries. But the political climate of Europe in the nineteenth century proved inhospitable—a situation that, in terms of staffing, was propitious for the development of Jesuit education in the United States. Displaced by the turmoil ravaging Europe,[22] Jesuits emigrated to the United States, where they staffed the growing network of Jesuit colleges. Exiled French Jesuits took the helm at Saint John's (now Fordham) and Spring Hill College. Ten years after its establishment, Belgian Jesuits assumed responsibility for Saint Louis University, the first institution of higher education west of the Mississippi. German Jesuits displaced by the *Kulturkampf* went to work at Canisius College in Buffalo, Saint Ignatius College in Cleveland, and Xavier College in Cincinnati. Italian Jesuits opened Woodstock College, the Jesuit seminary, in Maryland, while others went to the far West, staffing Santa Clara College, Saint Ignatius College in San Francisco, and Gonzaga College in Spokane (see table 1, in chap. 1).[23]

Like Georgetown, the College of the Holy Cross began with the vision of a Jesuit-turned-bishop. Benedict Joseph Fenwick, a Marylander, ended his recently begun tenure as Georgetown's president and his affiliation with the Jesuits when appointed bishop of Boston in 1825.[24] Yet his commitment to education ran deep, turning into aspirations for a residential college for Worcester and a day college for Boston. In 1842, an elaborate ceremony replete with ecclesiastics, dignitaries, speeches, a marching band, and cannon fire marked the realization of the first of Fenwick's academic hopes, as a local academy was transformed into the College of the Holy Cross, a Jesuit college under the direction of Jesuit Patrick Mulledy.[25]

As with other Jesuit and Catholic colleges, three factors played roles in the establishment of Holy Cross: a general commitment to the education of young men (the "proper work of the Society," according to Superior General Jan Roothaan),[26] a pronounced desire to foster vocations to the priesthood, and growing support for the strategy of separatism in education among Catholics. In the case of Holy Cross, the last was particularly strong, with Fenwick taking the unusual step of refusing Protestants admission to the college. This was unusual; although religiously affiliated, few colleges were religiously exclusive in terms of admission.[27] "Aware long since of the great disadvantage of mixing Catholic with Protestant students," Fenwick resolutely insisted on rigid separatism. It was, in part, a decision rooted in his belief that the college was more likely to attract students and produce vocations if it were a *"purely Catholic Institution."*[28] It was, as well, symptomatic of Protestant-Catholic relations during the middle decades of the nineteenth century as anti-Yankee sentiment burgeoned in the largely Irish Catholic population and, in kind, anti-Catholic sentiment flourished among New England Protestants.

Holy Cross faced its share of the typical vicissitudes of nineteenth-century colleges, including monumental financial difficulties and a devastating fire. It also faced strong anti-Catholic opposition. It had difficulty securing a charter from the Massachusetts legislature, and in 1855, in the heyday of Know-Nothingism, representatives of the Joint Special Committee on the Inspection of Nunneries and Convents scrutinized Holy Cross, their visit propelled by rumors that weapons were being stored and women were being held against their will at the college. Given the religious climate in New England, the very fact of a Catholic college proved occasion for satisfaction for Catholics. "We have achieved prodigies!" wrote one Jesuit to the superior general in Rome. "It pleases me to send you news of 'the Catholic College of the Holy Cross of the Society of Jesus'—in the midst of *Yankees!*"[29]

The students at Holy Cross marched through the seven-year classical course of studies outlined in the *Ratio Studiorum.* Like students at colleges both Catholic and Protestant, they devoted most of their energies to the study of the ancients—to Livy, Xenophon, Cicero, Virgil, Horace, and Sophocles. When not focused on the ancient tongues of Greece and Rome, they took up the study of mathematics, English, geography, history, and some natural science. But the Jesuits also offered, reluctantly, a commercial course, a concession to parents who desired for their sons more practical instruction in subjects such as bookkeeping and arithmetic.[30] By 1893, its student body numbered approximately three hundred, and in 1899 it held its fiftieth commencement exercises. It had over the course of a half century graduated 719 men, with 242 entering the priesthood, 103 pursuing careers in medicine, 94 in law, 51 in business, 32 in education, 8 in journalism, and 40 in other careers.[31]

In 1842, Bishop Fenwick broached the idea of a day school for Boston with his former Georgetown colleague John McElroy, S.J., a native of Northern Ireland. By the 1850s, discussion grew into resolve, ecclesiastical permissions were secured, and McElroy set out to purchase property on Leverett Street in Boston's West End for a day college and a church. His attempt proved futile. Some leading, liberally minded Boston citizens supported his efforts, including notables from Harvard such as Edward Everett (a former Massachusetts governor and former Harvard president), Rufus Choate (a professor and leading Boston socialite), and James Collins Warren (dean of Harvard Medical School), but other citizens, less than tolerant, were dismayed by the prospect of a Catholic church and college in the heart of the city. They successfully pressured the authorities responsible for zoning, thwarting McElroy's attempt to purchase the Leverett Street property. After years of wrangling and legal maneuvering, McElroy and the Jesuits decided on another site: a parcel of land on Harrison Avenue between Concord and Newton Streets in the South End. Opposition arose again, but McElroy's persistence paid off; in 1857 the Jesuits secured a site for a church and a college, and building began.[32]

In August 1864, the Jesuits announced the opening of Boston College with an advertisement in the *Pilot:*

A.M.D.G.

ON THE FIRST MONDAY OF SEPTEMBER THE FATHERS OF THE SOCIETY OF JESUS will open, for the reception of Scholars the lower classes of Collegiate Instruction, the building adjoining THE CHURCH OF THE IMMACULATE CONCEPTION, Harrison Avenue, between Concord and Newton Streets. It is their intention to add a higher class each successive year, until the course of studies is complete.[33]

The advertisement continued: "as in other Catholic colleges" the course of studies would last seven years. The full complement of courses would eventually include the familiar components of the liberal arts curriculum: "English, Latin, and Greek languages, Arithmetic, Mathematics, Logic, Metaphysics, Ethics, Natural Philosophy and Chemistry, with the usual accessories." The "chief aim" of the college was education in the "principles & practice of the Catholic Faith," and while clerical vocations were hoped for, profession of the Catholic faith was not a "necessary condition for admission" (as it was at Holy Cross). Students were, however, expected to be able to "read & write . . . understand the primary principles of Grammar and Arithmetic, and be of reputable character." Tuition, per term, was $30.[34]

The Jesuits made good on their 1864 pledge in the *Pilot* to expand the curriculum until a full complement of courses was available to their students. With the 1876 introduction of the philosophy course, the traditional capstone of the Jesuit curriculum, the course of studies was complete, and in 1877 nine men graduated from Boston College.

The Jesuits of the restored Society of Jesus brought the sixteenth-century *Ratio Studiorum* to nineteenth-century America. In 1897–98, readers of the catalog of Holy Cross College learned that the "Course of Studies . . . is that in vogue in all Jesuit Colleges, and is, therefore, based on the Ratio Studiorum, or official Code of Studies of the Society of Jesus."[35] The catalog from Boston College informed its readers that the "educational system of Boston College is substantially that of all other Colleges of the Society of Jesus," one based on the "principles as elaborated in the *Ratio Studiorum*." Like their predecessors who created the *Ratio*, the Jesuits who taught in the United States in the nineteenth century embraced the ideals of Christian humanism. They continued to advance the concept of education as an intellectual and moral enterprise, one preparing students to contribute to the good of society and bettering their chances for success in the next life. They would make that contribution to society through the exercise of "sound judgment, of acute and rounded intellect, of upright and manly conscience," faculties gained by an educational system that stressed the intellectual, moral, and religious.[36]

In 1894, Timothy Brosnahan, S.J. (1856–1915), the newly appointed president of Boston College, penned an elegant essay on Jesuit education destined for publication in the Boston College *Catalogue* and the catalogs of other Jesuit colleges through the 1950s. Born in Alexandria, Virginia, Brosnahan studied at Gonzaga College in Washington, D.C., and entered the Jesuit novitiate in 1872. His work at Boston College began in the early 1880s as a teacher; after additional studies and a stint as a professor at the Jesuit seminary in Woodstock, Maryland, he returned to Boston College as its president in 1894, serving in that capacity for four years.[37] The "Fathers of the Society," Brosnahan wrote, understood education "in its completest sense, as the full and harmonious development of all those faculties that are distinctive of man." The studies pursued at Jesuit colleges were carefully chosen to "further that end," and "only in proportion, and in such numbers, as are sufficient and required." Gradation, coordination, and subordination all came into play. "If two or more sciences, for instance, give similar training to some mental faculty," the Jesuits chose the science that "combines the most effective training with the largest and most fundamental knowledge." Further, studies were "graded and classified as to be adapted to the mental growth of the student and the scientific unfolding of knowledge" so that the student might "gradually and harmoniously reach, as nearly as may be, that measure of culture of which he is capable."[38]

The Jesuit system, Brosnahan explained, rested on the assumption that "different studies have distinct and peculiar educational values" and that the "specific training given by one" could not be "supplied by another." Mathematics and the natural sciences helped students develop the "inductive and deductive powers of reason." As "manifestations of spirit to spirit," language and history affected a "higher union" in which the "whole mind of man" was "brought into widest and subtlest play." Among languages, all of which called for "delicacy of judgment and fineness of perception, and for a constant, keen, and quick use of the reasoning powers," the ancient languages of Rome and Greece held a "position of honor" as "instrument[s] of culture" in the curriculum. As "languages with a structure and idiom remote from the language of the student, the study of them lays bare before him the laws of thought and logic, and requires attention, reflection and an analysis of the fundamental relations between thought and grammar."[39]

In practice, the seven-year course of studies at Boston College in the 1890s took students through an almost wholly prescribed curriculum. (At Holy Cross the catalog simply informed students "there are no elective courses.")[40] Students spent much of their day learning the ancient tongues of Greece and Rome and developing *eloquentia perfecta*. In this, the subject matter, texts, and manner of instruction at nineteenth-century Boston College bore notable similarities to instruction in the Jesuit colleges of sixteenth-century Rome, seventeenth-century Quebec, and eighteenth-century India. Yet there were subjects in the curriculum at Boston College that would have been unfamiliar to students at Jesuit colleges in previous times, including modern languages, chemistry, and some other cognate sciences. Recognizing the popularity of medicine as a career choice among graduates, Father Brosnahan went so far as to add anatomy and physiology to the curricular line-up, clear evidence that the Jesuit prescription to adapt had not been lost in slavish adherence to the *Ratio*.

By 1900 the Jesuits had gained the largest share of the field of American Catholic higher education. With two dozen colleges under their direction, they had established a network of institutions comparable in number to those sponsored by a number of Protestant denominations.[41] Yet the expansiveness of their enterprise did not guarantee its future. As the Jesuits were expanding their academic empire, a revolution in American higher education had given rise to a new academic order in which the universities—especially Harvard—had come to exercise considerable influence. The preceding chapter details how, through the efforts of Georgetown President J. Havens Richards, Georgetown, Boston College, and Holy Cross secured places on Harvard Law School's select list of colleges whose graduates were admitted automatically as regular students. Given Harvard's eminence and influence, its recognition was valuable. But the Jesuits had not actually gained a permanent spot on the Law School's list. As the controversy rekindled and intensified, the Jesuits encountered the great challenge of *time*. The challenge came in the person of Charles Eliot, whose disdain for the "famous Jesuit schools" derived not solely from the fact that they were Catholic but from his deeply held belief that the Jesuits had refused to adapt their educational practices to the wants of modern times.

As described in chapter 1, the faculty of Harvard Law School, in an effort to improve legal education, voted in 1893 to implement a policy during the 1895–96 academic year that would restrict regular admission to those men who held diplomas from a select list of colleges or were eligible to enter the senior class of Harvard. While the change in the admissions policy was "in line with the general policy of the School," it was hoped, according to the *Harvard Law Review*, that higher standards would also check the growth of the student body, which "threatened to outgrow the accommodations of Austin Hall." It had no such effect. Despite Harvard's unusually high entrance requirements and a notable increase in the number of law schools (with lower admissions standards), the number of students in the regular course at Harvard Law School more than doubled between 1893 and 1903, jumping from 328 to 678.[42] Among those making recourse to the increasingly popular Law School were graduates of Jesuit colleges. While the number of Georgetown graduates at Harvard Law School between 1893 and 1897 alternated between one and two, the number of men from Boston College and from Holy Cross increased from one to six. Although a mere fraction of the Law School's entire student body, the number of Boston College men at the Law School constituted a significant portion of the college's graduates during a decade in which graduating classes numbered between fifteen and twenty-nine. The six Boston College graduates who entered Harvard Law School in 1897 made up 26 percent of their entire graduating class.[43]

In 1897 the status of the Jesuit colleges on the Law School's list was about to change, and as a result the number of Boston College men at Harvard Law School would plummet; by 1902 there would be no Boston College graduates at the Law School. The first hint of trouble surfaced when J. Frank Quinlan, a student from Saint John's, applied for admission. The secretary of the Law School, E. A. Gilmore, informed Quinlan that the catalog from Saint John's was under review by the university's Committee on Colleges (also called the Committee for Admission from Other Colleges). Five days later, Gilmore informed Quinlan that a degree from Saint John's would admit him only as a special student. "Special students have all the rights and privileges of regular students," he wrote, "but stand on a different footing as to the degree." To earn an LL.B. degree as a special student, Quinlan would have to take admission and year-end exams and maintain an average 15 percent higher than that required of regular students.[44]

Quinlan pressed his case with the Law School dean, James Barr Ames, asking for information about the formulation of the list. Ames had a long history at the Law School: he entered as a student in 1870, became an assistant professor in 1873, popularized the case method of study introduced by Dean Christopher Columbus Langdell, and succeeded Langdell as dean in 1895.[45] Ames informed Quinlan, "In making up our list of selected colleges we have followed, in the main, the rule of putting on any college whose graduates would be admitted to the senior class of Harvard College."[46] Harvard considered no college its equal, so transfer students were regularly admitted a year or more behind where they stood previously. A student who had already earned a bachelor's degree from another university would at best be admitted to the senior year of Harvard College. The case of Boston College graduate

William Healey is illustrative. After graduation from Boston College in 1895, Healey applied to Harvard, where he was admitted as a sophomore. The ledger from the Committee on Admission from Other Colleges documented his case:

> Healey, William C. S.
> A.B. Boston College 1895
>
> Good testimonials.
>
> Admitted to sophomore, credited with two courses, but conditioned in German; if at the end of the first half year of work in approved courses is found to be thoroughly satisfactory, the Committee will credit him with two additional courses.

On February 25, 1897, another ledger entry appeared: "courses approved." To his A.B. from Boston College Healey added an A.B. from Harvard in 1898 and an M.A. in 1899. He then went on to a successful managerial career in East Boston.[47]

After explaining the "senior class rule," Ames informed Quinlan that "strict adherence to this rule would doubtlessly exclude Georgetown, Holy Cross and Boston College" from the Law School's list. And though all Jesuit colleges used the same curriculum, "it will hardly be claimed," Ames wrote, that Saint John's "ranks on an equality with Georgetown." Ames explained that an "exception in favor of Georgetown" had been made "from a desire not to exclude all Catholic institutions" and that the other two colleges were "added from the same desire not to appear sectarian." It was, however, "probably a mistake to add the last two." The Law School could not add Saint John's to the list; "indeed," wrote Ames, "if we make any change at all we shall remove the last two and possibly Georgetown from the list." This said, Ames reiterated the earlier determination that Quinlan's degree from Saint John's made him eligible for admission as a special student. "Of course," Ames added, "you will have no difficulty in entering as a regular student any other law school in the country."[48]

As he had four years earlier, Georgetown President J. Havens Richards took up the cause of the Jesuit colleges, writing to Ames about the correspondence with Quinlan. He reminded Ames that Eliot's review of materials from Georgetown in 1893 "had quite convinced him that Georgetown should have been included in the list" and that the Law School faculty "arrived at the same conclusion from independent considerations." Richards acknowledged that there were some Catholic colleges "unworthy of the position to which they aspire and pretend"—as were some other denominational and nondenominational colleges—but "the best colleges of our church are far from admitting . . . the slightest inferiority to other similar institutions." Georgetown and the Jesuit colleges certainly admitted no such inferiority. Though the course of studies was "almost wholly prescribed," it was a course "more thorough and more comprehensive than that of non-Catholic colleges." Furthermore, as it combined "the natural and scientific methods," Richards claimed that the Jesuit approach to teaching was "superior to any others in use." In fact, as a "preparation in particular for the study of law," he argued, "a more perfect scheme could scarcely . . . be devised." The "thorough training in systematic philosophy received by all our graduates in their senior year, is of itself an invaluable acquisition to a lawyer, and no where can it be obtained with a tithe of the thoroughness which characterizes it in this and other similar Catholic colleges."

Richards then urged Ames to acquaint himself with catalogs and examination papers from the "leading Catholic colleges of the East." He was confident that the result would be "an acknowledgement on your part similar to that so gracefully made by President Elliot [sic] some years ago." (Given Eliot's claim that the "lack of equivalence" in Catholic higher education stemmed from the "famous Jesuit schools," Richards seems a bit disingenuous at this point.) The Jesuits and their colleges would then be "relieved of the imputation of occupying through mere sufferance an undeserved place on your list, an imputation which we cannot but consider as certainly and decidedly (though assuredly not intentionally) unfair."[49]

Ames's reply to Richards differed little from his reply to Quinlan. He had checked with the Committee on Admission from Other Colleges, which felt that "Georgetown College distinctly outranks all other Catholic colleges in this country." Yet the Committee wanted additional information "in order to be satisfied that Georgetown comes up to the standard by which we have intended to be guided in framing our list." Ames agreed to look into the case of Georgetown and the other Catholic colleges, but the "absence of the Chairman of the College Committee on Admission from Other Colleges" made it impossible for Ames to provide Richards with "definite information . . . until after the opening of the academic year." The chair of the Committee was Hans Carl Gunther von Jagemann, professor of German and German philology (1889–1925). "Should the Harvard College Committee inform me that a Georgetown College A.B." met the standard of the senior-class rule, Ames wrote, "no one would be more gratified than myself."[50]

The Jesuits waited several months for the decision, during which time Richards and Timothy Brosnahan of Boston College considered possible explanations for their situation with regard to Harvard. Neither dismissed the possibility of bigotry out of hand. Both agreed that there was some "intense anti-Catholic feeling somewhere in Harvard," but it was "congested in one or two heads," perhaps even in Ames's. Brosnahan went so far as to dismiss sectarian antipathy, claiming the issue of the Jesuit colleges was "apparently decided a few years ago since & as apparently on its merits." But Brosnahan did not dismiss the seriousness of the situation. "I don't think there is a doubt that Harvard would, if it could, absorb all educational control of this neighborhood." And Brosnahan claimed, "This insistence on standards is only one weapon in the warfare."[51]

As far as Brosnahan was concerned, the "general feeling of Harvard is very kindly toward us." As evidence he pointed to Harvard's "athletic authorities," who had done "some very substantial favors" for Boston College, which lacked its own playing fields. ("Without their cooperation our athletic meeting would not only have been a failure, but would have been impossible.") He also wrote Richards about Harvard professors who were "present at one of our Prize Debates," who subsequently had "spoken to their classes in the highest terms of the work done at our college."[52] Brosnahan could also have pointed to Eliot's participation in the 1897 annual prize debate at Boston College as further evidence of cordial feelings between the two institutions. He did not need to remind Richards that Eliot and Richards had both addressed the 1896 Catholic Alumni Banquet in Boston; appropriately enough, at the banquet Eliot spoke on professional education, Richards on "Unity in Education." *Woodstock Letters*, a Jesuit newsletter, reported on their joint speaking engagement, noting that the "speech of Father Richards at the 'Catholic Alumni Association of Boston' deserves to be remembered. It is all the more worthy of note as it followed the speech of President Eliot of Harvard, who had made a plea for the students of Catholic colleges to attend the professional schools of Harvard."[53]

Eliot's plea to Catholic graduates to attend Harvard's professional schools stands as incongruous counterpoint to decreased access to the same by graduates of Jesuit colleges since what Brosnahan and Richards feared came to pass in March 1898. The letter from Ames to Brosnahan bearing the "really distressing" news, as Richards put it, read:

The Chairman of the Harvard College Committee on Admission from Other Colleges informs me that graduates of Boston College are admitted only to the Sophomore class of Harvard College. I am obliged, therefore, although with much regret, to write you that we must remove Boston College from our list of colleges whose graduates are admitted to this School as regular students. . . . [S]tudents graduating at Boston College in 1898, as well as all present holders of your degree, who may wish to enter this School will be admitted as regular students without examination. Persons who graduate from Boston College after 1898 will be entitled to register at this School as Special Students without examination.[54]

The Law School also removed Holy Cross from the list, but kept Georgetown on it. It was an unusual move, for the Law School regularly augmented the list of colleges but rarely removed any institution or program from it (see appendix B).

The tone of the Richards-Brosnahan correspondence took a turn with Harvard's unsatisfactory decision, and with it, the first hints of criticism of a temporal nature directed at the Jesuits surfaced; Richards sensed that the Jesuits' adherence to traditional forms of education rendered them antiquated relics of past ages in the eyes of some. Previously willing to give Harvard officials the benefit of the doubt when the possibility of bigotry arose, Richards wrote of a "systematic and deliberate intention on the part of these gentlemen to discredit Catholic education, and to drive us from the field." As far as he was concerned, "they consider us enemies, and they are determined to secure Catholic patronage for their University." Hypocrisy marked their approach to Catholics: "They will speak sweetly to Catholics in public, flatter them by commending their liberal spirit, etc., and at the same time they will do all in their power to represent Catholic colleges before the public as inferior institutions, mediaeval in character and methods, having only a high school standard, etc. etc."[55]

Richards urged Brosnahan to fight Harvard's decision "with all the means in your power," telling him, "you are fighting the battle of all the Jesuit colleges, and ultimately, of Catholic education." But for the immediate future, the task of defending the Jesuit cause fell to neither Brosnahan nor Richards, both of whom retired from their positions of president in 1898. Nor would it fall to John Lehy, S.J., president of Holy Cross (1895–1901), who was preoccupied with pressing problems, including dire financial circumstances.[56] The immediate challenge fell to Boston College's new president, W. G. Read Mullan, S.J. (1860–1910). A native of Maryland and a former student of Loyola College in Baltimore, Mullan served as president of Boston College from 1898 to 1903. An even-tempered man, he was described in 1899 by one of his fellow Jesuits as "kind and considerate, a good listener . . . a man of few words" and later eulogized as "mild and gentle of nature."[57]

In fall 1898, Eliot received at least two queries about the removal of Boston College and Holy Cross from the Law School's list, one from Holy Cross president, John Lehy, the other from Msgr. Thomas Conaty, a former Holy Cross student who, as second rector of the Catholic University of America, served as the informal leader of American Catholic higher education.[58] After consulting with Ames about the standing of the Jesuit colleges on the Law School's list, Eliot sent similar letters to Conaty and Lehy that drew heavily upon Ames's earlier letter. He informed his correspondents that the Law School faculty "found it extremely difficult to determine the right mode of dealing with the American colleges which are managed by the Society of Jesus." He then proceeded to explain that the colleges in question were removed from the list because their graduates "could not properly be admitted even to the Junior Class of Harvard College." Moreover, the Law School may have "made a mistake in retaining Georgetown," although few Georgetown graduates attended Harvard Law School, thus it was not a decision from which the "School suffers directly." Furthermore, Eliot pointed out that Boston College and Holy Cross graduates "do not make good records as a rule." Eliot offered to meet with Lehy to discuss the "whole matter of the relation of the Colleges in charge of the Society of Jesus to our professional schools," and some months later Mullan and probably Lehy met with Eliot. Unfortunately, if records of this meeting were made they have not been located.[59]

The issue then languished until a committee from the Boston College Alumni Association pressed it further. During the summer of 1899 they arranged a meeting with Maryland–New York Provincial Edward Purbrick and urged him to have the Jesuits bring the issue before the public through the press. They had prepared a resolution describing the removal of Boston College from the Law School's list as a "covert attack on higher Catholic education in New England" and an attempt by Harvard to drive students "from our colleges" by "dictat[ing] to Catholic students where they shall receive their preliminary training." They resolved to "protest against this action of Harvard University," and as they were convinced that it constituted a "grave injury" to their alma mater, they urged upon the Jesuits the "necessity of taking such action as will ensure the standing of the College and the recognition of her degrees."

Purbrick counseled patience and asked the gentlemen to take no action until a "committee of Ours" had "exhausted all the means at their command to bring about the desired retraction by the Law School of its decision."[60]

Apparently spurred by the alumni association, Mullan wrote Eliot on September 1, 1899, referring to our "interview of last spring." Noting that the Boston College men had yet to receive an adequate, consistent explanation for the removal of their college from the Law School's list, Mullan asked Eliot for an official statement explaining the exclusion. Eliot's response proved unacceptable, and thus, two months later, Mullan asked for and Eliot arranged a meeting between Hans C. G. von Jagemann, the chair of the Committee on Admission from Other Colleges, and representatives of Boston College.[61]

In its wake, von Jagemann provided Eliot with an account of his meeting with Mullan, Richards, and Dr. Francis Barnes, a Boston College ('84) and Harvard Medical School ('88) alumnus who lectured at Boston College and participated actively in the Boston College Alumni Association. Von Jagemann's report was mixed. He explained that the Harvardians easily convinced the representatives of the Jesuit colleges that the Committee on Admission "could not have acted otherwise than it has in the cases of students and graduates of Boston College that have heretofore applied for admission to Harvard College or the Graduate School." On the other hand, von Jagemann admitted to Eliot that they had not succeeded "in persuading the gentlemen that the list of approved colleges published by the Law School is just." Von Jagemann conceded to the Boston College delegation that some of the colleges on the list ranked "no higher than Boston College" and acknowledged that "any such list . . . will in many individual cases work an injustice." Von Jagemann then complained that the Law School placed the Committee on Admission (part of the Faculty of Arts and Science) in an untenable position: "The Committee on Admission from other Colleges is therefore convinced that its own policy of judging each case on its merits is the wiser one. . . . The list of colleges published by the Law School has caused the Committee considerable trouble. . . . If the Law School adheres to the publication of its list, it would seem just that it alone bear the responsibility for it and should not leave the task of defending it to a committee of the Faculty of Arts and Sciences."[62]

Two days after von Jagemann penned his version of the meeting, Mullan sent Eliot his account. He reminded Eliot that he had asked for the meeting with von Jagemann because the dean of the Law School laid responsibility for the evaluation of the Jesuit colleges on von Jagemann's committee. But von Jagemann abjured the responsibility. According to Mullan, von Jagemann told him that "his committee never thus rates a college as an institution, but investigates each application for advanced standing, and decides on the merits of each individual case." Von Jagemann "would not say that the Committee would not admit a Boston College graduate to Harvard Senior," but did say that the "Law School list was drawn up hastily and carelessly, and his committee was not responsible for it." Mullan then reported to Eliot that von Jagemann produced the records of fifteen Boston College students and graduates considered by the committee over the past eight or nine years, a review that, while supporting the claims that the committee treated cases individually, also suggested that Boston College men were suited for admission at least to Harvard junior, not Harvard sophomore. Mullan also informed Eliot that he had provided von Jagemann with copies of Boston College's entrance and final examinations, which fared well in comparison with those used at Harvard. Mullan closed his lengthy letter to Eliot by pointing to the records of nine Boston College students at Harvard Law School whose grades (an A, a B, a D, and six Cs) represented "altogether too excellent a record for Harvard to continue discrediting our graduates." "It is hard for us not to suspect Harvard of unfair discrimination," wrote Mullan. It was also hard to believe that "Boston College is inferior to everyone of the Colleges in the Law School list," especially since Mullan possessed an "official statement" that one such college admitted to "freshman after only one year of [high school] preparation."[63]

After discussing the matter with Ames, and after another query from Mullan, Eliot replied to Mullan. The case of the Jesuit colleges "has been reexamined," wrote Eliot. The Law School "adheres to its opinion that Georgetown is the best of the Jesuit colleges, and is entitled to stand in the Law School list if any Jesuit college is to be admitted to the list." Although Georgetown retained its place on the list, Eliot informed Mullan that it was initially included on the list "lest it should seem to some persons that the Catholic colleges had been excluded on religious grounds." As for the formulation of the list itself, von Jagemann was "absolutely right in telling you that his Committee does not grade colleges"; it dealt "singly with each case of admission from another college to Harvard as it presents itself." But over the years, the "record shows the manner in which a series of cases from a single institution was dealt with," forming the basis for a "practical rating of that institution, unless indeed the single cases show great diversity." Furthermore, having discussed the records of the Boston College men with Ames, Eliot did not feel their grades entitled Boston College to a "special claim." Eliot conceded, however, that the Law School's list "needs revision, and that some colleges are included in it that ought not to be there."[64]

Finding Eliot's reply unacceptable, Mullan fired off a lengthy reply on January 11, pointing out that he had not inquired about the Jesuit colleges as a group, but Boston College in particular. Moreover, Eliot had failed to explain the grounds for Boston's exclusion from the list and to reconcile the discrepancy between Ames's and von Jagemann's statements. Mullan informed Eliot that he had it on the authority of a Harvard professor that "C was considered by the Law School as a very satisfactory mark." The only "fair way" to evaluate graduates, Mullan contended, was to determine the quality of the "work done in our College" through an examination of actual courses taken by students, not by a review of the Boston College Catalogue. But Mullan feared that the set of examination papers he had given von Jagemann in 1899 had "met the same fate" as the set forwarded to Ames in 1898, which had been "politely ignored." Mullan continued that the Boston College degree represented "twenty-five hours of college work per week carried on through four years, under trained teachers employing a thoroughly tested system of instruction" that was at least as "efficient as that of Harvard" with its "much shorter weekly period, shorter yearly period, fewer advantages for individual instruction, fewer helps to enforce attendance, wider attraction to 'snap' courses." Mullan concluded that there must be some "strong anti-Catholic spirit at Harvard" and that suspicions that Harvard was "making a determined effort to discredit all Catholic education in order to fill its halls more surely with Catholic students" were justified.[65]

Mullan could not believe that "Harvard has shown the same zeal in the case of the other colleges" as it had shown in the case of the Jesuit colleges, and Mullan's incipient investigation into the ranking of "ten or twelve other colleges" on the Law School's list was, he argued, likely to strengthen his "argument of unfair discrimination." Indirect evidence suggests that Mullan surmised correctly; the Catholic colleges were subject to particular scrutiny. When asked by the dean to describe his responsibilities, Law School secretary Gilmore informed Ames that he was responsible for keeping records and developing statistical analyses. For example, he created tables showing the percentage of college graduates and the colleges represented in the different law schools and universities," adding that at "various times there are special tables and statistics to be prepared, such as a table showing the number of graduates of catholic universities in the law school during the last ten years and the character of their work."[66]

Eliot responded to Mullan's letter a week later, reiterating his previous response: the Committee on Admission from Other Colleges considered cases individually, but over the course of years a basis was formed for a practical ranking of a college. Eliot rejected Mullan's assertion that "an inspection of a set of your examination papers" would constitute "satisfactory ground for a verdict on the quality of the college." And he insisted that the decision to remove the Jesuit colleges from the list was not "influenced in the least by the fact that your college belongs to the Catholic Church." Nor was it an attempt to "discredit" Catholic colleges in order to gain students for Harvard. Harvard had no desire "to diminish in any way the resort of Catholic youth to the Jesuit colleges." Then Eliot told Mullan that "We should be heartily glad, however, if the Jesuit colleges would so amplify their courses of instruction and raise their standards of admission" such that they would compare to colleges such as "Dartmouth, Amherst, Williams, Haverford, Lafayette, Oberlin, Rutgers, Trinity (Ct.), and Wesleyan (Ct.). On this level, in the judgement of Harvard University, the Jesuit colleges in the United States do not stand, and have never stood."[67]

Unsatisfied with Eliot's response, Mullan wrote to Eliot a third time, asking him to reconcile von Jagemann's statements with Ames's. Eliot replied with a reiteration: "As I have already explained to you, that Committee takes no action on colleges, but only on the individual cases of applicants for admission from other colleges."[68] Then again, a week later, Mullan challenged Eliot for the fourth time to identify the party responsible for the evaluation of Boston College:

> Now, will you kindly tell me further:
> 1—What official or department of Harvard University has decided that graduates of Boston College can be admitted only to sophomore class in Harvard College?
> 2—What are the facts which justify such a decision in the opinion of that official or department?[69]

The Mullan-Eliot exchange then ground to a halt. Eliot reached the conclusion that "our correspondence had better cease for the present." He had given Mullan the "official reasons" for Harvard's decision "as plainly as I am able to state them." He did not wish to answer Mullan's second question, which would "involve my making a detailed statement concerning the inferiority of the Jesuit colleges." As far as Eliot was concerned, it was the "duty of Catholics, not of Protestants, to study the present organization and methods of the Jesuit colleges, and if, on comparison with the Protestant colleges, they find defects or evils, to suggest the remedies." A week later he told Mullan, "My sole interest in the discussion between us has been to contribute to the raising of the standard of the Jesuit Colleges, Boston College included, in order that their graduates might become admissible to the Law School just like those of a hundred or more Protestant Colleges."[70]

Even as he claimed that it was not the duty of Protestants to critique Catholic colleges, Eliot ironically found himself in the middle of a public-relations debacle precisely because he publicly denigrated the Jesuit colleges. Though he refused to answer Mullan's direct query about why Harvard deemed Boston College's course of studies inferior, in other venues, as we shall see, Eliot was quite clear and public about why he considered Jesuit colleges second rate. Jesuit education was, he claimed, unreformed and mired in the past. Clinging to a prescribed, classical curriculum formulated in the sixteenth century, the Jesuits had yet to embrace the wholesome influence of Protestant-inspired liberty that spun the engines of modern progress and encouraged young men toward maturity through liberty in education. "They are not advancing," noted Eliot in a local Boston newspaper.[71]

The interplay between long-held beliefs about religious liberty and the increasingly powerful sway of the modern mindset helped propel the university movement as it fueled Eliot's disdain for the Jesuits. Like their fellow Protestants, the leaders of the university movement defined Protestantism as the religion of liberty; this was nothing less than a bedrock conviction. According to a contributor to an 1837 issue of the *Princeton Review*, "Protestantism is liberty—the liberty wherewith Christ has made us free. Popery is a yoke of bondage—spiritual despotism."[72] Insofar as the Reformation had freed Christians from the tyranny of Rome, the university men argued that the new universities, as Protestant institutions, were to be infused with and shaped by a full measure of liberty not wholly realized in American colleges. "Above all," Eliot proclaimed in his inaugural, a university "must be free. The winnowing breeze of freedom must blow through all its chambers." With nineteenth-century Americans increasingly convinced that they were living in modern times and headed toward a progressively better future, the winnowing breeze of freedom assumed a more pronounced temporal hue. Freedom in education meant emancipation from the deleterious constraints of an outmoded, irrelevant past. "Are our young men being educated for the work of the twentieth century," asked Eliot in 1884, "or of the seventeenth?"[73]

As liberal Protestants with modernist tendencies, Eliot and other university leaders expressed serious reservations about the role that revealed religion played in denominational colleges, not merely because it undermined religious harmony but because it stymied academic quality, and with it, the holy cause of national progress. A college "under denominational control tends to make allegiance to its own form of belief a leading qualification," wrote Andrew Dickson White of Cornell. It might become a "tolerably good denominational college, like those keeping down the standard of American education," White asserted, but "it can become nothing more."[74] Eliot concurred. Sectarian-affiliated colleges, Eliot claimed, were "suffering" because they "have taken, and still take, their presidents from the clerical profession almost exclusively." A proponent of religious progressivism, Eliot criticized the clergy for holding fast to the tenets of revealed religion. While the "lay world believes in the progress of knowledge," the "bonds" of creeds that "most ministers" assumed at an "early age" had to be "worn all their lives." To Eliot, the creed or articles of faith espoused by ministers "may be somewhat vague and elastic, but cannot honestly be stretched much." Theologically inflexible and thus out of touch with the times, the clergy, Eliot claimed, necessarily experienced a "loss of influence," finding themselves subject to the "terrible stress of temptation to intellectual dishonesty." On those grounds alone Eliot could fault Catholic education; as he explained in 1893 to Richards, clerical leadership of Catholic colleges explained their "want of equivalence" with Protestant colleges.[75]

The university men's disparagement of sectarian affiliation, revealed religion, and the clergy occurred during a period of science ascendant. Science moved definitively into the honored epistemological position long held by the once-regnant queen of the sciences, theology, assuming the status of the foundational science upon which other activities and fields of inquiry were ordered and assessed. It was a revolution marked by an epistemological shift from deduction to induction, an explosion in the scope of scientific knowledge, and a proliferation in the branches of science. The nineteenth-century emergence of science as the functional equivalent of religion in some quarters signaled its newly realized cultural and intellectual status, with the scientist being compared to the priest, the laboratory to the temple, scientific inquiry to prayerful labor, and the scientifically minded to worshippers.[76] Americans' fascination with science as the engine of progress surfaced at the 1893 Chicago

World's Fair, where awestruck visitors marveled at the Yerkes tele-
scope, the Otis elevator, and the gargantuan Ferris wheel. Scientific
achievements, the "most comprehensive and brilliant display of man's
material progress which the ages have known," displayed in and among
architectural wonders, proved so evocative that commentators resorted
to religious language, calling the fair a "Heavenly City," a "New Jerusa-
lem," and a "Divine Exposition."[77]

The modernist tendency among the leaders of the university movement
clearly emerged when they spoke of science. They lived in an age in
which the development of historical criticism and its application to things
religious, an exercise suggesting that the tenets of religion were historically conditioned, would "dig up and unsettle the foundations of all belief," as a Rev. Mr. Burnap explained to his audience at Harvard in 1853.
So, too, had the findings of archeology, geology, paleontology, and the
1859 publication of Charles Darwin's *Origins of Species*.[78] Faced with the
task of reconciling competing and even contradictory truth claims, the
university men upheld the value of science. "Religion has nothing to fear
from science," Gilman claimed at his inaugural at Johns Hopkins, and
"science need not be afraid of religion."[79] Trained as a chemist, Eliot felt
no need to reconcile religion and science. Science itself was religious.
God was "so absolutely immanent in all things, animate and inanimate,"
Eliot claimed, that "no mediation is needed between him and the least
particle of his creation."[80] Study of the natural world brought scientists
"face to face with inscrutable mystery and infinite power." The "electric
light of science" made "white and transparent the whole temple of learning,"[81] while scientists, Eliot wrote, could

> show how physics, with its law of the conservation of energy, chem-
> istry with its doctrine of the indestructibility and eternal flux of at-
> oms, and biology with its principle of evolution through natural se-
> lection, have brought about within thirty years a wonderful change
> in men's conception of the universe. If the universe, as science
> teaches, be an organism which has by slow degrees grown to its form
> of to-day on its way to its form of to-morrow, with slowly formed hab-
> its which we call laws, and a general health which we call the har-
> mony of nature, then, as science also teaches, the life-principle or
> soul of that organism, for which science has no better name than
> God, pervades and informs it so absolutely that there is no separat-
> ing God from nature, or religion from science, or things sacred from
> things secular.[82]

The closing decades of the nineteenth century were an era of theological reformulations,[83] with many of Eliot's generation rejecting what he called "dogmatic teaching" (an approach serviceable perhaps for a "convent, or a seminary for priests," he claimed in his inaugural) in favor of the scientific method as the new *via sacra*. As it fostered an "open mind," it would, through the work of the university, serve the cause of "Christ and the church." For the University of Chicago, Harper claimed that "science and the scientific method . . . now dominate," and Eliot's bold 1883 claim on behalf of the scientific method, that "no other method of inquiry now commands respect," was not much of an exaggeration. As early as 1870, the Law School's Dean Langdell declared that law was a science; in that spirit he introduced the case method, challenging students to derive legal principles from the evidence of specific cases. He later threw down the methodological gauntlet: "If law be not a science, a university will consult its own dignity in declining to teach it."[84] His colleagues throughout the university also embraced the scientific method, with "scholars as widely divergent as Francis G. Peabody and Albert Bushnell Hart . . . Charles Everett and William James," as Paul Buck noted, deeming their respective areas of inquiry "scientific." Though it is far from clear that these men shared a common understanding of what they meant by the scientific method, few would have contradicted Eliot's claim that "the scientific spirit, the scientific method . . . prevails."[85]

University students also felt the effects of Protestant-inspired liberty, particularly as the winnowing breeze of freedom blew through the curriculum, leaving the traditional, classical course in disarray and the elective system in its place. The breezes that toppled seven centuries of curricular tradition were driven in large part by a prodigious growth in the number of sciences vying for inclusion in the curriculum. The disciplinary crowding of the curriculum created a taxing educational conundrum. What subjects, old and new, warranted inclusion in the curriculum? What courses should students take? Who should determine a student's course of study? While the scientific revolution helped create the curricular problem, Protestant-inspired liberty and the "doctrine of individualism," as Harper put it, helped produce one solution: having students select their own courses.[86]

In the very first sentence of his inaugural address, Eliot acknowledged disagreement in the academy: there were "endless controversies" about which subjects should be included in the curriculum. In the second sentence, he declared the issue moot: "This University recognizes no real antagonism between literature and science, and consents to no such narrow alternatives as mathematics or classics, science or metaphysics." In the third sentence, he bid all subjects enter: "We would have them all, and at their best."[87] It was no idle boast. Eliot—as the *"amplificator imperii,"* as historian Samuel Morison Eliot dubbed him—enlarged the "intellectual empire" prodigiously. In 1870 he hired the reluctant Henry Adams to teach history; within seven years Adams founded a department and increased the number of courses to ten, which was, by contemporary standards, a large offering. The number of courses in English and the modern languages mushroomed, while those in the natural and physical sciences increased exponentially. By 1907–8, a year before Eliot's retirement, Harvard's undergraduates could choose from 189 year-long and 254 semester-long courses.[88] In 1895 Eliot boasted that it would "take a single individual between 70 and 80 years to go through the courses offered at Harvard College." Should the university scale back its offerings? Eliot argued the negative. Unless an institution "resigns itself to teaching only some small parts of modern knowledge," election among courses was inevitable, according to Eliot. "The limitation of teaching is an intolerable alternative for any institution which aspires to become a university; for a university must try to teach every subject . . . for which there is any demand." He called this the "mechanical argument" for electivism, and he made it on more than one occasion.[89]

Historians have seen far more in Eliot's advocacy of the elective system than the logic of the mechanical argument. His views on electivism, Morison noted, have been linked to democracy, utilitarianism, and even romanticism.[90] However influential any or all of these were, any attempt to explain Eliot's advocacy of electivism apart from his religious convictions is incomplete. For Eliot, electivism was "not merely an educational device but an expression of a spiritual principle," according to one biographer, "not a pedagogic invention but a spiritual conviction." The elective system was, Eliot claimed, "in the first place, an outcome of the protestant reformation" (and in the "next place . . . an outcome of the spirit of political liberty"). As such, it stood as part of a broad revolt against the "sham monastic régime of the common American college," where students, treated as children rather than men, were denied the opportunity to elect their own courses.[91]

Unitarian anthropology shaped Eliot's views on electivism. One of liberal Protestantism's most distinctive features, clearly distinguishing it from its conservative counterpart, was its optimistic assessment of human nature. The "genuine Puritan" from whom Eliot descended, noted Irving Babbitt, had a "lively and even exaggerated sense of 'Old Adam'"; Eliot and his liberal coreligionists had no such sense. Human beings were fundamentally good and inherently oriented toward God. As such, man was a divine work-in-progress. Moreover, each individual was unique, the "duplicate of which neither does nor ever will exist," thus the path to perfection of nature was unique to each individual. "The natural bent and peculiar quality of every boy's mind," wrote Eliot in 1869, "should be sacredly regarded in his education."[92]

In the work of Ralph Waldo Emerson (1803–82), the Unitarian prophet of self-reliance and leader of the Transcendentalist movement, Eliot found the bridge between liberal Protestant anthropology and educational practice. Speaking at Symphony Hall in Boston in 1903, Eliot acknowledged his debt: "When I had got at what proved to be my lifework for education, I discovered in Emerson's poems and essays all the fundamental motives and principles of my own hourly struggle against educational routine and tradition." Among the lessons drawn from Emerson (a Harvard alumnus and overseer), Eliot found the "fundamental doctrines on which this elective system rests." He was taken with Emerson's conviction that the "object of Education should be to remove all obstructions" so that an individual's "natural force" might have "free play and exhibit its peculiar product." If allowed to elect their own courses, unencumbered students would develop self-reliance. Emerson was clear: "The secret of Education lies in respecting the pupil. It is not for you to choose what he shall know, what he shall do."[93]

Emersonian sentiments echoed throughout Eliot's pronouncements on electivism. In his inaugural address (with Emerson in the audience), Eliot noted that until recent times, "every man studied the same subjects in the same proportions, without regard to his natural bent or preference." Clearly, the "individual traits of different minds have not been sufficiently attended to." When a young man came to the "revelation of his own peculiar taste and capacity," Eliot urged him to "give it welcome, thank God, and take courage." Armed with an appreciation of his own natural bent, "a well-instructed youth of eighteen can select for himself . . . a better course of study than any college faculty, or any wise man who does not know him and his ancestors and his previous life, can possibly select for him."[94]

Students at Harvard had plenty of choosing to do. Only one fragment of the medieval curriculum survived the winnowing breeze of Protestant-inspired freedom under Eliot: a single required course in rhetoric for the freshmen. Unfortunately, Eliot claimed, there were still colleges where faculties insisted on a prescribed course of studies for their students, a practice that suppressed individual talents and interests, thus depriving individuals of happiness and society of their talents.[95] In 1899, the year that the elective system reached its fullness at Harvard, Eliot singled out the "famous Jesuit schools" of the "past four centuries" for public criticism, faulting them for adhering to the retrograde practice of curricular prescription. For Eliot, the failure of the Jesuit colleges to achieve the academic respectability found in the Protestant colleges largely stemmed from Jesuit unwillingness to grant their students the liberty to elect their own course of studies. Rather than sailing with the progressive currents of the modern academy, they had anchored their colleges to the religious tyranny of the curricular past.

In October 1899, the *Atlantic Monthly* published an essay by Eliot, "Recent Changes in Secondary Education," that, three months earlier, he had read before the American Institute of Instruction. Toward the end of the piece, in which he argued for the extension of the elective system into the high schools, he included, almost as an afterthought, two counterexamples.

There are those who say that there should be no election of studies in secondary schools,—that the school committee, or the superintendent, or the neighboring college, or a consensus of university opinion, should lay down the right course of study for the secondary school, and that every child should be obliged to follow it. This is precisely the method followed in Moslem countries, where the Koran prescribes the perfect education to be administered to all children alike. The prescription begins in the primary school, and extends straight through the university; and almost the only mental power cultivated is memory. Another instance of uniform prescribed education may be found in the curriculum of the Jesuit colleges, which has remained almost unchanged for four hundred years, disregarding some trifling concessions made to natural science. That these examples are both ecclesiastical is not without significance. Nothing but an unhesitating belief in the Divine wisdom of such prescriptions can justify them; for no human wisdom is equal to contriving a prescribed course of study equally good for even two children of the same family, between the ages of eight and eighteen. Direct revelation from on high would be the only satisfactory basis for a uniform prescribed school curriculum. The immense deepening and expanding of human knowledge in the nineteenth century, and the increasing sense of the sanctity of the individual's gifts and will-power, have made uniform prescriptions of study in secondary schools impossible and absurd. We must absolutely give up the notion that any set of human beings, however wise and learned, can ever again construct and enforce on school children one uniform course of study.[96]

Jesuit Provincial Edward Purbrick found Eliot's comments about Jesuit education "so insolent, offensive & yet so readily echoed in the Press" that he asked Timothy Brosnahan, then teaching philosophy at Woodstock Seminary, to prepare a rebuttal. When Brosnahan did so, the *Atlantic Monthly* refused to publish it. The editors explained to Brosnahan that "it is not the policy of the magazine to publish articles in controversy," yet two months later the *Atlantic* published an article by Princetonian Andrew F. West taking Eliot to task, specifically referring to Eliot's argument for electivism in the secondary schools and the Jesuit colleges.[97] That editorial decision left the *Atlantic* open to allegations of bigotry. More than sixty letters arrived in defense of Jesuit education, and a critic from the *Sacred Heart Review* queried, "Can it be possible that the *Atlantic Monthly*, in permitting Professor West of Princeton to defend Protestant institutions . . . and in refusing to allow Father Brosnahan to repel [Eliot's] more direct accusations against Jesuit colleges, has joined hands with Harvard's president in his crusade against Catholic classical institutes here in New England?" A contributor to the *Casket* commented that the "most literary of American magazines has made a heroic but ineffectual attempt to save President Eliot's reputation at the expense of its own." A contributor to the *Bookman* noted that the editor of the *Atlantic* ultimately deprived the readership of the "pleasure of a most interesting discussion carried on by men of marked ability, and at the same time he showed an apparent inconsistency."[98]

The *Sacred Heart Review*, a Catholic weekly, ultimately published Brosnahan's "President Eliot and Jesuit Colleges," first as part of its January 13, 1900, issue, then as a widely circulated pamphlet (appendix C). It was a persuasive, forceful, even stinging rebuttal. It undermined Eliot's theory of electivism even as it described how the Jesuits had made curricular adaptations without abandoning the method of the *Ratio Studiorum*. His defense of Jesuit education was twofold; he identified errors of fact, especially pertaining to Eliot's allegation of Moslem-like rigidity on the part of Jesuit educators, and argued that radical electivism need not be the *only* system of education intelligent men might support.

Eliot's factual errors suggested, as Brosnahan pointed out, a lack of familiarity on Eliot's part with easily available sources of information about Jesuit education and the actual practice of education at Jesuit colleges, a pointed criticism, given the concurrent conversation with Mullan about the Jesuit colleges on the Law School's list and Mullan's suggestion that Eliot should better acquaint himself with the work of the Jesuit colleges. Brosnahan began by noting that students in seventeenth-century Jesuit colleges spent 100 percent of their time mastering Latin and Greek; in 1900, students at Georgetown spent 53 percent of their time on the classical languages: the remaining 47 percent was devoted to modern studies, including English, mathematics, modern languages, and natural science. Brosnahan also pointed out that students in Jesuit colleges spent three to eight hours a week, out of twenty-seven and a half, on the natural sciences—hardly a "trifling concession." By contrast, a student at Harvard, taking advantage of Eliot's elective system, might totally avoid the natural sciences, making no concession to them whatsoever. He also argued that the Jesuit system of education could not be faulted for centuries of immutability since the expansion of knowledge that burgeoned the curriculum was a nineteenth-century phenomenon. The full elective system at Harvard, he noted, was a mere fifteen years old: "It would consequently have been more exact, though less telling, to have said that: For the last fifteen years the curriculum of Jesuit Colleges has remained practically unchanged." And finally, Brosnahan noted that the *Ratio Studiorum* was promulgated in 1599, and thus the Jesuit system of education was three centuries old—not four—as Eliot claimed.[99]

Brosnahan then argued that radical electivism was unsound and that there were other justifiable approaches to the curriculum, even absent Divine wisdom. He conceded that the expansion of knowledge in the nineteenth century had created a conundrum for educators; no longer able to approach anything near curricular comprehensiveness, educators found themselves pulled between the principle of unity, the basis for a prescribed curriculum, and the principle of individuality, the basis for an elective curriculum. As far as Brosnahan was concerned, Eliot had "bow[ed] down before individuality" and extricated educators from difficult decisions by throwing the "whole embarrassment to the individual student."[100]

The crux of Brosnahan's rebuttal to Eliot's arguments for electivism rested on the philosophical distinction between essence and accident. Brosnahan argued that within kind, that which unifies is essential and that which differentiates is accidental. The strongest argument for electivism rested squarely on the phenomenon of individual—or accidental —differences among boys. Contrary to Eliot, who believed in the utter uniqueness of the individual and the sanctity of differences, Brosnahan argued, "To fix one's eyes on accidental differences and close one's eyes to essential similitude would be an example of elective observation not creditable to a philosopher." Boys undoubtedly varied; yet by virtue of their faculties commonly held—"memory, powers of observation, of reasoning, of judgment, of imagination and of discrimination"—they were bound by a "specific unity," allowing them to be "scientifically classed as belonging to the genus *homo,*" although for "native or wilful reasons they may not be capable of equal culture." Accidental differences suggested the use of electivism, essential unity the use of a prescribed curriculum. Brosnahan concluded that for the good of the boy, the concomitant good of the country, and the sanctity of their students' souls, the Jesuits would not engage in educational experimentation nor offer a "go-as-you please program of studies and a haphazard and chaotic system of formation." Brosnahan set forth no specific plan, but he proposed that, with thought and time, intelligent men might produce a solution to the curricular challenges educators faced at the beginning of the twentieth century.[101]

Brosnahan's reply to Eliot circulated widely, garnering widespread attention among educators and, in the press, consistent kudos. Catholic and non-Catholic papers across the country, among them the Boston *Pilot,* the Pittsburgh *Observer,* the *Michigan Catholic,* the *Western Watchman,* and the Boston *Republic,* a pro-Irish weekly, carried the essay in whole or in part. More than one thousand copies circulated in pamphlet form by February 1900. Purbrick reported to Rome that Brosnahan's paper was "well received by leading newspapers, by some of the most eminent Professors on Eliot's own staff, & by authorities at Princeton, Yale &c." William T. Harris, the U.S. commissioner of education, requested twenty copies of the "valuable and interesting reply to President Eliot's theories about electivism in colleges," and E. Winchester Donald, rector of Trinity Church in Boston, sent his congratulations to Brosnahan.[102] The editorial writer for the *Bookman* praised it as a "model of courtesy and urbanity" and noted that "its style is clear as crystal . . . its logic is faultless; . . . its quotations, illustrations and turns of phase are apt, piquant and singularly effective." Conversely, Eliot's position was routinely derided. "It will be some time before President Eliot will stir up the Jesuits again," wrote one editorialist. "One dose of hornet is enough for any witless but mischievous boy." Eliot read Brosnahan's essay, but made no direct reply.[103]

Things went from bad to worse for Eliot when the alumni of Holy Cross and Boston College came to the defense of Jesuit education. On January 22, 1900, nine days after the publication of Brosnahan's essay and at the height of Mullan's letter-writing campaign, speakers at the well-attended Third Annual Holy Cross Alumni Banquet denigrated Eliot's educational theories and assailed Eliot himself. The rector of the Catholic University of America, Msgr. Thomas Conaty, reminded his audience of their college's links to the glories of the medieval past, to the religious culture that produced "Paris and Bologna, Oxford and Cambridge," as he criticized educational experimentalism and those who aspired to sever the links between the churches and higher education. More strident criticism bubbled up from Dr. Francis Barnes:

> Take off the mask of liberality which our opponents wear in public, and you will see that it is used to cover the black visage of bigotry. Even the liberal, broadminded president of Harvard University, in his venomous sneers at the Jesuit colleges, now displays a spirit of intolerance which up to this time he has wisely restrained. For years he has posed as an unprejudiced observer and fair-minded critic of educational methods; but now, when he deems the time is ripe for putting his schemes into execution, he appears in his true character—a dogmatizing bigot.[104]

The tone of the meeting of the Boston College Alumni Association on February 5 at the Parker House was less inflammatory. The remarks "proved to be of a moderate character, though, in the course of some of the speeches," according to one account, "sharp references were directed toward Harvard and the elective system."[105] A committee reported on Mullan's correspondence with Eliot, after which Barnes again criticized Eliot, claiming that his refusal to explain the removal of Boston College from the Law School's list undermined the man who "pretends to stand for tolerance and liberality." On the other hand, the *Boston Globe* reported that some at the meeting felt that the exclusion of the Jesuit colleges from the Law School's list resulted from a "misapprehension on their part concerning the quality of the educational work accomplished by Boston college," a situation they believed would be "reversed" when the Harvardians "came to a full understanding of the merits of the case."[106]

In this heated, acrimonious tumult, Eliot withdrew from the controversy surrounding the Jesuit colleges. Spurred by Barnes's allegation of bigotry in the press, Eliot wrote Mullan a confidential letter on February

6 claiming that his "sole interest" had been "to contribute to the raising of the standard of the Jesuit Colleges, Boston College included, in order that their graduates might become admissible to the Law School just like those of a hundred or more Protestant Colleges." According to Eliot, the press was assigning "opinions and motives in connection with the discussion we have been carrying on, which have nothing to do with the matter, and are not correctly attributed to me." He refused to "say one word in reply to it," but offered to "state to you privately for your own use . . . what seem to me to be the facts about the low standard of the Jesuit Colleges," but only after the "fruitless public onslaught . . . has subsided."[107] Eliot also refused to respond to Barnes's comments, except to say that "they know very well why Boston College is not in the list . . . and they know the only way in which their school can be put upon this list. It is for them to improve their course of study." According to Eliot, the problem with the Jesuit schools was their static nature: "The Jesuit colleges . . . possessed practically the same programme or curriculum which they set forth 300 years ago."[108] Eliot also declined an invitation made by the editors of the *Sacred Heart Review* to respond in their paper to Brosnahan's essay and explain the removal of the Jesuit colleges from the Law School's list, but in doing so he added that "Harvard University does not count the Jesuit colleges as equal to the Protestant colleges." He clarified his own position: "I have not the smallest desire to attack the Jesuit colleges. . . . Quite the contrary, I should like very much to see them greatly improved." But he declined to make a public statement, claiming that it would be more appropriate for a Catholic than a Protestant to comment on the quality of Jesuit institutions.[109]

Eliot withdrew from the controversy, but the criticism directed his way was not over. Months earlier, Conaty had asked Brosnahan to prepare a paper on the "Relative Merit of Courses in Catholic and Non-Catholic Colleges for A.B. Degrees," to be delivered at the April meeting of the Association of Catholic Colleges of the United States (ACCUS). The object was to determine whether Catholic colleges were "better, equal or poorer" and to address "indirectly . . . the question in which we are so much interested concerning the blacklisting of our Colleges by Harvard." Brosnahan's approach was not indirect. He chose to compare the course of studies at Boston College with that of Harvard. In the paper he criticized the whole concept of the equivalence of studies on which the elective system was based, particularly with regard to theology and philosophy. And then by comparing the course of studies a Boston College freshman took with a course of studies that an industrious freshman at

Harvard might take, he concluded that the former was in no "way inferior to the collegiate course or courses at Harvard" and that there were "solid reasons for believing it is superior." Indeed, Brosnahan claimed, there was "not a bona fide Catholic college in this country whose course of studies is not superior to the average course chosen by a Harvard student." Willing to generalize about Catholic colleges, his comparison extended only to Harvard: to "put all non-Catholic colleges on the same educational level as Harvard . . . would be an injustice to many excellent institutions in this country."[110]

Like Brosnahan's first paper, this one received widespread attention, including front-page coverage in the *New York Times*. But unlike the first, this one received mixed reviews. Brosnahan's audience at the ACCUS meeting did not support Harvard, but did wonder whether Catholic colleges were as good as they could be or claimed to be.[111] The Catholic press published generally positive reviews, but the secular press found the attack on Harvard and ad hominum remarks about Eliot "unjustified and impolitic." The editorialist from the *Bookman* who praised Brosnahan's first pamphlet as a "model of courtesy and urbanity," wrote of the second, "We now regret all the more keenly the absence of this latter quality from an address which he lately delivered before a conference of Roman Catholic educators": the comments about Eliot were "tart" and "ill-tempered," and Brosnahan may well have "succeeded only in estranging public sympathy from the cause which he has been so earnestly defending."[112]

The Catholic assault on Eliot culminated on May 25, the day Mullan penned another letter to Eliot. He rejected the offer Eliot had made some months earlier for a private conversation regarding the quality of Jesuit schools; Eliot had publicly impugned the Jesuit colleges and Mullan wanted to defend them publicly. That same day, Eliot found his previous correspondence with Mullan published in toto in the *Boston Globe* (it was reprinted in other papers in the weeks that followed). Very pleased, the Boston College Alumni Association at their June meeting thanked Mullan for his defense of their alma mater, which had, they claimed, emerged "triumphant and unscathed" in the altercation with a "wanton aggressor."[113]

Eliot wrote his final response to Mullan on June 2. He again claimed to have "no quarrel whatever with the Jesuit Colleges." He did not wish to "diminish their influence," nor was it his intention to "crush out Catholic education," as some had alleged. If anyone doubted such an assertion, he urged them to ask "any one of the hundreds of Catholic young men who are now members of Harvard University" whether they had a "cordial welcome" and experienced "fair play without the slightest interference with their religious beliefs or practices." And nothing further would "draw any answer" from him on the question of Boston College and Jesuit education.[114]

With the publication of the Eliot-Mullan correspondence and Eliot's final letter, the direct debate between the Jesuits and Eliot over the Law School's admissions policy came to an end. The Jesuits failed to secure a place for Boston College and Holy Cross on the Law School's list; neither did they obtain a consistent explanation for their exclusion from it. Harvard continued publishing the troublesome list until 1904, at which time prospective applicants were directed to contact the secretary of the Law School to ascertain whether their alma mater appeared on the select list of colleges. Soon thereafter, the Law School made another significant change: admission was restricted to those who had graduated from "colleges of high grade" or could certify that they had "ranked in the first third of their class on work of the senior year." Georgetown no longer appeared on the list of high-grade colleges and universities; like Boston College and Holy Cross, it too was eventually banished from the Law School's list. In 1906, Charles Macksey, S.J., of Georgetown (formerly of Boston College) complained to Dean Ames of the Law School that fewer Georgetown graduates were now eligible for admission. Georgetown could hardly be pleased, wrote Macksey, for "in the past all of her graduates were eligible to enter your Law School as regular students, hereafter only one third of them will be thus eligible." Not only did Harvard Law School misapprehend the quality of the academic caliber of Georgetown, but its new policy did a disservice to any applicant rendered ineligible for admission, regardless of his "absolute excellence in scholarship and examinations . . . who happens to be in a class where talent and industry averages uncommonly high." Macksey lamely protested that the leadership at Georgetown felt "beholden to dissuade as far as possible our students from entrance to a University whose treatment of our degree is so lacking in a just appreciation of our work."[115]

Although the Jesuits failed to win a place for their colleges on the Law School's list, they were not totally routed. As leaders of the university movement rallied around the cause of modern progress, the Jesuits held fast to traditional ideals and practices that had, through the centuries, stressed the value of logic and rhetorical excellence. It is fitting, therefore, that the Jesuits won the war of words over the Law School's re-

strictive admissions policy and Eliot's public criticism of Jesuit education. Brosnahan's "President Eliot and Jesuit Colleges" became a minor
classic, a clear exposition of Catholic educational philosophy, studied as
a model of rhetorical excellence by students in the twentieth century—
including students in a writing class at Harvard in the 1960s.[116] In 1905
the board of trustees of Tufts University unanimously voted to offer
Brosnahan an honorary degree (it is not known whether he accepted it).
As late as 1934, a speaker at a national gathering of Catholic educators
could announce with little explanation, "Many still survive to recall
[the] masterly refutation by Father Timothy Brosnahan" of the "essential
error" of Eliot's "ideas."[117]

In May 1900, Professor Thomas Dwight of Harvard Medical School
told Brosnahan that his papers "almost mark an epoch." A convert to
Catholicism and member of one of Boston's leading families, Dwight
pointed out that it had "so long been the custom for people to say what
they please about Catholics that it is startling to have a man like Eliot
called to account." Indeed, Eliot's reputation suffered for his comments
on Jesuit education. "Father Brosnahan, throughout this dispute, made
no pretense of being a gentleman, but showed himself a thorough one,"
claimed the Reverend E. Winchester Donald, the rector of Trinity
Church. On the other hand, "Dr. Eliot made all pretense to be a gentleman but failed evidently to be one at all." Eliot's biographer, Hugh
Hawkins, concluded that through the Law School controversy Eliot's
"often generous relations with Catholics and Catholic schools stood revealed as essentially paternalistic and lacking in true acquaintance."
Thus "partly through Eliot's own failings, Harvard probably stood lower
in the opinion of Catholics at the end of his administration than it had at
the beginning."[118]

While Brosnahan garnered praise for his defense of Jesuit education
and Mullan won support from the alumni for his efforts on behalf of
Boston College, there was little rejoicing among the Jesuits themselves.
Behind the scenes, Father Purbrick spoke of failure. When pressed by
the alumni to respond more vigorously and publicly, the Jesuits asked
the alumni to act judiciously and in concert with their own efforts; unfortunately, according to Purbrick, "Dr. Barnes' zeal got the better of his
discretion." His intemperate comments reported widely in the press undermined Mullan's efforts to engage Eliot, and thus, wrote Purbrick, "our
Cause is damaged, if not ruined, by the indiscreet zeal of a friend."[119]

Despite Eliot's poor showing, he stood no lower in the eyes of some of
his university peers. Although it certainly was an embarrassing episode

for Eliot, he continued to play a central role in reforming American education. Behind the scenes he also continued to shape perceptions about Jesuit education. In 1903, Benjamin Ide Wheeler, the president of the University of California at Berkeley (1899–1919), asked Eliot for information about Harvard's "current usage" in the "granting of University credit to graduates of Jesuit colleges in this country." Eliot's response has not been located, but a fair amount can be inferred from Wheeler's acknowledgement of it. "Our experience accords with yours regarding the Jesuit colleges," wrote Wheeler. "I am interested in your expression 'Archaic training.'" Wheeler did not believe that the Jesuits' problem derived from the "subjects they teach"—an understandable claim coming from Wheeler, a classicist—but rather from the "whole spirit of instruction" and the fact that their students were not "inspired to think for themselves."[120]

In the controversy surrounding Harvard's refusal to honor the degrees of Jesuit colleges and Eliot's disparaging remarks about Jesuit education in the *Atlantic Monthly,* two fault lines surfaced—one old, one new. On the one hand, antipathies as old as the Reformation came into play: the "famous Jesuit schools" that troubled Eliot's Puritan ancestors still drew pointed and quick criticism in many Protestant circles. On the other hand, a new fault line had opened in American higher education, separating those who upheld tradition from those who were convinced of the necessity of thorough reform.

For Eliot and the other university builders, the two great divisions in higher education were linked causally; the Reformation constituted not only liberation from ecclesial control but liberation from the "romish" past. In their efforts to reform the academy, reformers were freeing it from the vestiges of its medieval Catholic past on behalf of modern, Protestant America. Quintessential Protestant liberty, hard-won by their reforming ancestors, needed fuller expression in the academy, for clerical influence and ecclesiastical control thwarted personal development and stymied free thought, and with them the scientific engine of divinely ordained progress. "The professors of the Jesuit colleges keep up with the times," argued one Jesuit supporter—but the leadership of the university movement took commitment to traditional forms of education as incontrovertible evidence of a deplorable, antiprogressive spirit.[121] As the age of the college gave way to the age of the university, age-old criticism of the Jesuits assumed a temporal hue: not only were their colleges antithetical to liberty, they were unresponsive to the wants of the age. Jesuit James Fagan described the common perception: "The Catholic idea is centuries old, and so subject to suspicion as being moss-grown, un-adapted to modern needs, lacking in living force."[122]

The *Constitutions* of the Society of Jesus directed Jesuits to adapt their educational modus operandi as necessary to suit the times. This was a daunting challenge in an age in which modernity rendered the value of the past and tradition all too tenuous. But that was not the only challenge facing the Jesuits in the age of the modern university. The *Constitutions* also exhorted the Jesuits to adapt to the *persons* they en-countered. Embedded in the Law School controversy and the academic revolution of the late-nineteenth century was yet another great chal-lenge: the numerous Catholic collegians who turned to Protestant-in-spired universities for professional education and a collegiate experi-ence more attuned to their increasingly middle-class sensibilities.

II

AMONG CATHOLICS

CHAPTER THREE

Persons: The Bonds of Religion and the Claims of Class

Was it not Dr. Eliot, of Harvard,
who said a short time ago: "Why
do people say that I am opposed to
Catholic truth? I have the largest
Catholic college in the country";
and so he has, and why is it?

—Chair of the Association
of Catholic Colleges of the
United States, 1904

The age of the college closed as the modern American university came of age in the final decades of the nineteenth century. Liberal Protestantism helped underwrite the historic transition. The eventual and quite remarkable success of the newly created modern university reflects the religious momentum and legitimacy it derived from a general liberalization within nineteenth-century mainstream Protestantism that weakened the claims of revealed religion, undermined denominational boundaries, and supported scientific inquiry. Religion is, therefore, essential for understanding the success of the university, but its explanatory value is limited; in itself, religion cannot fully explain the institutional preeminence that the university achieved in a relatively short period. The modern university's success ultimately stemmed from its ability to respond to a broad array of social needs and interests, including those of America's middle class, who increasingly turned to the modern university for professional education.[1]

The strong connection that developed around the turn of the century between university-based education and the aspirations of the middle class draws attention to one the ironies of the Harvard Law School controversy: the emergence of a Catholic middle class whose propensity to emulate the Protestant middle class pulled many Catholics into the orbit of Protestant higher education, including Eliot's Harvard. Seeking an education suited to the aspirations and sensibilities of what contemporaries called the "better classes," most Catholic collegians bypassed Catholic colleges. The trend sparked widespread comment. While Eliot and the presidents of the Jesuit colleges waged a public war of words in which religion and conceptions of time figured prominently, members of the Catholic community carried on a parallel conversation about the Law School controversy and Catholic participation in higher education in which the issue of social class loomed large. Here, in the "interplay between private talk and public talk,"[2] the Law School controversy assumes its full significance.

The public debate between Eliot and the Jesuits and the intensity of the Catholic community's responses to Harvard's selective admissions policy can be fully appreciated only in the context of a wide-ranging discussion among Catholics about the social functions of higher education. For the Jesuits and other Catholic educators, the issue of class became arguably the most significant challenge of the era. As the largely immigrant church of the nineteenth century became a largely middle-class church in the twentieth, their conversations illuminate the ways in which social class was reshaping the American Catholic Church and its adherents' participation in higher education. They also help explain the vicissitudes of Catholic colleges at the turn of the century, which remained small and underenrolled when compared with many other institutions of higher education.

The postbellum revolution in higher education that gave rise to the modern university and a new academic order was both social and institutional. In the second half of the nineteenth century, the college population grew significantly and became more diverse. Students enjoyed an expanded menu of institutions devoted to advanced learning that included (among other things) normal schools, business institutes, trade schools, conservatories, the increasingly popular universities, and the familiar colleges.[3] Not all collegians, of course, enjoyed the same spectrum of choices; a variety of factors delineated, narrowly or broadly, the range of academic opportunities available to any given student or group. Geography, personal aspiration, social expectations, family circumstances, and cultural background opened the doors of higher education to some as they closed doors to others. Gender, race, and ethnicity limited options or pre-cluded college attendance altogether for some young men and women. Patterns of constraint and limited access reveal a great deal about the so-cial contexts in which higher education operated. But so too do patterns of choice. Ironically, while the Jesuits battled over the exclusion of their graduates from the Law School, there were more Catholics studying at Harvard than at any other college in the country, Catholic or Protestant, making it, in terms of Catholic enrollment, the largest Catholic college in the country. The large number of Catholics studying at Harvard and other institutions associated with Protestantism—in "odd social niches," to borrow a phrase from sociologist Bennett Berger[4]—points to the dynamic interplay between religion, ethnicity, and class and the increasing sa-lience of the last in shaping Catholics' academic choices and experi-ences.[5]

In the absence of large-scale involvement in higher education by the state, corporations, and philanthropy for most of the nineteenth century, religion and ethnicity played large roles in the social organization of higher education, particularly during the age of the college. Demograph-ics and faith traditions often factored in the establishment of colleges and the sustenance of symbiotic relationships between ethnoreligious communities and their academic institutions. The Lutherans, for exam-ple, sprinkled the upper Midwest with ethnoreligious colleges (e.g., Saint Olaf College for Norwegian Lutherans and Gustavus Adolphus College for Swedish Lutherans). Princeton's roots reached into the soil of Scottish and Scots-Irish Presbyterianism, while Franklin and Mar-shall College in Pennsylvania was closely connected to the local Ger-man Reformed community.[6] In turn, such schools served as powerful sites for identity and social group formation. As colleges educated young men in hopes of producing Christian gentlemen, they helped to sustain religious and ethnic communities by recruiting and training men for the ministry, preparing students to teach in community schools, promoting endogamous marriage, using Old World languages, observing ethnic customs, reinforcing religious norms, and inculcating religious beliefs. These small ethnoreligious colleges provided their students with valu-able resources, including rich networks of relationships forged through shared experiences, important bodies of knowledge (including the man-ners and mores of the referent social group), and increasingly important educational credentials.[7]

In America's Gilded Age, social class became an increasingly impor-tant means of social organization, a development with profound implications for higher education, including colleges organized largely along religious and ethnic lines. Americans were, as historian Robert Wiebe has described, searching for order in a world that seemed increasingly complex, decreasingly personal, and far less manageable. Mass transportation and marketing, rapid communication, and cities swollen by immigration created a "distended society" in which the informal and personal modes of social interaction and regulation that served antebellum "island communities" no longer sufficed. With this change, postbellum Americans increasingly turned to social class as a means to situate their lives and negotiate their social worlds.[8] The concept of the middle class emerged as a particularly powerful social construct, representing far more than realization of income falling within an arbitrarily defined bracket. More than the money one possessed, it was being possessed of a certain state of mind that defined the middle class. Nurtured in the cradle of nineteenth-century American Protestantism, the middle-class mindset dictated a great deal in terms of how individuals lived and constructed their social networks. It also began to affect participation in higher education and higher education itself, which began catering to the middle class and those who aspired to be part of it. "It is neither for the genius nor for the dunce," announced Johns Hopkins president, Daniel Coit Gilman, "but for the great middle class possessing ordinary talents that we build colleges."[9]

The modern American university functioned well in a socially complex, class-conscious "distended society" by offering its students valuable socioeconomic and cultural resources to help them succeed in a competitive world. Having assumed the task of educating professionals (which had largely been an apprenticeship venture in antebellum "island communities"), the universities became critical gateways into the professions and thus popular among the middle class, who had begun looking to professional work as a vehicle of status attainment. In a society becoming more dependent upon expert, scientific knowledge, university-based professional schools granted their students academic credentials. In a world that seemed less personal and that was more mobile, a student secured from his alma mater a potable, corporate identity; he became a "Harvard man" or a "Michigan man" or a "Stanford man," and with that corporate identity came access to socially and professionally attractive alumni networks within which to operate.[10]

The allure of the modern university for the middle class also derived from the quality of its social life. While Charles Eliot and other university builders reformed professional education in university settings in ways that dovetailed with the interests of the middle class, students re-shaped the collegiate experience in ways consistent with their mid-dle-class aspirations and sensibilities. As Helen Lefkowicz Horowitz notes, in the late-nineteenth century, college life for students assumed its "mythic shape." As noted earlier, more than anything else, college was supposed to be fun, a time for socializing and carousing. It was not, however, purposeless; myriad social activities with concomitant social pressures constituted new forms of socialization that served as a dress rehearsal for the complex, competitive world awaiting students in their postcollege years. There was nothing like a universal experience, but a general consensus emerged regarding the constitutive elements and dy-namics of "real" college life, and with it a cultural benchmark by which institutions and various patterns of collegiate experience (e.g., residen-tial versus commuter) could be measured. An image of college life caught on: students could embrace it or reject it, but rarely could they ignore it.[11]

Like other collegians of the era, Catholics desirous of an advanced education could avail themselves of a number of institutions, both Cath-olic colleges and institutions associated with Protestantism. Primarily second-generation Irish and German and almost always the first in their families to attend college, their religious faith and ethnic heritage led many to the doors of their local Catholic college. For Irish Catholics in New England, that almost always meant Holy Cross or Boston College, two institutions woven tightly into the warp and woof of the region's Irish Catholic subculture. Others, however, chose a different academic path, their decisions to attend non-Catholic institutions indicative of the grow-ing salience of class in the social organization of higher education and the Catholic community. For many Catholics, moving up into the middle class required greater interaction with Protestant America.[12] This chap-ter explores Catholic students' disparate experiences, first within the ethnoreligious world of Boston College, then within the class-conscious world of Harvard University. While religion and social class combined kept some within the Irish Catholic subculture at the turn of the century, social class proved particularly effective in pulling other Catholics into the nation's new, nonsectarian universities.

The need to interact with Protestant America was particularly true in higher education since the modern, nonsectarian university had staked an early claim to professional education. Universities with professional schools proved attractive to many Catholic undergraduates—often those from the "better classes"—who desired an elite, modern education and a full measure of real college life. Within the Catholic community, discussions about Harvard's refusal to recognize the degrees of Jesuit colleges often segued into discussions about class and the social functions of higher education, which today sheds light on the ways in which social class was shaping Catholic participation in higher education.

Embedded in the Harvard controversy was a dual object lesson for the Jesuits: not only did it point up the growing influence of the universities, it also drew attention to the changing needs and desires of their traditional constituency. As the claims of class began to pull against the bonds of religion in higher education, a number of Catholics were left wondering whether the traditional approach to education, so ably defended by Father Brosnahan, combining classical study with heavy doses of piety and discipline, was suited to the "modern American boy"—a phrase used by Father Mullan at the height of the Law School controversy. It was an exceedingly important issue for the Jesuits on a number of accounts, not the least of which was the injunction in their *Constitutions* to adapt the educational strategies set forth in the *Ratio Studiorum* to the persons they encountered.

Until well into the twentieth century, Catholics in New England lived in a social world defined in large measure by the division born of Martin Luther's reforming efforts. For the largest group of Catholics, those of Irish lineage, their world was largely a two-sided one, with Irish Catholics in one camp and Yankee Protestants in the other.[13] In any given situation, ethnoreligious identity defined who was an insider and who was an outsider in this region where religious mistrust and animosity were long-standing and deep-seated.[14] Father Brosnahan recognized as much. On March 8, 1898, just days before learning from Dean Ames that the Law School faculty had removed Boston College and Holy Cross from its select list of colleges, Brosnahan wrote J. Havens Richards at Georgetown: "If we are stricken from the list, it will be difficult for Harvard to make our graduates who are accustomed to measure themselves with the graduates of Harvard in professional life believe that bigotry did not exclusively give the decision."[15] Brosnahan was correct. In a community that rarely missed an opportunity to remind others of the wrongs it had suffered at the hands of the Protestant majority, the Irish-dominated alumni of New England's Catholic colleges quickly resorted to charges of anti-Catholic prejudice.

Well-attended alumni gatherings in the winter of 1900, held soon after publication of Brosnahan's "President Eliot and Jesuit Colleges," became public forums to impugn Eliot. Large headlines appeared in the local papers: "President Eliot Called a Bigot," "Harvard's Discrimination Denounced at Holy Cross Banquet," and "President Eliot's Discrimination Against Catholic Colleges."[16] Dr. Barnes insistently raised the specter of bigotry. A journalist wrote in one particularly colorful piece, "The challenge was thrown down and Dr. Francis J. Barnes of Cambridge lance in hand, as the champion of Catholicism, advanced to meet President Eliot of Harvard University, the Protestant knight." According to Barnes, academic quality was not the reason for the removal of the Jesuit colleges from the list: there were institutions on the list that "cannot properly lay claim to the title of college in any modern acception of the term." Nor was it because the Jesuit colleges rejected Eliot's "pet scheme of unlimited electivism": there were colleges on the list that "stubbornly resisted" the curricular innovation. Nor was it because the Jesuits devoted considerable energies to teaching the classics. According to Barnes, Catholic colleges were "being attacked . . . because they are Catholic, and because they are under ecclesiastical control." Barnes laid the whole affair at Eliot's feet: graduates of Jesuit colleges were, he claimed, "shut out" of Harvard "simply because Pres. Eliot wills it so."[17]

There were more positive notes. Graduates at alumni meetings voiced their devotion to alma mater. At meetings punctuated by "bursts of applause and pledges of fealty," they articulated what a Jesuit education meant to them. If, as Barnes alleged, Eliot faulted the Jesuit colleges simply because they were Catholic, it was for precisely the same reason that the alumni from Holy Cross and Boston College hailed them. At an enthusiastic gathering of fellow graduates of Holy Cross, the rector of the Catholic University of America, Msgr. Thomas Conaty, explained: "We Catholics who believe in positive religion, who adhere with all the tenacity of life to the traditions of revealed religion as taught us by the church . . . we cannot, for ourselves at least, safely accept any instruction which ignores religion." Not given to fads or experimentalism, a Catholic education was built upon the solid foundation of the true religion and oriented students toward that for which they were created: eternal life. But a Jesuit education was not simply preparation for life after death, but for life after college. The college diploma was "our passport to the professions, upon it our standing as college men rests. It is all we have," said Conaty. The diploma signified loyalty to, even identification with, their alma mater. "Enmity to her [Holy Cross] is enmity to every one of us," claimed Conaty, and "unkindness to her touches us keenly and forces us to rally around her with the love of children to a mother whose character has been questioned." The refusal of Harvard Law School to include Holy Cross and Boston College on its select list of colleges was extremely troubling. "Our diploma is as dear to us as the diploma of any other college in the land. The depreciation of that diploma touches deeply every one of us."[18]

The loyal alumni who gathered in the winter of 1900 at the Bay State House in Worcester and the Parker House in Boston to defend their schools were professional men from the region's nascent Irish Catholic middle class. Conaty reminded his audience that those who held diplomas from Holy Cross included "bishops and priests, judges of the courts, lawyers and doctors eminent in professional life, mayors of cities, business men, men of letters, honored in their communities."[19] When, in 1950, Msgr. Michael Splaine, an 1897 graduate of Boston College and high-profile figure in Catholic Boston, was asked to describe his days at Boston College, he waxed nostalgic about his classmates. "My companions & fellows at Boston College in those days were an exceptional group of earnest young men anxious to better their station in life. We were just one generation away from our hard toiling fathers & were the first generation of what was then called the collar and cuff generation. Many of them rose to high positions, in church, State, medical & legal profession. In the halls of legislation, state & Federal, they have all given a good account of themselves."[20]

More often than not, the hard-toiling fathers (and mothers) who sent their sons to Holy Cross and Boston College had arrived in the United States and Canada during the nineteenth century. Protestant and Catholic alike, immigrants often reorganized their lives in the New World along ethnoreligious lines. Villages, towns, and city neighborhoods proved critical, providing the newly arrived with a sense of identity, sustenance, a degree of familiarity, and a community within which to grapple with the new complexities of life. The development of ethnoreligious communities reshaped American cities, creating a host of ethnic enclaves with, as one 1867 commentator put it, their "own theaters, recreations, amusements, military and national organizations; to a great extent their own schools, churches, and trade unions; their own newspapers and periodical literature."[21]

The massive waves of immigration also swelled and diversified the population of the Roman Catholic Church. Between 1776 and 1906 the percentage of Catholics among religious adherents in the United States rose from 1.8 percent to 32 percent, and relative to the entire population, the percentage of Catholics rose from less than 1 percent to 17 percent.[22] There were millions of new members, often needy, whose arrival sparked a massive brick-and-mortar campaign to meet their spiritual, emotional, material, and physical requirements. This immense project created the institutional underpinnings of a Catholic subculture. Catholic churches rapidly proliferated, with parishes becoming a powerful means of social organization. Frequently wary of Protestant charitable endeavors and building upon the church's ancient philanthropic tradition, American Catholics developed an immense, multifaceted, cradle-to-grave network of charities. Staffed in large measure by women in religious orders, these charitable institutions cared for the sick and the dying, the orphaned and the delinquent, the hungry and the homeless, the destitute and the deranged.[23]

In a country where the state-run school system and much of higher education were identified or affiliated with Protestantism, the Catholic minority created a separate system of schools to educate their own. Although support and patronage varied regionally and by ethnic group, it was a tremendous effort. Developed and sustained through voluntary contributions that often entailed significant personal sacrifice, according to one historian the Catholic school system was probably the "largest project undertaken by voluntary associations in American history, with the exception of the churches themselves." Even as schools and colleges prepared students for work and citizenship, they transmitted the Catholic faith, and in many cases also passed on ethnic traditions and Old World languages. Many pinned their hopes for the vitality of ethno-Catholicism on the parochial schools. According to Father Wenceslaus Kruszka, Polish-Catholic schools were the "foundation of the Polish Catholic church." Without them the "Polish church might remain Catholic," but its Polishness could well "sink in the Anglo-American sea."[24]

Boston, the land of the Cabots, Lowells, and Lodges, became an Irish Catholic stronghold in the second half of the nineteenth century, a metamorphosis wrought by a simple, monstrous, historical quirk: the failure of a single crop—the potato—on a small island three thousand miles removed from that city.[25] The ensuing famine, coupled with oppressive British rule and rent laws, drove Irishmen and Irishwomen in the late 1840s to some five thousand famine ships, stripping Ireland of much of its population. By 1860, more than a million Irish had sought refuge in the United States, representing one-third of all immigrants during the late 1840s and 1850s. Compared with other areas along the eastern seaboard, immigration to New England was primarily Irish, thus the region's ethnic cast assumed a strong Celtic hue.[26] Between 1846 and

1850, Irish immigrants who survived the ocean journey debarked ships in Boston's harbors and spilt out onto the wharves, swelling the city's Irish-born population to 35,287, or approximately one in every four inhabitants.[27] With their arrival, popery, Romanism, and Jesuitism swept across a region whose inhabitants had, two centuries before, banned Catholics and Jesuits from their wilderness Zion.

By 1900, the Irish in Boston had overcome formidable obstacles endemic among those of the famine generation: abject poverty, high rates of pauperism and delinquency, cholera and other diseases, and a mortality rate rivaling that of the slums of Dickensian England.[28] Among a host of immigrant groups that swelled the population, the Irish of the late-nineteenth century were, in William Shannon's words, the "closest to being 'in' while still being 'out.'" Yet the Irish Catholic community did not operate en masse—that is, did not arrive at the banks of the American and middle-class mainstream in toto. Although the second-generation Irish did considerably better than the first, a number remained in poverty, and many were working-class. In fact, studies report that, relative to other ethnic groups, the Irish remained overrepresented in the working class, with Boston, as described by historian Paula M. Kane, a "swamp of Irish underachievement." On the other hand, some Irish had breached the middle class, and a few had amassed great fortunes.[29]

The Irish Catholic community in Boston created a remarkably vital subculture. Conceived in the crucible of immigration and strengthened in the face of discrimination, the bonds of ethnicity and religion held Irish Catholics together even as the community diversified economically. The mix of poor, middling, and wealthy Irish—the "shanty Irish" and the "lace-curtain Irish"—maintained a separatist subculture.[30] It was, in part, a subculture sustained informally. In "their constant flow of humor," wrote a turn-of-the-century settlement-house worker in Boston, the Irish could "develop in some narrow back street much of the social give and take, and many of the friendly amenities that are characteristic of a country village."[31]

Key to the development and maintenance of a cohesive subculture were institutions and associations. Even as Irish Catholics were relieved of the crushing burden of postimmigration poverty, they strengthened their communal ties and defined the boundaries of their subculture by developing institutions and associations that mirrored those of the Protestant majority. In 1898 the *Catholic World* detailed in celebratory fashion an impressive list of "monuments to the faith" established in "this old stronghold of Puritan intolerance and bigotry, where," the author elaborated, "at one time the hound on the street would be served with kinder treatment than a Catholic."[32] Already wanting for churches before the famine inundated Boston with Catholics, in the second half of the nineteenth century the Catholic diocese of Boston built a plethora of churches, dotting the once Puritan hub of the universe with congregations loyal to Rome. Catholics also established a notable array of institutions to care for the needy, including the Home for Incurables, the Industrial School of the Working Boys' Home, Saint Mary's Infant Asylum, the Carney Hospital, and the Home for Destitute Children.[33] As these institutions ministered to the needy, they provided better-off Catholics with a separate venue for middle-class charitable endeavors—a place to emulate the Protestant middle class without stepping outside the Catholic subculture into Protestant society. The popular, service-oriented Saint Vincent de Paul Society, for example, fostered bonds within the community transcending disparities of circumstance and means: "We of the second and third generation, we have a duty to perform to the children sprung of a common ancestry, born into a common faith." These new Americans also established a panoply of voluntary associations that strengthened religious commitments and ethnic identification: sodalities, Catholic reading circles, chapters of the Knights of Columbus, the Friendly Sons of Saint Patrick, the Society of Saint Brendan, the Gaelic League, and others.[34]

When the 1864 establishment of Boston College was announced in the *Pilot*, an editorial in the paper wove the soon-to-be-opened institution into the ethnoreligious tapestry of Irish Catholic Boston. *"Felix Faustumque sit!"* the piece began: happiness and good luck to it. The "point is decided," wrote the editorialist, on the "necessity of combining religious training with secular instruction." Catholics would be able to "confide [their] children to the Jesuit Fathers" with a sense of "security." The church would also reap the benefits: the college would channel some of its students into the clerical life, and the Jesuits in residence would "assist our clergy, at present so much overtaxed in the duties of the confessional and in instructing the people" and would "add by their very number to the splendor of religious ceremonies." But "we need not only priests, but thoroughly educated lawyers, doctors, merchants— men of every profession." Looking to the future, the editorialist imagined a network of Catholic professionals bound together by their Jesuit education at Boston College. "When our lads shall have thus been educated in common, we may expect that they will be welded together by common recollections, sympathies and life long friendships. They will be the better able to support each other in good, and advance the interests of the whole Catholic body."[35]

The region's demographics dictated that the school roster would be dominated by students of Irish descent well into the twentieth century. In 1893, for instance, the entries for the letter *D* in the *Catalogue* of Boston College indicate a preponderance of Irish students: Daley, Daly, Davis, Day, De Coste, Delany, Denon, Desmond, Devlin, Dierkes, Dixon, Dobbyne, Does, Doherty (five times), Dolahar, Dolan, Doland, Donahue, Donnelly, Doogue, Dorsey, Dowd (three times), Downey, Doyle (twice), Driscoll, Drum, Duffy (twice), Duke, Dunphy, and Duran. (It was the same at Holy Cross in Worcester, where the 1893 entries for the letter *H* read: Hackett, Halloran, Halpin, Hanrahan [twice], Harkins, Harrington [twice], Harris, Healy, Hennessey, Hennon, Hickey [twice], Hogan, Howard, Hughes, and Hussey.)[36] A survey of colleges and their students by the Immigration Commission in 1908 provides further evidence of Hibernian domination at Boston College. Among 125 students surveyed, 42 percent were sons of native-born fathers; 55 percent were sons of foreign-born fathers; 2 percent were themselves born in Ireland. Among the 69 second-generation students, 62 (90%) were of Irish descent, with the remaining 7 students hailing from Canadian, English, German, or Scottish homes.[37] (Boston College rivals claimed that IHS, the Latin acronym that appeared on the cover of the college catalog, actually stood for "Irish High School.")[38]

An analysis of residential patterns and accounts from alumni connect turn-of-the-century Boston College with a largely working-class constituency. The working class in Boston lived in what a social worker, Robert Woods, called a "zone of emergence," a ring of neighborhoods and towns surrounding the core of the city where first- and second-generation families tended to move after they quit their tenements and wharfside shanty towns. In this zone "few were poverty-stricken, employment was comparatively regular and often well paid, there was a high proportion of home ownership, most spoke English, and many had at least an American grammar school education," according to urban historian Sam Bass Warner.[39] The zone included Charlestown, East Boston, South Boston, and Roxbury (which became Irish Catholic strongholds), as well as East Cambridge, Cambridgeport, and Dorchester (where Catholics mixed with middle-class Protestants). Taken together, these areas were described by a settlement-house worker as the "great Irish belt of the city."[40] The bulk of Boston College students in the 1890s came from these working-class neighborhoods. Students in the 1894–95 *Catalogue* came from Boston or one of sixty-six cities and towns almost all of which surrounded Boston. Fully 62 percent came from the city or one of the towns in the zone of emergence. Represented were Charlestown (31 students), Cambridgeport (5), Dorchester (27), East Boston (23), East Cambridge (3), Roxbury (52), South Boston (42), and Boston proper (67). The remaining towns, including the wealthier suburbs, averaged only two or three students, with only a handful sending more than five to the college. "We were all, for the most part, boys from poor homes," recalled Msgr. Splaine. Although a few "thought they were entitled to special privileges because their parents had a little more money," on the whole Boston College educated the sons of hard-toiling fathers. According to alumnus Michael Scanlon, it was a "poor man's school"; as alumnus Timothy Ahearn put it, it was an institution for the "poor Irish."[41]

Boston College was not unique; Catholic colleges throughout the country served a large number of second-generation students, primarily of Irish and German descent. According to the Immigration Commission survey, fewer than half (47.5%) of the students in nine Catholic colleges surveyed (all Jesuit, save Duquesne in Pittsburgh, which was conducted by the Congregation of the Holy Ghost) were sons of native-born fathers; more than half were the sons of foreign-born fathers or were themselves immigrants (47.5% and 4.5% respectively). By comparison, only 24.5 percent of men enrolled in the twenty non-Catholic colleges in the survey were second-generation. In Catholic colleges, 60 percent of second-generation students were sons of Irish-born fathers; the second largest group (20%) were sons of German-born fathers. Only in cities with exceptionally large German populations did second-generation Germans outnumber second-generation Irish (as was the case at Canisius College in Buffalo and Saint Xavier College in Cincinnati).[42] At Vincentian-run Saint Vincent's College (later known as DePaul University) in Chicago, the Irish constituted approximately one-half, the Germans about one-third of the student body between 1898 and 1908. A history of Villanova offers additional, anecdotal, evidence of the strong headway made by the Irish in Catholic higher education: those with "identifiably Irish surnames" were said to make up "more than 50 percent of the 1,548 individuals who attended between 1843 and 1893." According to Andrew Greeley, by 1900 those of Irish extraction were attending college at or near the national rate; by 1910, the Irish and German Catholic figures either reached or superseded the national average.[43]

Boston College grew slowly, from twenty-two students in the first class of 1864 to more than four hundred in the 1890s, making it one of the larger Catholic colleges. In 1894, Brosnahan reported to Luis Martín, the Rome-based head of the Society, that there were "almost 400 pupils" in the college, and since enrollment was "growing in number day by day," he predicted that they would be "very tight" in terms of space within a few years. When enrollment did reach four hundred, Brosnahan declared a holiday. Apparently it was a memorable event: more than a half-century later, alumni remembered the occasion, although the effects of time upon memory created some variance in their accounts. Both John Johnson (A.B. '94, Harvard Law School LL.B. '99) and Msgr. Frederick Allchin (A.B. '99) recalled such a holiday, although Johnson placed the critical number at three hundred and Allchin put it at five hundred. Msgr. Splaine also remembered "good dear old Father Tim Brosnahan" proclaiming a holiday when enrollment reached five hundred, garnishing his account with what was perhaps apocryphal nostalgia: Brosnahan, he claimed, "never knew that it was by drafting a likely young fellow from the ash cart that circulated around the College we were able to reach the 500 mark."[44]

Students placed in Father Brosnahan's charge were already products of their culture; their families, associates, schools, parishes, their engagement with print material and various forms of popular culture had already taught them formative lessons about what it meant to be Irish and Catholic in Boston. The lessons they learned at Boston College, formally and informally, through the curriculum and extracurriculum, bolstered students' ethnoreligious ties, which in turn strengthened the bonds sustaining the Irish Catholic community. But their academic lessons also set them apart within that community. A student's successful completion of his course of studies, an education that was largely classical in substance and deeply Catholic in tone, lifted him above the intellectual fray of less-lettered men. He assumed a new identity, becoming a "college man" who carried a newly issued passport into the professions.

As the 1864 editorialist hoped, once "educated in common," students who attended Boston College were indeed "welded together" by "common recollections, sympathies and life long friendships." Their education was common, not in the pedestrian sense but, rather, as an experience shared by all. While students at Harvard cobbled together a highly individualized, Protestant-inspired course of studies from a panoply of options, students at Jesuit colleges moved together through a prescribed course of studies. They learned the same subjects, mastered the same materials, and used the same texts. Moreover, the small scale of operation further reinforced the common nature of their education. Students necessarily knew each other well; classes of fifteen to twenty-five studied together year after year, in a single building, with a faculty of numbering about a dozen. Tellingly, when interviewed fifty years after graduation, alumni recalled the same professors, offered like descriptions, and recounted similar anecdotes. Two alumni, for example, remembered the Irish-born Father Cormican chiding students ill-prepared for class. "Go sell your books," announced Cormican, with a pronounced brogue, "you're wastin' time."[45]

The concessions made to modern subjects by the Jesuits were not, as Charles Eliot alleged, "trifling." Nonetheless, students in the regular course at Boston College and other Jesuit institutions spent the bulk of their intellectual energies mastering the classical languages, long considered the backbone of a gentlemen's education. No longer requisites for statecraft or the professions, much of the academic world had become disenchanted with "useless" ancient tongues; Greek and Latin held little sway among many moderns.[46] But the ancient languages, especially Latin, were far from useless in Catholic circles and colleges. It behooved students to master Latin if for no other reason than that completion of their academic program required it, for philosophy, a daily, three-hour class in the final year, was conducted in the ancient tongue. *"Dice Latinae!"* rang out when students lapsed into English. (One alumnus remembered teachers of other subjects occasionally drifting into Latin.)[47] More broadly, Latin was a valuable cultural resource for Catholics. Unlike Luther's spiritual descendants who had embraced the vernacular, Catholics clung to Latin as their official communal language; it served as the language of liturgy, of theology, and the seminary. Carved into buildings, printed on devotional items, used in prayers and hymns, Latin was a cultural staple. Apparently it was also a social resource for Boston College students. Their use of Latin in social settings adds a twist to Walter Ong's argument that the acquisition of the Latin tongue served as a Renaissance puberty rite, separating boys from unlettered females by giving them linguistic entrée into the gender-exclusive world of their learned male elders. Apparently Boston College students used Latin to capture the attention of young ladies, for according to Michael White ('94), he and his fellow students "used to talk about the girls in Latin so as to bother them" as they rode to and from school on the transit system.[48]

At Boston College, as in other Jesuit colleges, the extracurriculum played an important role in advancing the academic and literary aims of the college. As historian Bruce Kimball points out, two traditions have dominated the history of the liberal arts: that of oratory, stressing the ability to communicate, and that of philosophy, stressing the ability to reason.[49] While the university movement evinced an affinity for the philosophical tradition, the Jesuits (and other critics of modern education) continued to emphasize the value of the oratorical. This commitment to the oratorical at Boston College found clear expression in both the curriculum and extracurriculum. In the literary and oratorical societies, noted the Boston College *Catalogue*, "the work of the classroom is supplemented, or special fields in the liberal arts are cultivated."[50] Such traditional societies, long-standing fare in American higher education, dominated extracurricular life at Boston College and the other Jesuit colleges, fostering esprit de corps, developing *eloquentia perfecta*, and deepening the classical lessons of the classroom. The Boston College *Stylus*, begun in 1883 at students' initiative, was intended to enrich students' literary sensibilities and skills. In the first issue, student writers queried, "Why should Boston College lag behind? All the leading Institutions of learning in the land are making an editorial effort; this is ours." Gently mocking college papers given over to "college wits" who "like the poets' muses, wander unrestrained" (perhaps the *Harvard Lampoon?*), Boston College journalists aimed for "worth, not wit," seeking "literary excellence, to fit ourselves to cope with the world of thought."[51]

The oratorical tradition within the liberal arts found further extracurricular expression in various forms of public speech. As early as the 1550s, the Jesuits recognized the pedagogical value of *exercitium*—the drama inherent in orations and disputations.[52] In the 1890s, students in Jesuit colleges still had occasion for *extraordinariae exercitationes*—that is, various forms of public performance. At Boston College, students held class reunions (pre- rather than postgraduation events) at which they delivered speeches, read poetry, sang, and performed musical selections.[53] The more enthusiastic thespians joined the Boston College Athenaeum, which performed Shakespearean plays.[54]

The extracurricular jewel of Boston College, the popular Fulton Debating Society, was limited to fifty students. Members enjoyed the privilege of having their own meeting room, where they were free to recreate. One of the highlights of the 1890s was the 1895 debate between Georgetown and Boston College, the first intercollegiate debate between Jesuit institutions. (Georgetown won.) Such debates were grand affairs, attended by leading clergy, alumni, and citizens, including Charles Eliot, who was present at the 1897 Boston College prize debate. The following year, the Fulton Debating Society met Harvard in Cambridge; the debate fittingly resolved with a decision in favor of neither team. For the Jesuits and their supporters, a win in 1900 by the Holy Cross Juniors over the "Junior Wranglers of Harvard," before twelve hundred people in Mechanics' Hall, Worcester, undoubtedly proved satisfying.[55]

In the 1890s, a Jesuit education was as much Catholic as it was classical. The spiritual care of students was incumbent upon the Jesuits; three centuries earlier, they had embraced education as a principle ministry as a means to "help souls." They remained convinced that true education was inherently religious. "Man's first and most sacred duty is to God," and educational systems that ignored this fundamental fact were "defective and incomplete," wrote a Jesuit in 1903.[56] His claim carried an apologetic overtone. Just as progressivism and utilitarianism weakened classicism's long hold on the academy, the rise of secular and state-sponsored education in the eighteenth and nineteenth centuries rendered a claim for the inherent religiosity of education less a truism than a proposition in some circles. But in Jesuit and Catholic quarters, the religious ends of education were taken as a given, a stance that created a powerful orientation ineluctably affecting the atmosphere and workings of their schools.

Integral to realizing the aims of a Catholic education, the Jesuits and other Catholic educators used classroom instruction to deepen students' understanding of Catholicism and imbue them with a Catholic outlook on life. Turn-of-the-century collegians did not study theology; philosophy capped their course of studies, with theology reserved for those who went on to study for the priesthood. Collegians' formal instruction in the tenets of the faith consisted of recitation of the "daily catechetical lesson" and attendance at the "weekly lecture on the doctrines of the Church." In the college course, students at Boston College used *Wilmer's* catechism for an hour each week, their attention directed to a long list of topics including "Creation of the World . . . the Work of Redemption . . . Grace, Actual and Sanctifying . . . Christianity as a Revealed Religion . . . The Church, the Dispenser of the Christian Religion . . . The Existence and Nature of God."[57] Alumnus Martin Welsh (A.B. '00) recalled that "in religion we had a weekly lecture given to the whole student body together, but besides that we had a daily lesson, taken from Wilmer's Catechism, which was divided into four sections, one for each college year, and was as a whole a masterly work on Christian doctrine, suitable for the educated laity." Welsh was generous: "We were really fortunate to have such a splendid volume."[58]

The study of Catholicism was not limited to catechetical instruction; students appropriated an understanding of the Catholic faith and Catholic outlook through the various disciplines. "Our books must be Catholic," argued Brother Azarius, "our historical knowledge must be studied from the Catholic point of view."[59] Speaking at the 1901 ACCUS meeting on the "Teaching of History in College," Father Laurence Delurey, president of Augustinian-run Villanova, told listeners that the study of the past "furnishes the student with powerful weapons in the defense of truth and religion." The Middle Ages, he suggested, "would seem a most interesting, and certainly most fruitful epoch" for study in a Catholic college. Conversely, developing a Catholic viewpoint entailed skepticism and wariness of all things Protestant. The "so-called Reformation," he claimed, "the personages and their characteristics, their principles . . . their motives . . . all demand a careful treatment at our hands." At the same conference, a Vincentian priest from Niagara University made a similar case for English, urging teachers to be steadfast in presenting a Catholic point of view. Indeed, he lamented, "we seem to be casting the minds" of students "from a literary point of view, in a Protestant mould." Use of Protestant-authored texts required extra care to "minimize the harm" to students. Better, he argued, that teachers made more extensive use of Catholic authors such as Newman, Vaughn, Manning, and Ward.[60]

The curriculum at Boston College blended the Catholic with the non-Catholic. In English literature classes, Protestant authors (e.g., Milton, Johnson, Addison) substantially outnumbered Catholic (e.g., Newman). In their course on the history of philosophy, students examined works variously Protestant (e.g., Hegel and Berkeley), Catholic ("Thomistic philosophy under Leo XIII"), and nominally theistic (Locke and Voltaire). Religious diversity notwithstanding, Catholicism left heavy tracks across the course of studies. In the first term of the sophomore year, for instance, students spent two hours a week studying "Church History, by Epochs," marching through "The Anti-Nicene Church—the Benedictines—Gregory the Great and the Missionaries—the Dark Ages —Charlemagne—Gregory III and the War of Investitures—Boniface and Philip the Fair—the Crusades—Scholasticism and Education in General—the Schism of the West—Renaissance and Reformation— Jansenism and Revolution—Modern Times." Readers of the *Catalogue* were informed that, in treating these topics, "special emphasis is given to the Church's conservatism and yet breadth, the Church's democratic spirit and sympathy with the poor, the Church as a binding force in the world."[61]

Throughout the nineteenth century, religious observances and worship were normative elements of a college education for America's young men and women. (Harvard's move to *voluntary* chapel services in the 1880s was considered by critics as a decisive step toward godlessness.)[62] In the Jesuit colleges, sacramental and devotional practices were part of the rhythm of the school day and the academic year, and far from voluntary. As in other Catholic institutions, students at Boston College began each day with mass, with some of their number being pressed into service as altar boys. Traditional devotional practices punctuated the remainder of the day; classes began with prayer, and students often penned religious acronyms (e.g., A.M.D.G. for *ad majorem Dei gloriam* or J.M.J. for Jesus, Mary, and Joseph) at the top of their papers. Students who excelled academically won prizes, often of a religious nature; for example, superior work in Greek prosody won a student a copy of *The Life of Christ* in Greek. Students made an annual retreat, observed sacramental obligations, and participated in the Sodality of the Immaculate Heart of Mary. The Saint Cecelia Choir, named for the patron saint of music, sang for special occasions.[63] According to the *Catalogue*, those who had not yet received the "Sacraments of Penance, Confirmation, or Holy Eucharist" were to "prepare for their reception," while those who had already made the Sacrament of Penance were directed to "present themselves to their confessor every month." Routine ensured that they did so, with teachers recast as confessors and students as penitents each month, giving students (at least potentially) what a consultor for the college described as "advantages which a personal and kindly influence on the part of the Confessor might secure for them."[64] Father O'Neill was confessor-of-choice for a number in the mid-1890s; "all students knew" that Father O'Neill had "one deaf ear, his left," according to alumnus Joseph Loughry (A.B. '99), and thus "40 to 50 boys would be in front of Father O'Neill's box until Father Brosnahan would appear and scatter them to other confessors."[65]

In an ideal world students would have had little need for the sacrament of confession since the Jesuits went to great length to enforce discipline conducive to upright living. Of course, all colleges needed discipline to keep students in line,[66] and the Jesuit colleges were no different. Although the older students sometimes chafed, discipline in the Jesuit colleges was largely a one-size-fits-all affair for students, who ranged in age from approximately 12 to 21. Students lined up and marched between classes and events. Gentlemanly conduct was expected, while smoking and boisterous behavior were prohibited. "Playing ball, snowballing, pitching, and all games that endanger windows" were not allowed.[67] For the Jesuits, "Order is the first law of heaven,"[68] but discipline was more than a case of ensuring good order for its own sake; good discipline spiritually protected students. In the Jesuit colleges, especially residential colleges such as Holy Cross, the Jesuits closely watched over their students lest they succumb to temptation and fall into serious sin. Consumption of alcohol and transgressions sexual in nature were paramount concerns.[69]

While a Boston College education in the 1890s was clearly common, classical, and Catholic, it was not explicitly Celtic. By the end of the century, Irish and Irish Americans had established organizations to celebrate their ethnic heritage (e.g., the Ancient Order of Hibernians, the Gaelic League, the American Irish Historical Society), but Boston College had no Irish-oriented club or activity. As Boston College historian Charles F. Donovan pointed out, Irish themes and causes were virtually absent in rhetoric and writing exercises; the *Stylus* and the Fulton Debating Society rarely mentioned anything Irish. In itself the ethnic homogeneity of the college inevitably reinforced ethnic identification, but the curriculum and extracurriculum did little formal ethnic work. To have done so would have marked a departure, for historically a Jesuit education aimed at the development of Christian gentlemen, not ethno-Catholics. If anything, nineteenth-century Boston College focused on creating American Catholics, not Irish Catholics.[70] In an era in which many native-born Protestants voiced doubts about immigrants' potential to assimilate and become "good" Americans, the emphasis at Boston College was on the national, rather than the ethnic. The college in its early years adopted the eagle as its mascot, and students memorized F. Scott Key's "The Star Spangled Banner" and practiced military drills as members of the Foster Cadets.[71] Only after the turn of the century, as alumni and the wider community grew more confident in terms of their presence in Boston, did they come to view the college as a platform to promote explicitly Irish identity and heritage. A grandiose plan that surfaced around 1909 to build a "Daniel O'Connell Memorial Building and Irish Hall of Fame" at Boston College went unrealized, despite support from various Irish American clubs. Among other things, supporters of the multifaceted plan considered placing a statue of Daniel O'Connell, the "Great Liberator" of Ireland, atop a prominent dome, no doubt meant to convey a message to Boston's Protestant citizens. (The plan devolved into a more modest venture; opened in 1913, the main building on the new campus housed a large assembly hall celebrating Irish history and culture.)[72]

While the Jesuits remained aloof from the reforms that swept through the academy in the second half of the nineteenth century, holding fast to classical and Catholic patterns of education inherited from their European predecessors, their students injected a very American element into the collegiate experience: athletics. Like students in other colleges of the period, those in Jesuit colleges enthusiastically embraced sports and competition. Students keenly followed their teams, linking their corporate honor with the wins and losses of the "baseball nine" and other teams. In 1884 Boston College students founded an athletic association, "to encourage the practice of manly sports, and to promote by these the *esprit de corps* of the College Students, who are its members." But athletics remained a small-time operation, in part because the students were commuters, in part because the school lacked playing fields. "We practiced when we played someone," recalled alumnus Michael Burke, captain of the baseball team.[73]

For students who persisted through the seven-year course at Boston College, graduation ceremonies marked completion of their studies. Between 1877 and 1900, the college held annual ceremonies for graduating classes that ranged in size from nine to twenty-nine, with ceremonies that usually included music, student addresses, the conferral of degrees, and a valedictory address. Graduation in 1891 was somewhat unusual; according to alumnus Charles Quirk (A.B. '91), Pierce J. Grace's father, "a millionaire," hired a symphony orchestra for the occasion. In contrast, Msgr. Michael Scanlon's 1895 graduation "was a simple one." The "students did not wear caps and gowns," Scanlon recalled, because Father Brosnahan thought it would be an "Imitation of Harvard." Nonetheless, the students donned elegant "Prince Albert suits and stove pipe hats," rented for $2.50, and those who could afford to do so "hired hacks" and "took their parents out to dinner" after the ceremony.[74]

But most Boston College students never enjoyed graduation day; they "sojourned within her sacred walls for a few years, drinking from the fountain of wisdom," as a journalist described it, but left, "reluctantly," before obtaining the "much-coveted diploma."[75] In 1900, no job or profession absolutely required a college diploma, thus, throughout higher education, it was quite common to leave college early. A college degree was certainly not needed for the types of jobs popular among second-generation Irish in Boston, such as clerkships and municipal jobs. For Boston College students, save those bound for the seminary, there was little reason to persist through the seven-year course of studies, and most did not. Between 1891 and 1900, students stayed an average of three to four years at Boston College—a retention rate consistent with other Catholic colleges. Class size for students in the first year of study (known as Rudiments) averaged eighty-five. With enrollment decreasing thereafter by an average of 16 percent annually, class size for students in the final year of study (known as Philosophy) averaged twenty-three. Over the course of the seven-year program, the persistence rate through graduation was 33 percent; for those who actually began college-level work, the rate was 42 percent. The attrition rate meant that only 35 percent of students taught by the Jesuits at Boston College during the 1890s were doing college-level work. Most of the Jesuits' work was with the 60 percent enrolled in the preparatory-level course and another 5 percent of students enrolled in a vocationally oriented English program (a course reluctantly offered by the Jesuits at the insistence of the Boston archbishop, John Williams).[76]

For almost all who did graduate from Boston College, a professional career in Boston lay ahead. At least 71 percent of graduates between 1877 and 1907 became priests, lawyers, or doctors; 24 percent became educators, journalists, or businessmen. Priesthood was the most popular profession among graduates. Between 1877 and 1890, almost two-thirds became priests; between 1891 and 1900, 43 percent migrated from Boston College to a seminary.[77] Some joined the Jesuits or another religious order, but most entered the local seminary, Saint John's, in Brighton. According to a journalist writing in 1893, it was a "well-known fact" that the sizes of the classes at Saint John's "vary with the graduating classes at Boston College." It seemed as if the "entire body of the younger clergymen of the archdiocese is made up of Boston College men"; they were, he added "performing the duties of their sacred office with piety and zeal." Enrollment data confirm the impression. According to one study, between 1884 and 1893, between 29 and 74 percent of the men entering Saint John's Seminary had studied at Boston College—on average, 43 percent per year.[78]

After the priesthood, medicine and law proved the most popular professions among Boston College men graduating between 1877 and 1907; respectively, they drew 11 and 12 percent of graduates (see table 2). A significant proportion of those who became physicians or lawyers secured their professional training at Harvard. Of the 171 graduates be-

Table 2

Career Paths of Boston College Bachelor's Degree Recipients
(Percent of Total)

	1877–1890 n = 202	1891–1900 n = 214	1901–1907 n = 184	1877–1907 n = 600
Priests*	63	43	36	48
Lawyers*	6	21	9	12
Physicians*	13	14	7	11
Educators**	4	5	20	9
Journalists	3	1	3	2
Business/clerks	5	14	20	13
Other	1	2	2	2
Unknown	4	2	1	2
Deceased	4	2	1	2
Total	100	103***	100	100

Source: Graduates of Boston College (1908).
*Includes those in professional schools and seminaries in 1907.
**Includes teachers, administrators, and librarians.
***Total is greater than 100 because some graduates followed two career paths; e.g., an individual who held a law degree and worked as headmaster of a school.

tween 1891 and 1900 who did not become priests, 74 (43%) became either doctors or lawyers. Of these 74, 42 (59%) attended either Harvard Medical School or Harvard Law School, with 23 going to the Medical School and 19 to the Law School. For those not going to a seminary, Harvard was a popular route into the professions. The notable decline in the percentage of Boston College graduates after 1900 who became doctors or lawyers is explained in part by the growing number who became educators and businessmen. It also suggests that Harvard's refusal to admit graduates of Boston College to the Law School as regular students after 1898 may have turned aspiring physicians and jurists toward other institutions for their undergraduate work.

Despite James Barr Ames's claims that Jesuit college graduates at Harvard Law School "made poor records as a rule" and that the grades of Boston College men were "not a very good exhibit,"[79] the last of the Boston College men to enter Harvard Law School enjoyed remarkable professional success. James Devlin, Arthur Dolan, Francis Fogarty, Joseph Walsh were in the class of 1897; Francis Carney, Bartholomew Coyne, Joseph Keogh, and George McLaughlin were in the class of 1898. All practiced law, many entered politics, and a number enjoyed distinguished careers. The son of a business manager, James Devlin left general law practice to serve as legislative counsel for the City of Boston and its police commissioners. He rose to the rank of assistant attorney general and served as judge for the municipal court. Arthur Dolan also combined law and politics. He was a member of the Common Council from 1900 to 1905, serving as president after 1902. That year, the *Boston College Stylus* reported Dolan's service as acting mayor of Boston for a day; the following year it noted his marriage to Christine M. Barr, of Charlestown, in "one of the events of the social season in Charleston."

Francis Carney was born in Cambridge, the son of a piano manufacturer. Carney eventually became a senior partner in the firm of Carney, Lynch, & Killion and taught at Boston College Law School from its founding in 1929 to 1936. Active in the American Bar Association, he served as its vice-president and chairman of the Committee on Ethics and Grievances. His *New York Times* obituary described him as a "leader in the national campaign beginning in 1935, to raise the standards of professional conduct." Bartholomew Coyne (LL.B. '01 cum laude) was the son of a farmer. A founding member of Abbott & Coyne, a firm known for work in admiralty law, he served as director and officer of several corporations. He also worked as attorney for the Danish consul, for which we was awarded a "noninheritable title" from the king of Denmark.[80]

As graduates of Boston College "rose to high positions," as Msgr. Splaine put it, "in church, State, medical & legal profession," they remained closely tied to the subculture of Irish Catholic Boston. They did so through their parishes and participation in a host of ethnic and religious activities and associations. Their success became a source of pride for the community at large. The case of James Francis Aylward (A.B. '84, Harvard Law School LL.B. '86) is illustrative. Like many who took law degrees, Aylward gravitated toward politics, serving on the Cambridge Common Council, the Board of Alderman, the Massachusetts House of Representatives, and as assistant U.S. attorney during the Wilson administration. A loyal alumnus who served as president of the Boston College Alumni Association in 1915, he was also a member of the Bishop Cheverus Council, the Knights of Columbus, the Clover Club, the Irish Charitable Society, the Cambridge Catholic Union, and the American Irish Historical Society.[81] Catholic Boston celebrated successful alumni such as Aylward. According to an 1893 contributor to *Donahoe's*, graduates of Boston College "reflected credit upon their Alma Mater by their civic and religious virtues." More broadly, Alyward and other successful alumni who assumed leadership roles in the community became personifications of Catholic success in Protestant America. An obituary for the eminent jurist Francis Carney in 1940 captures the broader symbolic role graduates played in the life of the community: "Catholic Boston claimed him among its own and knew him as exemplifying the best traditions and the best aspirations of Catholic culture."[82]

Graduates of Boston College stepped out into professional life and the Irish Catholic subculture welded together through a wholly common, largely classical, and deeply Catholic education. The Law School controversy, a significant moment in their self-understanding relative to their academic and professional lives, further bound together this generation of Boston College men. Years later, records concerning the Law School controversy kept by alumnus Eugene McCarthy ('84; Harvard Medical School '87) were compiled into a lengthy typewritten manuscript. The editor explained that even after the "lapse of thirty years," the records of the controversy that "startled New England and indeed many other parts of the country" were perhaps still of "interest for their educational value" and "historical importance."[83] Interviewed a half-century later, nineteen alumni from the 1890s regularly mentioned the "great controversy" sparked by Eliot's "attack upon the Ratio Studiorum." They remembered "quite a bit of feeling against Harvard"; as reported tersely in another case, there was "academic hostility toward Harvard (Ratio Studiorum vs. Eliot's Electivism)." Father Brosnahan emerged as the great defender, pitted against the "famous opponent Charles W. Eliot." The "general consensus of the intelligentsia," according to one alumnus, was that "Father Brosnahan had won a decisive victory."[84] The strong impression made on the Boston College men endured. A postmortem tribute to Bartholomew Coyne published in the *Boston College Alumni News* in 1938 linked the successes in his life with the Law School controversy. "Bartholomew B. Coyne was a member of the class of 1898," wrote the editorialist. "This in itself was a distinction." He "entered the Harvard Law School as one of a small band from Boston College" and by his "achievements" he "vindicated the claims indisputably made by the revered Reverend Timothy Brosnahan, S.J., that men educated by, and through the 'Ratio Studiorum' are the equals of other educated men."[85]

Claims of victory for the Jesuit cause surfaced immediately in the wake of the Law School controversy. Despite Brosnahan's and Mullan's failures to regain a spot on the Law School's list for Boston College and Holy Cross, alumni claimed that their side had won the great academic contest.

According to the Boston College Alumni Association, the "great tribunal of public opinion" had decided in favor of Jesuit education. Their alma mater emerged from the controversy with "more dignity and honor" than its "wanton aggressor," and "far from being injured by the attack upon its reputation by some of the authorities of Harvard University," Boston College came through the controversy "triumphant and unscathed." According to a contributor writing in 1900 under the pseudonym of Candor in the *Sacred Heart Review*, Eliot had unwittingly handed Boston College and Catholic education a psychological victory. "Instead of creating a panic among Catholics," Candor wrote, Eliot actually provoked what he was "probably . . . most anxious to avoid"—namely, "rallying Catholics to the defence of their educational institutions."[86] *Woodstock Letters*, the Jesuit newsletter, reported on one display of loyalty, recounting how a pastor traveled thirty-six miles to attend commencement exercises in 1900. "I never come to commencement," he reportedly told Father Brosnahan, "but this year I am here to show you that I am with you in your fight with Harvard."[87]

The numbers, however, tell a different story. They undermine the simple we-versus-them religious construct that sustained much of the public debate surrounding the Law School controversy. Catholics rallied rhetorically to the defense of the Jesuit colleges, but the controversy adversely affected enrollments, especially at Boston College. As higher-education enrollments nationally soared (72 percent between 1890 and 1900), the Jesuit colleges languished. After steady increases during the 1890s that pushed enrollment at Boston College to a high of 475 in 1899–1900, the year the Law School controversy erupted in the press, enrollment shrank precipitously to a low of 335 in 1904–5, a 29 percent decrease in five years. At Holy Cross, enrollments dipped between 1898 and 1900, then held relatively steady until 1903. Although Georgetown's distance from Harvard makes a direct connection between the Harvard Law School controversy and its enrollment tentative at best, it, too, experienced a drop in enrollment in the wake of the controversy. In the meantime, estimates of the number of Catholic students at Harvard increased sharply, from 325 in 1893 to 480 in 1907.[88]

A keen student of educational history and current trends, Fr. James Fagan, S.J. (1856–1906), turned to social class in explaining the Law School's adverse effects on enrollments at Boston College, describing the college's predicament in 1902 in a lengthy letter to the superior general in Rome about Jesuit colleges in the Maryland–New York Province. "In the beginning," wrote Fagan, Boston College "rightly enjoyed a satisfactory reputation." Its early students "could scarcely be called rich," yet they came from some of the "more distinguished Catholic families in the city" at a time when "almost all our Catholics were of humble circumstances." The College made "great progress" under the "leadership of Father Brosnahan" until it "came into conflict with Harvard." According to Fagan, "our men seemed to have waged their side with little prudence or discretion" and were, therefore, subject to "clever and smart opponents from Harvard," an institution that "enjoys considerable fame and influence even among Catholics." Some Catholics were "upset at Boston College and our men who had rudely attacked such a school and its president." He now reported the troubling consequences: "The number of students is fewer, especially among those of good families and income." Boston College, thought Fagan, seemed in "great danger" of "slowly and imperceptibly" being reduced from one of the Jesuits' major schools to a minor institution.[89]

Fagan was not the only one to introduce the issue of class into the debate surrounding the Law School controversy. In summer 1900, following the publication of the Mullan-Eliot correspondence, a series of letters to the editor appeared in the *Sacred Heart Review,* some penned by the above-mentioned Candor and others by his sparring partner, Veritas, who betrayed his loyalties by using part of Harvard's motto for his pseudonym.[90] In their first few exchanges, Candor and Veritas squabbled about Eliot's refusal to answer Mullan, the terms of fair play, and the validity of arguments in Brosnahan's second paper "The Relative Merit." Their subsequent exchanges focused on support for Catholic higher education among Catholics. Responding to Candor's claim that the "great body of Catholics" supported Catholic higher education, Veritas wrote:

Whatever may be said of the views entertained by "the great body of Catholics" regarding this educational question, it is certain that the most enlightened Catholics clearly recognize the necessity of educating their sons in non-sectarian colleges. What may be called the better class of Catholics in and around Boston are now educating their sons at Harvard. Those in other parts of the country send their sons to the nearest non-sectarian college, or, if their purse permits, to Yale or Harvard or one of the other great American universities. The less enlightened Catholics, who do not appreciate the evils of sectarian education, send their sons to Catholic colleges. Another very significant fact in this connection is the marked increase, dur-

ing the last few years, in the number of Catholic students attending
non-sectarian colleges. During the same period the Catholic colleges have not only been unable to increase their attendance to any
appreciable extent, but also in some instances have failed to maintain their former numerical importance. Thus we see that, with improved opportunity and greater enlightenment, Catholics are shun-
ning the narrow sectarian college for the more liberal American
institution. The tide has set in toward the broader culture; and the
Catholic college must soon face the dreary prospect of an untimely
end.[91]

In subsequent letters to the editor, Candor strongly criticized Veritas's
assertion that students from the better classes who attended non-Catholic schools were more enlightened. He also claimed that the "great majority of Catholic young men enter the Catholic college." But Candor was
wrong. They may or may not have been enlightened, but Catholics who
patronized non-Catholic colleges and universities such as Harvard did
so in great numbers, far greater than those who opted for Catholic colleges.[92] The claims of class, the desire to move up, were pulling Catholics out of the ethnoreligious worlds of their mothers and fathers and into
the Protestant worlds of education in pursuit of valuable educational
credentials, desirable social networks, and a full measure of popular
student life. As the age of the university dawned, social class was beginning to cut across the grain of religion and ethnicity in higher education
in quite significant ways.

The changing contours of the Irish Catholic experience in the United
States coincided with and were shaped by fundamental transformations
in the ways in which Americans understood and organized their lives
during the second half of the nineteenth century. As "island communities" and "walking cities" gave way to a "distended society," Americans grew more class conscious. "We are," one labor leader claimed,
"rapidly developing classes in society as well as in the industrial world
and . . . these classes are becoming more and more fixed."[93] At the apex
of Americans' increasingly fixed class ladder were the very, very rich—
the Vanderbilts, Carnegies, and Rockefellers—whose fabulous fortunes
and opulent lifestyles dazzled the American populace. At the bottom of
the ladder were the very, very poor—new immigrants, street urchins,
alcoholics, fallen women—whose misadventures and very existence
troubled and scandalized the more fortunate. For most Americans, the

prospect of amassing a great fortune was unimaginable; the more real possibility, of poverty, was appalling. The majority considered themselves part of, or at least on the cusp of, what they understood as the middle class.

Americans' increased recourse to class as a social construct grew in tandem with the size and complexity of society. In larger, more heterogeneous communities of the late-nineteenth century, the informal, personal modes of social intercourse common in antebellum communities became inadequate. Less likely to know their neighbors and their neighbors' histories in the personal and immediate ways of their small-town grandparents, Americans increasingly relied on social class as a means of social organization and regulation. Social class filled in the blanks created by size and diversity; one might not know a certain family personally, but one could assume much by virtue of its class. Middle-class status revealed a great deal, for being middle class was to be possessed of a powerful state of mind that regulated virtually every facet of everyday life: manner of deportment, organization of family life, choice of occupation, use of leisure time, location of residence, patterns of consumption, and modes of voluntary association. This middle-class state of mind took aspiration as a requisite, respectability as a norm. It also shaped attitudes toward money and masculinity. While their grandparents admired pious, virtuous men who were right with God and did right by their neighbors, middle-class Americans at the turn of the century came to admire successful men who did well for themselves and their immediate families. Far less likely than antebellum Americans to measure a man's worth by his piety, work ethic, and civic contribution, those who came of age during America's gilded years increasingly measured a man by his financial prowess. The esteem attached to communitarian-oriented values essential to the healthy social ecology of America's island communities shifted toward individually oriented virtues and charismata necessary for personal achievement in distended societies. The Gospel of Success, and its scientific corollary, social Darwinism, found many enthusiasts at the turn of the century.[94]

During the turn-of-the-century "search for order," higher education assumed greater importance and new functions. With the exception of the ministry, the world of work and higher education had been loosely coupled for most of the nineteenth century. Antebellum Harvard provides a case in point: at midcentury, the Yard was peopled in large part by aspiring ministers (though they were growing fewer in number) and the sons of Boston's leading families sent to Harvard to finish their studies with a gentleman's education. But this pattern changed quite quickly with the triumph of industrial capitalism. Postbellum Americans turned to educational institutions to prepare their children for the world of work. At the end of the century one could make a good living without a college diploma; in fact, according to some self-made men a college education actually hindered those who aspired to financial success. According to Andrew Carnegie, while collegians whittled away hours studying "barbarous and petty squabbles of a far-distant past, or trying to master languages which are dead, . . . knowledge . . . adapted for life upon another planet . . . as far as business affairs are concerned, the future captain of industry is hotly engaged in the school of experience, obtaining the very knowledge required for his future triumphs."[95] But this approach ran counter to what was becoming conventional wisdom, especially among the middle class. While Bostonians' genealogical fixation continued to bolster the social importance of the Brahmin class, across the nation "schooling had been replacing breeding."[96]

Lacking an apprenticeship system and an aristocracy (Brahmins notwithstanding), Americans thrust new social and vocational functions onto their colleges. A college diploma indicated that a man had a certain capacity for intellectual work and was, therefore, a candidate for white-collar and professional jobs. But college education was more than cognitive work and the mastery of texts; it was a multifaceted set of experiences that included the development of all-important college friendships. Aspiring to careers in business and the professions, collegians knew well that social connections were an immensely valuable asset. Moreover, as colleges carved out distinct reputations, the social sorting process in relation to educational affiliation became more refined. It was not merely obtaining a diploma, but obtaining it from a "good" school. Whom you knew and where you met them counted. Graduates began to trade on their alma maters' cachet, a disturbing development for Henry Adams, class of 1858, who studied at Harvard during more genteel, parochial days. Returning as a faculty member in the 1870s, he was taken aback when a student baldly announced that the "degree of Harvard College is worth money to me in Chicago."[97]

Changes in legal education, many inaugurated at Harvard during Eliot's tenure as president, reflect the growing centrality of higher education in American society, particularly for the middle class as they turned to university-based professional education for the credentials and networks necessary for a successful career. In the Jacksonian era, the "doors of access to the legal profession always swung open to anyone stung by ambition,"[98] doing so in the context of personal relationships. Law schools then were few in number, and for most aspiring jurists the first step in their legal education began with an apprenticeship. In that open, rather democratic process, an individual simply "read law" with a practicing lawyer for a period of time—a period that sometimes lasted several years. But that personal, informal system of legal education grew inadequate on two fronts. As society and the economy grew in scale and complexity, so, too, did the law; as it did, university-trained specialists in the "science" of the law became more useful than privately trained generalists. Furthermore, larger, more heterogeneous communities rendered the informal and personal modus vivendi of antebellum legal education inadequate. As the law became more scientific and technical, and society more complex, law schools and the credentials they provided became more important. By 1900, the law school—Harvard's, in particular—was becoming one of the "most important guardian of the gates to the legal profession."[99]

Given higher education's new social and economic functions, growing numbers of young Americans went to college. Compared with the general population, college-attenders were still few and far between; in 1870, only between 1 and 2 percent of college-age students pursued advanced education. But as Americans came to recognize the socioeconomic value of higher education, college attendance rates began a steep climb. Between 1870 and 1900, enrollments rose from 52,000 to 238,000, pushing the rate of college attendance to 4 percent among the college-age population. Gains in enrollments in professional schools accounted for much of the increase. The number of students in law schools, for instance, increased from 3,134 in 1879–80, to 4,518 in 1889–90, to 12,516 in 1899–1900.[100] Harvard's student population swelled during the Eliot years. The undergraduate population saw a fourfold increase, from 563 students in 1869 to 1,077 in 1886, and to 2,238 in 1908. Despite more rigorous admission and graduation requirements, enrollment in the Law School rose steadily and substantially, from 120 to 684, an almost sixfold increase during Eliot's presidential tenure.[101]

As Harvard's enrollment burgeoned, it became more diverse. Driven by his democratic principles, Unitarian optimism, and faith in the social efficacy of education, Eliot was particularly keen to create a more heterogeneous campus. Doing so meant undoing Harvard's reputation as a school that catered to Boston's elite. "Luxury and learning," he announced in his 1869 inaugural, "are ill bedfellows"; the "poorest and the richest students are equally welcome here, provided that with their poverty or their wealth they bring capacity, ambition, and purity."[102] In the middle of the nineteenth century, Harvard deserved its aristocratic reputation; having alienated part of its traditional clientele with its early-nineteenth-century conversion to Unitarianism, Harvard drew its students primarily from the insular ranks of Boston's gentry.[103] By the end of the century, Harvard had become decidedly cosmopolitan, more so than Yale or Princeton. Edwin Slosson, whose study of American universities graced the pages of the *Independent* in 1909 and 1910, made a direct comparison: Princeton held fast to homogeneity, while Harvard worked toward diversity. "The Harvard students are gathered from all over the world, admitted under all sorts of conditions, and given the most diversified training."[104]

True, Harvard was still top-heavy with representatives from the upper end of the socioeconomic scale; tuition, at $150 a year, coupled with living expenses, put Harvard beyond the grasp of many. Yet Eliot made good on his inaugural announcement. Harvard drew students from the public and the prep schools and offered scholarships and loans more generous than those at many other colleges and universities.[105] As Slosson put it, "that the future of the university is dependent upon the perpetuity of the Society of Mayflower Descendants is already disproved. The old stock has been successfully grafted with new life." By 1908–9, students in the college hailed from sixty-five states or countries.[106] Alumnus Rollo Walter Brown (A.M. 1905) reported that the "pampered youth" of the day "protested . . . that the over-aggressive Jews or the over-aggressive Westerners or over-aggressive sons of New England mill hands were disturbing the genteel atmosphere of the Yard," but such complaints, Brown claimed, warranted little attention, for though "socially important," the elite were a "declining minority."[107] Regardless, by the 1890s the Yard was filled with representatives of what Harvard philosopher George Santayana called "crude but vital America." Thus Brown counted among his friends a "German Catholic from Ohio; . . . a Quaker from Pennsylvania; . . . a Mormon from Utah; . . . a Presbyterian from Indiana; two were pure pioneers from the Dakotas; another was from Iowa; another from Virginia; another from Japan; another from France; another from Bulgaria."[108]

In its metamorphosis from the local, parochial institution of Eliot's student days into the large, cosmopolitan university of his presidency, Harvard became an academic analogue of Wiebe's "distended society." "It is a very large machine," wrote Santayana in 1894, "serving the needs of a very complex civilization." Slosson concurred. "Harvard University is so complex and diversified that almost any statement may be made about it with some degree of truth, except a general statement," he wrote. "Each department has an independent life and character, with its own theories, methods and traditions."[109] Size and diversity inevitably exacted a toll on class unity that had been sustained in earlier times by the intimacy of small classes, relative homogeneity of social background, and a largely prescribed curriculum. Whereas colleges in 1890 averaged 106 students,[110] in the 1890s Harvard undergraduates numbered more than a thousand. Writing for the *North American Review* in 1888, a journalist noted the parallel with "the great world outside." Harvard had "changed amazingly during the last four or five decades." Fifty years previous, when a class of "sixty men" was considered large, the "character and mode of life of every man were known to every other man," a "condition now [with classes averaging 250] impossible."[111] Nor would the students know the character of every faculty member. Though a number of instructors proved favorites among the undergraduates, the increase in the size of the faculty in the college (about fivefold between 1869 and 1908) rendered the degree of student-faculty familiarity of previous generations a bygone thing. The curriculum also undermined social cohesion. "The elective system has done its share," complained Santayana. "It has broken up the classes, the only natural unities in so great a mass of students." Students learned no common languages, histories, or texts; they went their own curricular ways.[112]

Unlike many colleges (including Boston), where a common education in intimate settings aimed at the development of Christian gentlemen fostered social cohesion, almost everything at Harvard—its size, demographics, curriculum, and Protestant-inspired, centrifugal-force individualism—pulled hard at the social fabric. New conditions strained older forms of social organization, requiring new strategies of Harvard students. But students received no help in these matters from President Eliot, who, having no more desire to organize their extracurricular lives than to choose their courses, left students to their own social ways.

There was a reason for leaving students to their own devices: it fit them to be men in the modern world. Whereas the Jesuits framed the ultimate purpose of education in terms of eternal life, the Harvardians' conception of the after life, with a teleological lens foreshortened by the worldliness of liberal Protestantism, had shrunk to life after graduation. The university was not vocational in any strict sense, but it did, some claimed, prepare students for life in the world, a world perceived to be more competitive and demanding, requiring greater decisiveness and action. Eliot explained: "It is in college that men begin to prepare for the strenuous competitions of the world, and win the mental power, the nervous power to succeed in them." Choosing their courses, forcing students to forge their own academic paths—this was a dress rehearsal for the modern world. Those who chose well were readied for the relentless competition of fin-de-siècle America. LeBaron R. Briggs, as dean of Harvard College, counted the elective system as an occasion for young men to "work their way out into clear-headed and trustworthy manhood," while his colleague Nathaniel Shaler noted that it placed "youth" in the "independent position of men."[113]

So, too, with discipline, for it was liberty befitting *men*, not discipline suited to *boys*, that preconditioned the realization of vital manhood. During Eliot's presidency, the book of disciplinary regulations symbolically shrank from forty pages to five, and with it the disciplinary role that the faculty played in students' lives.[114] Treat students as men and they will rise to the occasion and behave as men; such was the wisdom of the day at Harvard—a far different approach to discipline than that at Boston College and other Jesuit colleges. According to the Boston College *Catalogue,* "Religious motives being habitually appealed to, little need has been experienced of frequent or severe punishment." At laissez-faire Harvard, the faculty saw "so little necessity for severe discipline" according to Professor A. B. Hart, because "students seem on the whole to accept the responsibility of manhood."[115]

Collegians at Harvard and other universities, left largely to their own devices, mimicked their elders, turning to social class as an organizational framework for their educational experiences. Race, ethnicity, gender, and religion continued to affect individuals' participation (or lack of it) in higher education, but social class came to the fore during the Gilded Age. Collegians came to understand quite clearly that colleges and their diplomas were not created equal; institutional reputation and the type of social opportunities a college afforded would, in their futures, play critical roles in competitive, get-ahead America. In the meantime, late-nineteenth-century collegians created forms of student culture shaped by their class-bound sensibilities. As Horowitz put it, it was not the classroom but "college life" that "taught the real lessons."[116] Some of the more salient lessons collegians learned were the lessons of class, with students assuming the professorial role. Harvard historian Samuel Eliot Morison's account of his undergraduate experiences sounds naïve and even condescending to contemporary ears, yet it captures something critical: in the Gilded Age, class mattered.

Since 1890 it has been almost necessary for a Harvard student with social ambition to enter from the "right" sort of school and be popular there, to room on the "Gold Coast" and be accepted by Boston society his freshman year, in order to be on the right side of the social chasm. Family and race did not matter: an Irish-American, Jew, Italian, or Cuban was not regarded as such if he went to the right school and adopted the mores of his fellows; conversely, a lad of Mayflower and Porcellian ancestry who entered from a high school was as much "out of it" as a ghetto Jew.[117]

Ironically, Eliot's hands-off approach to student life helped create conditions conducive to social outcomes at odds with his democratic principles. Eliot recognized the democratizing role that higher education could play. Holding fast to the Unitarian and Brahmin idealism of his youth while others of his class lost faith, he helped open the doors of Harvard to new constituencies, including African Americans, the less-than-wealthy, Mormons (a particularly egregious decision to some), Jews, and Catholics (but not to women). But once students arrived at Harvard, Eliot the social engineer receded. In the lacuna, students created their own class-construed world. "A man who does not belong to the fashionable set may be a very worthy fellow," reported one observer, "but at best he is unfortunate, and he is treated with an air of patronage that is not always gracious."[118] In his 1901–2 *Annual Report,* Eliot addressed the issue, revealing some of his own ambiguities: "For some reasons one could wish that the University did not offer the same contrast between the rich man's mode of life and the poor man's that the outer world offers; but it does, and it is not certain that the presence of this contrast is unwholesome or injurious. In this respect, as in many others, the University is an epitome of the modern world."[119]

Collegians' financial circumstances varied. (Even Boston College had a few well-to-do students on its rolls.) But at Harvard both the excesses and disparities of means associated with the Gilded Age became strikingly apparent. There were among Harvard students young men of slender means, who with their parents struggled to meet the expenses associated with a college education. In 1903, 14 percent of students were sons of government workers, farmers, and manual laborers.[120] A large number of students, intellectually curious and personally ambitious, arrived at Harvard lacking both the time and money necessary for a rich extracurricular experience. It was not, however, these men who gilded Harvard and attracted attention, but rather the students whose lifestyles and spending bespoke tremendous privilege and immense wealth. Absent sufficient housing in the Yard (further evidence of Eliot's laissez-faire approach to student life), market forces prevailed, with well-to-do students transforming nearby Mount Auburn Street into a "Gold Coast" where standard accommodations consisted of spacious, comfortable quarters with private baths (a far cry from the spartan accommodation in the Yard). Servants, butlers, and exorbitant spending were not unheard of.[121] Famed journalist John Reed (class of 1910) wrote:

> Harvard University under President Eliot was unique. Individualism was carried to the point where a man who came for a good time could get through and graduate without having learned anything; but on the other hand, anyone could find there anything he wanted from all the world's store of learning. The undergraduates were practically free from control; they could live pretty much where they pleased, and do as they pleased—so long as they attended lectures. There was no attempt made by the authorities to weld the student body together, or to enforce any kind of uniformity. Some men came with allowances of fifteen thousand dollars a year pocket money, with automobiles and servants, living in gorgeous suites in palatial apartment houses; others in the same class starved in attic bedrooms.[122]

Neither horribly poor nor terribly rich, most fin-de-siècle students hailed from the middling ranks. Seeking higher education largely as a means to enhance their prospects for life after college, this generation of college students created powerful popular images and enduring forms of student culture. Situated squarely between the constraints of youth and home and the yet-to-be assumed responsibilities of adulthood, collegians deemed the college years as their time—four years of manly pleasures absent a full measure of manly responsibilities.[123] Books, classes, and intellectual life played second fiddle to the real work of college. Construed as a dizzying series of one social event after another, college life was to be fun, active, comfortable, social, and heterosocial.

A legion of joiners like their middle-class elders, most collegians took to extracurricular activities with a vengeance. While the "grinds" assiduously attended lectures and read books, the "activity men" scurried between their extracurricular and social obligations: the drama clubs, student newspapers, subject-matter clubs, glee clubs, choirs, bands, religious groups, social-service associations, and debating societies devoured their time. Dances, poker games, and evenings "at the wine cup" in the company of their chums sapped their energies. They went to college to have fun, make friends, meet members of the opposite sex, and forge connections with the right people. Fraternities, sororities, and exclusive clubs were *the* place to meet, and even become, one of the right people. But one did not simply join up: one was asked to join. The precious invitation often meant that one already came from the right social circles; for denizens of Harvard's "Gold Coast," after securing a well-appointed apartment came the business of appointment to a club, preferably one of the elite clubs such as the Porcellian, the "Apex of the social pyramid at Harvard." Wealth was an asset, but it was not the only criterion for membership. Making the cut also meant that one approximated the ideal college man: fun-loving and popular; if studious, only moderately so; athletic, but if not, then an ardent fan of the college's teams. Such club life was sweet: at Harvard it meant instant brotherhood, comfortable quarters (complete with bar, billiard tables, and card room), as well as entrée into Boston society life with introductions to eligible young ladies. Woodrow Wilson, then president of Princeton, was correct: "The side shows are so numerous, so diverting, . . . that they have swallowed up the circus."[124]

In the late-nineteenth century, a sports craze swept across American college campuses, adding a whole new, consuming layer to collegiate life. While size and diversity undermined social cohesion and the curriculum and extracurriculum pulled men helter-skelter, athletics drew the campus together. The exploits of the men who ran the bases and carried the ball transfixed students, alumni, and the public at large. A Yale-Princeton football game could create a "frenzy" in New York, while a Harvard-Yale game turned aloof, well-heeled Harvardians into raving fans.[125] If athletically gifted, even poor students could realize social success on campus, perhaps attracting the attention of desirable coeds or leveraging a notable record into a bid from a fraternity. The emergence of the athlete as an ideal college type, a veritable campus hero, was complemented by a coterie of types and texts spawned by the sports craze. Teams needed coaches, and by 1900 the position of the professional coach was a fixture in academe; the fact that his salary sometimes superseded the best-paid professors signaled the importance of sports. (At Harvard the football coach earned one-third more than the faculty, and just slightly less than Eliot.)[126] Athletes also needed fans and publicity, and thus the development of mascots, pep bands, cheerleaders, and student journalists covering the sports beat with a breathless, rarely flagging enthusiasm. And then there were the fans who loyally attended home games and took specially arranged trains to the away games. Decked out in the team colors, they purchased the programs, waved the pennants, sent up their cheers, and sang the fight song until hoarse.[127]

As Eliot and his presidential peers were building the modern university, late-nineteenth-century collegians were creating the paradigmatic image of what college life was supposed to be. Collegians' success in this arena arguably rivals that of the university builders': it played an immense role in shaping students' expectations of higher education and the ways they participated in it. Setting the terms of engagement socially and intellectually, student life taught lessons as potent as any of those to be learned in Eliot's idealized, academic laboratory of democracy. So often a cause of consternation for their elders in the academy, students' versions of college life captured the popular imagination through fictionalized accounts penned by recent alumni. Turn-of-the-century novels and serialized works appearing in leading magazines such as the *Saturday Evening Post* popularized images of college life and introduced the public to the social worlds that students had created. John O. Lyons notes that, predictably, the "novel of academic life really begins at Harvard." It was as if its own sense of importance found a "need to express [in print] this collective self to the rest of the nation."[128]

Waldron Kintzing Post's *Harvard Episodes* (1903) follows a cast of characters, primarily the socially busy, well-to-do students, described as a "typical set of Harvard men, hailing from various and distant parts of the nation, and of various characters" who had grown "very much alike in certain respects, after three years together around that Yard." In the first episode, they are introduced to Varnum, a "chap" with a mere "two dollars and forty cents in his pocket!" whose studies and part-time jobs limited his extracurricular activities to crew and the YMCA. "There are lots of men doing just that sort of thing," noted one of the characters. "Some day we'll be proud of having been in the same class with some of those fellows. It's a shame that we don't know all about all of 'em."[129]

The juxtaposition is acute: students approached extracurricular fun and frivolity with great earnestness. In a nation where the currents of anti-intellectualism ran deep, they dismissed academic achievement as the sole or even primary marker of success, cutting an anti-intellectual swath through institutions ostensibly devoted to the intellectual development of youth. "The most vulnerable point in our collegiate system is the diversion of the interests of the student body from the true aims of the college," wrote Slosson, in his study of fourteen universities. "Social life, athletics, dissipation, and the multitude of other student activities have cut down to the minimum the attention given to their studies."[130]

Slosson was correct, but he, like many others quick to criticize college life, missed an important point. Students took to college life not merely because it was fun; in fact, at times it was not fun at all. The high value that students placed on extracurricular life stemmed in large measure from its postgraduation value. Its frenetic pace, its competitive nature, and its various rewards were constitutive elements of the world that lay ahead; thus the college years were laying the groundwork for life after college, for life and work in the class-conscious, distended society that commenced when commencement exercises came to a close.[131]

By 1900 a sizeable number of Catholics were attending Harvard University, a highly symbolic change realized during the course of Eliot's presidency. In 1870, 98 percent of students identified themselves as Protestant, with Congregationalists, Episcopalians, and Unitarians comprising 80 percent of the student body. An 1881 poll of undergraduates and Law School students signaled an increase in religious diversity. The Congregationalists, Episcopalians, and Unitarians slipped to 70 percent, while Catholics, numbering thirty-three, rose to almost 4 percent. With the passing of another decade, the number of Catholics rose tenfold, to more than three hundred by 1893 and more than four hundred by 1908. By the time Eliot retired in 1909, 9 percent of the student body was Catholic and 7 percent was Jewish.[132]

The historical record provides ample evidence to support Harold Wechsler's droll observation that the "arrival of a new constituency on a college campus has rarely been an occasion for unmitigated joy." Members of new constituencies, including women, African-Americans, and Jews, often experienced difficulties on campuses once the almost exclusive domain of white, Protestant men.[133] Catholics inevitably encountered bias when it came to the Church of Rome; even in a more tolerant age, even among the most liberal of men, subtle and less-than-subtle prejudices endured. Moreover, ethnic and racial stereotyping, shored up by the nascent social sciences, was common. Convinced that the Anglo-Saxon was the most developed and civilized of the races, a number of faculty members at Harvard felt little compunction in explaining the inherent inferiority of other ethnic groups and races, including the Irish. Henry Cabot Lodge, who taught at Harvard in the 1880s and went on to a formidable career in Washington politics, deemed the early Irish a "very undesirable addition" for they were "hard-drinking, idle, quarrelsome, and disorderly," and thus poorly fit for the rigors of republican citizenship. In 1896 Professor Shaler informed readers of the *Atlantic Monthly* that the Irishman was possessed of "admirable qualities," yet "fails to fit into the complex of our civilization," for Celtic "talents" were "too little interwoven with the capacities which go to make up the modern successful man."[134]

The common biases of the day notwithstanding, the presence of Catholics at Harvard and other universities was more an occasion of liberal satisfaction than cause of social tension. Catholics slipped into the Yard and the social worlds of Harvard, causing little unease.[135] Inviting Bishop John J. Keane to speak in 1890 and 1892, and awarding him an honorary degree in 1893, sparked no protest, but symbolized to many, Protestant and Catholic, the success of the liberal agenda. Writing in the *Catholic Family Annual* in 1895, Paulist priest Peter J. O'Callaghan (A.B. 1888) insisted that "All good men, whatever their religion, are welcome to her halls. There is no such thing as discrimination." In 1904 the recently graduated John LaFarge, Jr. (A.B. 1901) wrote that Harvard was free of even "tacit discrimination" and that Catholics rarely if ever sensed a "shade of inconsiderateness or exclusiveness" in the classroom or extracurricular life. In responding to charges of bigotry, in his final letter to Fr. Mullan in June 1900, Eliot challenged Mullan: "Ask any one of the hundreds of Catholic young men who are now members of Harvard University if they do not have, first, a cordial welcome, and secondly, perfectly fair play without the slightest interference with their religious beliefs and practices."[136]

The Catholic presence at Harvard grew slowly over the course of the nineteenth century until the closing decades, when Catholic enrollment gathered momentum. Among the first Catholics to grace the historic Yard were a handful of rather cosmopolitan Catholics—well-traveled, well-educated, well-connected, and well-to-do—from the Anglo-Catholic homes of Maryland's gentry. In the eighteenth century Maryland Catholics sent their sons to the Continent or later to Georgetown for advanced education; in the nineteenth a number started sending their sons to Harvard, inaugurating family traditions that would see descendants at Harvard well into the twentieth century. The governor's son, John Lee, arrived in 1804 with a request from his father to a local Catholic priest to see to the spiritual welfare of his son. The same family that produced patriot Charles Carroll and Bishop John Carroll, the founder of Georgetown, sent two cousins to Harvard in the 1820s. The American branch of Europe's famous Bonaparte clan sent a son to Harvard as well; Jerome

Napoleon Bonaparte II (son of Jerome Napoleon I and Elizabeth Patterson of Baltimore) graduated with the class of 1826. His son, Charles J. Bonaparte, ('71, LL.B. '74), who held a number of important posts, including secretary of the navy and U.S. attorney general, became a Harvard overseer in 1891.[137]

Boston's Brahmin class also contributed to a Catholic presence at Harvard. A significant number of Americans in the mid to late nineteenth century, including many of old Puritan stock, converted to the Church of Rome. Hardly a Brahmin family remained untouched: the Abbots, Cabots, Forbes, and Warrens, to name a few, could count Catholics among their family members. Ironically, as Unitarianism helped get Catholics to Harvard, it helped get Harvardians to Catholicism, for Unitarianism's thin, pale character sent many searching for the positive, certain strains of revealed religion offered by the Roman Catholic Church.[138] George Foxcroft Haskins (class of 1826), Joseph Coolidge Shaw (class of 1840), Edward Holker Welch (class of 1840), and George Mary Searle (class of 1857), all converts, became Catholic priests after graduation, with Shaw and Welch joining the Jesuits. A descendant of General Joseph Warren of Bunker Hill fame, Dr. Thomas Dwight converted to Catholicism as a child. He held the Parkman Professorship of Anatomy at Harvard Medical School, an institution founded by his grandfather, Dr. John Warren.[139] John LaFarge, who became a well-known Jesuit, also came from an eminent New England family. LaFarge's father was a famous artist, his mother, Margaret Perry, a convert. Both parents were well connected; their social circles included the likes of Henry Adams, Henry and William James, and Edith Wharton. It was family friend Teddy Roosevelt who urged LaFarge to attend Harvard, and during his undergraduate years LaFarge often called upon family members in Cambridge, including Professor Thomas Perry of the English Department and family friends such as Emma Forbes Carey, another famous convert.[140]

The first Irish Catholics went to Harvard in the famine years. Onetime seminarian Francis Maguire left Ireland in 1846 and graduated from Harvard in 1853; Patrick Aloysius O'Connell, of Killarney, took an A.B. in 1857 and a medical degree in 1861. John Coleman Crowley began his studies at Holy Cross but finished them at Harvard with an A.B. in 1852 and a law degree in 1857. After taking a law degree in 1871, Patrick Collins took to politics with immense enthusiasm, serving as U.S. congressman, chairman of the Democratic National Convention, consul-general in London, and mayor of Boston. Other sons of Eire fol-

lowed, and with the converts and cosmopolitan Catholics they constituted an increasingly noticeable presence. By 1880, approximately fifty
Catholics had graduated from the Law School; by 1893, at least eighty-
four had graduated from the undergraduate college.[141]

The cosmopolitan, the convert, the Celt: like their Protestant counterparts, Catholics who attended Harvard around the turn of the century
participated in the life of the university in a variety of ways, often determined by their social class and aspirations for the future. For a number
of second-generation Irish students, financial circumstances limited
their ability to participate fully in college life or even college itself. The
five sons of James and Elizabeth O'Connell attended Boston College and
Harvard University when the family was financially solvent and withdrew when it was not. But their parents' investment in their children's
education paid off, for their sons eventually realized success in journalism, veterinary science, and law. They, like other Catholics, turned to
Harvard as a stepping stone into the professional middle class.[142] On the
other end of the spectrum, well-to-do Catholics (notably Marylanders)
enjoyed Harvard's vital club life. Catholics from Maryland in the 1820s
joined the Porcellian; their sons and grandsons followed suit. Charles
Carroll (class of 1887), for instance, was elected to the elite D.K.E. The
more ascetic John LaFarge, considering clerical life, abjured the excesses of the privileged clubs and the Gold Coast, working on the editorial board "of the Harvard monthly." (Upon his ordination as a Jesuit in
1905 a New Haven newspaper reported that he was "Born to wealth, the
son of a world-famous father, and through his mother a descendant of
Benjamin Franklin in the most direct line." Through "ancestry, birth,
wealth and fame of family," he was "classed among the exclusive circles
of New York and Newport" and "could have chosen to join the leaders of
the smart set.") Still other Catholics made their marks on the athletic
fields; James Parrish Lee (A.B. '91), the grandson of Harvard's first
Catholic student, was a stand-out football player.[143]

The lessons Catholics learned about the ways of the world from a
class-conscious university in a class-conscious society did not vitiate the
personal and communal bonds of religion. Even in the modern, nonsectarian university, religious affiliation affected the ways in which Catholics understood and deported themselves. Bolstered by the enthusiasm
surrounding the visits of Bishop Keane in the early 1890s, during the
1892–93 academic year Catholic students successfully broached the
idea of a club for Catholics with Eliot. Established in May of 1893 (as the
faculty of the Law School was formulating its soon-to-be infamous list of

colleges), the club was designed, according to its constitution, "to bring the Catholics of Harvard University into closer relationship with one another, to promote their religion, and to spread a knowledge of the Catholic religion at Harvard."[144] Among a handful of Catholic clubs that sprang up before the end of the nineteenth century in large non-sectarian universities (including Cornell, Berkeley, Pennsylvania and Wisconsin), the Catholic Club at Harvard took up quarters at Phillips Brooks House with other Protestant clubs. Its turn-of-the-century officers included undergraduates, graduate and professional students; its first president was Thomas Mullen, a law student. During the 1890s it reported membership of 175, with a large number of its members enrolled in the Law School.[145]

Just as Catholics in Boston developed associations and institutions to sustain their separate subculture in Protestant America, Catholics at Harvard established an association that helped members deepen personal identification with Catholicism as it strengthened the bonds of affiliation among adherents of a communitarian-oriented religion. They complemented social and service activities with "smoke talks" with recent Catholic alumni, Harvard faculty such as Protestant Charles Eliot Norton, a fine arts professor with an affinity for the Middle Ages, as well as notable Catholics such as Professor Dwight, future Cardinal William O'Connell, and the illustrious Charles Bonaparte. By the 1910s the Catholic Club (then known as the Saint Paul's Club) was quite purposeful in its efforts to provide members with a Catholic outlook. "The Social Research Committee," under the guidance of the club's spiritual director, took up issues central to social scientists of the day. Refracting their research through a Catholic lens, members presented on "The Church and Private Property," "Social Evils and Their Remedies," and "Socialism and Religion."[146]

Within American Catholicism, the transition from a largely immigrant church in the nineteenth century to the largely middle-class church of the twentieth was well under way by the 1890s. Catholics of Irish and German descent were most instrumental in tipping the socioeconomic scales. For the Irish, moving up, shedding immigrant rags for middle-class respectability, often entailed greater interaction with Protestants; the religious antagonist of former times was becoming a coworker, neighbor, middle-class role model, and often a fellow student. The great sectarian divide became more porous socially in the face of the powerful processes of generational assimilation. "The second generation has now become the clergy, teachers, doctors, and lawyers of the community, and its members are naturally widening their influence to include people of every sort," wrote one observer of the Irish in Boston at the turn of the century. "Many of them reach across all class and religious lines into that larger life which is above sectarianism as such."[147] But as they reached beyond, would they lose their grasp from within? As the claims of class tightened, would the bonds of religion hold?

The presence of Catholics at Harvard, the nation's foremost university, spoke to both the hopes and concerns of the Irish Catholic community in New England. On the one hand, Catholics at Harvard were cause for satisfaction; Catholics were successfully making their way in Protestant America. Just as it celebrated the successes of Boston College graduates, the Irish and Catholic press recounted in celebratory fashion the "Catholic Sons of Harvard" who had "added something to the glory of their alma mater while faithfully following the teachings of the Church."[148] On the other hand, those who attended Harvard and other non-Catholic institutions, who stepped outside or bypassed altogether the ethnoreligious circle of Catholic higher education, sparked concern in some quarters of the subculture. Though many upwardly mobile Irish in Boston "manifest a mania for the respectable and pious, the sober and genteel," those who appeared too socially ambitious or desirous of Protestant company found themselves subject to criticism. "The contemptible worldly pride of their parents—that is the whole of it," wrote the editor of *Donahoe's Magazine* in 1898. "These ignorant apes imagine that Mickey and Pat will mingle with 'better people' at Yale. . . . [Their] boys may see young Vanderbilt across the campus. Bliss! And they can in after years casually refer to 'my chum, Dick Astor don't y' know.' They can learn to play golf and to look like an Englishman."[149]

Commenced in 1893, the golden era for Catholic students at Harvard proved a casualty of the Law School controversy. The highly publicized war of words between the Jesuits and President Eliot complicated Catholics' relationship with Harvard University. A few individuals continued to invoke the ameliorative image of Bishop Keane at Harvard: writing in 1900 in the *New York Sun*, a contributor insisted that "no sensible Catholic" could impugn Harvard with bigotry over the Law School's admissions policy "since the day when the university invited Bishop Keane to its halls."[150] But the warm relations between Protestants and Catholics, symbolized by and celebrated during Keane's Harvard visits, turned decidedly chilly as the Law School controversy heated up. Celebratory articles about Catholics at Harvard and successful alumni disappeared, as did notable Catholic speakers, whose university-sponsored addresses had attracted large audiences and press coverage in the early and mid-1890s. Catholics at Harvard simply kept a lower profile, their enthusiasm dampened by the controversy surrounding the Law School's admissions policy and Eliot's disparaging comments about Jesuit education.

More than a decade later, Father John J. Ryan wrote, "Everybody recalls the legislation passed by the government of the University when it assumed to set a standard of value on the degrees conferred by many colleges, and . . . how the Catholic colleges in large number were made to suffer when the determined standard had been published." Based at nearby Saint Paul's and serving as chaplain to Catholic students, Ryan was no enthusiast for Harvard. The Law School controversy was still on his mind more than a decade after the fact. "The controversy that ensued was felt in every section of the nation," wrote Ryan in the *Harvard Alumni Bulletin*, "and aroused intense feeling, which is not yet allayed, and is like the banked fire, ready to break into fresh flame if stirred by the slightest provocation."[151]

As the claims of class continued pulling Catholics toward Harvard, the Harvard Law School controversy tightened the bonds of religion, especially among the clergy, where it tested their loyalties and limited their participation in the broader academic community. Msgr. Conaty, who had publicly defended Holy Cross, was well regarded in Catholic circles and much respected among his non-Catholic peers. His personal connections with men such as G. Stanley Hall, of Clark University, helped secure for the Catholic University of America an invitation to become one of the founding members of the elite Association of American Universities.[152] Given his prominence, Harvard officials understandably thought of Conaty when scheduling speakers. In summer 1898, they asked Conaty to speak at Appleton Chapel. Aware that Boston College and Holy Cross had already been removed from the Law School's list, Conaty informed them that he was not in a position to speak at Appleton Chapel. Two years later, Conaty turned down another request to speak at Harvard.[153] He did not, however, turn down a request to speak at Boston College. On May 25, 1900—the day that Father Mullan's correspondence with Eliot appeared in the *Boston Globe*—Mullan implored Conaty to speak at the Boston College commencement. Noting that Bishop Potter was scheduled to speak at Harvard, he pointed out that a "strong speech from a Catholic ecclesiastic would be a fine contrast at our Commencement. I ought not to say that I invite you to come, but I beg you most earnestly." Conaty accepted Mullan's invitation, delivering a "strong, uncompromising speech on Catholic education" before thirty-two hundred gathered at Tremont Temple. That year, twenty-seven young men graduated.[154]

What good graces Conaty accrued by his appearance disappeared a year later when the name of Dr. William Kerby, of the Catholic University, appeared on a list of those scheduled to lecture at Harvard Divinity School during the summer. The Boston College Alumni Association sent excoriating missives to Conaty. Given the "present juncture of the educational controversy between the Catholic colleges . . . and Harvard University," Kerby's scheduled address was "deplorable," even a "betrayal of our cause." Harvard was, they claimed, exploiting Kerby, who was "play[ing] into the hands of the enemies of Catholic education." Suggesting that Conaty must be unaware of the "deep feeling aroused in the Catholic body of New England by the unjust and unwarrantable attitude of the chief non-Catholic University in New England towards Catholic collegiate education," they exhorted Conaty, as rector of the foremost Catholic university in the nation, to use his influence on their behalf. As it turned out, Kerby fell ill with typhoid and could not fulfill his obligations.[155]

The bonds of religion also tightened around Father Thomas Gasson, professor of ethics and economics at Boston College. A convert to Catholicism, Gasson had been giving talks on the Catholic faith to members of the Harvard Catholic Club at the behest of John LaFarge, who had turned to Gasson for weekly spiritual direction when he arrived in Boston. According to LaFarge, Gasson's "informal conferences" were popular, and the "little room in which they were held was usually thronged." The provincial, Edward Purbrick, explained to Superior General Martín that "Fr. Gasson does much good amongst the young Catholics in Harvard University by his Conferences to them." But at the height of the Law School controversy, Father Mullan informed LaFarge and his fellow Catholics at Harvard that "he was not in a position" to allow Gasson to offer another series of talks. Despite "requests repeated from time to time, the Father Rector concluded that it was better not to permit Father Gasson to come out to Cambridge." Mullan's decision was not his alone. On October 2, 1899, the "subject of one of our Fathers giving occasional talks to Harvard Catholics and others at Harvard" was discussed among the consultors, a small group that functioned as an advisory board to the president. The minutes reported tersely, "one consultor for—three against."[156]

It was one thing to pull Father Gasson back from Harvard; it was wholly another to come to terms with the forces that were pulling Catholics toward Harvard and other non-Catholic institutions of higher education. During the nineteenth century, Catholics built a subculture in Protestant America sustained in large measure by institutions—its churches, social-service agencies, health-care facilities, and its schools. They built more than five dozen men's colleges to provide Catholics with an advanced education grounded in the Catholic faith. But the social walls that separated the Protestant from the Catholic did not hold fast in higher education. With the advent of the age of the university, Catholic higher education was found wanting; the separate system was found to be far from equal in the new academic order. Charles Eliot attributed the "lack of equivalence" evident in Catholic colleges to the fact that they were run by priests and heavily influenced by the Jesuits; in so doing, he created inequality by rendering them ineligible to serve as stepping stones to Harvard's desirable professional schools.

But Eliot was not the only one to recognize a lack of equivalence. Georgetown, Saint Louis, and Notre Dame notwithstanding, Catholic higher education could not offer, directly or indirectly, what many middle-class (or soon-to-be-middle-class) Catholics both wanted and needed; namely, a full measure of popular student life, respectable professional credentials, and access to elite social networks. "We have indeed a number of good Catholic colleges, but we have not, it should be frankly admitted," wrote one prominent Catholic in the *New York Freemans Journal* in 1898, "any Catholic university in the United States that is the equal of Harvard, Yale, Johns Hopkins, Columbia, Princeton, University of Pennsylvania, Cornell and some other prominent Protestant universities." What was needed, he argued, were Catholic institutions that catered to the well-to-do. Catholic colleges were "too much one price colleges." "Let us have, then," he suggested, "a few high price colleges" with "comforts and even luxuries." After all, he argued, Catholic higher education had a "mission to fulfill towards rich Catholics as well as towards poor Catholics." The "sons of prosperous Catholics" should not be forced to attend Catholic colleges with bad food, uncomfortable dorms, and overly strict discipline; but neither should they be forced to go to Harvard for an education. Nevertheless, they did go to Harvard. As a character in a work of Catholic fiction pointed out, "if Harvard and Yale give a training and prestige to their men unknown to the Catholic college, Harvard and Yale will get the student."[157]

Father Mullan well understood how social class was affecting Catholic participation in higher education and Catholic colleges. At the inaugural meeting of the Association of Catholic Colleges of the United

States in spring 1899, he did not speak about the admissions policy that kept Jesuit graduates out of Harvard Law School but about the factors that pulled Catholics toward Harvard and other non-Catholic colleges. In his talk on "The Drift Toward Non-Catholic Colleges and Universities," he acknowledged that some Catholics began their studies in public school and thus did not, as a matter of course, consider Catholic colleges.

Mullan was far more concerned with the "wholesale defection from our preparatory departments." Were one-third to persist through graduation, noted Mullan, "we should have a proud array of graduates, both in number and quality, on each commencement day." But, Mullan claimed, Catholic students bypassed or withdrew from Catholic colleges because the colleges were strikingly out of touch with the sensibilities and aspirations of the "modern American boy." As he was "accustomed to more or less luxury in his home life" and imbued with a spirit of "independence," he found Catholic colleges unappealing on a number of accounts. He chafed under the rigid discipline and found a seven-year course of studies under the same management "unbearable." Austere conditions, including unappealing food and spartan accommodations, drove some away. Conversely, non-Catholic colleges provided attractive opportunities, socioeconomic resources, and the "real college" experience. They offered, noted Mullan, financial aid, more humane room and board, looser discipline, and elective courses (so a student "may not only omit what studies he dislikes, but may select those which have a direct or indirect bearing on professional studies"). Non-Catholic colleges also catered to those seeking the social benefits of elite education. The "fear of loss of social prestige" led some Catholics to non-Catholic colleges with a "broader . . . more liberal education amid more refined association," according to Mullan. And even as he argued with Eliot about the integrity and quaity of studies represented by the Jesuit college diploma, Mullan admitted to his peers that the "degree of non-Catholic colleges is held in much higher estimation." This was, he acknowledged, "a matter of wide importance to young men who have their own way to make in the world," who understandably sought "every advantage which the college course and college associations are likely to bring them."[158]

A number of Jesuits wrote to Superior General Martín expressing varying degrees of disappointment and frustration with enrollments in the Jesuit colleges. Each seemed surprised that the bonds of religion did not work more effectively on behalf of Jesuit education in drawing more students into their institutions. In 1894, Brosnahan reported that there were nearly four hundred students at Boston College, but he added, "in this large city we should have 1000 students." A year later, William Pardow, head of the Maryland–New York Province, made a similar point regarding Fordham, in New York: "It seems marvelous that in a city of 600,000 we only have 150 students." In his lengthy letter to Martín (already quoted from above), Father Fagan explained how social class vied with religion in the social organization of Catholic higher education.

> Most of the faithful are poor or of very modest fortune. For the most part, those who are richer and of some prominence don't wish to send their sons to our schools because they would have to associate with poor and lower class boys. They prefer to send their sons to attend non-Catholic schools and universities because they may have the sons of the rich and powerful as friends and may, by design, form associations and friendships as they look forward to the world of life after college.
>
> For in their view it matters a great deal whether a young man attends a university of note or an obscure Catholic college. So it happens that with the exception of Georgetown, the sons of the foremost Catholic families are quite seldomly educated in our colleges.[159]

The *Constitutions* of the Society of Jesus directed the Jesuits to adapt their educational program as necessary to the times, persons, and places they encountered. In the Jesuits' interactions with Charles Eliot, an ardent enthusiast for the concept of progress, the challenge of time crystallized: how could their colleges respond to the wants of modern America without abandoning the wisdom and fruits of the past? Concurrently, a stream of conversation surrounding the Law School controversy among Catholics clarified another great challenge in the age of the university: that of persons. Brosnahan, Pardow, and Fagan expected religion to factor more prominently in the social organization of education, but it did not; it found potent competition in social class. The Jesuits were coming to understand that their colleges, with their traditional course of studies and strict discipline, were not well suited to the needs and sensibilities of the nascent Catholic middle class. Mullan best understood the new challenge confronting the Jesuits. His choice of words, *modern American boy*, is telling. Bypassing the religious referent, Mullan situated the Jesuits' traditional constituency in terms of time and place: he is modern and he is an American. This boy, Mullan implicitly argued, is possessed of multiple identities that factored into his academic decisions. This modern American boy's decision to patronize institutions of higher education associated with Protestantism, to ensconce himself in an "odd social niche," sparked intense conversation among Catholics, conversations inseparable from the great work and crisis of the Roman Catholic Church in the 1890s: figuring out how to be a Catholic community in a place acknowledged to be Protestant.

CHAPTER FOUR

Place: Americanism and the Higher Education of Catholics

> The question, plainly stated, is
> this: Is it proper or prudent to
> send Catholic boys to Protestant
> or non-sectarian colleges? . . . I
> am fairly convinced that Eliot's
> real reason for excluding Catholic
> colleges was his desire to freeze
> them out, and I am further
> strengthened in my belief by his
> personal views as expressed in
> his printed addresses. The Catho-
> lic mind has been poisoned and
> Protestantized by all this insis-
> tence on broad views, the spirit
> of true Americanism, the great
> gain realized by different classes
> from their association together in
> the school and college.
>
> —"Candor," in the *Sacred
> Heart Review*

A stream of correspondence from the United States to Rome kept the Jesuits' superior general, Luis Martín, apprised of the Jesuits' troubles
with Charles Eliot and Harvard Law School. At the height of the controversy, Martín penned an uncharacteristically gentle note of consolation
to Father Mullan. Having "heard about the trouble with Harvard," he
told Mullan to "dismiss any concern." Boston College "would not suffer
much," provided the course of studies was "promoted with greater energy." As for students considering Harvard, they "should be urged not to
attend this irreligious university." Martín then encouraged Mullan to
practice traditional forms of Catholic piety, such as fasting, to help en-
gender a religious spirit among his students through his personal exam-

ple.[1] It was pious, paternal advice from a religious superior to a priest in his charge. But is was also simple advice from a European superior out of touch with the complex challenges facing Mullan and his American colleagues. Recommending that Mullan simply direct students away from "irreligious" Harvard signaled a failure on his part to recognize the profound challenge of adapting to place—namely, modern Protestant America—faced by the Jesuits at the turn of the century.

The Jesuits' extraordinary and successful global exploits—in the villages of Latin America and the courts of China, in the palaces of Europe and the missions of Quebec—derived from their distinctive approach to *space* and commitment to adapt to *place*. ("Few spectacles are so grand as that of Ignatius surrounded by a handful of obscure men in a little church of Paris, and dividing among themselves a world to conquer," wrote a Protestant in the *American Church Review* in 1875.[2]) The Society's corporate pledge to travel wherever needed to help souls, the very heart of the Jesuit mission, marked a distinctive undertaking and nothing less than a turning point in the history of the church. Whereas their clerical predecessors, the monks, took a vow of stability, the Jesuits, in essence, took a vow of mobility.[3] They were not the first religious order to abjure the monastic commitment to a life circumscribed in space; the Franciscans, Dominicans, and other thirteenth-century mendicants had adopted a peripatetic modus vivendi in order to preach the gospel and minister more effectively. The Jesuits, however, caught up in the Age of Discovery, radically reconceptualized the spatial dimensions of religious life, claiming the entire world as their "house" and the journey itself as a constitutive element of their mission and communal life. "It must be noted that in the Society there are different kinds of houses or dwellings," wrote Jerónimo Nadal, an early, highly influential Jesuit. "These are: the house of probation, the college, the professed house, and the journey—and by this last the whole world becomes our house."[4]

The Jesuits' success derived not merely from their embrace of an immense theater of operation; swept up in the spirit of the age, a number of other religious orders had taken to the high seas and made for exotic lands. What the Jesuits of the sixteenth and seventeenth centuries understood more thoroughly than other religious orders was the importance of adapting their ways to the specific places in which they were working. Other religious orders sometimes limited their efficacy as missionaries by insisting that non-Europeans adopt European ways, without themselves adapting to local cultural norms. In contrast, the Jesuits learned native languages, read indigenous literature, donned native dress, and adopted local customs, sometimes struggling against the temptation of going "too native." Their strategic adaptation to place proved tremendously effective. "No one, now-a-days, ever hears of Franciscans, or Dominicans, while the Jesuit is every where, and is every where at work," wrote a contributor to the *Princeton Review* in 1845. The ubiquitous Jesuit could be found "amid the cloisters and scholars of Oxford, in the newly christianized islands of the Southern Ocean, in the fastnesses of the Nestorian mountains, among the turbulent millions of Ireland, and the education boards of New York and Philadelphia." This productive, intertwined space/place dimension of Jesuit life provided Father Brosnahan with bragging rights; in his famous rejoinder, "President Eliot and Jesuit Colleges," he did not neglect to mention the international scope of their educational enterprise, noting that Jesuit colleges could be found "at Georgetown College in Washington, at Stonyhurst College in England, at Feldkirch in Austria, at Kalocsa in Hungary, at Beyrouth in Syria, at the Ateneo Municipal in Manila, at Zi-ka-wei in China."[5] Charles Eliot's empire might be modern, but the Jesuits' was vast.

In the late 1880s and 1890s, Catholics in America struggled intensely with the issue of adaptation to place, their disparate views on Protestant America pulling them in opposing directions and into a series of conflicts known as the Americanism controversy.[6] Concerned for the spiritual welfare of Catholics and the religious integrity of the church, conservatives counseled caution when it came to Protestants and American society. Convinced that the Roman Catholic Church was the one true church, and cognizant of the long history of animosity between the descendants of Luther and the followers of Rome, conservatives were prone to portray Protestants as irreligious, unredeemed, and relentlessly hostile to Catholic interests. They were also convinced that Protestant values, principally individualism, shaped American society. Thus in adapting to America, Roman Catholics and their church incurred the unacceptable risk of being Protestantized. Faced with a Protestant majority and believing the United States to be spiritually dangerous, they argued for watchfulness and a strategy of separatism in order to inoculate Catholics from the threat of religious declension. Keeping the church free from deleterious Protestant influence required vigilance. Though Catholic institutions and associations were not wholly conservative endeavors, conservatives' guarded, separatist approach proved conducive to the establishment of parochial schools, ethnic parishes, Catholic social services, devotional groups, and Catholic professional organizations.[7]

The winds of liberalism that fostered religious toleration and openness to modern culture in much of mainline Protestantism (discussed in chapters 1 and 2) blew through the Catholic church as well, creating a liberal wing by the 1880s. Like Catholic conservatives, liberals remained steadfast in their belief that the Roman Catholic Church was the one true church; they parted ways in their assessments of Protestants and American society. To liberal Catholics, Protestants were at least partially redeemed and usually genial to Catholics; if hostile on occasion, it was largely because they were unfamiliar with a "better class" of Catholics and ignorant of the actual tenets of the Catholic faith. Enamored of modern America, liberals considered the political order, particularly as shaped by the principle of separation of church and state, an ideal milieu in which Catholicism might flourish, a belief bolstered by the vicissitudes of the European church and its loss of temporal power in the nineteenth century. Compared with Europe, America's newness and innocence, its energy and vitality, bespoke a healthy, rich environment conducive to a revitalized church that would help renew the church worldwide.[8] Thus they argued for rapprochement with and adaptation to American society as a means to ameliorate bigotry and promote fuller, richer participation in American life by Catholics. In the long run, improved Catholic-Protestant relations would help boost the social, economic, and political status of Catholics, creating occasions to expand the beneficent influence of the church on society. Finding affinities between the richness of Catholicism and the spirit of America, and adapting church discipline along those lines, would make the church more attractive to potential converts. Missiological strains ran deep in the liberal camp.[9]

During the last two decades of the nineteenth century, high-profile ecclesiastics from the liberal and conservative camps clashed, sometimes acrimoniously, disagreeing over the founding of the Catholic University of America, Catholic membership in secret labor organizations, clerical participation in ecumenical events, the need for ethnic parishes, and Catholic enrollment in public schools. After early liberal advances, including the establishment of the Catholic University and Catholic participation in the 1893 World's Parliament of Religions, with the promulgation of Leo XIII's *Longinqua Oceani* in 1895 the ecclesiastical tide turned in favor of the conservatives. Leo announced that, contrary to liberal thought, Catholicism and the American political order did not complement one another. Holding to the politically battered conviction that the supreme pontiff was rightful in his claims to and exercise of power over the temporal order, Leo informed the faithful that it would be "very erroneous to draw the conclusion that in America is to be sought the type of the most desirable status of the Church."[10] Four years later, Leo issued another letter, *Testem Benevolentiae,* in which he condemned Americanism, effectively silencing the liberal camp. Leo defined Americanism carefully. He praised American Catholics for their efforts on behalf of their church and their country and identified an acceptable form of Americanism—namely, "characteristic qualities which reflect honor on the people of America," along with the "condition of your commonwealths" and the "laws and customs which prevail in them."[11] Yet Leo harbored deep concerns for an unacceptable, theologically aberrant form of Americanism; it consisted of "new opinions" that, taken together, suggested that the church, in an effort to attract converts, "ought to adapt herself somewhat to our advanced civilization, and, relaxing her ancient rigor, show some indulgence to modern popular theories and methods." It was, Leo noted, an approach misguidedly applied not only to the "rule of life, but also to the doctrines in which the *deposit of faith* is contained." Here Leo ruled against adaptation to place: there is but one church, Leo noted, not one "church in America different from that which is in the rest of the world."[12]

As the church at large struggled with "Americanism," so the Catholic educational community wrestled with the challenge of *place:* in Protestant America, where should Catholics pursue an advanced education? Beginning in 1898, while the Jesuits were battling with Eliot and Harvard, surveys and anecdotal evidence documenting extensive Catholic patronage of non-Catholic colleges and universities began piling up. The large numbers of Catholics found studying in non-Catholic colleges and universities—including Harvard—sparked widespread discussions among Catholics that were inseparable from the community's wider conversation about the church's relationship with American society. Heated debate about the "drift" of Catholics toward non-Catholic higher education was not part of the Americanism controversy proper, for much of the discussion about the issue occurred after the 1899 promulgation of *Testem Benevolentiae,* which is historically understood as the culmination of the controversy. Yet Catholic patronage of non-Catholic institutions carried religious import to a community struggling to come to terms with its place in Protestant America, and debate over Catholic collegians' enrollment patterns divided along the same conservative and liberal lines of thought. Would a Protestant education unacceptably transform Catholic students? (Would they go "too native"?) Or would Catholics in

Protestant institutions of higher education help transform American society by fostering religious harmony and giving witness among Protestants to the one, true faith?

The "drift" toward non-Catholic higher education attracted widespread attention and comment. Prominent Americanists and conservative bishops weighed in on the subject, as did clergy, editorialists, and fiction writers. Arguments for and against Catholic patronage of non-Catholic higher education found expression in the press and the pulpit. Given their institutional commitments, the men from Catholic colleges —faculty, students, and alumni—understandably made common cause with conservatives on the issue, arguing that Catholic students should attend Catholic colleges. For some, including a number of Jesuits, their stance on the issue was not solely born of institutional considerations; leaning heavily toward the conservative end of the religious spectrum, they were deeply convinced of the spiritual dangers of Protestant higher education. But not all within the circles of Jesuit higher education adopted such a thoroughly negative stance toward Protestant America and its educational institutions. Provoked by the Law School controversy, a number, including students from Holy Cross and Boston College, thought carefully about place and the role of Jesuit higher education in American society. They saw spiritual dangers in Protestant higher education, but they blunted the edges of separatist rhetoric by arguing that Catholic higher education served America well through its soundly educated, civic-minded, morally grounded, and religiously committed alumni. In other words, separatism in the form of Jesuit higher education was a plank for constructive engagement with and the betterment of American society.

In Jesuit circles this line of argumentation, that the education offered by the Jesuits served the public good, hearkened back to the ideals of Christian humanism that inspired the earliest Jesuits in their turn toward education. They conducted schools *ad civitatis utilitatem,* arguing for the establishment of schools on the grounds that they would produce virtuous and learned men for the good of church and state. They would serve society by leavening it with a Catholic intelligentsia.[13] But the Jesuits of the late-nineteenth century entered the academic revolution that gave rise to a new academic order largely lacking the imagination and openness to culture characteristic of the early Jesuits. Aligned with the conservatives during the Americanism controversy, the Jesuits were, on the whole, quick to point to the faults of others, whether non-Catholic educators like Eliot, liberal Catholics, or Catholic students in non-Catholic colleges. Lacking imagination during this critical period in American and Catholic higher education, they failed to produce a constructive argument in defense of Jesuit education in Protestant America. Noticeably absent among the sons of Loyola was sympathy for the project of adapting to place.

Yet the challenge of place was unavoidable for the Jesuits at the turn of the century. Coupled with their troubles with Harvard, their newly gained understanding of the extent of Catholic patronage of non-Catholic institutions brought home the realities of a new academic order. In the age of the university, could they create Jesuit colleges attractive to students and respectable to non-Catholic educators? Or would they, as writer Candor put it, "deliver over to Protestant institutions the education of those who will be the leaders of our people?"[14]

In chapter after chapter, the fictional characters in Lelia Hardin Bugg's *The People of Our Parish* (1901) took up issues of importance to Catholics of the "better classes" that, more often than not, involved some debate about how Catholics should interact with Protestants and Protestant society. Did well-to-do Catholics (the "pink tea" set) seek the company of well-to-do Protestants too eagerly? Should Catholics marry non-Catholics? Should women work outside the home? On one occasion, those seated in the "easy chairs" before "an open fire in Mrs. Driscoll's pretty drawing-room" for tea and conversation launched into a discussion about Catholic higher education after Captain Claiborne suggested that an advanced education obtained in a "denominational school" such as Notre Dame "handicapped a boy in the race with modern life." Horace Norrison rejoined: there were strong Catholic colleges and weak, but "adverse criticism" and "comparisons with Harvard and Yale" advanced by "carpers" were simply "illogical" since "struggling" Catholic colleges that relied on "ridiculously cheap" tuition could hardly be expected to provide "all the advantages of a great Eastern University, with its millions of endowment and its high charges." Mrs. Driscoll then chimed in. Even weak Catholic colleges were "quite as good as the 'half-baked' institutions of our non-Catholic brethren," she argued, and in one respect they were "infinitely better, for they teach religion and morals, and purely secular institutions do not." But, Horace argued, weren't Catholic colleges too strict for our "twentieth-century American young men"? Overly rigid discipline, he claimed, pushed Catholics toward the "great secular universities instead of to our own." What an unfortunate reality, countered Dr. Mordant, for with "the immorality, drunkenness, gambling, and midnight carousals and debauches that go on at the secular universities you would thank God for the Catholic college and its restrictions." What Catholics needed, argued Mordant, were some "really good colleges" and "at least one representative university" in order to realize overall improvement. "Dr. O'Malley, in his able articles on the Catholic college, insists upon this."[15]

Dr. Austin O'Malley (1853–1932) was not a fictional character; he was a professor of literature at Notre Dame who published articles and editorials at the turn of the century about Catholic colleges and enrollment patterns. The Jesuit-educated son of Irish immigrants, the one-time Jesuit possessed a wide range of interests. A physician with expertise in bacteriology, he was appointed to the U.S. Department of Health in 1893; in 1895, after contracting small pox, he left for Notre Dame. A holder of a Ph.D., he was an accomplished Latinist and Dante scholar who published on a variety of subjects for scholarly and general audiences. He left Notre Dame in 1902 to study and practice ophthalmology.[16]

Publication of O'Malley's article "Catholic Collegiate Education in the United States" in the June 1898 issue of the *Catholic World* created a great stir in the Catholic educational community. In particular, his figures on Catholic collegians studying at non-Catholic colleges jarred Catholic educators and played a likely role in Msgr. Conaty's decision to schedule two talks on "The Drift Toward Non-Catholic Colleges and Universities" at the inaugural meeting of the Association of Catholic Colleges of the United States (ACCUS) in 1899. At that time, Catholics were not completely unaware of Catholic students' presence at non-Catholic colleges. In 1906 Francis B. Cassilly, S.J., published an article about Catholics at state universities, noting the establishment of "Catholic clubs" and other early "indications" antedating O'Malley's report that suggested "colonies of Catholic students in these colleges were growing to considerable proportions." In personal correspondence in 1893, J. Havens Richards wrote of "Catholic young men trooping to Harvard." But until the publication of O'Malley's article, few Catholic educators would have surmised the extent of the drift toward non-Catholic institutions by Catholic collegians. As Father Delurey, of Villanova, put it at the 1899 ACCUS meeting, "That there has been and is, not only a drift but a rapid flow of Catholic students into non-Catholic colleges is a fact which educational statistics bring very forcibly to our minds. The drift we admit. We must do so."[17]

The survey that startled the Catholic educational world included a review of enrollments in Catholic colleges. In 1897, O'Malley sent surveys to fifty-one Catholic colleges listed in *Hoffmann's Directory* and received replies from thirty-five. Finding, on average, two preparatory students for each college-level student, he estimated the total number of collegians in Catholic colleges at 4,764. His numbers approximated those in the 1900 report of the U.S. commissioner of education; sixty-one Catholic colleges providing information enrolled 12,376 students, but only 5,396 (44%) were enrolled in college-level courses. But O'Malley's analysis went further; he considered some Catholic colleges so weak that if the enumeration of collegians was limited to those institutions truly "worthy [of] the name of college," the actual number of bona fide collegians would drop to 973.[18]

O'Malley also obtained information about the number of Catholics enrolled in thirty-seven non-Catholic colleges and universities. In just 5 percent of the nation's non-Catholic institutions, he found 1,452 Catholics. Some of the schools with large numbers of Catholics included Harvard (300), the University of Pennsylvania (201), the University of Michigan (120), the University of Wisconsin (118), and Yale (115); smaller numbers of Catholics could be found at Indiana University (9), the University of West Virginia (6), the University of North Carolina (3), and the University of Idaho (2). He recognized that large schools were overrepresented in his sample, yet he was certain that there was "no inconsiderable number" of Catholics "scattered throughout the remaining 95 per centum" of the nation's non-Catholic institutions.[19] Catholic educators and others could easily infer from O'Malley's data that the number of Catholics in non-Catholic colleges significantly outstripped the number in Catholic institutions. The large numbers of Catholics at institutions such as Harvard and the University of Michigan stood in sharp relief to the small number of collegians in Catholic colleges. Among the Catholic colleges whose officials responded to O'Malley's survey were Saint Mary's University in Galveston, Texas (34 college-level students), Saint Peter's in Jersey City (90), Fordham (67), Saint Ignatius in Cleveland (47), and Villanova (85). Among O'Malley's respondents, Boston College, with 189 collegians among its 456 students, enrolled the largest number.[20] (See table 3.)

Other studies and pieces of evidence suggested that O'Malley's research had not fallen wide of the mark. In an 1897 study of Presbyterians in sixteen state universities, O'Malley's correspondent Francis W. Kelsey, a classicist from the University of Michigan, found 530 Catholics among 14,637 students (4 percent of the total). In 1906, Cassilly

Table 3

Students in Jesuit Colleges as of October 1, 1898

Institution	Total	A.M. (in Course)	College Course	Grammar Course	Latin Rudiments	Commercial	Preparatory
Boston College	441		188	188	8	16	41
Canisius College	239		64	142	33		
College of the Holy Cross	283		175	103	5		
Creighton College	169		56	68	45		
Detroit College	220		60	79	81		
Georgetown College	228	15	102	57	32		
Gonzaga College, Spokane, WA	110		23	34	331		22
Gonzaga College, Washington, DC	147		32	47	49	19	
Immaculate Conception	305		61	78	61	76	29
Loyola College	174		62	55	57		

College							
Marquette College	211		58	115		38	
Sacred Heart College	119		29	37	22	10	21
St. Francis Xavier College	612	31	187	140	106		148
St. Ignatius College, San Fransisco	331		63	102	53	71	113
St. Ignatius College, Chicago	411		114	202			24
St. Ignatius College, Cleveland	206		35	139	32		
St. John's College	257	2	88	81	22	46	18
St. Joseph's College	185		41	73	71		41
St. Louis University	348		85	109	64	49	
St. Mary's University*	116		12	64			40
St. Peter's College	180	13	65	45	57		
St. Xavier College	440	35	113	132	91	57	22
Santa Clara College	182		90	36		43	13
Spring Hill College	111	6	34	36		30	5

*Destroyed by a storm in 1900.

found more than two thousand Catholics enrolled in forty-two state universities.[21] At the 1907 meeting of the College Department (ACCUS became the College Department of the Catholic Educational Association in 1904),[22] Catholic educators discussed a survey conducted at their behest by Father John Farrell, a Catholic chaplain at Harvard and member of the American Federation of Catholic College Clubs. Farrell found 8,671 Catholics studying at 229 non-Catholic institutions. The following year they discussed a report by Louis Mercier, who found only 4,232 college-level students in the nation's Catholic colleges. The results of the Mercier study reflected so poorly on Catholic higher education that leading Catholic educators felt it best to circulate the report *subjecta oculis fidelibus*—only "for the scrutiny of the faithful"—and thus kept it from publication in the proceedings of the annual meeting and the *Bulletin* of the Catholic Educational Association.[23]

Thus Catholics discovered Catholic collegians in large numbers in unexpected places. Religious orders, particularly the Jesuits, with support from the Catholic community, had expended considerable energies and resources building dozens of colleges for the faithful, yet Catholic students flooded non-Catholic institutions. Given their personal commitments and corporate investments, the Jesuits and other Catholic educators were understandably dismayed. But the phenomenon of the Catholic drift toward non-Catholic education was not solely a concern for those involved in the day-to-day operations of the Catholic colleges. Catholic patronage of non-Catholic colleges and universities spoke simultaneously to liberals' hopes and conservatives' fears, becoming another point of contention for a church struggling to craft a satisfactory relationship with Protestant society and already beleaguered by a decade of internecine wrangling between liberals and conservatives.

Some of the heartiest seeds of liberal Catholicism were contained in the efforts of Catholic immigrants to become Americans. Moving to America and assuming a new identity required a certain psychic fortitude; to leave behind the familiar for the unfamiliar deeply tapped the wells of individuals' emotional resources. For nineteenth-century Catholic immigrants, many native-born Protestants' insistent attention to the differences between themselves and immigrant Catholics further complicated their assimilative efforts. Ethno-Catholic enclaves, coupled with many Protestants' firm belief in the fundamental incompatibility of Catholicism and republicanism, gave less tolerant Protestants occasion to portray the growing Catholic minority as an inassimilable, indigestible lump of humanity cast upon American shores. "There lurks in the minds of not a few Americans," wrote Archbishop John Ireland of Saint Paul, "a suspicion that the Catholic Church is unfriendly to civil and political liberty and to the republican form of government which obtains in this country."[24] Yet despite these challenges, Catholics did not count themselves out of the national project, insisting all the more adamantly over Protestant claims to the contrary that they were indeed Americans and good ones at that, whose religion constituted no detriment to civic participation. "American liberty and Catholic dogma are in accord," claimed an 1897 contributor to the *Catholic World*.[25]

Catholics' efforts to embrace an American identity and convince skeptics of their patriotism fostered a self-consciousness about being American conducive to the development of liberal Catholicism, a religious outlook characterized by a firm, optimistic belief in the compatibility of the ancient faith with its New World milieu. As Robert Cross pointed out in his study of liberal Catholicism, the combination of intense devotion to their faith and commitment to their new country spurred some toward a vision of a "consciously 'American' Church" that brought to the New World the best of Old World Catholicism even as the latter adapted to and appropriated the best that the New World had to offer.[26] Liberals' understanding of the relationship between the two was symbiotic: America was good for the church and the church for America. The marvelous growth of the church during the nineteenth century provided liberals with plentiful evidence that America was fertile soil for the church. At a mass in 1889 marking the centennial of the church in the United States (held on the anniversary of John Carroll's appointment as bishop of Baltimore), Archbishop Patrick John Ryan of Philadelphia informed those assembled, according to a journalist, that "Catholicism had above all other religious bodies been benefited by religious liberty" and had the "honor of having inaugurated this freedom in Maryland." The journalist further reported how Ryan, filled with "patriotism," noted a "mysterious affinity between the cosmopolitan democracy of the United States," which "weld[ed] together the most diverse races in order to emancipate them," and the church, which "call[ed] all men without distinction of origin to liberty and equality as children of God."[27]

Catholics from the liberal end of the religious spectrum came to believe that the church in America had been given a special role to play in salvation history. Like other Americans, liberal Catholics were convinced of the superiority of the New World over the Old. With the nineteenth-century church in Europe sapped of much of its spiritual vitality and stripped of its temporal powers, liberals claimed for the flourishing church in the United States a mission with uncanny Puritan overtones. Their errand in the New World was to revitalize the church at large, to accept the spiritual mantle of leadership as it migrated from the Old World to the New. Archbishop John Ireland of Saint Paul, the most prominent of the "Americanists," clearly understood the role of the American church in those terms. Born in Ireland and raised in America, the "consecrated blizzard of the Northwest" was an immense enthusiast for his adopted homeland.[28] At the centennial celebration, where Archbishop Ryan reviewed the history of the nineteenth-century American church, Ireland looked to the church's future, speaking on "The Mission of Catholics in America" in the twentieth century. For Ireland, the task at hand was "to make America Catholic, and to solve for the Church universal the all-absorbing problems with which religion is confronted in the present age." The mission was global in its scope. "The Church triumphing in America, Catholic truth will travel on the wings of American influence, and encircle the universe."[29]

Liberals construed the church's mission largely as an outreach to American society and the Protestant populace.[30] They were a people, liberals claimed, possessed of natural virtues, "some of them in a high degree." The divinely authored natural virtues "most prominent" among Americans, such as their love for liberty, were, argued Father Walter Elliott, a member of the missionary-oriented Paulist order, "the result of providential environments of race, country, and form of government." And yet Protestants were not possessed of a full measure of virtue, for in adhering to Protestantism they were deprived of the supernatural virtues inherent in the one true faith—the "deifying treasures of supernatural life," as Ireland described it.[31] To some liberals, bringing the spiritual riches and resources of Catholicism to the masses was nothing less than a religious imperative. Thus the church ought to adapt to American culture, shedding nonessentials that Americans found unattractive. "To force a foreign religion on an American is like setting him down in his own home," wrote Elliott, "to a distinctively German dinner, *nudels* and *blutwurst* the only dishes; or to a French feast, serving only broiled frogs and stewed snails; or to an Italian one, forcing him to eat *polenta* and macaroni or starve in his own house." To Elliott, "the Catholic religion should neither be foreign nor look foreign in any country."[32]

The Paulists (formally known as the Society of Missionary Priests of Saint Paul the Apostle) were founded by convert Isaac Hecker in 1858.[33] Missionaries committed to bringing the Catholic faith to the American people (until 1908, the United States was an official mission territory of the church), they were enthusiastic proponents of greater interaction between Protestants and Catholics, particularly of the better classes, for they believed it would help them realize their ultimate goal of the conversion of America to the Catholic faith. Elliott boldly staked out the goal before those assembled at the Catholic Congress at the Chicago World's Fair. "Denominations, and 'creeds,' and 'schools,' and 'confessions' are going to pieces before our eyes," announced Elliott. In the "collapse of dogmatic Protestantism," he saw both an opportunity and a providential mission for Catholics. "God would have us missionaries to the American people," he announced, and with "American bishops, priests, and laity working together in an apostolic spirit [we] will missionize the entire land in half a decade of years."[34]

As Ireland put it, in this critical missionary work Catholic laymen and laywomen had a "special vocation," for it was they who, day to day, interacted with Protestants in everyday affairs. Articles in the *Catholic World* and the *Missionary* urged Catholics to pray for the conversion of America to Catholicism, while those with Protestant associates were exhorted to use "whatever power they possess to induce their non-Catholic friends and neighbors to examine the teachings of the Church."[35]

In the arena of higher education, liberals' propensity for rapprochement with culture and society surfaced in their support for the establishment of the Catholic University in 1889.[36] Convinced that universities were "one of the most real, and potent influences in shaping our national character and destiny," Bishop John Lancaster Spalding of Peoria envisioned an "American university" situated at the cultural intersection of religion and nation, "where our young men, in the atmosphere of faith and purity, of high thinking and plain living" would become "intimately conscious of the truth of their religion and of the genius of their country."[37] Few could fault the concept of a full-fledged, modern university conducted under Catholic auspices, yet their plan for a national university in Washington was not without critics. Bishop Bernard McQuaid, an outspoken conservative, argued that the need for seminaries, like his in Rochester, was greater. His conservative friend and ally Archbishop Michael Corrigan of New York wanted the university to be located in New York and conducted by the Jesuits. The Jesuits themselves were concerned when talk of relocating Georgetown's medical and law schools to the new university surfaced; J. Havens Richards ably negotiated a situation that could have become quite contentious.[38]

Bishop John J. Keane was appointed the first rector of the Catholic

University, an institution construed as the foremost institution in the world of American Catholic higher education. Among his liberal episcopal colleagues, Keane stood out as the Catholic goodwill ambassador, speaking regularly and making friends in Protestant circles. More than anyone else, Keane was responsible for Catholic participation in the World's Parliament of Religions, the "crowning event" among a series of congresses held in conjunction with the 1893 Chicago World's Fair. Participation in the parliament required serious politicking by liberals; conservatives charged that Catholic involvement would suggest that all religions were equally valid and that Catholicism was merely one among the many. "Comedy of convocations!" wrote the conservative editor of *Church Progress*. "Think of putting a creed upon exhibition as at a Fair, as one might bring cattle to a show!" Liberals successfully countered, with one bishop arguing, "St. Paul must have been a big fool! Why didn't he act like a respectable Catholic? . . . Why didn't he stay among his own?"[39] Dismissing conservative criticism, a liberal Catholic entourage, including Cardinal Gibbons of Baltimore, joined hundreds of representatives from the world's Eastern and Western religions. Participants, often in colorful, exotic garb, listened to talks and mingled informally for seventeen days along the shores of Lake Michigan. Keane, whose name became "synonymous" with Catholic participation in the parliament, reveled in the ecumenical gathering: "And the old Church has come here, and she is rejoiced to meet her fellow men, her fellow believers, her fellow lovers of every shade of humanity and every shade of creed."[40]

Keane brought this liberal openness and ecumenical zeal into his personal relations and professional responsibilities. He developed warm relations with other university leaders. In 1891, President Andrew Dickson White of Cornell invited Keane to be his houseguest during the Third Annual Convention of the College Association of the Middle States. Charles Eliot also invited Keane to stay at his home during one of Keane's visits to Harvard; in thanking his host for the "charming hospitality," Keane described his stay with the Eliots as one of the "most pleasant incidents" of his life.[41] A gifted orator, Keane also accepted invitations to speak at the University of Michigan, Brown University, the University of Pennsylvania, and the Brooklyn Institute of Arts and Science. In 1891 he received an invitation from William McQuaid of Yale (not to be confused with Bishop Bernard McQuaid of Rochester), inviting him to be part of an annual lecture series; the previous years' speakers included the "Hon. Theodore Roosevelt . . . & Prof. Woodrow Wilson of Princeton." McQuaid asked Keane in making his decision to consider "upwards of one hundred" Catholic students at Yale, claiming they would undoubtedly benefit from his presence. McQuaid also asserted that a "still more potent benefit" would be realized by those "outside the Church but in high places" who would have occasion to see that a "broad and liberal culture" was "not inconsonant with a belief in the tenets of the Church of Rome."[42] Keane accepted the invitation, speaking in February 1892 on "The Church and the Social Problems of the Day," just two weeks after speaking on "The Wisdom of the Ages" at Harvard. "If there were a dozen men like Bishop Keane to travel over the country to call out the people," wrote one Catholic observer, "thousands could be brought into the Church."[43]

In 1889, Keane accepted an invitation to speak at Cornell, but he subsequently withdrew, his decision illustrative of some of the tensions surrounding the liberal agenda. The invitation was made by a representative of the Catholic Union. Formed in the wake of a mission conducted by a Paulist priest in the town of Ithaca, the Cornell Catholic Union aimed to protect Catholics from the "evil effects of liberalism and protestantism" and, on a more positive note, "enlighten protestants in regard to the Catholic religion, reverse their prejudices, and work toward the reunion of Christendom in the apostolic church." Cornell was located in the Diocese of Rochester, and Bishop McQuaid was little enthused for the university. He chastised Keane for agreeing to speak at Cornell without consulting him: "This should have been your first step," he emphatically told Keane. McQuaid informed Keane that he himself had declined such invitations on the grounds that his presence might appear to "sanction" Catholic patronage of Cornell, an institution he considered full of "Danger" and "peril" for Catholics. Given the increase in the "number of Catholic young men who turn from our Catholic Colleges to resort to non-Catholic institutions," McQuaid felt that Keane's presence would exacerbate an "evil." "Patting on the back those who take these risks will not be a help."[44]

Keane's aborted plans to speak at Cornell rose and fell on disparate views of Protestants. In interacting with Protestants in higher education, did Catholics risk their very souls? Was Protestant-sponsored higher education full of dangers for Catholic collegians? In addressing these issues, liberal Catholics held up a version of a kinder, gentler Protestant whose prejudices stemmed more from ignorance than animus. "There was a time," claimed an essayist for the Ave Maria, "when tirades against the Church of Rome were freely indulged in by professors and preachers," but those days were "happily passed" with the exception of "professors of second-rate sectarian institutions, and preachers whose voices echo only in the backwoods." It would be quite erroneous to assume, the essayist claimed, that professors at state universities were mostly "infidels and agnostics" who held deep prejudices against the church. Indeed, many were "deeply interested in religious questions, sincerely desirous to know the truth, and curious to hear what any one may have to say in explanation or defence of the Catholic religion." A contributor to the *Catholic World* concurred: Protestants from the better classes were amiable, even-tempered individuals "ready to abandon" any "false idea" about the Roman Catholic Church they may have inherited from their "ancestors."[45] At the University of Wisconsin, a priest working with Catholic students claimed they experienced no "disadvantages on account of their faith," while a Catholic professor at the University of California at Berkeley reported that he had "never noticed any discrimination on account of religion." At Yale, a "man's religion is never questioned," wrote one Catholic, and as far as the faculty was concerned, "a more liberal body of men I have never met with."[46]

The liberal defense of Catholic patronage of non-Catholic colleges rested not only on the broad-minded views of Protestants but on the good that Catholics might do among the descendants of Luther and Calvin as they mingled with them in the halls of academia. If strong in their faith, wrote the Catholic professor at Berkeley, Catholic students "have a chance to do a great amount of good." A contributor to the *American Ecclesiastical Review* held forth that "daily association" between Protestants and Catholics would be an "invaluable aid . . . to the Catholic cause," fostering a "feeling of trust and confidence . . . between the Catholics and Protestants which will continue and mark their whole subsequent relations in society."[47] An alumnus of Cornell described how Catholics helped dissipate bigotry in the old "burnt-over" district of western New York State, where the fervor of the Second Great Awakening had stirred the red-hot flames of anti-Catholicism in the early-nineteenth century.

> The most marked feature at Cornell to a Catholic was the general air of surprise that a man desiring education should be a Catholic. . . . That Catholic students at Cornell have been an influence for good in the village life of Ithaca I firmly believe. They have been the cause of the removal of much of the old-time prejudice against Catholicity. Their entrance and continuance at Cornell shows that they are not lacking in intellectual capacity, and that settles the prejudice that only the ignorant are Catholic.[48]

A Catholic alumnus of Harvard claimed that Catholic collegians had the same positive effect upon religious relations in Cambridge. James Gallivan, class of 1887, was buoyant. Less than a year after Harvard awarded Bishop Keane an honorary doctorate, university officials asked one of its alumni, Paulist priest Peter J. O'Callaghan (class of 1888), to lead religious services in Appleton Chapel. The first Catholic to lead regular religious services in the university's 258-year history, O'Callaghan spoke before an "immense audience," including Eliot, who congratulated him after the service.[49] Writing in *Donahoe's Magazine,* Gallivan described this "new precedent" as yet "another barrier swept away from mutual understanding and sympathy between representatives of different religious denominations." Growing tolerance, so evident at Harvard, derived, Gallivan claimed, from "increased knowledge of the mother of all the churches" for which the "Catholic sons of Harvard College, both past and present" deserved credit. They were doing "their share towards enlightening their fellow-students at the university . . . as to the true claims of the Church," and through their daily efforts were helping "dissipate that prejudice which has heretofore kept many good people outside the Church." The significance of their religious endeavors was acute, for as Harvard was the "pulse of America's highest intellectual life," it would play an outsized role in "changing of the attitude of the American mind towards the Church."[50]

Raised in Salem, Massachusetts, O'Callaghan joined the Paulists soon after graduating from Harvard, his passions running strong for the work of evangelization. Converts to Catholicism and the tremendous increase in the Catholic population of New England made O'Callaghan tremendously optimistic about the prospects of converting America to the Church of Rome. The church had, O'Callaghan wrote, "captured a stronghold which had been for two centuries in the possession of those who hated her very name." In the bosom of the one-time Puritan stronghold, O'Callaghan hoped to bring those "in darkness and in the shadow of death" into the light of the true faith through "missions to non-Catholics" of the type regularly conducted by the Paulists. And there was, according to the Harvard alumnus, "no more fruitful place than in Cambridge" for a mission among the "future leaders of men!"

Most of the sons of Harvard take places of prominence in the professions and in society. They become leaders where the Church most needs to make its future conquests, if we are "to make America Catholic." They are intelligent men hungering for Truth—for the Bread of life—and shall we not break it to them? Win a dozen such men to the Church and you have won hundreds. That America will be Catholic—who can doubt it who believes that Truth must prevail? . . . Who can doubt it who knows the story of past heresies and sees that story beginning to repeat itself in the disintegration and decay of Protestantism? And if America is to be Catholic, the Harvard of the [future] will be a Catholic Harvard. In those days there will be room for many Catholic Universities in America, and the cause of none will be injured by laboring to build up others.[51]

For O'Callaghan, the work of evangelizing Harvard would ultimately contribute to the revitalization of the church at large. Here O'Callaghan's enthusiasm for the task of evangelization reached an almost feverish pitch:

Great faith and great projects give birth to great achievements. The timid must fail because they dare not hope for success. . . . Splendid prognostic of what the world will be,—once more Catholic,—once more recovered from the shock of religious anarchy which has so much delayed its progress! Our own America holding the place the honor in a regenerated world! "Win America for the Church and you have won the world," has been said by a great bishop after Leo's own heart. It might be said with equal truth, "Make Harvard Catholic and you have converted America," for she is the chief intellectual centre of our country, and to win the intelligence of a nation is to win the nation.[52]

For liberal Catholics, higher education represented an important platform for engagement with modern, Protestant America. The Catholic University of America institutionally embodied their commitment to wrestle with and contribute to the great intellectual challenges of the day. As for Catholic patronage of non-Catholic colleges, liberals thought it boded well for the cause of the church in America. Much good would come, they claimed, from greater interaction between Protestants and Catholics of the better classes: bigotry would wane and conversions would be realized. But this was not the conclusion reached by conservatives and a number of individuals working in Catholic colleges, who variously saw in the university movement spiritual dangers for Catholic students and adverse institutional effects for Catholic higher education.

Like the liberal element, conservatives within the church firmly believed that the Roman Catholic Church was the one true church. But where liberals saw mission territory and religious opportunities, conservatives were prone to see spiritual risks. Conservatives were not completely averse to American society. America had great strengths, but it was not without its weaknesses. Protestantism, they claimed, had deeply suffused American culture, rendering it vulnerable to excessive individualism and blatant materialism. Unlike liberals who believed that society would be transformed through constructive engagement with the church, conservatives feared that the church would be malformed through uncritical engagement with society. Thus conservatives adopted a vigilant stance and argued for separatism, particularly in education.

The debate over Catholic patronage of non-Catholic colleges built on a surfeit of anecdotal evidence. While liberals offered up examples of improved religious relations and images of mass conversions, conservatives countered with reports of religious declension among Catholics attending non-Catholic colleges. Although not all cut of the same theological cloth, the Jesuits and other Catholic educators often joined with conservatives in pointing to the spiritual dangers of non-Catholic education. Msgr. Conaty, a practical-minded moderate, acknowledged that there were some Catholics who made it through non-Catholic colleges spiritually unscathed, but a "thousand and one others" had "lost faith altogether," or had "drifted into absolute indifference in religion."[53] In his article documenting Catholic patronage of non-Catholic institutions, Austin O'Malley also reported religious declension. Like Conaty, he acknowledged exceptions; there were, he noted, "good priests and devout laymen . . . graduated at Harvard and Yale and similar institutions." But there were far more of whom their "neighbors" said, "Those men should be Catholic, but they are not." And while one Cornell alumnus reported on the salubrious effects that Catholics had on the population of Ithaca, another reported on the deleterious impact Cornell had on Catholics, with claims that only "one-tenth of the number" of Catholic men "who enter Cornell practise their religion faithfully throughout their life at that institution." ("Women students and foreigners" at Cornell were, the graduate claimed, "apparently free from contamination as regards their religion.")[54]

Those sympathetic to Catholics in non-Catholic schools warned against causal arguments facilely linking the collegiate experience with spiritual ruin. If Catholics did in fact fall away from the practice of their faith, it was "not necessarily . . . the college course that corrupted them." It was far more likely that there was a connection between their home life and their faith life; as one Catholic at the City University of New

York put it, "if the parents were lukewarm, the boys were not zealous." After all, noted the chaplain of the Harvard Catholic Club, "indifferent Catholic parents usually develop indifferent Catholic children." At the very least, Catholics at non-Catholic colleges faced no more serious religious temptations than young Catholics who went into business and gave "themselves up to money-making," who became, as an essayist described it, "liars and cheaters like the great majority of those with whom they are brought in daily contact."[55]

Despite such objections, those with conservative views on the subject continued to draw close connections between non-Catholic education and the Catholic collegians' fall from grace, arguing that students should avoid non-Catholic colleges where they were likely to make a "shipwreck of their faith and their virtue," as Jesuit Rudolph Meyer put it.[56] The source of the problem was twofold. Inside the classroom, Catholics faced misconceptions and errors espoused by prejudiced Protestants and "infidels"; outside the classroom they faced moral laxity and unethical behavior that flowed from either Protestantism or secularism. One of Austin O'Malley's informants reported that a Catholic at Ohio State "must expect to hear many things which grate harshly on his religious sensibility." Another reported that scholasticism, the bedrock of Catholic philosophy and theology, was "violently opposed" in philosophy courses at Yale. (His correspondent naively believed, O'Malley contended, that this did not actually constitute "opposition to Catholicism.") Villanova's President Delurey feared that students in history courses at non-Catholic colleges were taught to "treat with contempt a venerated antiquity and to proudly despise holy things and persons." Instilled in their minds at a "tender age," it was an intellectual "poison" nearly impossibly "eradicated" in later life.[57]

The assault upon the faith of Catholic students extended beyond the walls of the classroom. Popular student culture, filled with club life, parties, athletic events, class rushes, and a fair amount of foolishness and misbehavior, gave conservatives further cause to rail against Catholic patronage of non-Catholic colleges. Unlike Catholic colleges, which had strict discipline, non-Catholic colleges and universities exercised too little oversight, placing students in temptation's way in the name of misguided, Protestant-inspired liberty. Critics of Catholic patronage of non-Catholic colleges pointed to cheating scandals, drunken fraternity parties, sexual escapades, and violent clashes, claiming that they inevitably exacted a toll on the moral rectitude of students. Yale was a case in point. Readers of the *Catholic World* learned from Dr. O'Malley how "intoxicated young men, to the number of nearly a thousand, thronged the lower streets of New Haven, while lewd women carried off scores of them to their resorts." This was no place for Catholic youth concerned with their eternal salvation. As the fictional Doctor Mordant in Bugg's *The People of Our Parish* put it, "no Christian parent" had the "right to expose his son to needless temptation."[58]

In Catholic moral theology, to have knowingly placed oneself in the "immediate" or "proximate" occasion of sin absent sufficient cause was in itself sinful. This was, according to critics, exactly what Catholics were doing. According to Jesuit Rudolph Meyer, the church had "declared" that non-Catholic schools were "usually proximate dangers to faith and morality." Thus "Catholic parents and guardians usually commit a grievous sin by sending the young to such schools, unless," he noted, "they have grave reasons for so doing, approved by the proper ecclesiastical authority, and unless moreover they take precautions, in each individual case, that the proximate dangers be made remote."[59]

For conservatives and supporters of Catholic higher education, the powerful temptation of worldly success was, more than anything else, luring Catholics into non-Catholic universities and the "immediate" or "proximate" occasion of sin. The "social element," claimed Father Delurey, was the most salient factor in explaining Catholic patronage of non-Catholic institutions. "Purse-proud parents," he announced, sent their sons to "Yale, Harvard, Pennsylvania, Chicago or Columbia" so they could "get a peep, even from afar, into society." Archbishop Corrigan admonished those who sent their sons to non-Catholic colleges out of a "desire to ascend the social scale, to mingle in fashionable circles," among "companions deemed desirable." There were, he claimed, "evil" and "deplorable" consequences, for when children lost the "gift of faith" it was a "bitter cause [of] regret" for parents.[60]

Those against Catholic patronage of non-Catholic colleges had a stronger theological case than those favoring it. It was certainly easier to argue that such institutions were immediate or proximate occasions of sin, and thus should be avoided, than it was to demonstrate that they posed little spiritual risk and afforded occasions to realize positive religious outcomes. Moreover, unlike American Protestantism, Catholicism had no "Gospel of Success," no positive theology of upward mobility or economic progress. Many late-nineteenth-century Catholics, including leading educators such as Conaty, were sympathetic to the concept of upward mobility, but Horatio Alger had no Catholic counterpart. Thomas Kernan, a prominent layman from the State of New York, argued that the sincere desire of parents to see their children "rise in the world socially" and move in the "best society" was "laudable and excusable," and constituted neither venial (i.e., minor) nor mortal sin.[61] But Kernan was a rare Catholic voice, making a weak theological claim. Shaped by preindustrial and premodern views of labor and social relations traceable to the Middle Ages, Catholic teaching on the socioeconomic order was fundamentally conservative on the issues of social inequities and economic disparities. *Rerum Novarum*, Leo XIII's 1891 encyclical on the rights of workers, marked a departure from this traditional stance, but there was little in nineteenth-century Catholic theology to sanction upward mobility.

Given formal schooling's increasing importance in the socioeconomic order, theological questions about the purposes of education naturally arose. As early as 1866, U.S. bishops were concerned that Catholics might turn to education to boost them beyond their "station in life." At the Second Baltimore Council, they issued a pastoral letter to their flock explaining that

> Education, to be good, need not necessarily be either high or ornamental. . . . Prepare your children for the duties of the state or condition of life they are likely to be engaged in: do not exhaust your means in bestowing on them an education that may unfit them for these duties. This would be a sure source of disappointment and dissatisfaction, both for yourselves and for them. Accustom them from their earliest years to habits of obedience, industry, and thrift: and deeply impress on their minds the great principle, that happiness and success in life, as well as acceptance with God, do not so much depend on the station we fill, as on the fidelity with which we discharge its duties. Teach them, that the groundwork of true happiness must be placed in habitual and cheerful submission of our wills to the dispensations of Providence, who has wisely consulted for the happiness of all, without, however, bestowing on all an equal share of the goods of fortune.[62]

The Catholic press also weighed in on Catholic patronage of non-Catholic colleges, with most of it taking a conservative position. Catholic literature—magazines, advice manuals, and fictional works—grew substantially in the second half of the nineteenth century, partly because the hierarchy supported it. In an 1884 pastoral letter, the bishops urged Catholics to subscribe to "one or more Catholic periodicals" and adorn their homes with "chaste and holy pictures, and still more, sound, interesting, and profitable books." This episcopal exhortation toward proper Catholic domesticity bespoke a growing middle class, whose lifestyle and financial resources allowed for leisure reading of newspapers such as the *Pilot* and the *Sacred Heart Review,* journals such as the *Ave Maria* and the *Catholic World,* and fiction penned for Catholics by Catholics (including members of the Guild of Catholic Authors). This literature was not unsubstantial. According to one study, 558 Catholic titles appeared between 1876 and 1890; 1,300 appeared between 1885 and 1890. It was grist for popular groups such as the Columbian Reading Union and the Catholic Educational Circle, which, combined, by 1893 consisted of 250 local units and ten thousand members.[63]

Catholic advice literature, a barometer for tracing the vicissitudes of the Catholic community, regularly enjoined Catholics from seeking success and garnering wealth if it required sacrificing religious principles, neglecting family obligations, or associating excessively with Protestants in business, social settings, or in education. It also discouraged parents and young men from attending non-Catholic colleges. In one of the most popular books of the period, *True Men as We Need Them: A Book of Instruction for Men in the World,* Msgr. Bernard O'Reilly held up for approbation the time-tested principles shaping Catholic education and the men devoted to them. According to O'Reilly, good parents saw that their sons attended Catholic institutions. "An unerring instinct in the heart of a Catholic parent will direct him, in seeking for his boy the guides who can lead the latter safely through the walks of classical antiquity, and the bewildering mazes of modern science . . . to select the men who have sought eminence in learning through a holy ambition, and who impart it for His love." Parents themselves, who in all likelihood had only secured rudimentary or elementary education, whose Old World ancestors had been denied the opportunity of a Catholic education, would naturally, O'Reilly claimed, relish the opportunity "to be able to give their sons, their money, and their heartfelt sympathy" to Catholic colleges "struggling against the most adverse circumstances."[64]

Catholic fiction writers in the second half of the nineteenth century reacted to Protestant America with varying degrees of openness, enthusiasm, and suspicion; they rarely approached it uncritically. As early as the 1850s, they began writing about Catholics attending non-Catholic schools and colleges, and nowhere are the spiritual pitfalls of non-Catholic education more clearly or colorfully presented. Catholic authors were particularly critical of socially ambitious Catholics who sent their sons to the likes of Harvard and Columbia, where Catholic collegians succumbed to all manner of evil and appropriated Protestant manners, values, notions of history, perhaps a Protestant spouse, even the Protestant faith. Zealous in visiting onerous punishments upon their misguided Catholic characters, Catholic authors offered up to readers evidence of how non-Catholic education destroyed students' spiritual lives, ripped asunder familial ties, encouraged vice, distorted truth, and even threatened the Republic. The non-Catholic college was a sure road to spiritual, emotional, physical, and economic ruin.

In *The Blakes and Flanagans: A Tale Illustrative of Irish Life in the United States,* popular writer Mary Ann Sadlier described two branches of a family working out issues surrounding schooling, success, and salvation. Published in 1855, with at least four reprints to follow, the story tells of brothers-in-law Miles Blake and Tim Flanagan and their disparate views, aspirations, and fates. Miles and his wife "were more anxious for making money than anything else; and though they professed to be good Catholics, and were so considered by many people, yet religion was, with them, only a secondary object." With hopes of living the good life, Blake sent his son Harry to the public school to "make acquaintances with them that's above—not below him!" Blake's intense desire that his son succeed in life led his son toward a career in law; that, coupled with his son's growing disdain for things-Catholic (commenced in public school), led Harry to Columbia Law School for professional training.[65]

Harry's non-Catholic education sealed his spiritual fate. He capitalized upon his Columbia connections and experience and soon launched a successful political career. But his religious and moral compass was terribly awry, his political success depending on deceit and manipulation of the Irish in New York. Ignoring church precept by eating meat on Friday, he blithely announced that "my stomach lost its Catholic tone at old Columbia, and has never since recovered it. Indeed, I fear it never will." Harry never recovered religiously, and his family life suffered for it. His marriage to a Protestant socialite disdainful of Catholicism created tensions between Harry and his father, Miles. Tragedy followed as Harry's first-born child died without the benefit of baptism and was thus eternally denied access to heaven. A surviving son unfortunately followed in his father's academic and spiritual footsteps: "Henry T. Blake came from Columbia College a very bad Catholic, his sons went into it without religion of any kind, saving a sort of predilection in favor of the Baptist sect—what they came out may well be guessed."[66]

Things went quite differently in the Flanagan household. Tim Flanagan's children attended Catholic schools, where priests and sisters taught them not only their academic lessons but the catechism, religious practices, and right from wrong. In his later years, Tim was thus blessed. Two of his sons became priests, an immense honor for Catholic parents. Another became the ideal family man who, blessed with a good Catholic wife and healthy children, remained emotionally and physically close to his parents. When Flanagan dies at the end of the novel, he does so satisfied with his life, surrounded by his family, and in a state of grace. Thus readers knew that Tim Flanagan was bound for heaven. Sadlier concluded with a direct exhortation:

> Ah! it would be well if Catholic parents would think more of these things than they do. If they would only consider that they are accountable to God and his Church for the precious gift of faith, and are bound, under pain of deadly sin, to transmit it to their children pure and undefiled, they would not dare to send those children to godless schools, where they are almost sure to lose that precious inheritance, or to have it so shorn of its splendor, so poor and so feeble, that it is no longer worth having.[67]

John Talbot Smith added his warnings about non-Catholic higher education in his short story "One of Many," published in 1891. Tom, the story's protagonist, broods over the fate of his one-time college pal Algernon Murphy. The two met at a Catholic college, but Algernon left prematurely, largely because his mother wanted him to mingle with "the sons of the great people." Tom tried to dissuade him, but the allure of non-Catholic higher education was strong and that of Catholic higher education weak. "Had we cultured professors, elegant quarters, grand libraries and aristocratic pupils, instead of a Spartan simplicity in our very vices," lamented Tom, "my arguments would have prevailed." Tom was unable to save Murphy from the effects of non-Catholic education: religious indifferentism and skepticism. Young Tom considered Algernon's fate:

> In following the curiously uncertain path which Mr. Murphy trod for a few years, often a soul is lost. The losing of a soul is an idea which brings a smile to many a lip in our day. It is known to be an idea which causes mental suffering to Catholics, but not to certain scientists who know there are no souls to lose, and not to certain Protestants who know of no desert in which to lose them. Mr. Murphy was often willing to accept the conclusions of these parties, and, had he

been a cleverer or less clever man, might to day have been a Unitarian or a sceptic.[68]

In the years following publication of O'Malley's data on Catholic enrollment patterns, a sense of crisis set in among the Catholic college men. Those who penned editorials, advice manuals, and fictional works failed to persuade; as subsequent surveys made all too apparent, Catholic collegians continued to patronize non-Catholic colleges in great numbers. The drift toward non-Catholic colleges and universities riveted the attention of the ACCUS; it was discussed, often heatedly, every year between the inaugural meeting in 1899 and 1908.[69]

By 1908 the college men's concern about enrollments spurred them to seek episcopal support. Led by Jesuit John Conway, of Georgetown, then serving as head of the College Department, they drafted a memorial to the bishops of the United States asking them to support the cause of Catholic higher education. In effect they were asking the bishops to extend to higher education the position they adopted in 1884 at Baltimore Council III on elementary education. At that council, the bishops adopted separatism in education as an ecclesial norm, with an instruction that each parish sponsor a school and a directive to parents to send their children to them. Less emphatically, they urged parents to send their older children to Catholic academies and colleges. The bishops recognized that Catholic schools were not always "perfect" and exhorted those responsible for them to make them so. Imperfections notwithstanding, they directed parents to send their children for a "Christian education," one that would protect them from the "noxious errors of popularized irreligion" and equip them for the "coming combat between truth and error, between Faith and Agnosticism." Uncomfortable with the sweeping mandates, a number of prelates helped temper the strong language issuing from the council by insisting on exemptions and enjoining against "excessive zeal," a move directed toward clerics willing to excommunicate parents who did not send their children to Catholic schools.[70]

The bishops and the clergy applied the directives and sanctions of Baltimore III unevenly. Many pastors did not build a school, and those directed to improve the schools sometimes did not and often could not, lacking either the will, competence, or resources. Parents who sent their children to non-Catholic schools often went unchallenged and undisciplined by their clergy. On the other hand, some bishops and pastors applied the precepts of Baltimore III vigorously, even zealously. Rochester's McQuaid wielded the threat of excommunication, even against collegians. In 1903, *Outlook* magazine reported that McQuaid had directed twenty Catholic women studying at Cornell to withdraw from the university or face excommunication. Responding to a query from the magazine, McQuaid explained that Catholic women at Cornell were in great spiritual danger: they were exposed to false teaching, compelled to attend non-Catholic chapel services, and subject to the "perilous" practice of coeducation. "In the judgment of the Bishop of Rochester," McQuaid wrote, "a young lady needlessly exposing her religious faith to danger, sins; sins unrepented of cannot be absolved in the tribunal of penance." He instructed them to attend "high grade" Catholic colleges for women. While there were hundreds of Catholic academies for women and dozens of colleges for men, there were in fact only a handful of bona fide Catholic colleges for women (and none in his own diocese). Women's choices were, therefore, more circumscribed than men's; with few exceptions it was either a Protestant-sponsored college or a Catholic-run academy.[71]

"The case of young men is different," McQuaid wrote. He would have preferred Catholics to avoid Cornell altogether, but felt it prudent to deal with conditions as they were by tending to the spiritual needs of Catholic men at Cornell. With a handful of other bishops, McQuaid argued for the establishment of Catholic halls at non-Catholic universities, where chaplains could counsel students, provide formal instruction in the Catholic faith, and celebrate the church's sacraments. McQuaid was, in essence, arguing for the establishment of social, intellectual, and religious enclaves for Catholics within Protestant universities. Pius X's encyclical *Acerbo Nimis*, in which he urged church authorities to establish "schools of religion . . . to instruct in truths of faith and in principles of Christian life youth who attend public Universities, Lycea, and Gymnasia wherein no mention is made of religious matters," provided justification, while the English hierarchy's permission in 1893 for Catholics to attend non-Catholic universities with Catholic chaplaincies provided a precedent of sorts for Catholic halls or colleges attached to non-Catholic universities.[72] Some of the more notable ventures developed at the University of Wisconsin at Madison, the University of California at Berkeley, and the University of Texas at Austin. McQuaid's own plan for a Catholic hall at Cornell never materialized; thwarted by opposition, it withered after his death in 1909.[73]

The bishops promoting Catholic halls—McQuaid, Archbishop Patrick William Riordan of San Francisco, Archbishop Sebastian Messmer of Milwaukee, among others—did not want to encourage additional Catholic attendance at non-Catholic universities. Nor were they inspired by liberal visions of improved Catholic-Protestant relations. Largely from the conservative camp, their approach was pastoral and practical. Along with a number of clergy, they were concerned for the spiritual welfare of Catholic students in non-Catholic institutions.[74]

The development of episcopally sanctioned support for Catholic students at non-Catholic colleges provoked deep concern among the Jesuits and other Catholic educators. They were grappling with competing interests: saving souls and saving institutions. The tension surfaced at the 1906 and 1907 meetings of the Catholic college men. Harvard chaplain John Farrell's paper "The Catholic Chaplain at the Secular University," presented at the 1907 meeting, spelled out the conundrum: "He [the chaplain] feels that the Catholic students attending these universities must be protected in their faith, and yet in doing this he must not in any way encourage other Catholic students to risk the same dangers." As priests, those in his audience could not easily dismiss the pastoral obligations to tend to the faithful, regardless of where they studied. After all, the "Good Shepherd . . . left the ninety and nine to go in search of the one." Yet the college men did not wish parents and students to construe the presence of a Catholic chaplain or a Catholic hall as tacit approval of Catholic patronage of non-Catholic universities. Timothy Brosnahan took a moderate course at the 1907 meeting: "Nobody is advocating the abandonment of those young men who unfortunately are making their undergraduate studies at non-Catholic universities." Nonetheless, Catholic parents were remiss in sending their sons to non-Catholic institutions, particularly at the undergraduate level, "in order to get an education which can equally well be obtained in Catholic institutions." The risks, especially for impressionable undergraduates, were far too great: during the course of their schooling, the "Catholic instinct is lost, and the loss is manifested in speech and action."[75]

Shortly after Brosnahan spoke, a parish priest, Father Peter Yorke, took the floor. Hoping that his audience would not take offense, he respectfully suggested that the college men were "parochial," putting their institutional interests over the needs of the faithful and even the broader good of the church. There was, he argued, no reason to do so. "I might say here that the discussion . . . seems to suppose a certain amount of competition between the Catholic and non-Catholic college, and that the increase of Catholic students at secular universities means a diminution of students at Catholic institutions." Yorke had his doubts. "I think there is enough to go round and that Catholic colleges are far from having exhausted the resources of their constituency." They would, he claimed, "be taxed to the breaking point to provide for students who should be in them and are not in them, neither in any institution of learning." But Yorke found no sympathy for his position; the Catholic college men were convinced of the opposite. Many Catholic colleges were at the breaking point precisely because Catholics turned to non-Catholic colleges in such large numbers.[76]

Large-scale Catholic patronage of non-Catholic colleges with growing support for Catholic halls and chaplains propelled the leadership of the College Department to seek episcopal support in 1907, crossing "the great abyss," as Bishop Denis O'Connell, the Catholic University rector, described it, "that for so long has kept them divided from the hierarchy and the hierarchy from them.[77] The leadership presented the bishops with a memorial seeking support for Catholic higher education. Crafted by Conway, the memorial made a case against Catholic halls; the situation in England, they argued, did not apply in the United States, where Catholic colleges were numerous. Nor was the presence of a Catholic chaplain any kind of substitute for a Catholic education or remedy for non-Catholic education. Unfortunately, great numbers of Catholics attended non-Catholic colleges, with a significant number following a classical course. Pointing to the success of Catholic lower education, which, they claimed, owed much to the bishops' support, they "beg[ged]" for a "little encouragement and like zeal" for Catholic higher education, hoping for a directive from the bishops to parents to send their children to Catholic colleges.[78]

For reasons that the historical record does not make entirely clear, the support that the college men sought failed to materialize. The college men were initially heartened by the appointment of a subcommittee of bishops, but a subsequent meeting between the subcommittee and a delegation of the college men proved unproductive. Cardinal Gibbons may have scuttled prospects for episcopal support before the meeting was held, sending a message to the bishops to adopt a "passive attitude" after hearing the college men out. Given "the present condition of things," Gibbons felt an episcopal mandate "would be untimely and fruitless." And at least one member of the subcommittee, John Farley, archbishop of New York, was a known critic of Catholic colleges, his derogatory comments on their quality having been published two years earlier in the *New York Times*.[79]

For the Jesuits, their students, and alumni, the closing years of the nineteenth century were immensely troubling on two critical fronts.

Austin O'Malley's 1898 article drove home convincingly one point: Catholics were flocking to non-Catholic colleges. A student editorialist in the *Boston College Stylus* put it succinctly: "The drift of our youth to non-Catholic institutions has been constantly on the increase, while our own universities and colleges have lacked support in a quarter where it was most naturally expected."[80] And while large numbers of Catholics were bypassing Catholic higher education, prominent non-Catholics were criticizing it. The removal of Boston College and Holy Cross from Harvard Law School's select list of colleges in 1898 set in motion a series of events culminating with highly publicized charges of bigotry leveled at Charles Eliot and allegations of academic inferiority leveled at the Jesuit colleges. The president and alumni of Holy Cross attempted to dismiss the seriousness of the situation with claims that graduates of Catholic colleges would not be "seriously embarrassed" by Harvard in their pursuit of advanced studies, for there were "other universities which would warmly welcome them, and whose good will would be an earnest of honorable treatment."[81] But the goodwill of other institutions could neither undo the damage nor change the facts: in Protestant America, in the age of the university, the Jesuits' base of support was weak, and their reputation was suffering.

In June 1900, the Boston College Alumni Association appealed to the Boston-area clergy in the form of a letter linking the Harvard Law School controversy with Catholic patronage of non-Catholic colleges. They began with a preemptive strike: "As a Catholic priest" the recipient of their letter would de facto "view with deep concern the indifference and, in some cases, the hostility of certain Catholics toward our schools and colleges." The "defection among our own people" combined with "powerful opposition of Protestant and infidel educators in various parts of the country" made "active measures for the encouragement and support" of Catholic higher education "imperative." They quickly referred to the event at the forefront of many Catholic minds: the "recent attack on Catholic colleges made by the president of Harvard University" that revealed "the strength and character of the antagonism which threatens the existence of our higher institutions of learning." Ignoring Eliot's claim that his only interest was the eventual improvement of Catholic colleges, the alumni depicted Eliot's attack as nothing more than an effort to "compel Catholic students who are desirous of entering the Harvard Law School to obtain their collegiate training in a non-Catholic institution" and to "degrade Catholic education in the estimation of the public." For Catholics to "quietly submit to attacks of this kind upon our colleges" would be "tantamount to surrendering the education of our youth to the enemies of our religion" and leaving the "leaders of our people in the future . . . tainted with all the errors of modern liberalism."[82]

The alumni continued with their plea for support. Unfortunately, the "number of Catholic students attending Protestant institutions" was "already very large" and would probably "rapidly increase" unless parents came "to realize the moral dangers to which they subject their sons in sending them to non-Catholic colleges." What was needed, they argued, was a "united effort on the part of the clergy and educated laymen with the view of inducing the Catholic public to patronize their own schools and colleges." It was a "pressing need," given that "almost two-thirds of the total number of Catholic students in Harvard College this year came from Boston and its immediate vicinity." Unwritten but quite clear was the inference: these men should have been at Boston College. The alumni then asked the clergy for their "earnest co-operation in furthering the cause of Catholic collegiate education," in particular "to see to it, as far as you can, that the young men of your parish who are to receive a collegiate training shall attend a Catholic college."[83]

It is difficult to assess clergy support for Catholic higher education.[84] Given the number of Jesuit-college alumni among the local priests, including a number active in the Boston College Alumni Association, there was certainly some support to be found among the clergy. Yet Father Mullan laid some of the blame for the "drift" on the "open encouragement or the inaction of Catholic men in authority."[85] Catholic conservatism and even anti-intellectualism among clergymen may have vitiated support for the very idea of advanced education for the laity. Moreover, given that many priests were local and of Irish lineage, they may have taken satisfaction in a Catholic presence at Harvard or, like the evangelically minded liberals, seen it as a step in the right religious direction. Regardless, appeals made little difference; enrollment at Boston College continued to decline.

Together, Catholic patronage of non-Catholic colleges and charges of academic inferiority deeply troubled those invested in Jesuit higher education. While Brosnahan's spirited and public defense of Jesuit higher education admitted no weakness, among themselves those closer to the Jesuit educational enterprise would, as a Boston College student did, "freely confess that our own colleges are not without their drawbacks." But more often than not, those admitting to limitations blamed extrinsic factors, especially paucity of funds and lack of endowment. In an age of large-scale academic philanthropy, "Alma Mater has no Rockefeller, no Stanford, no Clark to endow her and enable her the easier to hold aloft the torch of enlightening truth," observed a Holy Cross alumnus.[86] Conversely, supporters of Jesuit higher education attributed its strengths to intrinsic factors. The student editors of the *Holy Cross Purple*, for instance, passed on to its readers the comments of R. Ross Perry, a noted Washington lawyer and Georgetown law professor. In "the classics, Greek and Latin, in humanities and belle lettres," the Jesuit colleges were "superior" to "Harvard, Yale or Princeton," while the leading universities were, when compared to the Jesuit colleges, "deficient . . . in their instruction in ethics and natural law, which lie at the bottom of all law." There was, Perry concluded, "no ground for the action of Harvard."[87]

But claims of academic excellence in themselves were not sufficient to surmount the challenges facing Jesuit higher education at the turn of the century. The Law School controversy, coupled with Catholic patronage of non-Catholic colleges, required a compelling religious apologia for Jesuit education directed at the Catholic community itself. "Why should we Catholics choose a Catholic college for our training instead of a non-Catholic one?" a student queried in the *Stylus*, looking for an "honest reason," rather than an answer born of "blind prejudice."[88] As Georgetown's Conway put it in 1907, "The only reason—valid reason— we had to urge for parents to send their children to Catholic colleges was the religious one. In everything else the great colleges of the country are better equipped than ours are; state universities appeal to local pride, charge less, give greater liberty, have greater social advantages."[89] Harvard Law School's refusal to recognize the degrees of Jesuit colleges (save Georgetown) only exacerbated the issue; students' diplomas— their "passport to the professions," as Msgr. Conaty described them—no longer gained them passage to a particularly popular and important academic port of call. Given the high academic and professional costs, it was thus critical to find a religious answer to the question posed by the student journalist (i.e., to forge a compelling rationale for attending a Catholic college). It made for a tidy juxtaposition. While Fathers Brosnahan and Mullan were arguing the academic merits of Jesuit education with Eliot and Law School officials in order to secure access to Harvard for their graduates, the Jesuits and their supporters were arguing the religious merits of Jesuit education among Catholics in order to foster loyalty to their own schools. Making simultaneous arguments for the integration of Jesuit education into the academic mainstream and the distinctiveness of Jesuit education (i.e., for mainstreaming and separatism) was sometimes difficult. Austin O'Malley exemplified the tension. Though committed to Catholic higher education, O'Malley felt that good Catholic colleges were still a year behind their non-Catholic counterparts, but, he noted, "there is the compensation of religious influence, discipline, and philosophy to atone for the feebleness of the course."[90]

Students enrolled in Jesuit colleges at the height of the Law School controversy understood, in various ways and to different degrees, that they were close to the eye of a larger storm. When, at Boston College, the editors of the *Stylus* reprinted articles about the Law School controversy from Catholic periodicals, they did so as a matter of "justice," so that readers would "know that the discussion" about Harvard's admissions policy and Catholic participation in higher education was not only "local." They were not, the editors claimed, the only Catholics facing "the curious opposition which savors of intolerance rather than of liberality."[91] For students at Boston College and Holy Cross, their problem actually stemmed from a curious admixture of liberality and intolerance—from the liberal vision that opened the doors of nonsectarian universities to Catholics and the intolerance that closed the doors of Harvard Law School to graduates of Jesuit colleges. Writ small in their responses to this complex situation were the disparate strands and ambiguities of the Americanism controversy. In higher education, what was the proper course for Catholics? Was Protestant America hostile or genial to the interests of Catholics? The questions were immediate and acute for Catholic collegians and their parents. While leading liberals held forth a vision of a Catholic America and a church renewed, and as well-known conservatives held forth on the manifold evils of non-Catholic education, it was parents and their college-bound children who had to make and come to terms with their academic choices. While Keane and Ireland and McQuaid and Corrigan were drawn ever closer into the Americanism controversy proper, the laity, as historian Thomas McAvoy noted, "continued to associate with their non-Catholic neighbors in all things that were not essentially religious—in labor unions, in chambers of commerce, in business firms, and in sports."[92] The case of higher education was distinctive and important in this regard since, unlike those other venues, it stood uniquely at the intersection of society and religion, secular goals and sacred pursuits, worldly success and heavenly rewards. Student journalists at Boston College and Holy Cross, though lacking the theological acumen and vocabulary of some of their clerical elders, keenly understood what was at stake. Finding themselves pulled between the poles of separatism and rapprochement, rather than adopting an either/or stance on higher education, they began to frame a both/and response—one in which a separate Catholic education served the nation's broader social goals.

Eliot's public disparagement of Jesuit education and the Law School's decision to remove Boston College and Holy Cross from the Law School's select list of colleges ineluctably drew Catholic students to an issue at the heart of the Americanism controversy; namely, Protestants' fundamental disposition toward Catholics. Given that they, as college students, were headed toward professional education and work, it was an important question for students to consider. But there was no consensus among them. Almost entirely from Irish Catholic households in New England, they were, like religious conservatives, sensitive to discrimination. Like the alumni, they quickly saw in the situation with Harvard the hand of intolerance. "It is impossible not to feel strongly at the evidence of such unfair discrimination," confessed a contributor to the *Stylus*.[93] Eliot was a misguided pedagogue bent on exercising his influence in a manner detrimental to the cause of Catholic higher education, spurred by the "enviable progress made in the past by the graduates of Catholic colleges . . . to check, if possible, the further advance of our colleges and universities." In reporting on Dr. Barnes's inflammatory speech impugning Eliot, the editors of the *Stylus* concluded that "in the light of events we do not hesitate to say that his vigorous language was entirely justifiable."[94]

Yet the students could not dismiss the entire Protestant population in this manner. On the one hand, editors of the *Holy Cross Purple* reported on a speech at Yale that was peppered with anti-Catholic sentiment— further proof, they claimed, that nonsectarianism was a guise for anti-Catholicism in higher education. Yet on the other hand they knew of honorable Protestants. Moreover, for a large number of Boston College and Holy Cross students, those Protestants would soon be their classmates and instructors in various professional schools. "Since reading . . . Dr. Barnes' effective reply to the now widely known President of Harvard," wrote a one-time Holy Cross student studying at Yale Law School, "I have been even more observing while among the students and professors and have tried to find any sign of bigotry, so noticeable elsewhere"; but, he said, he searched in vain. The men of Yale were "too broad-minded," with "too keen a sense of gentlemanly character to be bigots." Rather than undermining a Catholic's commitment to his faith, Yale actually "broadens his mind and strengthens his belief in the Catholic faith."

Yale faculty, he claimed, "care but little for a student who is not man enough to stand by his religion and openly practice and profess it." Yale was, therefore, "more American, more cosmopolitan and more endearing to her students" than other universities—"Harvard, in particular."[95]

Unlike the liberals of the day, with their highly optimistic views about society, the students were less sanguine about the world. In a defensive mode, it was understandably easier for them to focus on the spiritual dangers of non-Catholic colleges than religious opportunities for evangelization therein. Young men, claimed one editorialist, had to make their way in a world that would not "adjust itself to the needs of their souls," a spiritual reality requiring vigilance on the part of young Catholics. It was, he claimed, "an unwise and unholy thing to thrust ourselves . . . into temptations even for great advantages of a wholly worldly character." Unfortunately there were large numbers of Catholics who did precisely that, including the "unambitious sons of socially ambitious parents" whom the "laxity and irreligion of a large university will most effect." In making their case for separatism on the grounds of spiritual risk, the Boston College editorial staff invoked LeBaron R. Briggs, the dean of Harvard College, who acknowledged in an article in the *Atlantic Monthly*, "Fathers, Mothers, and Freshman," that "beyond what is spent for the chapel" and "the maintenance of decent order, there can be very little visible outlay" relative to the protection and development a student's character.[96]

Students followed their elders' lead with claims that the Catholic college offered precisely what the non-Catholic college did not: a *true* education rooted in religion. "The Catholic college cannot make mad experiments with youth," wrote a student journalist, his words echoing those of Brosnahan in "President Eliot and Jesuit Colleges." "It is responsible to God, and not to a changing age and to the flickerings of a mad electivism for the souls of youth."[97] While Jesuit education kept its eyes firmly set on the religious prize, other systems of education had lost sight of fundamental truths, mistaking innovation for discovery, change for progress, knowledge for wisdom.

In making a case for educational separatism based on the religious distinctiveness of Catholic higher education, students recognized a vulnerable point in their argumentation. They were open to charges that their separate, religiously oriented education left them unfit for the manly work of the world. The Catholic college could be construed as a "petite seminaire," whose "spirit represents aloofness from the practical problems of the day," where "students are prepared to meet the demands of the cloister only, and not of the world."[98] The feminization of religion during the second half of the nineteenth century rendered religious men open to allegations that they, like women, were better suited to private spheres of influence—like the cloister—than the public worlds of modern men.[99] Thus the students rejoined. "We are essentially placed in a religious atmosphere," wrote a Boston College student in 1899, "but this does not mean that we are made pious idiots." They were, he argued, surrounded by instructors who served as role models of "noble Christian manhood." In a Catholic college, with its classical curriculum and strict discipline, where "self-reliance, honor, conscience, responsibility" were emphasized, "boyishness" naturally gave way to "manliness."[100]

Students smoothed over the sharper edges of conservatism with liberal strains by linking their education with the needs and temper of modern America. They did not take up the evangelical goal of mass conversions, nor did they aspire to a Catholic America. But they did argue that Catholic higher education was suited to the times and fitted to America; like liberals who claimed that Catholicism had vital spiritual resources to offer America, Boston College and Holy Cross students argued that Catholic colleges had a critical role to play in society. Given the connections developing between higher education and the world of work, students argued that Catholic education, as a *true* education, offset some of the spiritually corrosive culture of aspiration taking root in the academy.[101] Their colleges did not make "undue concessions . . . to the 'American point of view,'" which the author quickly noted was "not American at all, but only the materialist point of view of a materialistic age." Catholic higher education did not stymie progress; it recognized true progress. Even as Catholic colleges kept young men "abreast of the last fleck of foam that the wave of progress has tossed upward," it taught students that "true conservatism is simply a method of progress." This was, the Boston College student claimed, the "function of the Catholic college, especially in a democracy."[102]

And the Jesuits themselves? Strikingly absent during the course of the Law School controversy and in their reactions to Catholic patronage of non-Catholic colleges was an apologia for Jesuit higher education in Protestant America. During this critical period in American educational history, in which reformers argued successfully for transformative changes in higher education based on the needs of a modern nation, the Jesuits produced no statement linking the classical course of studies offered in their colleges with the needs of America. Their students, whose futures necessarily entailed greater interaction with Protestant society, began articulating a rationale for Jesuit education in which separatism served the cause of engagement; armed with the resources garnered through their Jesuit education, they would bring to American society the beneficent influence of the Catholic faith. But the Jesuits merely responded to the exigencies at hand with a defense of classical education as offered in the Jesuit colleges. In "President Eliot and Jesuit Colleges," his great statement on Jesuit education, Brosnahan defended classical education's value in terms of its potential to develop mental culture, not on its responsiveness to the needs of the nation. In point of fact, while he offered a convincing critique of the elective system advocated by Eliot, Brosnahan offered no alternative solution to the curricular conundrum of the day—namely, the vast expansion of knowledge and "useful" courses vying for inclusion in the curriculum. For Brosnahan it was sufficient that education be sound; the issue of relevance to place—and to time—went unaddressed.

The Jesuits' failure to explicitly connect Jesuit higher education with the wants of the nation was symptomatic of the conservative spirit within the Society that precluded support for the task of adapting their educational enterprise to America. Throughout the course of the Americanism controversy, Jesuits repeatedly took a conservative stance. Walter Elliott, the well-known liberal Paulist cleric, considered the American Jesuits "fine men, full of peace and good will," whom he counted "among our warmest friends." Yet on issue after issue throughout the contentious Americanism controversy, the Jesuits, nationally and internationally, sided with the conservatives.[103] Jesuits involved in the popular Catholic summer-school program, for example, saw to it that those leaning toward modern, liberal ideas were kept off the roster of speakers. In another instance, when a faculty member from Catholic University published a pamphlet arguing that the state also had a right to educate children, a Jesuit instructor at Woodstock, René I. Holaind, issued a rebuttal, *The Parent First*, in which he reiterated the traditional Catholic teaching that the parents and the church have the right to educate children.[104]

Rather than craft a positive relationship between Jesuit education and the needs of the Catholic community in the United States, the Jesuits became critics not only of modern education as offered at Eliot's Harvard but of Catholic patronage of non-Catholic schools. To many Jesuits, modern education was rife with pedagogical debacles and intellectual chaos. Faddishness, materialism, and experimentalism had supplanted sound educational tradition. Other Jesuits expressed dismay over the Catholic populace itself, whose patronage of non-Catholic institutions bespoke misplaced values. Something must be "wrong with the spiritual temper of a Catholic home or a Catholic community," claimed Jesuit John Poland, "when its well-to-do young men" opt for "Yale, or Harvard, or Cornell" instead of "the Catholic University, or South Bend, or Georgetown."[105]

In the turn-of-the-century campaign for the soul (and matriculation) of the Catholic collegian, there were no clear-cut winners. The liberal vision of a Catholic America and a church renewed quickly evaporated in the wake of *Testem Benevolentiae*. Catholic students continued to attend non-Catholic colleges, but how, and the degree to which, their interactions with Protestants in the halls of academia affected Protestant-Catholic relations is difficult to ascertain. It certainly helped Catholics to improve their socioeconomic standing, but it resulted in no large-scale conversions to Catholicism among their Protestant classmates. In other words, the vital current ran toward Protestant America, not the Church of Rome.

More immediately, in the mid-1890s the liberals began to lose ground in what would evolve and become known as the Americanism controversy. Keane, the academic goodwill ambassador, was an early casualty. The Catholic University of America was rife with conflicts during its early years, with its officers and faculty embroiled in fights over the operation of the university and various aspects of the Americanism controversy. In 1896, conservatives scored a significant coup when, as the result of their politicking, the pope removed Keane as rector. Keane humbly acceded to the pope's decision. Only in 1900, when appointed bishop of Dubuque, did Keane return to a leadership role in the American Catholic Church.[106]

Leo XIII's 1899 condemnation of Americanism in *Testem Benevolentiae* effectively undermined the liberal agenda. While conservatives such as McQuaid heartily thanked the pontiff for his efforts to ensure orthodoxy, Keane and his liberal colleagues did what was expected of bishops: they thanked the pope and submitted to his teaching on the subject. Like other liberals, Keane assured the pope that the type of Americanism the pontiff found unacceptable was, as a later writer described it, a "phantom" heresy. Liberals' disavowal of theologically aberrant Americanism angered conservatives, who considered the liberals' response disingenuous at best. McQuaid complained from the pulpit: "It is very unbecoming to treat with flippancy an encyclical of the Pope, and insinuate that it was uncalled for, that no such errors infected the American church, and that much ado was made about nothing." Arguing that Americanism was indeed a very real heresy, McQuaid offered up four pieces of evidence, including Catholic participation in the World's Parliament of Religions (an "unholy alliance with enemies of the true church"), weak support for Catholic schools among liberals, and Catholic involvement in secret societies. Within a few months of the promulgation of *Testem Benevolentiae* and the first meeting of the ACCUS, McQuaid singled out Keane, denigrating his liberal engagement with non-Catholic higher education:

> The fourth exhibition of advanced Catholic Americanism came before the American public when a Catholic ecclesiastic took his stand before [a] non-Catholic university in his clerical robes to advertise to the community the new born liberalism of the Catholic church in entering into the halls and chapels of non-Catholic universities. It was an advertisement well worth paying for, as it was an encouragement to Catholic parents to send their sons to universities of such liberal tendencies that they were glad to rank among their alumni the veriest papists in the land. It was an innovation that effected the whole eccelestical [*sic*] body, yet the leaders in these exceptional proceedings never condescended to take counsel except from their superior wisdom.
>
> To-day, the rector of the Catholic University of America at Washington [Conaty] came to explain the paucity of members in his institution. He and many presidents of Catholic colleges and universities are discussing how to withdraw young men from non-Catholic universities and win them to their own. I did not notice in their deliberations, as published, that any one put his finger on the sore spot.
>
> This misfortune for the Catholic church when next a Baltimore council meets will have to be studied, and the problem for its solution will have to be met.[107]

Those arguing that Catholics should not attend non-Catholic colleges also failed to realize their objectives. While promulgation of *Testem Benevolentiae* affected the collapse of the liberal platform, conservatives and the Catholic college men proved largely ineffectual in bolstering Catholic patronage of Catholic colleges. Warnings spelling out the spiritual dangers of non-Catholic higher education—in sermons, editorials, advice literature, and fiction—went unheeded; claims for the academic and religious superiority of Catholic colleges failed to convince. Catholic students continued to turn to non-Catholic colleges and universities in ever greater numbers. Thus for conservatives and the Catholic college men, large numbers of Catholic students remained academically out of place in modern, Protestant America. Their displacement left many Catholic colleges underenrolled, with some struggling to survive.

Writing of the Jesuits of the sixteenth century, historian John O'Malley pointed out that "whatever authority they enjoyed derived from their own ability to persuade others and to present to their 'clientele' options more attractive than the alternatives."[108] Their finely honed skills of persuasion, which served the Jesuits so well throughout the world and through the centuries, faltered in turn-of-the-century America. Much of their traditional constituency abandoned them in favor of Protestant and secular academic alternatives, leaving some Jesuits pondering the very future of Jesuit higher education in the United States. According to one account, in 1907 Conway found "only 650 Collegians, or at the outmost, 700, in all the Jesuit Colleges of the New-York-Maryland [sic] Province, that is to say, from the Canadian line down to Alabama." He was led to ask, "Can we stem the tide? Can we stand up against fate?"[109]

The future of Jesuit higher education clearly rested on the Jesuits' willingness and ability to adapt to the circumstances they encountered in Protestant America in the age of the university. It would require finding ways to refit the *Ratio Studiorum* and the culture of their institutions in order to make them attractive to American Catholics and legitimate in the eyes of other American academics. In itself, this adaptation to place was an immense challenge. But rising to the occasion would prove difficult in light of Rome's increasingly strident campaign against modernity, their own general conservatism, and their superior general's suspicions about America.

III
AMONG JESUITS

CHAPTER FIVE

Novus Ordo Academicus *and the Travails of Adapting*

> Is it possible that men who . . .
> had such "a clear insight into the
> needs of their time" do not adapt
> their system to the needs of our
> age? Or is their system not capa-
> ble of being suited to modern
> times?
>
> —Robert Schwickerath, S.J., 1903

Having made a historic and unprecedented decision to devote their energies to the work of educating youth, Ignatius of Loyola and the Jesuits
of the sixteenth century developed an educational strategy with which
subsequent generations of Jesuits conquered the world academically.
Armed with the *Ratio Studiorum* and a directive in the *Constitutions* of
the Society to adapt their educational practices to the times, places, and
persons they encountered, the sons of Loyola succeeded on a grand
scale. They sprinkled the globe with hundreds of schools, colleges, and
seminaries and in them provided a classical education for the sons of
commoners and the elite, scholars-in-the-making, royalty, and future
princes of the church. Widely emulated by those who recognized the
efficacy of their approach to education, they thus exercised influence in
the field of education well beyond the scope of their own work. But as
noted, they were also widely criticized and often subjected to vitriolic attacks. In the annals of religious history, they appear with the greatest of
regularity at the center of controversy. Indeed, as one historian wryly

noted, "turmoil has been so chronic throughout the history of the Jesuits that getting into trouble, both in and outside the church, might be interpreted as a latent function of the order."[1]

At the turn of the century, the Jesuits working in colleges in the United States were in deep turmoil. The preceding four chapters have, through an examination of the Jesuits' troubles with Harvard and patterns of Catholic matriculation, taken up the great challenges that confronted the Jesuits as the age of the college gave way to the age of the university and a new academic order emerged. First was the challenge of *time*. In the second half of the nineteenth century, being timely, modern, and progressive became compelling cultural ideals, a change with profound implications for higher education, which had, for six centuries, privileged the wisdom and ways of past generations. The second great challenge faced by the Jesuits was that of *persons*. Near the turn of the century, the Jesuits and other Catholic educators discovered that most Catholic collegians were drifting away from Catholic colleges and into Protestant institutions more responsive to their middle-class aspirations and sensibilities. The third challenge was that of *place*. In a church struggling to define an appropriate relationship with Protestant America, those concerned with the higher education of Catholics wrestled with the question of where Catholics should study and whether a separate education obtained under Catholic auspices made students unfit for the work of the world. The confluence of these three significant challenges shook Jesuit and other Catholic educators; the arrival of a new academic order could no longer be ignored.

"Looking back," wrote historian Laurence Veysey, "it could be seen that the decade of the nineties witnessed the firm development of the American academic model in almost every crucial respect." Jesuit James Fagan lived in those times; as a contemporary he did not have the historical luxury of looking back, but he sensed the emergence of the new academic order that Veysey would chronicle more than sixty years later. "Just at this moment we are at the parting of the ways. In spite of all the efforts of educators and of educational associations," wrote Fagan in 1901, "education . . . is in a fluid state still; but it is like a solution which has passed the point of saturation. A slight jar, and, lo! a crystallized mass, a system definitely and finally shapped [*sic*] and imposed." Concerned about what this meant for Catholic higher education, he asked, "Have we Catholics nothing to fear from such a consummation?"[2]

In their first great encounter with the new academic order, the Harvard Law School controversy, the Jesuits learned precisely what they had to fear: institutional tarnish and marginalization. Of course, the implications of the academic revolution that transformed American higher education would have and indeed did become clear to the Jesuits and other Catholic educators in other critical ways, but it was through the battle with Eliot and Harvard, more than anything else, that the Jesuits came to understand the challenges and high stakes inherent in the emergence of a new academic order. The Law School's refusal to admit Jesuit college graduates as regular students and Eliot's disparaging remarks about Jesuit education in the *Atlantic Monthly* became a call to arms for J. Havens Richards, Timothy Brosnahan, W. G. Read Mullan, and their supporters. But more importantly, the Law School controversy was a wake-up call for the Jesuits, making all too apparent the newly realized power of the universities in setting standards for colleges and defining the mores of the academy.

Were it not for the large numbers of Catholic students flocking toward Harvard and other non-Catholic institutions, Eliot's comments and the Law School's admissions policy would have been little more than another example of sectarian bickering. If Catholic colleges had been fully subscribed, if they had been bustling with students satisfied with a course of study built largely around the study of the ancients, the Jesuits could have suffered Harvard's insult and savored Brosnahan's rhetorical success in "President Eliot and Jesuit Colleges." After all, the Jesuits thrived on criticism. But Harvard's influence was both institutional and social; it was setting standards and drawing Catholic students. As one Jesuit described it, "there is a strong current towards Harvard, which seems to sweep nearly everything before it."[3] Harvard had what the Catholic colleges largely lacked and Catholic students wanted: a broad range of studies, professional education, prestigious academic credentials, popular student culture, and occasions for social networking. Harvard and the other universities, as well as a number of Protestant colleges, were far more responsive to the social functions of higher education in a distended, class-conscious society than were the Jesuit colleges.

In the public debate, three Jesuit presidents asked the same thing of Eliot: academic vindication of the Jesuit colleges through their inclusion on the Law School's select list of colleges. Among themselves, the Jesuits in the United States and Rome asked something quite different: how should they respond to a new academic order and paltry enrollments in their colleges? Should they adapt the *Ratio Studiorum* and emulate the Protestant colleges and universities in order to make them more respectable and attractive? Extensive correspondence among superiors, provincials, rectors, consultors, and other Jesuits during the two decades spanning the turn of the century documents the Jesuits' in-house discussions about Eliot and Harvard and their wrenching struggles to come to terms with new academic realities. During this period of storm and stress,[4] their correspondence gives evidence of confusion, differences of opinion, and even anguish about how to proceed. It also reveals a *mentalité*—a collective mental framework that shaped their responses to fin-de-siècle exigencies. Unsurprisingly conservative, this mentalité evinced an affinity for the past and for tradition, skepticism about innovation and "novelty" (a word used frequently and with disdain), and a pronounced contempt for all things modern. This collective mindset was oppositional vis-à-vis the world and as such marked a departure from the Ignatian approach to the world. Ignatius, of course, understood opposition; toward the end of his life, as the Society was ineluctably drawn into the heat of the Reformation, enemies abounded and came to be understood as part of the burden and even to be an ironic measure of its success in fulfilling their mission. But separated by three centuries, the world-affirming spirit of Ignatius had been replaced in his successors (especially among those in leadership positions) with a world-suspicious outlook that saw the modern world as radically disordered by Protestantism and its legacy.

In terms of intensity, this conservative, oppositional mentalité was distributed unevenly within the Society and thus became instrumental in sparking disagreements about the ways they should respond to the new academic order. It was most intense and consistent in Rome, where the leadership of the Society played an integral role in the church's campaign against modernity that culminated with the promulgation of Pius X's *Pascendi Dominici Gregis* (1907), a broad condemnation of modern politics and intellectual life. The same conservative, oppositional outlook was present among the Jesuits working in the United States, although generally less intensely and certainly less consistently. Although Jesuits regularly sided with the conservatives during the Americanism controversy, and though they advanced no compelling public defense of the *Ratio Studiorum* relative to modern America, a number of Jesuits privately expressed the need for adaptation to new realities facing them. Thus disagreements arose, frequently and often vigorously, between European-based and American-based Jesuits, and among the Jesuits in the United States, about how they should adapt their educational strategies to the times, places, and persons they encountered in modern, Protestant America.

This chapter takes up what Martin E. Marty described as the important historiographic project of "fusing *l'histoire des mentalités* to narrative lines"—in this instance, exploring how the Jesuits' mental framework shaped their responses to Eliot and Harvard and, more broadly, the fruits of the academic revolution. Some Jesuits were inclined to ignore new, pressing academic conditions, but this was the generation of Jesuits forced into the unavoidable work of, as Philip Gleason put it, "contending with modernity."[5] The necessity of reform became patently and often painfully clear as the twentieth century opened. But could the Jesuits reform their colleges so as to attract students and satisfy large universities and the state without abandoning the *Ratio Studiorum* and sacrificing their religious principles? Could they adapt to the new academic order without appropriating aberrant, modern ideals spawned by the Protestant-dominated university movement? These were the fundamental issues with which the Jesuits struggled for more than two full decades in the wake of the academic revolution in Protestant America.

By the early 1890s, the revolution that fundamentally reshaped American higher education was coming to fruition. The modern research university, unknown just a few decades earlier, now sat at the apex of the American educational system, where it was beginning to assert its influence over the wider academic order. Greater numbers of young men and women were going to college. But in the early 1890s, most Jesuits failed to grasp the significance of the academic revolution. Though clearly aware of the university movement, they had yet to recognize its implications for their colleges. There certainly was no sense of crisis. The rectors of American Jesuit colleges, like college presidents everywhere, busied themselves with the everyday work of running colleges, tending to enrollments and finance, space needs and buildings, faculty and curriculum. On one broad front there was reason for general satisfaction: enrollments at the Jesuit colleges were holding steady or, more often, were on the increase. *Woodstock Letters* reported an increase of 128 in the enrollment in the colleges in the Maryland–New York Province between 1888–89 and 1889–90; between 1890–91 and 1891–92, enrollment rose by a satisfying 233.[6]

Enrollment figures fostered a false sense of confidence in at least one Jesuit writer. In a celebratory article, "About Teaching" (published in *Woodstock Letters* in 1892), the writer created two fictional Jesuit characters, Philosopher and Theologian, who are spurred by recently published statistics about increased enrollment in their colleges into a discussion about pedagogy. To Philosopher's inability to explain the "sudden appreciation of our colleges and of our system, which the large increase certainly bespeaks," Theologian replies: "The reason is not far to seek. Our system must always prevail in as much as it is a system, but chiefly because it is a perfect system. Our success may for a time be slow, but under ordinary circumstances doubtful never." Theologian further explains that "the *Ratio* administrated by zealous and loyal Jesuits will always win, even . . . against mere monied institutions and eclectic systems." After the Jesuits "have perfected a few details, our colleges will occupy their proper position—they will be models, which even Protestant Universities will not be ashamed to imitate." While Philosopher acknowledges that the "spirit of reform is strong within me," Theologian takes a conservative stand, arguing that through steadfastness to "our system which has been so eminently successful during three centuries, we shall in the end attract more students than by trimming our sails to every popular breeze." He granted that the "temptation to yield to the spirit of the times is very enticing," but to do so would constitute a betrayal of the "lofty thoughts of our fathers."[7]

Signs of an impending crisis for the Jesuits began to surface in the mid-1890s. The brash confidence of Philosopher and Theologian disappeared in short order. More prescient than many of his colleagues, J. Havens Richards was among the first to appreciate the significance of the university movement. As early as 1890 he asked the provincial to consider providing "young Fathers opportunities for acquiring scholarship in special branches."[8] Although his protests to Eliot had secured a place for Georgetown, Boston College, and Holy Cross on the Law School's list of colleges, Richards was not lulled into complacency. Late in 1893 he wrote to Rudolph Meyer (1841–1912), who having served as provincial of the Missouri Province and rector of Saint Louis University in the 1880s had become a key assistant to Superior General Luis Martín in Rome in 1892.[9] In arguing for the wisdom of including a few modern subjects in the curriculum ("Latin is good, but it is not *everything* at the present day"), Richards explained to Meyer by way of illustration how Eliot justified the absence of the Jesuit colleges on the Law School's list on the "ground chiefly that their studies were on lines so different from those of 'Protestant and nondenominational institutions' as not to be equivalent." For Richards, the episode illustrated "what a battle we have to fight."[10]

By the late 1890s, the equanimity found among many Jesuits just a few years earlier had dissolved. Confusion set in. As far as Richards was concerned, "the state of Catholic Collegiate education in the United States is almost chaotic."[11] The words *battle, controversy,* and *crisis* appeared with increased frequency, especially when the subject of Harvard arose. Presenting a united front and admitting no weakness in Jesuit education in public, behind the scenes there was neither unity nor consensus about the cause of their troubles and how to proceed. "Consternation" about the situation with Harvard was "considerable," wrote Provincial Edward Purbrick.[12]

According to Purbrick, the consternation ran in a number of different directions among the Jesuits; the troubles with the nation's foremost institution of education represented a whole host of different problems. In a lengthy letter to Martín in February 1900, Purbrick explained how a number of Jesuits wrote off the controversy as yet one more example of "sectarian bigotry."[13] Still others placed some of the blame on their students: "Our boys who have been to Harvard have not been satisfactory as students & have damaged themselves by drink—in plain English our students 'are low Irish.'" (Purbrick's words echoed a report received from Holy Cross President John Lehy—a report that Purbrick passed on to Martín in an earlier letter—that students accustomed to "strict surveillance" during their years at Holy Cross "are apt to run wild when they find themselves in the freedom of Harvard & are apt especially to indulge in the fatal weakness of men of Irish extraction for whiskey.")[14]

Other Jesuits' consternation derived from more substantive academic concerns. The Law School controversy awakened a number of them to the newly realized power of the universities and increased involvement of the state in educational affairs. Purbrick told Martín that in itself the Law School controversy warranted "serious consideration & debate," but so, too, did the "cognate difficulty beginning to loom large," in particular a "combination of large non-Catholic Universities with the authority of many of the States." The desired end, Purbrick claimed, was to "bring all secondary education under the full control of the State & so kill the small colleges for the glory & advantage of the large Universities or as men phrase it for the unification & progress of education as a public interest."[15]

Purbrick's concern over centralization was not ungrounded. In an age of large corporations, trusts, and monopolies, education was subject to the same centralizing tendencies. Progressive educational reformers, a cohort top-heavy with university presidents such as Eliot, looked to improve education at large by rationalizing and bringing order to what they perceived as a chaotic, inefficient nonsystem of education. An unregulated and largely local affair, education in the late-nineteenth century seemed woefully inadequate to meet the needs of a growing and increasingly urban population in an industrial age. To reform the nation's educational system, in the latter part of the nineteenth century numerous associations sprang up seeking improvement through standardization. In 1893 the Committee of Ten, under the leadership of Charles Eliot, issued its influential report to the National Educational Association on the relationship between the high school curriculum and admission to college. Accrediting bodies interested in entrance requirements were formed, among them the New England Association of Colleges and Preparatory Schools (1885), the North Central Association of Colleges and Secondary Schools (1895), and the Middle States Association (1887). The College Entrance Examination Board was established in 1901.[16] By the mid-1890s, the New York State Board of Regents had decided that four years of high school was to precede admission to college. Harvard did its part, insisting that those admitted to its Law School hold bachelor's degrees from reputable institutions.

The growing power of the universities and the state throughout the academic order alarmed a number of Jesuits and other Catholic educators who feared for the autonomy and even the survival of Catholic education. Fagan closely followed the issue of educational legislation relative to private education. "Some fifteen years ago the government exercised no or merely nominal authority over private schools," he wrote to Martín in 1902, but "now . . . officials regard nothing as more established than to claim for themselves complete power over education."[17] Msgr. Conaty shared his concerns. Speaking on "The Catholic College in the Twentieth Century" at the 1901 ACCUS meeting, the Jesuit-educated Conaty deemed it a "critical period" for Catholic colleges in light of the "trend . . . toward national unification and national education." He bolstered his argument with a report of an assertion by a "prominent educator" that the "past century has witnessed the organization of system in education, and that the State and State alone has been the controlling influence in educaiton; adding that, before this century the Church controlled it." The "mighty machine of secularized education," claimed Conaty, was "threatening to destroy all effort on the part of the individual or the Church in the fields of educational endeavor."[18] More immediately, a number of Jesuits and their supporters concluded through the course of the Law School controversy that Eliot was set on bringing all education in New England under his control. Dr. Francis Barnes, in a widely reported speech before the Holy Cross Alumni Association in which he called Eliot a "dogmatizing bigot," derogated what he took as Eliot's educational aspirations. "This is one of the men," complained Barnes, "who aspire to form a trust which will control the education of American youth."[19]

Given the international scope of the Society of Jesus and the vicissitudes of church-sponsored education in Europe during the nineteenth century, the Jesuits had particular reason for concern about government involvement in education. The state did indeed increase its role in U.S. higher education during the late-nineteenth and twentieth centuries, but not to the degree that Conaty and others feared; relative autonomy, localism, and the free market continued to shape higher education in ways ensuring significant institutional heterogeneity. In 1900, however, the Jesuits could not foresee the future and were all too aware of the toll that state intervention had taken on their educational enterprise in Europe. "Europe is driving us out," wrote Thomas Gannon, the Maryland–New York provincial, in 1903, "or so hampering us that the full work and proper development of our Society are there impossible." Ever the student of government, Fagan regularly reminded his correspondents, readers, and listeners of the dangers of government interference. The "recent happenings in France," for example, where Catholic clergy had been forced from their work in education, were a "sharp lesson" for Catholic educators in America.[20]

An encounter with the New York State Board of Regents had already taught the Jesuits a sharp lesson.[21] The regents of New York were entrusted with considerable powers: in addition to their responsibilities as board members of the State University of New York, they were charged with chartering and inspecting schools, academies, and colleges, setting standards for instruction and discipline, and regulating professional education, which included setting admission requirements. "How do we like the system?" a Catholic asked rhetorically in 1892: "Greatly," he replied. For in cooperating with the board of regents Catholics experienced no discrimination; to the contrary, he claimed, it provided occasion to disabuse Protestants of erroneous notions about Catholic education, even as it bolstered Catholic confidence in their own schools.[22] But the Jesuit experience with the board of regents was not so benign. Unlike their troubles with Harvard, their difficulties with the regents did not become a cause célèbre; moreover, it resolved in their favor. But the Jesuits often linked the two as cases demonstrating the challenges and perils of the new academic order.

In 1895 the Jesuits discovered that graduates of Fordham and Saint Francis Xavier in New York City were no longer admitted to law schools on the same footing as they once had been. They also learned that a student who had completed one year of the college course at Georgetown had been refused admission to Columbia Medical School even though admission to medical school in New York required but four years of high school. Once again, J. Havens Richards took up the cause, sending a long letter to the Regents Office describing the Jesuit course of studies in detail. The Regents Office responded by sending two of their examiners to Fordham and Saint Francis Xavier. The examiners were quite impressed, and the Jesuit schools were restored to the academic status they once enjoyed. For Richards, the episode demonstrated "the rapid growth of conditions altogether different from those under which our colleges have thus far existed." Had any of his fellow Jesuits any doubt that the conditions they faced were substantially altered and threatening, he alerted them to the fact that the "president of one of the largest and most widely known universities in New England has not hesitated to urge against us in the public prints the want of equivalence of our courses with theirs, and this in a tone plainly indicating that by want of equivalence he understands inferiority."[23]

There was yet another cause of consternation among the Jesuits stirred up by the Law School controversy. Rather than looking beyond their own walls—at prejudiced Protestants, tippling students, aggressive universities, and an intrusive state—some Jesuits turned their attention within, laying a good portion of the blame for their troubles with Harvard at their own feet. Even as Brosnahan and Mullan wholeheartedly defended their course of studies in public, among themselves a number of Jesuits criticized its quality. Criticism among Jesuits about their work in the classroom was nothing new, but it increased as the troubles with Harvard intensified, even at Boston College. The house diarist for 1898–99 noted that some of the Jesuits at Boston College ("neither few in number nor particularly unfamiliar with the views which pertain to our colleges") spoke of "negligence" on the part of "many of our rectors and prefects of studies" who manifest laxity in "the admission of students, their promotions at the end of the year, and particularly with regard to the awarding of grades." Moving then from description to prescription, the diarist set forth a number of resolutions and challenges. It was, he argued, "incumbent" that the general and provincials seek a "remedy." In according with the "spirit of the Society," the Jesuits should be "considerate and paternal, and even merciful" with students, but neither "tears nor gifts ought to entice us to reward lazy students who are undeserving." Among the rectors and prefects of studies there should be "unity" and a "clear and well-defined method of procedure and organization of studies." All colleges should "conform," lest any given college, through poor leadership, sully its "reputation" and, by extension, cause "irreparable damage to our other schools."[24]

As the exigencies of a new academic order became apparent and the extent of Catholic patronage of non-Catholic institutions became clear to the Jesuits, the issue of adaptation ineluctably arose. As Richards put it, how should they respond to "conditions altogether different from those under which our colleges have thus far existed"? To Richards, the "practical inference" was clear: "we must be on the alert to adjust our colleges to the altered circumstances of the times."[25] In like vein, the Jesuits' eminent alumnus Conaty exhorted the Jesuits and other Catholic educators to adapt to modern conditions. In his address "On the Teacher," delivered at the 1900 ACCUS meeting, he invoked the memory of "college teachers of the past," a corps of "self-sacrificing, simple-minded, scholarly men who trained whole generations without the advantages of modern methods, or the opportunities of university preparation," who "laid the foundations of our recent successes." As "men for the times in which they lived," these teachers of old would be, Conaty claimed, the "first to recognize the new conditions" facing Catholic higher education as the twentieth century opened and the necessity of adapting "along all approved modern lines, in order to meet the just demands of a Catholic people constantly progressing in comfort and culture."[26]

But the Jesuits were not of one mind on the issue of adapting. Ignatius of Loyola had enjoined his brother Jesuits to adapt as necessary their educational practices to the times, places, and persons they encountered. Three centuries later, the sons of Loyola in America were divided over the issue of adapting the *Ratio Studiorum* and their traditional ways to the conditions encountered in the wake of the academic revolution that had given rise to the age of the university.

After 1900, especially in the wake of the controversy with Harvard and publication of surveys about Catholic patronage of non-Catholic schools, Catholic educators could no longer ignore modern educational realities. Only in public, in essays, editorials, and speeches, did the Jesuits and their supporters hold forth unequivocally for the *Ratio Studiorum* as a perfect system of education and its ultimate vindication in an age seemingly gone mad for fads and experiments. In private, among themselves, they stewed over modern education and its implications for the future of the *Ratio*. Some among them counseled resistance, rather than adaptation. "We must resist the tendency to fads, novelties, displays, showy things etc.," concluded a committee on studies of the Missouri Province.[27] In 1898, Purbrick complained, "In this country everything is in such a state of flux, fads are taken up and imposed for a time, found to be failures & exchanged for a new fad & so on," a process that "makes it extremely difficult to devise remedies for real or supposed deficiencies." At the 1902 ACCUS meeting, Jesuit John Poland railed against the modern academic order. "And we must plunge ourselves into this confusion, and strive to keep up with these ever varying conditions. Why?" he queried. The Society's "traditional methods, *when properly carried out*," were not to blame, for they prepared students well for professional studies. The fault lay with "a few Eastern universities, in which faddery is rampant," that "object to our courses and make a difficulty about admitting our graduates on the testimony of their diplomas."[28]

By early in the twentieth century, most Jesuits came to recognize that they could neither wholly resist nor withdraw from the modern educational world, continuing on as if nothing had changed. Though Poland facilely launched into diatribes directed at modern educators and education, he knew, as did a number of others, that it would be unwise to "go to extremes in our conservatism." Even as he and others railed against the powerful Eastern universities with their unbridled enthusiasm for innovation, he admitted that "we have to take into consideration the circumstances of time and place; we have to make some concessions to the spirit of the age in order that we may be able to do good." Fagan reached the same conclusion: "Unless we embrace in one way or another innovations . . . I fear that shortly we . . . will be finished."[29] Fagan also counseled judicious adaptation, acknowledging difficulties.

> But we Catholics are conservative. We are slow to change, slow oftentimes to realize that changes are demanded of us. All around us is an educational ferment, which we for the most part calmly disregard or view with languid interest. Before it subsides, if we are not watchful, on one pretext or another—on the score, for instance, of lack of modernity (sit venia verbo) or on the charge that we are not alive to the educational needs of the hour, or that we lack efficiency or fail to prove our efficiency—our privileges may be withdrawn.[30]

Thus, as Brosnahan and Mullan publicly defended the quality and integrity of Jesuit education, an inchoate reform agenda surfaced. Cautiously and often reluctantly, the Jesuits considered curricular and extracurricular changes that would better fit Jesuit education to the American system and attract more students to their colleges. For some implementing reform was but an expression of compliance, a begrudging acknowledgement that they were no longer free to set their own autonomous academic path. For others, the academic revolution occasioned deep consideration about education, the American people, and what a well-adapted program of education would entail in modern times. In other words, conservatism had not completely overshadowed the Jesuits' historic commitment to adapt to time, place, and person.

The work of reform was difficult and contentious. Those Jesuits proposing reforms met resistance; every reform had vocal critics. Reform-minded Jesuits repeatedly made a case for change based on the character of American students and conditions in America. A cause for dissension among Jesuits based in the United States, the case for reform was particularly difficult to make to Jesuit officials in Rome, especially Martín. Deeply conservative, Martín could see in America and American education the deleterious influence of Protestantism, and thus in adapting to America, the Jesuits incurred the unacceptable risk of contamination by Protestant, liberal, and modern ideas.

Born in 1846 into a prominent Spanish family, Luis Martín Garcia entered the Society of Jesus in 1864 and was ordained twelve years later. He knew firsthand the political tumult ravaging Europe and the effects upon the Society of Jesus. In 1868 he and his fellow Jesuits were forced to flee Spain, traveling in disguise, only to return a short time later when France expelled the Jesuits and Spain adopted a more lenient stance. He subsequently proved an able provincial for Castile, and in 1892 was elected the twenty-fourth superior general of the Society of Jesus. Headquartered in Rome, he quickly became a valued confidant for Leo XIII and Pius X (Pius compared their relationship to that of a father and son) and an important figure in the church's campaign against modernity.[31]

A profound crisis in authority running along two broad fronts spurred the church's crusade against modernity, which it waged with increasing vigor in the second half of the nineteenth century and the early-twentieth. On one hand, the crisis was political. The maturation of the secular, autonomous nation-state, resting on the pillars of Enlightenment philosophy (rather than the divine right to rule) and the market economy, affected a dramatic, almost wholesale, loss of temporal power for the church. On the other hand, the crisis in ecclesial authority was intellectual. Modern science not only relied on evidence rather than revelation, but its findings were increasingly at odds with the tenets of revelation itself. Historical consciousness, another defining feature of modern intellectual life, substituted the contingent for the determined, progress for the eternal, the natural for the supernatural. The development of these potent, extraecclesial forms of authority provoked grave concern among church leaders, who understood quite clearly the inherent threat to the church's very foundations—its theological tenets, ecclesial structures, and symbol systems.

The church's efforts to neutralize the corrosive effects of modernity entailed identifying dangerous, modern errors and their antidotes. Toward the first end, the popes of the period issued official condemnations of manifold heterodoxies, most of which could be linked in some way with liberalism, that rather comprehensive philosophy built from the Protestant-hewn timbers of individualism and personal judgment. As the perceived dangers were legion, the scope of the response was broad. Pius IX found eighty modern fallacies to condemn in his 1864 *Syllabus of Errors,* which he concluded by roundly anathematizing the proposition that the "Roman Pontiff can and should align himself with progress, liberalism and modern civilization."[32] Other condemnations followed, including that of aberrant Americanism in 1899. The antidotes for these and the other grave errors of modern times were to be found in the restoration of proper, divinely ordained authority. (Pius X took as his papal motto, "to restore all things in Christ.") Vatican Council I (1869–70) produced a powerful statement on ecclesial authority by setting forth the doctrine of papal infallibility. In his 1879 encyclical, *Aeternis Patris,* Leo XIII provided an intellectual antidote to modernity, launching a neoscholastic revival lasting well into the twentieth century. The Jesuit-educated Leo directed the church to the writings of Thomas Aquinas in particular, declaring him the fountainhead of Catholic philosophy and theology. "We . . . exhort all of you, Venerable Brothers, with the greatest earnestness to restore the golden wisdom of St. Thomas," wrote Leo, "and to spread it as far as you can, for the safety and glory of the Catholic Faith, for the good of society, and for the increase of all the sciences."[33]

The campaign against the errors of the modern world culminated in 1907 with the promulgation of Pius X's *Pascendi Dominici Gregis,* a sweeping condemnation of "modernism." For Pius, modernism was the "synthesis of all heresies" presented "without order or systematic arrangement." The theological perpetrator, the modernist, "comprises within himself many personalities": he was the philosopher adopting an agnostic stance; the believer insisting on the primacy of personal experience; the historian excising the supernatural; the apologist resorting to the methods of the rationalists; the reformer rejecting the immutable.[34] Though inchoate in their approaches, modernists of various stripes evidenced common propensities for the empirical, individual, experiential, developmental, and rational. Together, they created an unholy chasm between faith and reason, church and state. And like common descendants bearing noticeable similarities, this wayward lot could trace their lineage to a single source: the reforming impulse of Martin Luther. The original sin of the modern world, Luther's insistence on the primacy of the individual and private judgment, had (via the Enlightenment and liberalism) given rise to modernism and set in motion a trajectory headed toward the destruction of religion. "The first step in this direction was taken by Protestantism; the second is made by Modernism; the next," Pius argued, "will plunge headlong into atheism." Civilization itself was at stake, for as Roman Catholicism was the true foundation of the social order, whatever threatened the church threatened civilization at large.[35]

As Lester Kurtz noted in his sociological study of the modernist controversy, the enemy without is potential cause for solidarity, the enemy within nothing less than a crisis.[36] Indeed, the incursions of modernism *within* the church greatly concerned Pius: the "partisans of error" he wrote, "are to be sought not only among the Church's open enemies; they lie hid, a thing to be deeply deplored and feared, in her very bosom and heart." Thus the campaign against modernism focused sharply on errant Catholics, especially clerics in positions to educate others, formally or informally, in the classroom or through their writings. The troublesome party was a "rationalist and Catholic" who gave evidence of "difficulties" with "scholastic philosophy, the authority of the fathers and tradition, and the magisterium of the Church."[37] Pius's distinct contribution to the campaign against modernism was strengthening the mechanisms of vigilance. He directed responsible parties to particular care in staffing seminaries and Catholic universities, decisively rooting out those sympathetic to modernism. Bishops were instructed to exercise greater oversight over Catholic publishing ventures and to permit congresses of priests only rarely. Diocesan watch committees ("Councils of Vigilance") were to be established as quickly as possible.[38] In 1910, concerned about the tenacity of modernism within the flock, Pius required those in holy orders to sign an oath against modernism.

In the nineteenth century, the papacy and the Society of Jesus worked closely in mutually beneficial fashion. Having been suppressed by one pope and restored by another, the Jesuits were politically cautious and keen to develop close, protective ties with the papacy. Conversely, the increasingly beleaguered papacy looked to the Society, whose members took a special vow of loyalty to the pope, to help squelch the pernicious effects of modernity. The popes tapped Jesuits to draft a number of important statements; Joseph Kleutgen, for example, drafted *Aeternis Patris*, in which Leo set forth the philosophy and theology of Aquinas as remedy for an intellectually disordered world; Camillo Mazzella drafted *Providentissimus Deus* (1893), wherein Leo identified the dangers of modern science and biblical criticism.[39] A handful of Jesuits, including Martín and Meyer, his assistant, had a hand in crafting and seeing to the promulgation of the hierarchy's joint pastoral letter "The Church and Liberal Catholicism" (1900), an unequivocal condemnation of liberalism and harbinger for what would come in *Pascendi*.[40] Liberal Americans blamed European Jesuits for Keane's dismissal from the Catholic University. The Jesuits' Roman-based *La Civiltà Cattolica* did its part to stem the modernist tide. Its editors and contributors published pieces supportive of the papacy and the neo-Thomist movement and watched for incursions of liberalism and modernism among the faithful. They were vigilant regarding the Catholic Church in the United States, quick to point out what they considered excessive liberalism and incursions of unacceptable "Americanism"; Gibbons, Ireland, O'Connell, and Keane all felt the sting of its criticism at various times. For example, the editors roundly criticized Keane and Gibbons for participating in the World's Parliament of Religions in 1893. When liberals sidestepped criticism by disavowing the existence of the type of Americanism identified as unacceptable in *Testem Benevolentiae*, the Jesuit editors heatedly claimed that the liberals were being disingenuous, noting that the word *Americanism* had "originated in America . . . to designate, in general, the 'new idea,' which was to rejuvenate the Church." Not surprisingly, the American liberals complained among themselves about the Jesuits.[41]

Martín's tenure as superior general of the Society, from 1892 to 1906, coincided with the crucial years leading up to *Pascendi*, although he did not live to see it promulgated. Ardent in his support for the church's campaign to curtail heterodoxy and restore proper religious authority, Martín's worldview mirrored that of Leo XIII and Pius X. He was gravely concerned for the fate of the church in a world he saw as radically disordered. What Luther began by substituting the authority of man for that of

God had grown like a hydra into the many faces of liberalism, which Martín considered the foremost heresy of the age. It was the very work of the archdeceiver, providing an arsenal of weapons to those bent on the destruction of the church.[42]

Martín was convinced that abominable liberalism had already claimed England and the United States, where Protestants dominated numerically and culturally. Insufficiently vigilant, Catholics in those countries had grown too tolerant of Protestants and their errors, thus rendering themselves and the church vulnerable to Protestant influence and heresy. For evidence, Martín needed to look no further than the Society's troublesome English province. Particularly disturbing was the highly publicized case of Jesuit George Tyrell, whose liberal writings and modernist commitments resulted in his dismissal from the Jesuits and subsequent excommunication from the church in 1906. To Martín, Tyrell's sympathy for Americanism was one of the more damning pieces of evidence against him. Indeed, the warm reception the Americanists received among the English was, according to Martín, indicative of the degree to which Catholic England had fallen under the sway of Protestant-inspired liberalism.[43]

Insofar as he understood it as yet one more manifestation of liberalism, Martín's disdain for Americanism was predictable. But Martín's reactions to Americanism were also byproducts of his upbringing and culture. As a Spaniard supportive of the tradition of monarchy, he was both unfamiliar with and unsympathetic to republicanism and democracy and thus was antipathetic to the Americanists' political sentiments and celebratory posture about things American. The Spanish-American War in 1898 only "worsened Martín's already sour disposition toward Protestant America," according to David Schultenover. At the very time during which the Americanists were claiming that a vital America was poised to assume the religious mantle from a languishing Europe, the quickly resolved war shrank Spain's empire precipitously, as the young, Protestant nation emerged ever more fully as an international power.[44] Deeply aggrieved, Martín called 1898 his "year of martyrdom." Spain's defeat distressed him so deeply that he found it difficult even to speak to his assistant Meyer, who was an American. Moreover, as superior of an international order with provinces in the United States, he found "having to deal with the Americans" equitably extremely difficult.[45]

Martín's first letter to the Society of Jesus as a whole, "On Some Dangers of Our Times," reveals clear antipathies toward the modern world. Published in 1896, four years after he became superior, it became an important document among the Jesuits, part of their annual spiritual reading for decades.[46] Therein Martín repeatedly exhorted the Jesuits to vigilance. He wistfully recalled that in the earliest days of the Society, when the "faith was everywhere strong," how their "forefathers often enjoyed the protection and munificence of both peoples and rulers"; among their friends they counted "Roman Pontiffs . . . princes of the Church, bishops, kings, noblemen, magistrates." But conditions were far different for Jesuits in the late-nineteenth century. Their friends were fewer and far less powerful. Their enemies were legion, the times were evil, and dangers were manifold. With every reason to be wary of the world and its pernicious spirit, Martín counseled circumspection, for the "artful deceiver" (who apparently had learned from the wisdom of the Jesuits) was "wont to suit himself to the times, conditions and manners of each country and to adapt his snares to the character and circumstances of the individual."[47]

Martín wrote at length in "On Some Dangers" about threats to the integrity of the Society itself. He feared that a liberal, worldly spirit had made inroads among the Jesuits themselves, noting two particularly troubling manifestations. The first was a "natural levity of mind and character" that prevented "solid truths . . . from striking deep roots in the soul," leaving the mind "unsteady and changeable . . . fickle and inconstant." Seeking "excitement" and "glamor," a Jesuit imbued with such levity was, Martín argued, prone to follow the "natural impulse of the senses" rather than "God and the laws of our Institute." Martín's second concern was for a "specious" or "false" love of liberty, which, "becoming impatient of the bridle of authority, seeks to throw off all restraint" in favor of private judgment or personal opinion. To allow the "worldly spirit of unbridled liberty, knocking at our gates . . . to creep in among us," he announced, would be nothing less than "fatal."[48]

Young Jesuits' intellectual interests concerned Martín quite immediately. Rather than following the "time-honored and approved *Ratio Studiorum*," there were those who wished to devote the "best of their talent and the most precious hours of their time to the modern sciences," justifying their departure from tradition with claims that they would be able to use the very weapons "which the Church's foes abuse in attacking her" in her defense. Martín was not persuaded. To give one's energies to a "multifarious, shallow science, which is called *encyclopedic*," was dangerous and foolhardy, for an individual would need a "whole life-time" to master but one branch of science; any who attempted to study all "would acquire a true and thorough knowledge neither of the old nor of the new sciences," and be left with nothing but "flimsy and

flashy notions." Those "entrapped by the deceits of the devil and capti-
vated by the charms of novelty," who pursued the new sciences instead
of the old, who held that the "philosopher, the theologian, and the can-
onist must stand second to the mathematician, the naturalist, and the as-
tronomer," were deeply misguided and in "variance with our Constitutions." Inherent in their consecrated lives as members of a religious
order was an obligation to study philosophy and theology (the "sacred
science"), the foundations upon which the other sciences rested. The
"last General Congregation" was wise, Martín concluded, to "earnestly
recommend anew that all Ours should devote themselves to the serious
and solid study of the old scholastic theology" and "insist on a faithful
carrying out of all that is prescribed in the *Ratio Studiorum.*"[49]

Martín's concerns for the education of young Jesuits spilt over into
commentary on the nature of modern higher education. The "insane
method of teaching and the foolish system of education which are almost
everywhere forced upon us" clearly frustrated him. Modern students,
whose studies included "a slight sprinkling not only of letters but of almost all the sciences," graduated from college as "little encyclopedias"
who had "skimmed the surface of the whole field" without acquiring
anything "solid." A student certainly would not be possessed of the
"foundation of literary culture" that "would little by little make a man of
him." This, Martín lamented, was the "kind of education that our enemy
would represent to us as something superior . . . straining his utmost to
persuade us to train our young scholastics according to the methods and
programmes enforced in the public schools."[50]

The church's campaign against modernity, in which Martín and the
Jesuits figured prominently, profoundly affected Catholic intellectual
life. As American Catholics had not developed anything near the scholarly attainments of their European counterparts, the church's campaign
to stymie modernism was a low-profile affair in the United States as compared with Europe, where condemnations and suspicion riddled Catholic intellectual circles for decades. Nonetheless, the impact in the
United States was "chilling." Already chastened by the condemnation of
Americanism in *Testem Benevolentiae,* the American hierarchy and all
but a few scholars submitted to *Pascendi* quietly. Intellectual life perforce took the Thomistic turn. While the campaign against modernism
fueled the neoscholastic revival of the twentieth century, it also checked
Catholic engagement with and contribution to the main currents of
American intellectual life for most of the twentieth century.[51]

For Jesuits in the United States, the church's campaign against modernity had more immediate impact in institutional and practical matters than the elite world of scholarship.[52] The Jesuit community in the United States was not devoid of scholars; Georgetown, for instance, ran an internationally respected observatory.[53] But on the whole, the German research ideal that was transforming much of American higher education remained alien to the American Jesuits. In their seminary training at Woodstock, the Jesuits were schooled (often by conservative Jesuits exiled from Europe) in Thomistic thought, not modern scientific methods or historical criticism. They understood themselves not as researchers or scholars per se, but as priests and teachers, and conservative ones at that. When it came to modernism, the American Jesuits' intellectual house was in order. Nevertheless, Rome's conservatism and opposition to the modern world was felt in American Jesuit higher education at the turn of the century as American Jesuits struggled to come to terms with the emergence of a new academic order. Not infrequently they found themselves at odds with their European and European-based superiors, who considered modern American higher education riddled with Protestant-inspired, modern ideas.

In "On Some Dangers of Our Times," Martín made it clear that he was no friend of the new academic order, but his clarity on the subject did not foreclose weighty and frequent discussions about it with the American Jesuits over the next ten years. Awakening to the significance of the new academic order and the penchant of Catholic collegians for non-Catholic education, the American Jesuits turned to Rome for permission to conform the curriculum, extracurriculum, and discipline in their colleges more closely to that in vogue at other American colleges and universities. It occasioned lengthy explanations to the leadership in Rome about the challenges of time, person, and place in the age of the university and serious discussion about adapting to circumstances in the United States. A 1903 letter to Martín from Thomas Gannon, the Maryland–New York provincial, poignantly captures some of the tensions of these conversations. Gannon's letter displays an openness to America that was also to be found in a number of other Jesuits who were native born. While Europe was driving the Jesuits out, wrote Gannon, America "opened up to us a vast country, unlimited resources, full freedom of action." Unfortunately, he claimed, the governance of much of the American Jesuit enterprise was in the hands of Europeans who could "hardly be expected to understand or sympathize with the conditions, needs and aspirations of this growing and complex country." This was out of step with the Society's "own principles and spirit and in response to the requirements of time & place." He continued:

> It must not surprise us if, as we are at present, the peculiar influences of European Provinces do not produce the most benign and desirable effect through their dependent American Missions upon studies, or vocations, upon priests or people!
>
> Naturally and justly too in all legitimate matters Americans wish to cherish their own customs, ideas and language: sensible foreigners too, who come to live permanently among us, desire likewise to become thoroughly American in the best sense of the word. Why should our Society alone hold itself, as it were, aloof and remain a stranger in the land, especially as it is the great practical working principle of our Society to adapt itself freely and fully to the country where it exists and is doing apostolic work.[54]

In the two decades straddling the turn of the century, American Jesuits wrote frequently to Rome about popular student culture and the ways in which students' insistence that college be "fun" was transforming collegiate life. They wrote with some passion because they understood the ways in which popular student culture adversely affected their own colleges by pulling Catholic students toward non-Catholic institutions. Thus they sought permission from their European superiors to expand the extracurriculum and loosen discipline in ways that would bring their institutions into closer alignment with other American colleges. If for no other reason, reform was necessary to stem the drift toward non-Catholic education. But a number of Jesuits recognized something deeper. Reforming student life was, they claimed, an adaptation on the part of the Jesuits to one of the defining characteristics of the American people—namely, their love for liberty.

A number of the American-born Jesuits wrote sympathetically of their fellow citizens' penchant for freedom and liberty. At the first ACCUS meeting, Mullan spoke nonjudgmentally of the "modern American boy . . . with his spirit of independence and freedom from restraint." In communication between the United States and Rome, Richards became an ardent defender of American liberty (perhaps not a surprising development given his familial roots stretching into the soil of colonial New England). He wrote to Meyer in 1896 of the "character and habits of the American boy, which differ very greatly from those which, as I am informed, prevail in other countries." American students were, he explained, "accustomed to a great degree of freedom from early childhood," and while it made "them somewhat independent in spirit and impatient of minute control," it also occasioned a "certain maturity of character, self-respect, and self-control which are often surprising to observers of other nationalities."[55]

Like college administrators throughout the country, the Jesuits inevitably had to contend with athletics, a veritable "craze" (as one Jesuit described it)[56] that swept through American higher education in the late-nineteenth century. Should they, in order to attract students, build athletic programs? A number of Jesuits harbored reservations on the grounds that athletics diverted students' attention from their studies and often encouraged pride and cheating. But even the most lukewarm among them conceded the tenets of muscular Christianity, admitting that if properly supervised a moderate approach to athletics could develop virtue and character.[57] Those enthusiastic for athletics praised them for their potential to develop character and the good they might do for the college in fostering school spirit.

The strongest overtures for athletics came from Richards, who implored Meyer and Martín to allow the team from Georgetown to travel to compete against other teams. "Some enthusiasm over athletics is a great factor for good in a college," he wrote to Meyer, a Midwesterner by birth and provincial affiliation. "You perhaps can form little idea of the place athletics occupy in the eastern colleges." A year later, in 1896, he told Meyer that the "fever for athletics which has prevailed for several years among the young men of America, and particularly of the Eastern states, can scarcely be imagined by any one who has not been in the midst of it." A fan of baseball, Richards made his case for the all-American pastime to Rome by stressing the good their students realized (they "behaved with so much prudence and discretion and self-control as to be a source of edification not only to Catholics but to Protestants").[58] In an extended syllogism, he connected athletics with Catholic enrollment patterns and the success of the Society in its apostolic work. To disallow Georgetown students' participation in athletics would, Richards argued, drive students "elsewhere"—including to Harvard, where more than three hundred Catholic students were crowding its halls and endangering their souls. The stakes were high, for it was "not merely a question of the financial prosperity or bankruptcy of our colleges; it is a question of loss of immeasurable souls. We cannot make the world over; we must accept the material and conditions which we find and endeavor to work upon it for the good; but if all, or nearly all our boys leave us, we certainly cannot influence them, and through them society at large for good."[59]

While Richards argued on behalf of the baseball team, Brosnahan pled on behalf of the debate team, asking Martín to allow the Georgetown debaters to continue meeting their Boston College counterparts. This type of competition, Brosnahan explained, which brought "renown to both schools" and "glory befitting our System," was "practically necessary . . . on account of the peculiar ways of this region." The students were in no moral danger; during a "trip of twelve hours . . . the students were under the 'guardianship' of our men; they slept in our college and after the debate they returned the same way they came." Thus in their trip from Washington to Boston, there was "no greater danger" for students "than if they had passed from one room into another within the same college."[60]

The Jesuits also approached Rome about the issue of supervision and curfews in their boarding colleges and the conditions under which their students could be allowed to go unsupervised beyond the walls that separated, in monastery-like fashion, the denizens of their colleges from the world without. To protect students from moral contagion, it was not uncommon for nineteenth-century colleges to be sited away from cities. But in this, the Jesuit tradition was somewhat different: according to a Jesuit proverb, "Bernardus valles, montes Benedictus amavit; oppida Franciscus, magnas Ignatius urbes" ("Bernard loved the valleys, Benedict the mountains; Francis the towns, Ignatius loved great cities").[61] Thus in the spirit of their founder, the Jesuits built their colleges in the booming cities of nineteenth-century America—in Boston, New York, Washington, Cleveland, Saint Louis, Chicago, San Francisco, and New Orleans. But the city that held such great appeal for Ignatius presented problems to his followers three centuries later. As other colleges and universities loosened their disciplinary standards, granting students greater liberty, should the Jesuits follow suit, allowing their students to come and go unsupervised?

As priests, the Jesuits had a "most sacred obligation to prevent, as far as possible, their charges from coming into contact with moral contamination,"[62] as one Jesuit described it; thus, the Jesuits never considered loosening discipline significantly. Yet, as Purbrick explained to Martín, their students "know perfectly well what liberty is allowed" at Harvard, Yale, and Princeton, "and very naturally aim at obtaining something of the same latitude of freedom." They were, as a number of Jesuits pointed out, accustomed to freedom and liberty from their youth and tended to be older than the students in the Jesuits' European colleges. As Purbrick noted, "in this country" students "are rather young men than mere boys," who "would be better trained without this French military surveillance."[63] Richards, too, argued for less austere discipline: "If we attempt to confine them too closely . . . they become morose and resentful, all moral influence over them is lost . . . and finally they leave us . . . and go to the non-Catholic universities, where they are subject to no control at all and where every temptation both to faith and morals, besets them at every step." Gannon wrote to Rome along the same lines: it was futile to "restrain . . . the liberty of our American College Students," who were, he pointed out, "18 to 23 years of age." They were "men in habits, dress and social life" who were "wont to attend . . . dinners, receptions, and the theatre." In American colleges, he reported "moderate attendance at such public gatherings and amusements is demanded and conceded," adding that he and others as students at Holy Cross twenty-five years earlier had gone to lectures and the theater and returned to the college quite late. He entreated Martín: "Your Paternity must judge us Americans with due consideration and indulgence for our American ideas of propriety and decorum and not force us to conform to the more conservative and perhaps more excellent standards of conduct which obtain in good, old Europe."[64]

A few years later, in an attempt to make their colleges attractive to students, the Jesuits broached the issue of room and board with their European superiors. "During the last 20 years a great change has been forced upon us in the management of our Boarding Colleges here in the Eastern part of the United States," wrote Gannon to Martín in 1903. It used to be that their students were "content to live in a common Study Hall, a common Dormitory, and a common Play Room." But they were no longer. Being "accustomed to more or less luxury in his home life," as Mullan put it, the "modern American boy" expected his collegiate life to be similarly comfortable. The Jesuits were competing with institutions, such as Harvard, that had well-kept dormitories and dining halls; thus Mullan had become convinced of the "necessity" of "rooms in the place of common study halls and common dormitories" and "more humane attention to the matter of meals." Indeed, with changes in student culture and the upward mobility of Catholics, Catholic colleges soon felt the pressure to conform. "Gradually," wrote Gannon, "the students of the highest class began to request, then to demand private rooms, in which to live, study and sleep," for which students were willing to pay extra. The Jesuits were "forced to grant this demand or lose their students."[65]

Recognizing that student life and discipline in their colleges were ill-suited for modern collegians, provincials and rectors from the colleges in the East sought permission from Rome to adapt to the conditions they encountered—in particular, to their primary constituent, the American student. Following the lead of non-Catholic institutions, they argued for opportunities, privileges, and discipline suited to men, not boys. It proved a difficult case to make with Martín, who was convinced that society and culture in the United States had fallen lamentably under the sway of Protestantism and a host of modern errors. In responding, Martín was cautious at best. When he said no, he did so clearly; when he said yes, he did so equivocally. Writing to Brosnahan in 1895, he criticized Brosnahan for having "defended the debates . . . between students of Georgetown and Boston College as if in America they were somehow necessary." But he could not see that the value of the debates could "compensate for the dangers and expense of such a long trip."[66] As for athletics, the "whole business has pleased me little." He informed Richards that the team could travel, but "only during vacations." Unsupervised trips to the city were "occasions of sin" and thus should be curtailed. Providing private rooms to students diminished the Jesuits' capacity to supervise students; thus, Martín directed the Jesuits at Fordham gradually to abolish the practice.[67]

Repeatedly, Martín claimed that the discipline either in force or as proposed was but a "false liberty" or a "ruinous liberty" or an expression of "excessive license." Reports reached Martín of Georgetown students who, allowed unsupervised trips to the city, had frequented taverns, gotten drunk, used impure language, and even visited the "houses of ruined women." Allowing students such "false liberty" put their very souls at risk as well as the reputation of the Society. "Let us suppose," wrote Martín to Pardow and Richards, "there is only a spark of truth in these rumors and accusations, still what a firestorm this spark could arouse against the Society if things of this sort were brought by our enemies to the Bishop or Apostolic Delegate?" It was, Martín claimed, "no longer a question of expanding the freedom of the student" to conform with practices in other American colleges, but rather "extinguishing it and confining it within due limits, and conforming the practice of the whole college to the rules of the Society."[68]

Martín understood the rationale advanced by the American Jesuits, both in its positive iteration, stressing the wisdom of adapting to American circumstances, and in its negative iteration, stressing the need for adaptation in order to stem the Catholic drift toward non-Catholic colleges and comply with state regulations. But he was extremely critical of both. Frustrated with the Jesuits in the Maryland–New York Province, he bridled at claims that he did not understand the American character or context. Pardow, he said, was "restricted . . . to one part of America," while the superior general received "numberless letters from every region of North America in which the character and needs of America are clearly set out"; he thus argued that he was quite familiar with America and the character of its people and well-prepared to render judicious decisions. "In those parts differing from yours, there is also an American character and students are considered American. Yet they do not seek the things you ask for at times." Indeed, Martín found the argument for adaptation to the circumstances in America "hollow." "We ought not adapt our plan of action on the basis of non-Catholic universities but on the basis of the rules and tradition of the Society, or the letters of the Generals, or the universal practice of our colleges." For Martín, "even if the number of students should decrease by half," the Jesuits would still be "bound in conscience to remove as far as possible . . . all occasions of sin based on that false liberty."[69]

Correspondence with other American Jesuits, such as the consultors, had given Martín reason to believe that a number of their colleges had conformed too closely to non-Catholic models. As the rector of Fordham, Gannon had reported to Rome an apparent "inclination among some to increasingly order our colleges by the more liberal discipline and manner of acting of non-Catholic colleges." This would, he noted, "please the boys and young men," but gradually their colleges would "become practically identical with all other schools" and thus lose their "reason to exist."[70] Martín had also received a rather dire report from a "serious Father" about Georgetown. "To understand what is going on in Georgetown, one must represent to himself the idea of a Protestant American university." It was "Protestant" insofar as the "boys ranging from 14 years up, go where they like within the grounds and out in the city—only a formality is required, as to notifying authorities." It was a "University" insofar as every one was "treated as a formed man, as to times of study and recreation; everyone . . . may have a private room by paying for it. . . . There is a fine luxurious table; the boys rise from table as they like and drop in as they like." The cause of the greatest concern for this father was athletics. "Above all . . . the standard of the American University [has been adopted] in regard to the "Teams."

All the classes are rushed in between 9 A.M. and 3 P.M.. From 3 to 6 the "Teams" are free to train; a man from Princeton has them for three hours every day. All the other students likewise have recreation from 3 to 6. . . . To feed [sic?] the "Teams," men are engaged to life gratis at the College; and they are called Post-graduates. The Assistant Librarian, engaged on salary to attend to the Riggs Library, to be always there, pleaded by way of apology for not being at his post, that he was summoned several times by the Rector to the foot-ball field, to play. The Rector himself has little use for books and libraries. But he will sit for hours on a bench of the base-ball or foot-bal [*sic*] field, "like a big school boy," remarked one of the Fathers. The base-ball "Team" went forth in May on its long tour, to conquer the country. Every evening at 4 P.M., the long-looked-for telegram arrived: "Beaten Princeton," "Beaten Yale", "Beaten Harvard." A Prefect had gone with the boys. While in New York they had the hospitality of our College, and were supposed to sleep there; in other places they lodged in hotels. One of the boys, while in New York went to a . . . . house, and himself related that there the woman drawing a pair of beads from his pocket, instead of money, exclaimed, "You are a Catholic." For the one simpleton who told on himself, how many others did not tell on themselves.[71]

Martín feared that the Jesuits working in the American colleges were not equal to the challenges they faced, not solely because of the magnitude of the challenges but because of their own lack of spiritual discipline, which hampered the development of the Society and its ability to advance its mission. To Martín, the Americans appeared to have succumbed to pernicious modern temptations—that "worldly spirit" and propensity for "levity" and "novelty" about which he had written so emphatically in "On Some Dangers of Our Times." In 1895 he wrote Richards about a "worldly spirit" so "averse to the spirit of the Society" making inroads among the Jesuits. In 1904 he wrote again about a "worldly spirit" that had "crept in among very many of our schools." This spirit distracted the Jesuits and eroded their willingness and ability to provide their students with a solid and spiritual education.[72] He enjoined them to guard assiduously against a "specious liberty and secular spirit" and to refocus their energies on matters more important than the "lack of athletics." By promoting studies vigorously, asserted Martín, the Jesuits would find themselves beyond the reproach of non-Catholic educators and their schools would become increasingly attractive to Catholics and non-Catholics.[73]

In "President Eliot and Jesuit Colleges," Timothy Brosnahan responded to Eliot's allegations of curricular intransigence on the part of the Jesuits by invoking an address that Martín had delivered in Holland on January 1, 1893. "He warns his hearers not to confound the Jesuit *method* of studies with the *matter* to which that method is applied," wrote Brosnahan. "For the first he claimed stability, to the second he conceded change." As Martín himself put it, "As to the content we are not free at the present day . . . if we should try to retain the same content as before, we could close the doors of our colleges." And yet, Martín asserted, "we are still free in the spirit and method of teaching."[74] It was a quick but substantive concession to modernity—to modern subjects relentlessly vying for inclusion in the curriculum and political forces increasingly orchestrating educational affairs along national lines. Though Martín conceded control of subject matter to the forces of modernity, both the method and matter of Jesuit education proved ongoing subjects of discussion between the European and American Jesuits well into the twentieth century. The same topic was cause for dissension in the Maryland–New York Province as the Jesuits there attempted to develop a curriculum that was attractive to students, satisfactory to the state, and true to the *Ratio Studiorum*.

The two decades spanning the turn of the century were particularly difficult years for the American Jesuits in this regard. Unable to hold to the letter of the *Ratio,* they struggled to adhere to its spirit as enthusiasm for the ancient subjects waned and the modern subjects waxed. Martín's and Brosnahan's claims for freedom and stability notwithstanding, even the method of the *Ratio* proved problematic, with the Jesuits evincing occasional vagueness and disinterest in their own pedagogical traditions. Moreover, amid growing confusion about matter and intermittent uncertainty about method, a fairly widespread consensus developed: that the overall quality of studies was low and needed improvement. Institutional, provincial, and interprovincial meetings were held, reports were issued, new schedules of studies were developed and sent to Rome for comment and approval. In the age of the university, the Jesuits soon learned that adapting the curriculum and improving studies were just as taxing as the adaptation of discipline and the extracurriculum.

Modernity's challenges to the *Ratio Studiorum* were already apparent upon the restoration of the Society of Jesus in 1814. "In the very first assembly after the Restoration of the Society," explained Superior General Jan Roothaan (1814–53), "a petition had been received from the Provinces, and daily experience since then has shown it to be more and more necessary, that the System of Studies should be accommodated to the exigencies of the times."[75] Arguments surfaced for the inclusion of the vernacular, history, additional math, and a full program in the sciences, in part that students might be able to recognize and refute modern errors and heresies. But in revising the *Ratio*, the Jesuits of the early-nineteenth century largely stayed the course, leaving the aims, methods, and discipline of the *Ratio* largely untouched. They accommodated the "exigencies of the times"—new modes and expanding areas of inquiry—by augmenting the curriculum, adding some mathematics and physics, while designating other subjects, such as history and geography, as "accessory" subjects. But the *Ratio* of 1832 was never formally ratified; mandating a single course of studies for Jesuits teaching in diverse circumstances had already proved impossible. Yet the Jesuits were directed to conform to the *Ratio* as closely as possible. "The adaptation of the *Ratio Studiorum*," wrote a cautious Roothaan, "means that we consult the necessities of the age so far as not in the least to sacrifice the solid and correct education of youth."[76]

In building their colleges across the United States during the nineteenth century, the Jesuits (among them many Europeans, especially during the early decades) came to understand Americans as an impatient, results-oriented people, often desirous of a practical education. The *Ratio Studiorum*, so clearly classical in its orientation, remained at the heart of their educational enterprise, but most Jesuit colleges began adapting to American students' practical temperament, acceding to market demands by offering a commercial course or, as Boston College did, an "English course" de-emphasizing Latin and Greek. The father of an early Holy Cross student, upset by his son's affinity for Latin rather than English (English being "all important to his success in business"), asked that his son be allowed to forego Latin in favor of more useful subjects.[77] Americans' propensity for the practical also explained the push for inclusion of sciences in the curriculum that intensified in tandem with the rapid progress of the industrial revolution. In the late 1880s, Richards wrote to the superior general of the "character of the American people, so given over to the natural sciences."[78]

Fagan explained at some length to Martín the practical nature of the American people and some of its implications for Jesuit education. As they were "especially attracted by material and sensory things," they cared little for the intellectual life. All Americans conflated "success" with the "acquisition of wealth"; thus, parents wanted a "practical" education for their children that would help them realize the worldly form of success as quickly as possible. Indeed, why waste time in college when their "competitors have already crossed the finish line"? Given Americans' drive for material success achieved by practical means, arguments "against classical studies . . . and in general against all education and disciplines suggestive of antiquity" found a receptive audience, even among Catholics. Mostly the "sons of the foreign born and less cultured," they, too, "intensely desire . . . success." So, reported Fagan, they somewhat misguidedly sent their sons to the Jesuit colleges hoping they "would not learn Greek, or that in learning Latin they not waste so much time but attend instead to modern languages or mathematics or whatever."[79]

Committed to classical education, the Jesuits offered nonclassical programs reluctantly, especially in colleges east of the Alleghenies. "The English Course, or Commercial, is humbugging," wrote Maryland Provincial Charles Stonestreet in 1854.[80] Even as the great intellectual currents of the age found institutional expression in the modern, utilitarian university, the Jesuits continued "humbugging" about nonclassical studies. Richards was one of the few Jesuits who understood the times, arguing for the inclusion of modern subjects in the curriculum for their own sake; he also noted the concomitant need to train Jesuits along specialized, disciplinary lines. In 1889 he wrote, "It is a matter of the very greatest importance, not only to this college, but to the reputation and success of the Society in this country that we should have, *during the coming year,* able men, *specialists,* who can be called upon in an emergency to do something handsome in their respective lines." These lines, Richards suggested, should include not only the traditional disciplines of philosophy and rhetoric, but physics, mechanics, geology, astronomy, French, and German.[81] In like vein, Holy Cross president Joseph Hanselman (1901–06) argued that there was a great need for men "who know other subjects beside Latin, Greek, and the basics of English," who were versed in "English, French, German, and Spanish, or History or Natural Sciences, Math, Political Economy, History of Philosophy." Unless the Jesuits developed disciplinary specialists, he argued, "we will scarcely be found to be the rivals of non-Catholic schools, among which these studies are of such great value, perhaps more than is right, but nonetheless for this reason they attract many Catholic students."[82]

Richards and Hanselman were exceptions; in Jesuit circles, "humbugging" about nonclassical education endured well into the age of the university. Even in the colleges west of the Alleghenies, the nonclassical course existed largely as a concession to the market. Tellingly, as the provincial of the Missouri Province, Rudolph Meyer oversaw a revision of the *Ratio Studiorum* in 1887 that admitted little revision in the curriculum; it set a conservative course that lasted two decades. The Jesuits held fast to the ancient languages, their traditions, and—at least rhetorically—to their pedagogical traditions. "Other methods may have their merit," wrote Meyer, in the cover letter accompanying the 1887 schedule, "but not all of them can be engrafted on the method of the Ratio Studiorum, which binds us like other parts of the Institute, and which, though capable of being accommodated to the exigencies of the times, cannot be set aside or ignored by us without risk of abandoning all method."[83]

The *Ratio Studiorum*, Meyer asserted, *bound* the Jesuits as did other parts of the Society's institute; it stood along side the *Constitutions* and the Spiritual Exercises of Saint Ignatius as a foundational document for Jesuit life. But in the 1890s, concerns developed to the effect that the Jesuits were becoming disengaged, "unbound" as it were, from their own academic principles and traditions. Commitment to the *Ratio Studiorum* seemed to be flagging in some quarters. In 1896 correspondence with Pardow about the poor state of studies, Martín wrote of Jesuits who preferred preaching and hearing confessions to "preparing and giving lectures in the school." If such Jesuits were more devoted to the academic life (instead of the "freer life" of giving talks in parishes), "we would have professors, prefects and superiors of houses such that the colleges would fear nothing from Protestant and Catholic schools, because our students would surpass those of Protestant schools," claimed Martín. A month later, he wrote to Pardow that he and a number of rectors found it "regrettable" that "teachers are regarded as untrained and unfit, instructed by no method, lacking direction, left to themselves to work out their own method." He shared with Pardow the opinion of one consultor who felt that the "root of troubles in the colleges of the province is ignorance, neglect, indeed, contempt for the Ratio."[84]

Amid allegations of ignorance of and even contempt for the *Ratio* among the Jesuits, in 1893 the Woodstock Academy for the Study of the Ratio was "inaugurated by the authority and with the fullest approval of superiors." Based at the Jesuit seminary in Woodstock, Maryland, where Jesuits from different provinces mingled, seventeen active members met, over an eighteen-month period, seventy-one times, their object being increased familiarity with traditional methods of teaching among the Jesuits. The scope and results of their work were impressive; academy members studied every regulation of the *Ratio* through rhetoric (i.e., the penultimate year of study), along with various commentaries. They published the results of their work in six lengthy articles in *Woodstock Letters* ranging widely over curricula, authors to be studied, pedagogy, and discipline. Holding fast to the original object of increasing understanding of the *Ratio* within the Jesuit community, a contributor noted, somewhat defensively, at the academy's conclusion that it had been the "constant object of the Academy to learn, not to reform."[85]

Though the Jesuits were bound to the *Ratio Studiorum*, the new academic order relentlessly insisted on their attention. While the new order was easy for many to criticize and tempting for others to ignore, by the 1890s the academic revolution was a force with which to reckon, as the Jesuits' experience with Eliot and Harvard made clear. Father Fagan was particularly consistent and insistent in arguing for greater Jesuit engagement with the broader academy. At the very least, he argued, the Jesuits should closely study educational trends; optimally, they should participate in the educational associations of the day. In 1900, for instance, he encouraged his fellow Jesuits to participate in the National Education Association, not only to keep abreast of and learn from others but to have a hand in shaping American education. "Are we not lacking in zeal, at least, in not striving as the men opposing us strive to gain the attention of these men and women?" he queried in *Woodstock Letters*. "To have any influence in such a meeting, one must be known to the delegates. . . . As they so rarely hear anything from us, they little by little come to forget our existence, or to imagine that we are mere survivals from some antiquated growth which would hardly repay examination or study."[86]

Like that of other Catholic educators, the Jesuits' participation in non-Catholic associations and educational forums was limited and informal, with the notable exception of the Catholic University of America, which was invited to inaugural membership in the elite Association of American Universities.[87] In an age when educational associations proliferated—when "everyone seemed to be banding together," as historian Hugh Hawkins described it—Catholics established their own association, the Association of Catholic Colleges of the United States, and the Jesuits created their own forums.[88] In 1896, as the Woodstock Academy came to a close, Pardow, the provincial, convened the "Conference on Studies," with two delegates from each college in the province taking up an agenda too long to finish. According to Richards, what those gathered found most beneficial was the "comparison of ideas." Though representatives of Catholic colleges bypassed associations like the NEA in which they would have interacted with educators from non-Catholic institutions, at the Jesuit Conference on Studies they discovered that "many of the Fathers had been making themselves familiar with the movements and tendencies of the educational world outside of the Society, and had been carrying on unknown to one another, studies and investigations along similar lines."[89]

The Jesuits attending the Conference on Studies spent considerable time discussing entrance requirements, a facet of educational policy scrutinized intensely around the turn of the century. Under the auspices of the NEA, the Committee of Ten, headed by Charles Eliot, had issued its influential 1893 report discussing the relationship between high school curricula and college admissions. A number of educational associations, including the North Central Association and the National Association of State Universities, took up the issue. The College Entrance Examination Board was in the making.[90] With growing attention to entrance requirements and a regularized educational ladder of four years of high school followed by four years of college largely realized, the Jesuits faced a serious problem: articulation. How could they fit their seven-year, integrated program of studies to the U.S. system? They could divide the preparatory from the collegiate after three years of studies or after four; either way, they shortchanged students, leaving them vulnerable if they sought admission to other colleges or (in the case of Harvard and the New York State regents) professional schools. Thus the Jesuits reluctantly voted to add an additional year of studies to their program and push "down the chief Latin and Greek authors . . . by one year." They did so in order that students in Jesuit schools would be able to transfer into "Harvard, Yale, Dartmouth, etc." on the same footing as "graduates of New England High Schools." They also adopted American nomenclature—freshman, sophomore, junior, and senior—for the college course. They made these changes, Richards informed a correspondent, not because the program of studies in the Jesuit colleges was inferior, but rather "in order to conform more closely to the methods of the colleges with which we are in competition."[91]

The adoption of the four-plus-four-year course and American nomenclature marked a significant adaptation to American-styled education by the Jesuits, but they had not yet tackled the sticky issue of the *matter* of education (i.e., what to teach and when). In large measure, their problems were market driven; the classical liberal arts education was simply losing its appeal in the wake of new, modern options. "Any reductions of our course by eliminating modern branches," wrote Richards to Meyer in a letter about studies and the situation with Harvard, "will make it harder for us to compete with these great non-Catholic institutions."[92]

But reaching a consensus about what to include in the curriculum proved elusive since, as Brosnahan noted, "the Jesuit system of education has unwaveringly kept Language in a position of honor as an instrument of culture."[93] Moreover, significant alterations had the potential to undermine the integrity and cohesion of the *Ratio*, which built on the principles of gradation and subordination. Yet the issue could not be avoided: the addition of an eighth year of study forced it, as did students clamoring for modern subjects. The result was a series of "new schedules" at the turn of the century that created frustration and consternation among the Jesuits at home and abroad.

Attempts to preserve the *Ratio Studiorum* while adapting to new circumstances in the age of the university resulted in a long series of new "schedules," and with the schedules came aggravation for the Jesuits. Resistance consistently trumped reform efforts. In his lengthy 1902 letter to Martín, Fagan described the Jesuits' tumultuous experience of trying to adapt the *Ratio Studiorum* in Maryland–New York Province. According to Fagan, in the mid-1880s Provincial Robert Fulton (1882–89) "designated some eminent and very learned men to discuss the whole issue of studies and suggest what should be done." But, Fagan reported, the "Fathers finished the business in one or two days, as if it were a joke," making only a "few trivial suggestions." The next provincial, Father Pardow, convened a Conference on Studies "at which all the doubts and difficulties which our men had experienced over the previous years, as well as the causes of strife between us and the government, were examined and discussed at great length." But the resulting Committee of Five met only three or four times, offering the provincial "some minor suggestions" on how to proceed. (Recognizing the conservative leanings among his fellow Jesuits, delegate Brosnahan wrote Richards that "if we wish to do any good for the studies of the province . . . we must avoid even the *appearance* of innovation; consequently we must for the present leave much in status quo.")[94]

Like his predecessors, the next provincial, Purbrick, appointed a committee—this time a group of three, one of them Fagan. He directed them to develop a plan that would "preserve the directives of the Ratio," while adapting "in light of the circumstances of the times" and in a way that "would be acceptable to the government and as far as possible leave no . . . pretext for further harassment." Toward that end, Fagan and his colleagues worked "diligently," developing a schedule that satisfied the government. "Still we took the great care," wrote Fagan, "that even here the spirit of the *Ratio* and its methods be preserved." To promote greater "uniformity" among the colleges in conforming to the *Ratio*, they spelled out the "material to be taught in each class," expanded the scope of material to be covered in Latin and Greek classes, and "assigned for each class exercise books and tasks to instruct students in a better, more orderly, step by step manner."[95]

Fagan's 1902 letter to Martín was at once an apologia for reform and a litany of failures that had brought the Jesuits to the brink of disaster. Fagan laid much of the blame for their troubles on the Jesuits themselves, noting repeatedly their failure to adapt to new academic realities. "On the one hand," he wrote, "it is necessary to resist our external foes, and, on the other, to put up with domestic opponents." Those opponents regularly undermined efforts to respond to academic exigencies. Conservatives, Fagan claimed, quashed the Woodstock Academy. The goal of the academy was "to pore over the Ratio, investigate its true character and scope, and arouse its spirit throughout the province." An excellent plan, the academy had opened with the blessing of the superiors, but they "suppressed" it in the wake of complaints from "some professors and older (more weighty) fathers" who felt that young Jesuits should be studying theology rather than spending "time uselessly" in an academy that fostered a "pernicious spirit" (i.e., a "love of things too new"). In like vein, said Fagan, the new schedule of studies imposed by Purbrick had been roundly criticized as a "radical" departure, the work of three inexperienced men who "favored novelty"; the schedule's critics claimed that it was imposed without sufficient consultation and that the material laid out in the course of studies was "too heavy" for students. Fagan rejoined that its critics, when pressed, were unable to explain how the new schedule actually departed from the *Ratio.* For the charge that it was imposed without consultation, Fagan explained: "In our Province we were almost in the final crisis. Boston College and Holy Cross were at war with Harvard. . . . So there was no time for consulting any of the elders or for engaging in useless arguments and disputes," but rather, a dire need "for acting quickly and resolutely."[96]

Martín was well aware of the troubles stirred up by the "new schedules." In 1900 he had passed on to Purbrick complaints he had received: the new schedule was "destroying" the *Ratio Studiorum* and abandoning "tradition" by emulating "bad models." In 1902 he wrote to Gannon along the same lines, passing on the comments of a consultor: "We seem day by day to be pulling further away from our Ratio Studiorum." To another consultor, the new system of studies was "displeasing" on a number of counts: it was a retreat from the *Ratio;* it forced students to cover too much material; it sacrificed solid learning for "superficiality"; it fostered "cramming" among students; it yielded to the "spirit of the times" with its penchant for "novelty" and "experiments." Such a schedule, Martín concluded, should be imposed only if absolutely necessary, for it was "upsetting" and virtually "destroying" the *Ratio Studiorum* in the Maryland–New York Province.[97]

As provincial, Gannon tried, like his predecessors, to develop a workable, acceptable schedule of studies. Learning from Purbrick's mistake, Gannon formed a committee of fifteen and consulted widely before proceeding; thus, he explained to Martín in 1905, "I have been able to send out a *'Revised Schedule of Studies'* which thus represents the full wisdom and interested suggestions of the whole Province." He intended to improve the schedule year by year, and thus while the "spirit and form of our *Ratio* are kept *intact* . . . we shall be able to avail ourselves of all that is best and really valuable and progressive in our modern civilization—we shall be fully up to date, ever active with eyes wide open."[98]

In the revised schedule of 1906, it is fidelity to the *Ratio Studiorum* that is apparent—far more so, that is, than openness to the progressive elements of modern civilization. The cover letter accompanying the new schedule noted, "No essential change was called for by the twenty-seven reports sent in from the various colleges of the Province"; and claims that "our old and approved methods of teaching" had been abandoned were "misconceived."[99] By that time, American nomenclature for the names of the classes and an eight-year program divided equally between high school and college were now standard features in most Jesuit colleges; at Boston College and Holy Cross, the separation between the preparatory and college level began to emerge in the late 1890s.[100] But modern subjects? In "President Eliot and Jesuit Colleges," Brosnahan had responded to President Eliot's charges that the Jesuits were academically moribund by pointing out that during the nineteenth century, 47 percent of class time at Georgetown had been "wrested from the domain of Latin and Greek" by "English, mathematics, modern languages and natural sciences." But the modern subjects had difficulty gaining further ground as the twentieth century opened. When the Jesuits augmented the course of studies by an additional year, they added more philosophy, history, and English, with mathematics and the sciences barely retaining the ground they already held. Electives won but a handful of hours in the junior and senior years, and then were limited to a small range of choice among calculus, physics, chemistry, or one of the modern languages.

Though they had conformed more closely to American colleges structurally, the commitment to the classical and humanistic remained a potent force in determining the *matter* of the Jesuit curriculum.[101]

Despite Gannon's province-wide consultation and the strong showing for the classics in the 1906 schedule, the newest schedule still had its critics. On the surface, the 1906 schedule and those that followed in 1908 and 1910 made the classics paramount, with actual increases in the amount of time spent on mastery of the ancient languages. For example, between 1906 and 1910 the number of hours sophomores spent on Latin increased from six to ten hours per week.[102] But the increase in time spent studying the language of the ancient Romans did not produce the desired outcome. Complaints surfaced regularly about the inability of students to master Latin. Instructors for the senior-level course in philosophy, traditionally conducted in Latin, often turned to English to ensure that their students understood the material. It was a linguistic shift of great import and serious concern for many, including Brosnahan, the great apologist for Jesuit education.

In 1900, Charles Eliot informed the Jesuits that their colleges would be candidates for inclusion on Harvard Law School's list of select colleges if they would emulate the Protestant colleges. "We should be heartily glad," wrote Eliot to Mullan in January of 1900, "if the Jesuit colleges would so amplify their courses of instruction and raise their standards of admission, that they could be fairly put upon a level with such institutions as Dartmouth, Amherst, Williams, Haverford, Lafayette, Oberlin, Rutgers, Trinity (Ct.), and Wesleyan (Ct.)." Two weeks later, he wrote that it was "the duty of Catholics, not of Protestants, to study the present organization and methods of Jesuit Colleges, and if, on comparison with the Protestant Colleges, they find defects or evils, to suggest the remedies."[103] By 1906, Brosnahan was concerned that the Jesuits had indeed, albeit unwittingly, followed the example of the Protestant colleges, voicing his concerns in a lengthy letter to Pardow that was forwarded to Rome.

The vicissitudes of Latin in the Jesuit colleges concerned Brosnahan most immediately. "Without passing any judgment on individuals, their motives or purposes," wrote Brosnahan, "I do not hesitate to say, that there is a concentrated action (which would be a conspiracy, if the actors knew what they were about) on the part of some . . . to change our ideal of studies . . . and specifically to eliminate the Latin language, as a language of use, from our schools." This, Brosnahan noted, went "directly against the highest law of the Society." This unfortunate turn, he argued, suggested that the "spirit of the world . . . is beginning to leaven us." The troubles began "in the last five, or six years, or since the introduction of the schedule." Without fluency in Latin, students were unprepared for the study of philosophy and theology, their "treasures . . . locked up from them in a language to which they have not the key." Thus deprived, they "never acquire the true 'spiritus theologicus,' or the true 'Catholic instinct' for Catholic dogma." When students are illiterate in the language of the church, wrote Brosnahan,

> the spirit and thought of the Church gradually become unfamiliar, and the tendency is to drift towards a nationalized church. Shall we cooperate to bring about a similar condition of affairs in the United States, and indirectly foster that "Americanism" which we disapprove of in its conclusions and results? Yet in its last analysis this "Americanism" is simply unsound theology, due mainly to ignorance of the classic treasures of Catholic theology. . . .
>
> The *general causes* of this deterioration of studies in our Colleges is the idea of assimilating ourselves to Protestant Colleges, where it is notorious that solid study is neglected. And as you know, some of the better Protestant Colleges have recognized the deplorable condition of their studies and are making efforts to correct it, and in so doing are getting nearer and nearer to our ideals. We have, following the lead of the retrograde ones, adopted the ideal of school training which Father Roothaan reprobated in his letter introducing the new Ratio Studiorum. . . . There is scarcely a principle of study or scholarship . . . which the schedule imposed on the Province by the private authority of Fr. Purbrick and Fr. Gannon has not thrown to the winds. . . . In a word this movement is due to abnormal reverence for the methods of the modern world and its spirit, and to a disregard for our own laws and the ordinations of our Generals. . . .
>
> . . . I beg of you—and I know I am the voice of many—to do something to prevent the final degradation of our Colleges and studies. . . . You know of course that I am not opposed to progress and to adapting our studies to the need of our times. They are after all only means to get the Catholic youth into our Colleges. But we cannot give up the teaching of Latin—the efficient teaching of it, that is—without harm to ourselves and the church. The language of Rome is in our care in this country.[104]

After a protracted bout with cancer, Martín died in 1906, and with his passing the Jesuits convened the twenty-fifth General Congregation.[105]

Congregations were occasions not only to elect a new superior general but to engage in discussion about the Jesuits' shared life and work as a religious order. In some ways, the twenty-fifth General Congregation staked out a path of continuity: the delegates elected another conservative, Franz Xavier Wernz (1906–14), to be superior general. In his interactions with U.S. Jesuits, Wernz followed Martín's lead, voicing concerns over American Jesuits' increased engagement with the modern world, whether in the form of their fascination with athletics, late curfews for students, or members of the Society studying for doctorates at non-Catholic universities.

But the twelfth decree of the twenty-fifth General Congregation also effected a rather significant departure: the Jesuits formally conceded the universality of the *Ratio*. In 1832 they had recognized that the *Ratio* could not be mandated universally; thus, exceptions were allowed. By the twentieth century, chaotic, ever-changing circumstances rendered even a flexible rule for the entire Society an impossibility. The goals of Jesuit education spelled out in the proceedings of the twenty-fifth General Congregation harked back to the earliest days of the Society: "not only to develop all the faculties" in students, but "to lead them toward faith, piety, and good morals, and accustom them to discipline, and to teach them to act out of virtue." The method of instruction outlined in the *Ratio Studiorum* was to be preserved "as far as possible." Classical studies were to be emphasized as "far and away the most suitable instrument for the development of abilities and the most conformable to our institute." Where "necessity of great utility" made it "advisable," non-classical studies could be offered, provided classical studies did not suffer. But given the "variety and instability in legislation concerning schools and the subject matter taught there," a universally applicable "new edition" of the *Ratio Studiorum* "should not be attempted." Provincials, "after listening to their consultors and their most experienced teachers," were to craft a version of the *Ratio* fitted to the circumstances in their particular region and then submit their plans to the superior general for approval.[106] With this directive, primary responsibility for the *Ratio* shifted from Rome to the provinces.

It was in the two years following the election of the new superior general that the extent and implications of the Catholic drift toward non-Catholic colleges began to sink in among the Jesuit community at large. As late as 1906, Francis Cassilly, S.J., who was surveying Catholic students at state universities, wrote to Denis O'Connell of the Catholic University of America, "it seems to me that there is no reason for us, who

are engaged in Catholic education to take a gloomy view of the subject."
But Father John Farrell's 1907 report on Catholics at non-Catholic colleges and Louis Mercier's 1908 report on Catholic college enrollments
spawned deep gloom among the Jesuits and other Catholic educators.
"Nowhere can I find an optimistic feeling about the future of our colleges," wrote O'Connell early in 1907.[107] Throughout Catholic educational circles, morale was very low.

On the first day of 1908, amid deep confusion, Provincial Joseph
Hanselman sent a letter to members of the Maryland–New York Province inviting them, once again, to the work of crafting a new schedule of
studies. Referring to the decree of the recent General Congregation that
placed responsibility for studies on the provinces, he wrote, "We all recognize the opportuneness and the importance of this direction. The
difficulty is how best to carry it out." The challenges were formidable.
"School education is nearly everywhere in all but a chaotic state. The
colleges of our Province, as far as college education proper (from Freshman to Senior) is concerned, are in most cases [well nigh] deserted."
Through committee work, wide consultation, and review of programs of
study in use at the various colleges, the provincial hoped to realize a
"general outline along the lines of our Ratio Studiorum with such
modifications in the *matter* as modern and local conditions demand."
Exhorting his flagging troops, he urged each to "make a personal effort,"
adding in closing that "we want light and energy and generosity and
hearty cooperation."[108]

In 1908, yet another committee, with fifteen members, including
Brosnahan, began work on another schedule, their efforts culminating in
the "Schedule of Studies for the Colleges of the Maryland–New York
Province, 1910." The explanatory remarks accompanying the schedule
did not mention "prelections, reviews, repetitions, recitations, examinations, marks, etc." (i.e., aspects of Jesuit method); "all these and the
time-honored methods of the Ratio Studiorum are supposed," the document said.[109] Like the schedules preceding it, the 1910 schedule focused primarily on the *matter* of Jesuit education. The proceedings from
an early meeting reveals a host of substantive issues on the committee's
agenda. "Is the eight years' course . . . to be retained?" "Should a
non-Greek or scientific course be allowed along with the classical?"
"Should the degree of A.B. be restricted to the classical course?" "How
many branches (prescribed and elective) should be required in the High
School course[?] . . . the College course? Name them." "How many hours
(or periods) should be assigned for each week?" "In case of the eight

years' course, should Latin, Greek and English be taught in the Junior year?" "Should Solid Geometry be retained as a prescribed study?" "Should there be a fixed, uniform nomenclature for the names of the classes?" "How can a uniform and efficient sanction for the examinations . . . be best secured? Is a Central Examination Board or something similar feasible?" "Should Philosophy be taught in Latin?"[110]

Yielding little to the new academic order, the Committee of Fifteen crafted a schedule that represented the last great stand for the *Ratio Studiorum* in the eastern United States. The differences between the schedules of 1906 and 1910 were few and minor: the classical languages, philosophy, religion, and the sciences made small gains, while mathematics and English realized slight losses. With the exception of ethics, philosophy was to be taught in Latin. But the schedule of 1910 proved unworkable. Complaints soon surfaced. Between 1914 and 1917, the prefects of studies met annually to wrestle with the problems inherent in their latest attempt to fit the *Ratio* to the twentieth-century academic scene. As early as 1914 they dropped their own Latin syllabus in favor of that in use in the public schools. In 1915 they finally admitted that they could no longer teach philosophy in Latin.[111]

From within and without, the Jesuits of the Maryland–New York Province were challenged to forego their traditional educational practices in favor of American-styled education. During the late-nineteenth and early-twentieth centuries, the factors pushing (and largely resisted by) the Jesuits were, in essence, external to the Society. The forces of modernity that gave rise to the new academic order and the Jesuits' troubles with Harvard relentlessly demanded attention. Their traditional constituency's flight toward the modern universities and other nonclassical institutes emptied their colleges of students. But during the first two decades of the twentieth century, the forces militating in favor of reform came closer to home. The Jesuits of the Maryland–New York Province, where the presidents of Georgetown and Boston College had created an international stir by defending the tradition of Jesuit higher education, began to fall behind, even within Catholic circles. Increasingly, they found themselves among Catholic educators willing to broach modest reforms. Their involvement in the ACCUS exposed them to reform-minded Catholics from other religious orders who responded more favorably to the academic revolution.[112] While the Jesuits labored over the issue of dividing the seven-year course of studies into distinctive preparatory and collegiate-level programs, other Catholic educators accepted the four-plus-four-year model and began a successful push for the establishment of independent Catholic high schools. Even within Jesuit circles, the Jesuits in the Maryland–New York Province lagged behind. Though the Jesuits in the Missouri Province also resisted reform (especially during the years in which conservative Rudolph Meyer headed the province), during the 1910s they moved toward modern educational structures and accepted the American norms of standardization and external accreditation.[113]

In the Maryland–New York Province, curricular concession to the new academic order came in the 1920s. Those who crafted the schedule of 1910 stood by the *Ratio Studiorum*. In 1920, the next major attempt to revise the *Ratio* failed miserably, with the committee rather resentfully arguing for the reduction in the amount of course work for collegians on the grounds that the Jesuit colleges must concede to students' "craze for pleasure" and their "passion for earning money" and "concessions universally made by other colleges and universities to 'this-easier-way-of-doing-things' spirit of the times."[114] With the 1920 schedule quickly rejected, those who crafted the schedule of 1923 took the turn toward American-style education, adopting the curricular modus operandi of their non-Catholic counterparts. The high schools and the colleges finally went separate ways.[115] The "unit," "credit," and "semester hour" —mechanisms of curricular structuring formerly resisted by the Jesuits—were adopted. ("To secure uniformity among ourselves, as well as to come into accord with the way of speaking of colleges, universities, and the educational world generally, the committee recommends the employment of the term *Semester Hour* as a unit or standard for computing the student's work.") Majors were introduced, electives were increased, and Greek became optional.[116]

By the early 1920s, the Jesuit colleges in the United States were beginning to look more like their contemporary Protestant counterparts than nineteenth-century Jesuit colleges. Though Jesuit officials in Rome had slowed the processes of change, Jesuit campuses gradually assumed an American feel. Religious discipline remained rigorous (mandatory daily attendance at mass was common) and the role of in loco parentis was taken seriously, if not by all students, then by faculty and staff. But popular student culture had reshaped the Catholic campus along more American lines. Athletics flourished, discipline loosened. American-styled dormitories were erected, and heterosocial culture flourished; to wit, Catholic women's colleges, which sprang up by the dozens and then the hundreds in the twentieth century, were often sited in proximity to men's colleges.

In little more than a decade, the *Ratio Studiorum* so ably defended by

Brosnahan was largely undone. The coherent program of studies and integrated approach to education that served Ignatius and his followers for more than three centuries was supplanted as the Jesuits finally fit their colleges to the challenges of time, place, and person that they encountered in the age of the university. The changes were made often with the greatest of reluctance, for not infrequently they entailed sacrificing what was perceived as pedagogically sound and culturally valuable in favor of the untried and superficial. Yet circumstances demanded it. "Were Catholics in this country many times more influential than they are, they might succeed in enforcing educational standards different from those actually in vogue," wrote a Jesuit from the Midwest in the early 1920s. "In all that pertains to the fixing of educational standards whether by legal enactment or public opinion, the determining voice is that of the non-Catholic elements of the country."[117]

Still, the principles and commitments of the *Ratio Studiorum* continued to shape Jesuit education in powerful ways throughout the twentieth century. While expanding their graduate programs and professional schools, the Jesuits remained strongly committed to the education of undergraduates. The humanistic and philosophical traditions laid claim to much of the curriculum. Though crowded by other subjects, the classical languages retained a place of honor in the Jesuit curriculum until the middle of the twentieth century; at Boston College, the study of Greek was required for graduation until the 1930s, the study of Latin through the 1940s. Moreover, the Jesuits held fast to an educational philosophy rooted in the moral and religious. While the moral and religious education of students, a central facet of nineteenth-century American higher education, was pushed to the margins in the pace-setting universities of the twentieth century, the Jesuits and other Catholic educators remained committed to a countercultural vision of education that aimed at the education of the whole student.

The adaptations that the Jesuits made to time, place, and person as the academic revolution of the late-nineteenth century gave rise to a new academic order in Protestant America seriously strained the Jesuit system; modern education required significant concessions. But the philosophy of education and principles of pedagogy espoused and defended by Brosnahan were vindicated in some important ways. The policy of radical electivism, which Harvard's Eliot claimed as one of the greatest achievements of his presidency, was rolled back by his successors. The growing inability of the modern academy to address moral issues and engage religion, a trend ironically set in motion by early university re-

formers, proved persistently discomforting in various quarters throughout the twentieth century.[118]

The Harvard Law School controversy was a defining moment in the
history of Jesuit and Catholic higher education. It was the first great
encounter with the modern academic order in Protestant America.
Therein, modern academic realities and the challenges of time, place,
and person became strikingly clear, the necessity of reform sharply apparent, the strengths and weaknesses of Jesuit education increasingly
obvious. Though the transformation was often difficult, contentious, protracted, begrudging, and uninspired, occasional judicious resistance
and politic adaptation by early-twentieth-century Jesuits to modern,
Protestant-inspired education gradually obtained for their successors a
viable future for Jesuit higher education in the United States.

Conclusion

I foresee that we shall have to
get a clear definition of what a
Catholic college is.

—F. Heiermann, S.J., 1906

Following the revolution that produced a new academic order in American higher education at the end of the nineteenth century, the Jesuits took their first substantive steps into the world of modern higher education during the first two decades of the twentieth. In reorganizing and implementing curricular and extracurricular changes, their colleges came to resemble more closely the Protestant institutions that Harvard President Charles Eliot urged them to emulate at the height of the Law School controversy. Setting aside a number of traditions and practices inherited from their predecessors in Europe, Jesuit and other Catholic colleges assumed an American hue. But in conforming their colleges institutionally and organizationally to standard practice in American higher education, had they resolved the fundamental conundrum that surfaced in the 1890s? Had they set their institutions on a trajectory toward academic respectability while ensuring that they remained vitally Catholic? Or in following the example of Protestant higher education, did the Jesuits render the religious soul of their educational enterprise vulnerable to the corrosive effects of modernity? A brief overview of the events described in earlier chapters and a review of subsequent developments in Catholic higher education during the twentieth century (necessarily drawn in broad strokes) suggest that the Jesuits' conservative responses to the rise of a new academic order slowed their pursuit of academic respectability. Nonetheless, Jesuit conservatism also helped to protect their colleges from the secularizing currents of modern intellectual life, positioning them to reassert their religious identity in a postmodern period.

This book has examined the Jesuits—primarily those from the Maryland–New York Province—as they weathered the academic revolution that gave rise to the age of the university. For these Jesuits, two interrelated crises constituted the most immediate points of engagement with the postbellum academic revolution: the refusal of Harvard Law School to recognize the degrees of Jesuit colleges and the decision by large numbers of Catholics to patronize non-Catholic colleges and universities. These two crises were symptomatic of three broader challenges facing Catholic higher education at the turn of the century: that of time, in the form of the modern mindset; that of persons, in the form of upwardly mobile Catholics; and that of place, in the form of Protestant America. For the Jesuits, having to respond to immediate crises and broader challenges required various strategies. Before their modern-minded public critics, it necessitated an apologia for the *Ratio Studiorum* and traditional education. Within Catholic circles, it required a defense of separatism in education. Among themselves, it entailed serious debate about the ways in which they should adapt their colleges to a new, increasingly regularized academic order and the academic propensities of their traditional constituency.

In describing this period in American religious history, Martin Marty rightfully notes, with other historians, that the "great theorists of modernization displayed an all but sovereign indifference to the high cost of change because they belonged to the Protestant core-culture."[1] For those who stood outside this core culture, the changes effected by the forces of modernization were often perceived as threats to what the outsiders held as sacred, and thus the changes often created anxiety and confusion. The same analysis easily applies to the individuals who appeared in the preceding pages. Charles Eliot and the other great university builders stood squarely within the Protestant core culture (although it is certainly better to situate Eliot within that of Boston Unitarianism). From their liberal Protestant vantage, change seemed evidence of the hand of God and reform in education nothing less than a religious mandate. For the Jesuits and other Catholic educators, the same forces of modernity celebrated and marshaled by liberal Protestant academic reformers looked like nothing less than an assault on what they considered sacred, inviolable bedrock in education.

There is poignancy in recounting the Jesuits' struggles to come to terms with the academic revolution. Like other Catholic educators, they operated beyond the pale of Protestant culture and responded to the emergence of a new academic order without the resources of religious liberalism and theological modernism. But the Jesuits also entered this critical period in American higher education largely lacking what traditionally had been one of the Society's greatest assets: a willingness to adapt their educational practices to the circumstances they encountered. Corporately, and on numerous counts, members of the Society that had known great success in the sixteenth, seventeenth, and eighteenth centuries were unprepared to deal with the challenges that beset them in late-nineteenth-century America. As Jesuit historian William Bangert described it, nineteenth-century Jesuits "lost the feel for the pulse of the times and the sense of change in history." Their approach to education suffered, wrote John O'Malley, from a "tired and defensive formalism."[2]

Of course, the ideal of adaptation to time, place, and person developed by the earliest Jesuits had not completely disappeared; a number of American Jesuits recognized not only the necessity but the inherent value of adapting their schools to the academic standards and mores of higher education in America. But on the whole, this was a particularly conservative and unimaginative period in the history of the Society, with many, including its European-based leadership, far more disposed to resist than to adapt to new academic realities.

Despite the Jesuits' slow, often begrudging responses to the rise of a new academic order, the history of Jesuit higher education in the twentieth century is not one of decline and retrenchment but one rather of substantial growth and gradual improvement. By aligning their colleges more closely with American standards and practices during the century's early decades, the move toward academic respectability and institutional viability commenced. In 1900, the Jesuits enrolled 6,613 (preparatory, collegiate, and masters) students in their twenty-six American colleges; in 1999–2000, full- and part-time enrollment reached 188,892, in twenty-eight institutions.[3] Once limited to a prescribed curriculum, undergraduates' curricular options expanded dramatically. Following the lead of Georgetown and Saint Louis, which already offered postgraduate courses and professional education in the nineteenth century, almost all Jesuit colleges added graduate programs and professional schools in the twentieth. But rapid expansion exacted a serious toll. Through midcentury, several Jesuit colleges had difficulty securing accreditation for their professional programs, and few graduate programs were well regarded. The Jesuit colleges still had a long way to go toward reaching accepted academic norms, partly because of their late response to the academic revolution, partly because a persistent insular posture among a number of Jesuits retarded their engagement with the academic mainstream.[4] Only in the last third of the twentieth century did Jesuit higher education achieve academic respectability, with a number of Jesuit institutions and programs garnering national and even international recognition for their rigor and high standards. One hundred years after Charles Eliot accused Jesuit higher education of academic inferiority, the three Jesuit colleges at the center of the Law School controversy were, in terms of admission, among the most selective colleges in the country. Within their respective categories, Holy Cross, Boston College, and Georgetown University appeared in the top fifty in *U.S. News & World Report* rankings in 2002. Established in 1929, Boston College Law School ranked twenty-second among law schools (while Harvard Law School ranked third).

It is important to note that Jesuit adaptation to American higher education through the mid-twentieth century did not entail a complete concession to modernity, but rather a mix of adaptation and resistance that ensured Jesuit higher education of a distinctive Catholic identity until well into the twentieth century. Historian Philip Gleason notes that contending with modernity consisted of institutional adjustments, not ideological alignment. Institutionally and organizationally, the Jesuits and other Catholic educators conformed. They divided the seven-year course of study into four years of high school followed by four years of college. They developed majors, professional programs, and even offered elective courses. They made significant concessions to popular student culture, particularly through athletic programs. But by holding epistemologically to neo-Thomism,[5] they resisted the currents of modern intellectual life. While secular academics put their faith in science and Protestants sought ways to reconnect Christ and culture, Catholics believed that they were possessed of an integrated, all-encompassing philosophical and theological system.[6] Though Catholic intellectual life was largely cut off from the wider academic community, within Catholic academic circles Leo XIII's 1879 identification of the work of Thomas Aquinas as the foundation of Catholic scholarly life blossomed into a period of great intellectual vitality that helped create and sustain a Catholic subculture within American higher education. Catholic faculty developed their own professional organizations and published their own journals. Not only did students study Catholic philosophy and theology, but their faculty advanced a "Catholic point of view" on a wide array of issues, from literature to economics, family life to politics. As Julie Reuben convincingly demonstrates, one of the ironic outcomes of the university movement was the marginalization, by the mid-twentieth century, of moral concerns in the mainstream academy. Concurrently, a Thomistic-inspired approach to intellectual life among Catholic educators found practical expression in the development of a midcentury social action movement, with Catholic faculty, students, and alumni aiming to better society through various strategies and programs shaped by the church's teaching on the social order.[7]

Yet ideological resistance to the intellectual iteration of modernity could not sustain the *Ratio Studiorum*. In 1999, on the four-hundredth anniversary of the *Ratio*, a writer for the *Boston College Chronicle* celebrated the ancient, influential document by enumerating illustrious students of Jesuit education—not only Descartes, Moliere, Francis de Sales, and Charles Carroll but, in more recent years, Tip O'Neill, Fidel Castro, and Bill Clinton.[8] The claim for the influence of the *Ratio* on the latter group stretched the imagination. By the time Tip O'Neill graduated from Boston College in 1936, the *Ratio Studiorum's* claim on the curriculum was waning; by the time Bill Clinton graduated from Georgetown with a bachelor's degree in foreign policy in 1968, the *Ratio* had been quietly and gradually shelved. Yet the vision of the early Jesuits that gave rise to the *Ratio Studiorum* in the sixteenth century continued to shape Jesuit higher education in the twentieth. The Society's deeply held belief in the "humanizing potential of the humanities," so evident in the *Ratio*, endured;[9] the liberal arts, including philosophy and theology, continue to hold curricular primacy of place in Jesuit colleges. Moreover, the Society's commitment to education *ad civitatis utilitatem* continued—recast, in the late-twentieth century, in a corporate commitment to form "men and women for others." The modern Jesuit parlance describes a commitment that has been most strikingly evident in numerous university-community partnership initiatives, popular volunteer programs, flagship service-learning courses, and highly regarded ethics courses.[10]

The *Ratio Studiorum* went into "semi-official but definitive retirement" during the twentieth century,[11] but Jesuit and other Catholic colleges entered the 1960s with their religiosity intact, their Catholic identity taken for granted.[12] Religiously, institutional adaptation and intellectual resistance to modern intellectual life had proven themselves an effective mix, insofar as Catholic colleges had resisted the trend toward secularization evident in much of Protestant higher education. According to historian George Marsden, Catholic educators made a judicious "tradeoff." By holding to neo-Thomism and resisting the currents of modern intellectual life, Catholic higher education continued to suffer the taint of second-class citizenship within the broader academy, but "emerged from this era with one thing Protestants did not: universities with substantial religious identities."[13] Marsden made this claim in his influential *The Soul of the American University: From Protestant Establishment to Established Nonbelief* (1994). Garnering widespread attention throughout the academy, in Catholic circles his work was quickly incorporated into lively, widespread, often heated conversations about the most compelling question of the day: were Catholic colleges still Catholic? During the three preceding decades, had they lost what Marsden claimed they still had in 1960—a distinctly Catholic identity? Or had Catholic intellectual resistance to modernity merely forestalled the inevitable processes of secularization? Had the quest for academic respectability ultimately cost Catholic colleges their soul? Given their prominent place in American Catholic higher education, the Jesuit colleges, along with Notre Dame, found themselves subject to intense scrutiny. Relative to this study, it makes for a tidy inversion. In the 1890s there was no doubt that the Jesuit colleges were Catholic; the issue was whether they were sufficiently American. By the 1990s there was no doubt that they were American; the issue was whether they were adequately Catholic.

"Development may be forecast; revolution cannot."[14] Having weathered the revolution that gave rise to modern, American higher education, revolutionary forces buffeted Catholic higher education once again in the 1960s. Like other colleges and universities throughout the United States, they endured the tumult that rocked the nation's campuses in the 1960s. But Catholic higher education faced another kind of upheaval, as the Roman Catholic bishops of the world gathered in the eternal city launched their own revolution: Vatican Council II (1962–65). Turning from historic patterns of triumphalism and defensiveness vis-à-vis the world, council participants declared that the ancient Church of Rome was a church engaged in and in service to the modern world. Thus ended the church's "cold war with modernity," as one contemporary described it.[15]

In 1960 no one could have anticipated the radical nature of Vatican

Council II nor foreseen its profound impact on Catholic higher education in the United States (that impact can only be summarized here).
Along a sweeping front, the council's surprising rapprochement with the
modern world set forth in the council's *Pastoral Constitution on the
Church in the Modern World, Gaudium et Spes,* stirred enthusiasm for articulating a comparable vision for the Catholic university. Responding
to a 1965 call from the International Federation of Catholic Universities
to discuss the nature and role of the Catholic university, twenty-six
church leaders and academics in the United States, including a significant number of Jesuits, gathered to discuss the issue. Their "Land
O'Lakes Statement: The Nature of the Contemporary Catholic University" signaled a decided turn toward modern academic norms; while
they reaffirmed the importance of Catholicism within the university,
they asserted the necessity of academic freedom and institutional autonomy.[16] Five years later their work was joined with that of other regional
groups, and under the leadership of Notre Dame President Theodore
Hesburgh, C.S.C., the International Federation of Catholic Universities
issued "The Catholic University in the Modern World." It, too, asserted
the need for "true autonomy and academic freedom" that flowed from
the "very nature and purpose" of a university.[17]

Vatican Council II's theology of the laity, stressing their call to holi-
ness and Christian vocation to the world, also affected Catholic higher
education, providing theological impetus for greater lay participation in
leadership. Along these lines, the most significant and startling change
in the postconciliar period occurred in the area of governance. Following
the lead of Saint Louis University and the University of Notre Dame,
which created primarily lay boards of trustees in 1967, the Jesuits and
other religious orders abandoned governance structures in which board
membership was limited to members of the sponsoring religious order;
moving toward models of shared governance, they rewrote their by-laws
in ways ensuring significant lay representation.[18] Invoking the language
of the council, a contributor to the Jesuits' *America* magazine explained
that boards that included lay persons "more accurately reflect the shar-
ing of responsibilities that ought to characterize the People of God."[19]

Revolutions rarely lack for unintended consequences, and thus it is
not surprising that Vatican II changed the church and its institutions of
higher learning in unanticipated ways. The same forces inspired by Vatican II that pushed Catholic higher education into greater engagement
with the modern world made it more difficult for Catholic colleges and
universities to sustain their religious commitments. Traditional sources

supporting the religious life of Catholic colleges weakened following the council. As noted above, while institutionally and organizationally conforming to American higher education, Catholic higher education retained its distinctively Catholic character by holding fast to a worldview rooted in neo-Thomism. Already showing stress fractures by the 1950s, this intellectual system, championed by the Jesuit-educated Leo XIII, thoroughly collapsed in the immediate wake of Vatican II.[20] With its sudden demise, the intellectual system that bounded Catholic higher education, grounded a Catholic worldview, and sustained a vital subculture, all but disappeared. Though the postconciliar period was a time of theological ferment, no comprehensive philosophical or theological system emerged as a replacement to neo-Thomism.

The second unforeseen consequence of Vatican II for Catholic higher education was its laicization. Religious orders, the backbone of Catholic higher education, went through tremendous upheaval in the wake of Vatican II. Thousands of priests, sisters, and brothers left religious life altogether, while other religious left college classrooms for parishes and social ministries. Concurrently, the number of young men and women entering religious life dropped off markedly. The decline in vocations to religious life became increasingly and acutely apparent on Catholic college campuses after 1970 as the men and women who corporately embodied the religious mission of their respective institutions steadily and dramatically decreased in number. In many cases, on campuses once almost entirely staffed by religious, the sight of a priest, brother, or sister, even in the president's office, became a rarity. A survey of presidents of Catholic colleges and heads of religious orders published in 2000 found that 43 percent of Catholic college presidencies were held by laymen and laywomen; 28 percent of respondents predicted that, within ten years, virtually no members of the founding religious order would be involved in the work of their respective colleges.[21]

Thus within a few decades, internal and external forces reshaped the religious face of Catholic higher education dramatically. Vatican Council II played a major role in the transformation, not only in terms of staffing and intellectual matters but in liturgical life as well. As in the church at large, Vatican II profoundly affected devotional and sacramental practice on campus. Voluntary attendance at masses in English replaced compulsory attendance at masses in Latin; folk groups supplanted choirs. Weekly confession fell out of favor. Powerful external forces, including important legal cases and legislation regarding hiring and funding, also played important roles in reshaping religious life in

Catholic higher education. Moreover, the traditional college constituency changed: the student body became more religiously diverse, coeducation became common, and nontraditional, older students came to form a large segment of the student body.

Given such profound changes, by the 1980s a number of commentators began wondering whether Catholic higher education had, in the midst of so much change, lost its soul, or at least its religious bearings. Observers could quickly point to the academic successes of Catholic higher education, even as the salient issue concerning religious identity of Catholic colleges and universities came to the foreground. A number of observers and critics cast changes in Catholic higher education during the second half of the twentieth century as evidence of secularization.[22] Given demographic changes, the head of the Association of Jesuit Colleges and Universities, for example, wondered whether he was presiding over the demise of Jesuit education. And while lay presidential leadership was commonplace by 2001, the appointment of a layman to head Georgetown University, the flagship Jesuit school and the nation's oldest Catholic college, generated widespread comment. Many questioned whether Georgetown could forestall secularization and retain its Jesuit character without a Jesuit at the helm.[23]

It was in the midst of these changes that the Vatican became involved in conversations regarding the religious identity of Catholic higher education in the United States. Although wide-ranging in scope, discussions between American academic leaders and the hierarchy in the United States and Rome were dominated by the publication of two key documents: the revised Code of Canon Law (1983) and *Ex Corde Ecclesiae* (1990), John Paul II's apostolic constitution on Catholic higher education. The implementation of both documents, which gave church officials greater oversight in Catholic higher education, provoked widespread discussion within Catholic educational circles and beyond. Roman officials, U.S. bishops, college presidents, national leaders, and faculty vigorously debated what made a Catholic college Catholic and who was responsible for ensuring that identity. Rome's efforts to ensure that Catholic colleges remained Catholic through juridical measures often sparked tension between the college presidents and the hierarchy. Just as a number of forward-looking Jesuits in the late 1890s struggled to explain to their Roman superiors the distinctive challenges and opportunities Jesuit higher education faced in the United States, academic leaders in the 1980s and 1990s often struggled to explain to Rome the constraints under which American Catholic higher education operated. Academic leaders were concerned that Rome's juridical approach would create serious legal and financial challenges, threaten academic freedom, and undermine Catholic higher education's standing within the broader academic community. The long, often contentious process culminated in 2001 with Rome's approval of guidelines for implementation of *Ex Corde Ecclesiae.* Most noticeably, the guidelines direct Catholic theologians in Catholic colleges who teach subjects with a substantive Catholic content to secure a *mandatum,* or license, from the local bishop; it indicates that their writing and teaching accord with that of the official church. The outcome of decades of discussion—juridical in its approach—was, on the whole, poorly received in Catholic academic circles. Not only were the juridical norms, as developed, difficult to implement and troublesome in themselves, they were considered by many to be unsatisfactory mechanisms for ensuring the Catholic identity of a Catholic college.

It has indeed become challenging for many Catholic colleges to assert a robust Catholic identity. But like the story of Jesuit higher education in the twentieth century, the story of religion on the Catholic campus in the post–Vatican II period is not one of straightforward decline. Quite simply, salient questions and pressing issues notwithstanding, religion did not disappear from Catholic campuses during the late-twentieth century. Like religion in the broader public square, religion on campus refused to abdicate completely to the forces of secularization. While certainly not as thickly religious as before Vatican Council II, Catholic colleges are far from being wholly secular. While presidents and other national leaders focused their attention on implementation of *Ex Corde Ecclesiae,* Catholic campuses, like their non-Catholic counterparts, witnessed a notable surge of interest in religion and spirituality among faculty, staff, and students. Indeed, growing and widespread interest in religion on campus, secular and religious, constitutes one of the more interesting and notable developments in American higher education in recent years.[24]

At the end of the twentieth century, religion made a strong showing in Jesuit higher education. While administrators considered how to "hire for mission"—a growing concern given the waning number of Jesuits—a number of faculty have quietly sought ways in which to integrate their personal religious commitments with their work in higher education. For some faculty, religion has become an important object of study; for others, their religious and spiritual commitments function epistemologically, as another "way of knowing."[25] Their interest in religion finds expression through their participation in numerous conferences and symposia on religion, membership in Christian professional organizations, and their interactions with students inside and outside of the classroom. And though they are not as traditionally religious as many of their elders would like, students also give strong evidence of interest in religion and spirituality. Like their baby-boomer parents, they are a "generation of seekers," as one sociologist put it,[26] who variously swell enrollments in theology and religion classes, crowd into chapel, flock to service-learning programs, join religious and spiritual groups, and participate in traditional Catholic sacramental and devotional practices.[27]

Each generation of academics has had its own challenges and opportunities. To Charles Eliot's generation fell the immense task of responding to the vast expansion of knowledge and the industrial revolution. At the beginning of the twenty-first century, to denizens of an academic world shaped in large measure by the great nineteenth-century university builders has fallen the task of wrestling with one of the ironic outcomes of the academic revolution. Though clearly convinced that they were reforming higher education in the service of a Protestant America, Eliot and the other academic leaders of his generation set the stage for the eventual marginalization of religion and moral concerns in the academy. To the Jesuits and their lay colleagues now at work in the Society's American colleges has fallen responsibility for securing a vital place for religion in their academic enterprise. It is tempting to fault the Jesuits of Timothy Brosnahan's generation for resisting modernity and retarding the development of Jesuit higher education. But perhaps in their delay they created a critical temporal window, positioning Jesuits a century later to realize academically respectable and vitally Catholic colleges.

Harvard Law School's Select List of Colleges, 1893

The following is the list of colleges as it appeared in the 1893–94 *Harvard Annual Catalogue* (pp. 352–53). When the faculty voted in April 1893 to create a select list of colleges, they came up with sixty-nine institutions. Before publication of the list in the catalog, forty-four were added, including Georgetown, Boston College, and the College of the Holy Cross. Only one school was dropped: Adelbert. *Italic type* has been added to indicate the schools added between the April meeting and publication of the list.

TERMS OF ADMISSION AFTER THE ACADEMIC YEAR 1895–96

After the academ[i]c year 1895–96 the following persons will be admitted as candidates for a degree without examination:—

I. *Bachelors of Arts of the following Colleges:

Acadia,
University of Alabama,
Allegheny,
Amherst,
Antioch,
Bates,
Beloit,
Boston,
Boston University,

Bowdoin,
Brown University,
Buchtel,
Bucknell,
University of California,
Carleton,
Central,
University of Chicago,
University of Cincinnati,

Clark University,
Colby University,
Colgate University,
University of Colorado,
Columbia,
Cornell,
Cornell University,
Dalhousie,
Dartmouth,
Delaware,
Denison University,
DePauw University,
Dickinson,
Drake University,
Earlham,
University of Georgia,
Georgetown (D.C.),
Griswold,
Hamilton,
Hanover,
Harvard,
Haverford,
Hobart,
Holy Cross,
Illinois,
University of Illinois,
University of Indiana,
Iowa,
State University of Iowa,
Johns Hopkins University,
University of Kansas,
Kenyon,
Kings,
Knox,
Lafayette,
Lehigh University,
Leland Stanford Jr. University,
Marietta,
McGill University,
Miami University,

University of Michigan,
Middlebury,
University of Minnesota,
University of Mississippi,
University of Missouri,
Mt. Union,
University of Nebraska,
University of New Brunswick,
College of the City of New York,
University of the City of New York,
University of North Carolina,
Northwestern University,
Oberlin,
Ohio State University,
Ohio Wesleyan University,
Olivet,
University of Oregon,
University of Pennsylvania,
Princeton,
Racine,
University of Rochester,
Rutgers,
Saint Lawrence University,
University of the South,
University of South Carolina,
Swarthmore,
Syracuse University,
University of Texas,
University of Toronto,
Trinity,
Tufts,
Tulane University of Louisiana,
Union,
Vanderbilt University,
University of Vermont,
Victoria University,
University of Virginia,
Washington University (Mo.),
Washington and Jefferson,
Wesleyan University (Ct.),

Western Reserve University,
Western University of
   Pennsylvania,
Williams,

University of Wisconsin,
Wittenberg,
University of Wooster,
Yale University.

II. *Bachelors of Literature of the following Colleges:*

University of California,
University of Cincinnati,
Cornell University,
Dartmouth,

University of Michigan,
University of Minnesota,
University of Wisconsin.

III. *Bachelors of Philosophy of the following Colleges:*

Beloit,
Brown University,
University of California,
Delaware,
Drake University,
Iowa,

State University of Iowa,
University of Michigan,
Oberlin,
Sheffield Scientific School,
University of Vermont,
University of Wooster.

IV. *Bachelors of Science of the following Colleges:*

Amherst,
Bowdoin,
Cornell University,
Harvard

State University of Iowa,
Knox,
Massachusetts Institute of
   Technology.

V. *Persons Qualified to enter the Senior Class of Harvard College.*

*This list has been made chiefly from the Colleges whose graduates have entered the School in recent years. It is accordingly not intended to be exhaustive, and will doubtless be enlarged from time to time. Graduates of Colleges not here mentioned are advised to communicate with the Librarian before making formal application for admission as candidates for a degree.

Colleges and Programs Added and Removed from Harvard Law School's Select List of Institutions, 1894–1903

Year	Added	Dropped
1894–95	Centre (A.B.), University of Notre Dame (Ind.) (A.B.), Wesleyan University (Ct.) (B.Ph.), Wharton School of Finance and Economy (B.Ph.).	
1895–96		
1896–97	Hillsdale (A.B.), Lake Forest University (A.B.), Mt. Allison (A.B.), Cornell University (B.Ph.), Ohio State University (B.Ph.), University of Pennsylvania (B.Ph.),	Clark University (A.B.), Wharton School of Finance and Economy (B.Ph.).

Year	Added	Dropped

Union (B.Ph.),
Yale University (B.Ph.),
Carleton (B.Sc.),
Dartmouth (B.Sc.),
University of Cincinnati (B.Sc.),
Ohio State University (B.Sc.),
University of Pennsylvania
   (B.Sc.),
DePauw University (B.Ph.).

1897–98

Albion (A.B., B.Ph.),
Alfred University (A.B., B.Ph.),
University of Missouri (B.Lit.),
Northwestern University
   (B.Lit., B.Ph., B.Sc.),
Boston University (B.Ph.),
University of Chicago
   (B.Ph., B.Sc.),
University of Michigan (B.Sc.),
University of Minnesota (B.Sc.),
Oberlin (B.Sc.),
Columbian (A.B.),
University of Missouri (B.Lit).

Boston College (A.B.),
Griswold (A.B.),
Holy Cross (A.B.),
Knox (B.Sc.),

1898–99

Adrian (A.B.),
Pennsylvania (A.B.),
Illinois (B.Ph.),
University of Rochester (B.Ph.).

1899–1900

Franklin and Marshall (A.B.),
Kansas Wesleyan University
   (A.B.),
Lawrence University (A.B.),
Missouri Valley (A.B.),
Princeton (B.Sc.).

1900–1901

Manhattan (A.B.),
St. John's (Md.) (A.B.),
Western Reserve University
   (B.Lit., B.Ph.),
Iowa (B.Sc.),
Pennsylvania (B.Sc.).

Year	Added	Dropped
1901–2	Colorado (A.B.), University of Colorado (B.Ph.), Ottawa University (A.B.), Pomona (A.B., B.Lit., B.Sc.), Central University (B.Lit.), Illinois Wesleyan University (B.Sc.).	
1902–3	Alma (A.B.), University of Indianapolis (A.B.), Iowa Wesleyan University (A.B., B.Lit., B.Ph., B.Sc.), Wheaton (A.B.), Denison University (B.Ph.), Dickinson (B.Ph.).	
1903–4	Coe (A.B., B.Sc., B.Lit.), University of Maine (A.B.), State University of North Dakota (A.B.), Ohio University (A.B.), Central University of Kentucky (B.Lit.), Pacific University (A.B., B.Lit., B.Sc.), Colorado (B.Ph.), Lafayette (B.Ph.), Drake University (B.Sc.), Illinois University (B.Sc.).	Centre (A.B.)

President Eliot and Jesuit Colleges, by Timothy Brosnahan, S.J.

A DEFENCE

I

Mr. Charles W. Eliot, President of Harvard University, published some time ago in the *Atlantic Monthly*, an article advocating the extension of his elective system to secondary or high schools. Before dismissing his subject he saw fit to transgress the proper scope of his paper, as indicated by its title, in order to express his views on Moslem and Jesuit Colleges. What peculiar association of ideas is responsible for the yoking of Moslems and Jesuits in the same educational category it would be unprofitable to inquire, since it is a question of merely personal psychology. The present writer, having no brief for the Moslems, is concerned only with the strictures on the Jesuit system. These he thinks are unfounded, singularly inexact, and merit attention solely from the fact that they are the pronouncements of a man standing high in his profession.

The convictions of one holding the position of the President of Harvard University will naturally carry weight in educational matters. President Eliot has been at the head of one of our most prominent universities for over thirty years. It is no doubt due largely to his executive ability that the institution which he has governed so long has been so successful financially, and received that organization to which it owes, in part at least, its present popularity. It will be presumed therefore that he has made himself acquainted with a system of education which he thinks proper to criticize publicly. It will scarcely be expected that an educator of his prominence would thoughtlessly, or under the stress of any undue feeling, commit himself in a magazine article to adverse comments on a system which he did not deem worth his study.

President Eliot's estimate of the Jesuit system is expressed in the following passage in his paper: "There are those who say that there should be no election of studies in secondary schools. . . . This is precisely the method followed in Moslem countries, where the Koran* prescribes the perfect education to be administered to all children alike. The prescription begins in the primary schools and extends straight through the university; and almost the only mental power cultivated is memory. Another instance of uniform prescribed education may be found in the curriculum of the Jesuit Colleges, which has remained almost unchanged for four hundred years, disregarding some trifling concessions to natural sciences. That these examples are both ecclesiastical is not without significance. Nothing but an unhesitating belief in the divine wisdom of such prescriptions can justify them; for no human wisdom is equal to contriving a prescribed course of study equally good for even two children of the same family between the ages of eight and eighteen. Direct revelation from on high would be the only satisfactory basis for a uniform prescribed school curriculum. The immense deepening and expanding of human knowledge in the nineteenth century, and the increasing sense of the sanctity of the individual's gifts and will-power have made uniform prescriptions of study in secondary schools impossible and absurd."

Aside from the derogatory insinuations contained in this passage, the average reader will carry away from the perusal of it two main assertions: (1) that the Jesuit system of education implies a uniform prescribed curriculum of Moslem-like rigidity; (2) that the natural disparity of the individual student in gifts and will-power, the finite wisdom of the educator, and the increase of human knowledge are such as to necessitate the widest application of the elective system.

The first proposition enunciates what is claimed to be a fact, the second asserts a theory. These propositions, as we shall see, are extreme, and certainly not correlative. The negation of one does not infer the other. But in the truth of either the Jesuit system is condemned, not necessarily as a system of education, but as a system adapted to modern requirements. If the Jesuit system is as

---

*Though not directly bearing on the issue met by the present paper, it would, nevertheless, for the sake of erudition, interest many to have President Eliot cite or at least give references to the passages of the Koran where this comprehensive prescription of studies is found.

rigid in its prescribed matter as the system attributed to the Moslem, then it has failed to keep up with the modern development of knowledge, and to utilize modern sciences that possess educational values. If on the other hand all uniform prescriptions of study are "absurd and impossible," if no two individuals even of the same family can be submitted to the same uniform course of study, if only unlimited "electivism" is wise and possible, then undoubtedly the Jesuit system, and the system of many colleges wholly independent of the Jesuits, are condemned. In fact, if the principles of "electivism" must be applied to the education of every child of eight years and upward, it looks as if the President of Harvard had rung the death knell of all system, not only for colleges and high schools, but for primary schools as well; and we shall yet witness the exhilarating spectacle of "tots" of eight or ten years of age gravely electing their courses under the guidance, or rather with the approval of their nurses.

The state of the question as regards Jesuit Colleges may be clearer, if attention is directed to a distinction which the present General of the Society of Jesus thought it advisable to emphasize in an address delivered by him at Exaeten in Holland on January 1, 1893. He warns his hearers not to confound the Jesuit *method* of studies with the *matter* to which that method is applied. For the first he claimed stability, to the second he conceded change. The distinction is, of course, obvious, but not necessarily always present to those who discuss Jesuit or other systems of education. Now, I understand President Eliot to disapprove of our method in so far as he advocates the elective system of Harvard, and to maintain that, even in the subjects studied, the Jesuit system has adhered to the curriculum of four hundred years ago, excepting some slight concession to the natural sciences.

There is one way and only one way of investigating the truth of this last assertion. It is purely a question of facts. The records are published. He who runs may read. In the second, fifth, ninth, and sixteenth volumes of the *Monumenta Pædagogica Germaniæ* the history of the formation and growth of the Jesuit system, finally embodied authoritatively in the *Ratio Studiorum* of 1599, is given in all its details. One who wishes to find the facts need only contrast the studies indicated by the old *Ratio Studiorum* with the studies taught today in the various colleges of the Jesuits in various countries. One has only to compare, for instance, the program of studies at Georgetown College in Washington, at Stonyhurst College in England, at Feldkirch in Austria, at Kalocsa in Hungary, at Beyrouth in Syria, at the Ateneo Municipal in Manila, at Zi-ka-wei in China, in order to get a general, yet a fair idea, of the studies pursued in the Jesuit Colleges of today. By contrasting the courses employed in these colleges with those employed in the seventeenth century we may decide the question of fact. Whether our recent critic made an investigation of this kind or something equivalent I have no means of knowing. He gives us no intimation of the grounds on which he builds his statements. He simply asserts, with authoritative confidence and in a tone of finality, that for four hundred years there has been practically no change in the curriculum of studies in Jesuit Colleges. He may have thought the expenditure of time required to find the facts would be ill-repaid by the results; and in so thinking he may or may not be right. But in case he looked upon it as an unconscionable waste of time to explore the arid wastes of the Koran or the *Ratio Studiorum*, being an educated man, and having an educated man's dislike for facts that are constructed out of fancy, he might with decorum have abstained from all positive statement on the matter.

The bare facts are these. In the Jesuit schools of the seventeenth century the classes, which correspond to the college* classes of Jesuit schools today, were the three higher classes of the Gymnasium, with one class from the Lyceum, viz., *Suprema Grammatica, Humanitas, Rhetorica* and *Philosophia.* These classes, except the first two, were not necessarily each to be completed in one year; though it is the aim of the system in this country, when applied to diligent students, to have the courses, at least of the first three classes, finished in three years. The course of Philosophy may sometimes be extended beyond a year. The studies of the first three classes, by the *Ratio* of 1599, were the Latin and Greek languages and literature. The preparatory studies for these classes were made in the Grammar classes, corresponding in some respects to our modern Latin high school. The student entering the class of *Suprema Grammatica,* was reasonably familiar with the Latin and Greek languages, was able to read these languages, and to write Latin correctly, idiomatically and with some degree of ease. The purpose of his studies thereafter was to acquire the mental training and culture that came from an intelligent study of his authors as literature. The scope of the classes is indicated by the technical terms by which they are designated. In the judgment of those who planned the courses of 1599, that scope could be best attained by using the classic languages—at that time almost the only available instruments of college education. It is true, that in these classes, there were collateral studies—called *eruditio* in the *Ratio*—comprising the historical, geographical, ethnographical, critical, or other learning required to use the author read in accordance with the scope of the class. The character of the class was determined, however, not by the authors read, but rather the authors were selected in keeping with the purpose of the class. In this connection, it may not be out of place to note a fallacy which the writer from personal experience knows to obtain in places where one would judge it little likely to be found. The fallacy consists in measuring the grade of a class in a college course, by the author studied in that class. A mistake of this kind would indicate a very confused notion of educational ends. It ought to be quite clear that Caesar's Commentaries, for instance, studied in the first year of a high school, for the purpose of acquiring a Latin vocabulary, and a knowledge of Latin construction and idiom, is a vastly different thing from the study

*I use the word "College" in the sense which attaches to it in this country.

of the same Commentary by a body of young men, familiar with the Latin language and of some maturity of mind, in order to acquire a knowledge of historical style; that Homer's Iliad, studied by the high-school boy with one eye fixed on grammar and dictionary, is another book from that same Iliad, when read by a college student, in order to feel its epic power. Yet, undoubtedly, any one acquainted with the mechanical way of measuring class grades which is widely prevalent, at least in certain parts of this country, must confess that even those, who by their position ought to know the purpose of education, will attempt to determine a student's grade by the author he studied, and not by the end he had in view when studying that author, the method of studying, and the consequent mental results.* The scope of these three classes, therefore, is a distinct thing from the studies, or authors, which the Jesuit educators of the seventeenth century used to attain their end. Keeping these precautionary remarks in view, it is admitted that the twenty-five hours a week, constituting the class work of Jesuit schools in the seventeenth century, were practically devoted to the exclusive study of Latin and Greek.

With these twenty-five hours a week employed in the studies of Latin and Greek, let us contrast the studies and hours in the Jesuit College of today. For brevity's sake I take one American college. Georgetown University in its Collegiate Department exacts twenty-seven and a half hours a week of class work from every student who is a candidate for a college degree. But instead of one hundred per cent. of this time being given to Latin and Greek as in the schools of the seventeenth century, only about fifty-three per cent. is given to those studies today. Three hundred years later, then, forty-seven per cent. of class time is conceded to modern studies. Evidently there has been some change in the last "four hundred years," for nearly half of the class time has been wrested from the domain of Latin and Greek. This time is proportioned during four years to the study of English, mathematics, modern languages and natural sciences; specifically, three hours a week, exclusive of laboratory work, are assigned during the Sophomore and Junior years to natural sciences and eight hours a week during the Senior year. These facts are not difficult to obtain. Similar data may be had regarding the class hours in other Jesuit colleges. In view of them I shall permit the reader to surmise on what ground the declaration is made, that "another instance of uniform prescribed education may be found in the curriculum of Jesuit colleges, which has remained *almost unchanged for four hundred years,* disregarding some *trifling* concessions *to natural sciences.*"†

---

*The most lamentable confusion is manifested regarding the natural sciences. Physics, for instance, is taught in some of our high schools before the boys know even geometry. The result is not scientific education, but conceit. It is true some so-called laboratory practice is annexed. But in so far as any training of the mind in science, in inductive reasoning, in synthesis, and the faculty of observation is effected, the whole thing bears about the same relation to the teaching of science, that catechism does to theology.

†The italics are the present writer's.

Considering the scope of a college education, as distinct from university study; if we measure the concessions made to natural sciences by the time given, by the maturity of mind brought to the study of them, I believe these periods devoted to the natural sciences are in excess of the amount required for graduation in most colleges. Every one knows that a young man may graduate and receive a college degree from Harvard without having given any time whatsoever during his four years to the study of the natural sciences. And it would seem that in such cases Harvard has made no concession at all, either trifling or important, to natural sciences.

This suggests an old fallacy apparently underlying the strictures on Jesuit Colleges—the confounding of the number of studies taught by a given college and the number which the individual student must complete before he is declared a Bachelor of Arts. In the first sense Harvard has made large concessions to natural sciences; in the second, it has made large concessions to individual students—the concessions to let all science largely alone. If a college is distinguished from a university in this, that a college gives "a systematic discipline in liberal studies"*—and this distinction has not as yet become obsolete—then the value of a college curriculum ought to be settled by its application to the student, and not by vast programs announcing a multiplicity of studies which the student is at liberty to neglect. No wise man will estimate the value of a student's degree by this program, but by the studies which in fact the student does elect and master. And it is evident that that degree varies in significance to such an extent as to render it almost meaningless. It is a fact, however, that the unobservant, not necessarily the uneducated, judge the educational standard of a college by these elaborate programs, and not by the minute parts which the candidate for a degree undertakes to study. It would be very interesting to know, but it is difficult to discover, what courses the main body of students do actually elect in colleges in which studies are elective; what percentage of those who obtain a degree, do so on what they irreverently call "snap" courses. Until we have this information in detail, it is useless to write of "trifling concessions to the natural sciences," or in fact to any other sciences.

"Four hundred years" is, it seems to me, another misleading phrase in the criticism I am examining. "Four hundred years of unchanged uniformity" has an impressive sound in this mutable age when progress is in danger of being identified with change.† We must first note that the expanding of knowledge—whatever may be said of its deepening—the growth and differentiation of sciences are of recent development. Consequently it may be safely asserted that up to about forty years ago the curricula of all colleges were substantially

---

*Johns Hopkins Register, 1888–89, p. 145.

†There is some arithmetical confusion here, which I notice merely to dismiss it. The Jesuit Order was instituted in the year 1540, three hundred and fifty-nine years ago. The Jesuit method of studies was not fixed until 1599. The difference between 1599 and 1899 is three hundred.

in accord with that elaborated by the Jesuits during the two hundred years that preceded their suppression in 1773.

It is quite clear that the old curriculum could not have made use of instruments of education not yet invented. If the old program was retained, the reason evidently was that there was no new developed and coördinated body of learning or science to supplant it, or to claim equal rights with it. As soon as a new science was recognized to have reached a stage of coherency that gave it an educational value, we find that it was introduced into the curricula of nearly all our American colleges. But a complete change from the uniform described course is a policy of recent date. Until the school year of 1872–1873 there were prescribed studies for each of the four college years at Harvard. About that time it was discovered that no "human wisdom was equal to contriving a prescribed course of study equally good" for all Seniors. Thereafter this conviction gradually grew in extension until it comprehended at successive intervals the Junior, Sophomore and Freshman years. About fifteen years ago, then, after two centuries and a half of successful work in the field of education, Harvard recognized that "direct revelation from on high would be the only satisfactory basis for a prescribed school curriculum," and the present elective system that characterizes that institution was finally introduced. Fifteen years is a very short time in the history of an educational movement, yet within that brief span of years the elective system has become to its advocates an educational fetich, which whoso does not reverence is deserving of anathema. Nevertheless, it would be too much to expect that it should have been adopted before it was invented. In so far, therefore, as it is a reproach to Jesuit Colleges not to have accepted that system, the "four hundred years" dwindle to fifteen. It would consequently have been more exact, though less telling, to have said that: For the last fifteen years the curriculum of Jesuit Colleges has remained practically unchanged.

I am not citing these facts in praise or blame of either class of institutions. Nor am I claiming or denying or conceding a higher educational efficiency for the new program than for the old. There were brave men before Agamemnon. There were educated men graduated from Harvard before the advent of the system at present there in vogue. The number of graduates annually was not so large then as now. But it would certainly be folly to intimate that the old system did not produce proportionately as large a percentage of men, who in the very best sense of the word were educated scholars. In like manner the old program of the Jesuit College did somehow, in spite of its alleged disregard for the "sanctity of the individual's gifts and will-power," and without "a direct revelation from on high," result in giving to the world trained, cultured, and investigating minds. None of this concerns the issue I have raised, or rather attempted to meet. My contention deals exclusively with facts. I have endeavored to show that these facts are other than those proclaimed; that the Jesuit curriculum has not remained unchanged for four hundred years; that its concessions to natural sciences are not trifling; that even as a recalcitrant against the wisdom of Harvard's elective system these four hundred years "writ" small mean at the most fifteen.

II

But let us turn to the method of Jesuit education. It undoubtedly has remained unchanged for the last three hundred years. Do the exigencies of modern education call for its rejection in favor of the elective system of Harvard? Will anything short of "an unhesitating belief in the Divine wisdom" of its prescriptions justify non-compliance with this call? Aside from a "direct revelation from on high" can any satisfactory basis be found for it?

About forty years ago a new problem began to present itself to educators. Human knowledge in certain lines had widened marvelously. New sciences sprang into being, old ones grew in amplitude and extent, until no longer possessing a cohesive centre, they burst into a number of distinct and specific sciences. Coincident with this increase and multiplication of sciences, man's intellectual sympathies, interests, and bents varied and widened in range. President Eliot's premises began to confront every one on whom the direction of an institution of higher education devolved. "The immense deepening and expanding of human knowledge in the nineteenth century and the increasing sense of the sanctity of the individual's gifts and will-power" rendered the old solution of the problem inadequate on its practical side. The old solution had, it is true, the merit of unity, but the new problem demanded a fuller recognition of individuality. The difficulty that perplexed educators was to combine the principle of unity and the principle of individuality. The various departments of human knowledge had become so manifold that it was utterly impossible for any one mind to master them all. An attempt to do so even partially would have resulted in mental dissipation and loss of power. On the other hand awakened interests and broader outlooks would not be cramped within the precincts of the old curriculum. Some modification was therefore necessary.

It was possible, of course, to ignore either of these two principles by fixing one's mind so exclusively on the other as to exaggerate it out of all due proportion. One might adhere to a rigid unity on existing lines, or one might give free rein to individuality. One might, from an educational point of view, look on the learning of the century as a vast "sphere having its circumference everywhere and its centre nowhere;" or one might retain a centre and the old circumference, and doggedly refuse to enlarge one's horizon. Either solution of the problem would be extreme. The first, among a people feeling the thrill of new intellectual life and the exultation of widening intellectual vistas, would probably for a time meet with more general popularity. As usual in a transitional era the pendulum would swing from extreme conservatism to extreme liberalism. Not all would distinguish between the lifeless unity of a crystal and the living unity of an oak, which, unchanged in kind, varies within its species in different environments of climate, soil, and cultivation. A sane conservatism and a wise liberalism would run the risk of being dubbed antiquated, retrograde, reactionary.

The problem is not easy of solution. That solution will necessarily be the outcome of years of thought and experience. The selection from such a mass of educational matter, and the coördination of the same to definite educational ends is not to be effected by a priori theories, and exaggerated rhetoric on the sanctity of one principle to the exclusion of the other; nor by sweeping indictments of those whose heresy does not happen to be our heresy. There may be a medium between the alternatives of rigid uniformity and extreme "electivism," and it may be possible to discover that medium without the immediate and direct interposition of Divine wisdom. Some tolerant self-restraint, some wise distrust of one's own infallibility, some deference to the experience of the past—which is not wholly worthless—with experience, hard thinking, and mutual coöperation may solve this problem. It is not more difficult than others which the human mind has solved.

President Eliot's method of solving the difficulty is simplicity itself. He banishes unity from college education and bows down before individuality. And the curious phase of the matter is, he fancies this is a solution. He cuts the knot by having the educator abdicate his pretended functions, and by committing the whole embarrassment to the individual student, who panoplied in "the sanctity of his gifts and will-power" casts it aside with the ease and grace of youth. The young man applying for an education is told to look out on the wide realm of learning, to him unknown and untrodden, and to elect his path. To do this with judgment and discrimination, he must know the end he wishes to reach; he must moreover know himself—his mental and moral characteristics, his aptitudes, his temperament, his tastes; and finally, he must know which of the numberless paths will lead him to the goal of his ambition, what combination of studies will open up the Via Sacra that leads to success. There are some restrictions, it is true, which hamper his election. For instance, he must avoid in his choice of studies any conflict between the hours appointed for recitations and examination. He is "strongly urged to choose his studies with the utmost caution and under the best advice." But these provisions do not modify the general character of the system. He must distinctly understand that it is no longer the province of his Alma Mater to act as an earthly providence to him. Circumstances have obliged her to become a caterer. Each student is free to choose his own intellectual pabulum, and must assume in the main the direction of his own studies. If he solve the problem wisely, to him the profit; if unwisely, this same Alma Noverca disclaims the responsibility. The blame lies with himself, and for the present—until the elective system is introduced into our high schools—with those who had charge of his secondary education. If he is a careless student, having as yet no definite purpose to guide him, let him assume a purpose and reform. Is he not eighteen years of age?

This is the solution of the problem by the present elective system of Harvard. Now, the only question raised in this paper is: whether all educators are obliged to choose between this system and a prescribed system based on "direct revelation from on high"; whether a refusal to accept this system is "absurd and impossible." I am not, therefore, inquiring into its merits or demerits except in so far as I am compelled to do so in defense of the Jesuit system. It may be, for all I now care, a makeshift, hopelessly adopted by those who were nonplussed by the intractable elements of the problem, or a step in the evolution of a plan devised for the elimination of the college from our American education. If there are any who are satisfied with it, to them the Jesuits have nothing to say beyond the words of St. Paul, "Let every man abound in his own sense." But they discount the implied challenge either to reject their system or to adduce "direct revelation from on high" in its favor.

The most persistent argument advanced in proof of the elective system is drawn from the individual differences of students. We sometimes hear Leibnitz quoted in this connection as having said that no two leaves of the same tree are alike. It may be doubted whether a man of Leibnitz's intellectual balance ever made such a lop-sided assertion. Any woodman could have told him that an oak leaf may be recognized at sight. This could not be done, if they were not similar. To fix one's eyes on accidental differences and close one's eyes to essential similitude would be an example of elective observation not creditable to a philosopher. It may seem trifling to insist on this truism, and in fact the matter is trifling. But what other confusion is implied in the absolute certainty, that "no human wisdom is equal to contriving a prescribed course of study equally good for even two children of the same family, between the ages of eight and eighteen," except that which comes from emphasizing accidental differences and ignoring essential conformity? St. Thomas Aquinas holds that no two angels are in the same species. President Eliot comes perilously near predicating the same specific diversity of children. That boys vary in talents, in powers of application, in mental tendencies and aptitudes, is quite obvious; but we must also admit that they have intellectual faculties essentially similar, unless we are willing to maintain that they are kindred to the angels of Aquinas. Their specific unity is essential; their individual difference are accidental. All boys have those faculties by which they are scientifically classed as belonging to the genus *homo;* memory, powers of observation, of reasoning, of judgment, of imagination and of discrimination; though for native or wilful reasons they may not all be capable of equal culture.

A system of education which neglects either aspect of the subject is defective; and it is not evident that that is least defective which discards unity. The same arguments that are offered for "electivism" in mental education will apply to "electivism" in physical training. Man is a unit mentally as well as physically. The exclusive and abnormal development of one side of his mind is as destructive of the "whole man, the polished man and the rounded man" when consequent on partial mental education as would be the specialized training of an athlete which neglected certain classes of muscles. Prior to specialization in athletics the wise director of a gymnasium will demand rounded physical development. The man whose whole education has been special or elective is as pitiable an object as a hollow-chested acrobat who can toss barrels with his feet. Both have undergone "training for power," both have made a thorough study of a few things, but both will remain to the end of their days educational curiosities. If the elective system were applied to the visible and material, its absurdity would be instantly detected. Because the region of its application is supersensible it is foisted on us with a cloud of sophistry arising from a jumble of political economy and psychology. One wonders sometimes whether the reasons adduced in its favor were really premises by which convictions were formed, or merely arguments to shore up a foregone conclusion.

This is the fundamental ground on which the Jesuit method is at variance with the system of elective studies in use at Harvard. That system of itself has no unity. No quantity of theory, no frequent profession of educational principles speculatively correct, can obscure the fact that in practice President Eliot has abandoned the doctrine of unity in education. The Jesuits hold that doctrine of prime importance in collegiate training and formation. The causes assigned as motives for its desertion are not of such evident cogency as to put the only excuse for loyalty to it in "a revelation from on high." Relying merely on the light of reason, its desertion universally in this country would in the judgment of the Jesuits be disastrous. It would tend to lower the standard of education, to lessen the intrinsic value of a college degree, to give one-sided formation, to unfit men for effective University work.

President Thwing, of the Western Reserve University, in a recent paper declares that the "bane of our educational system is *haphazardness* in the choice of studies." President Harper, of Chicago University, in his address at the inauguration of the new president of Brown University, is even more emphatic, characterizing our present educational system as chaotic. Other citations might be added from men of equal standing in the world of education. Inevitably with haphazardness and chaos as notes of the system, the standard of education is going to depend on those who direct their own education. The present writer's experience does not cover the period "between the ages of eight and eighteen," but he does know from some years of observation, that between the ages of fourteen and twenty the average boy will work, like electricity, along the line of least resistance. And he is confident that his experience is not peculiar. To apply to their education, therefore, university methods applicable only to men of intellectual and moral maturity, before they are able to feel judiciously the relations of their studies to their life's purpose, must necessarily put to some extent the standard of education under their control, and almost wholly commit to them the character of their own formation.

Here I may notice the appeal that is made in behalf of this policy to the "sanctity of the individual's gifts and powers." "The greatest reverence is due to boys," cries the old Roman satirist, and who will dare gainsay it? But an abiding sense of that very reverence inspires the Jesuit educator with the belief, that it is an unhallowed thing to make the plastic souls and hearts and minds of those entrusted to their care the subjects of untried, revolutionary and wholesale experiment. Precisely because they believe in the sanctity of the individual they will not admit the advisability of subjecting them—though they were small quadrupeds—to novel experiments in educational laboratories. Because they know that the boy of today will be tomorrow the maker of his country's destiny, will fashion its future, will shape for good or ill the forces that will give it stability or bring it ruin, they have hesitated to announce a go-as-you-please program of studies and a haphazard and chaotic system of formation. Because they believe the soul of a boy a sacred thing destined for an eternal life hereafter, to be attained by a noble life here, they have recognized the delicacy and responsibility of their functions, and have been satisfied with a safer and more conservative advance. In this regard for the moral aspects of education, they do possess the note "ecclesiastical," which President Eliot finds significant. Fortunately, however, in this respect the Jesuit Colleges do not consort with the Moslem alone, but find themselves in the company of many excellent non-Catholic Colleges, in this country. It seems strange, and would be incredible had we not evidence, that any one professing to be an educator and acquainted with human nature in its formative period, should in this century maintain with such dogmatic intensity the exclusive wisdom of permitting boys to elect the studies by which their manhood will be moulded.

The distinction between the functions of a college and a university has been so often, so fully, and so definitely exposed that it seems impertinent to call a reader's attention to it again. Yet recognized truths in the presence of active adversaries need reiteration. The elective system retains the distinction in name; but has in the first place brushed aside all real distinction between them, and in the second, is by trend, if not by purpose, tending to eliminate the college from our American system. It was apparently to this President Hadley referred in his inauguration address, when he said: "I cannot believe that any one who has watched the working of the boy specialist;* it lays before him in large outline a map of the realm he may afterwards traverse in part and

*"There is no doubt that the tendency to specializing in our educational system, even from the beginning of the studies of youth, as contrasted with childhood, is excessive, and that if the best education is to continue, this tendency must be counteracted."—President Dwight, in his Report of 1899.

in detail, and it coördinates and relates his after specialty to other learning. A college is aware that a boy has idiosyncracies as well as sanctities; that by education these sanctities are brought out and the idiosyncrasies gently rubbed off and their wild exuberant growth pruned. The college is, therefore, in its method of teaching primarily tutorial, not professorial. The formation it proposes to give is not by accident in individual cases, but by design universally effected by personal and intimate relations between small groups of pupils and a teacher, whose duty comprehends guidance, advice, and encouragement, as well as instruction. Such a scheme of education gives the college student time and opportunity to study and compare his capacities and inclinations, and helps him to make a life decision which shall be founded on observation, experience, and reason. An opponent of this view would miss or confuse the scope of secondary and college education, if he argued that this system "has compelled the determination of the pupils' life destination at the early age of ten to fourteen." To recur to an illustration already used, the general training of an athlete in a gymnasium does not determine his after specialty, rather it manifests to him and his directors aptitudes and grounds for a discreet determination. The whole contention of this paper is summed up in a very apt metaphor of President Stryker, of Hamilton College. Contrasting the disciplines of a college and the investigations of a university, he says: "The processes have different conclusions. One should make iron into steel and the other make steel into tools. Specialization *not* 'based upon a liberal culture' attempts to put an edge on pot-iron."

The elective system of Harvard, carried into secondary schools and colleges to a logical and consistent issue, would be the application to education of the economic principle of the division of labor, which sinks the individual for the sake of the product. It might produce experts, but could not develop a man. We should have a crop of those specialists whom Oliver Wendell Holmes so genially portrays in his Breakfast Table series, but the elective system would not give us a Holmes. We might have ministers, theologues, but we should not be indebted to the elective system for a Phillips Brooks. We might get from such a system educators, knowing books and the science and history of education; but we should scarcely get a Father Fulton, knowing boys and skilled in the art of education. Lawyers too it may produce, but scarcely a Rufus Choate; bankers, but not Stedmans; literary men skilled in the technique of their art, but with no horizon outside of their sphere. In a word:

"Knowledge comes, but wisdom lingers . . .
And the individual withers, and the world is more and more."

In conclusion we submit with all due deference that President Eliot's reflections on Jesuit schools need recension. His declaration that the Jesuit curriculum has been marked by four hundred years of almost changeless uniformity is unfounded. His exaggerated statement that the method of Jesuit schools is justified only by "an unhesitating belief in the Divine Wisdom" of such a method is somewhat humorous, but not convincing. His implied challenge demanding either evidence of a "direct revelation from on high" as a basis of that method, or its rejection as "absurd and impossible" is a defective dilemma. Why may not a body of men by the mere light of human reason be persuaded of the unwisdom of haphazardness and chaos, and the necessity of unity in college education without being challenged to show their credentials from on high? They must confess they have no such credentials. Then abandon your method and adopt my elective system, is President Eliot's implied inference. There is a *non-sequitur* here so surprising that perforce we are driven to surmise that behind this paralogism there is an esoteric reason for this attack which we have not discerned.

President Eliot's whole career heretofore forbids us to put any interpretation on it which would imply that he was even subconsciously motived by unreasonable hostility. What inspired this criticism of Jesuit schools, therefore, we can not even conjecture. We can only await further enlightenment, assuring the President of Harvard that if he give reasons for his dislike of our methods they will always get that respectful consideration due them because of his position and personal worth.

TIMOTHY BROSNAHAN, S.J.
Woodstock, Md.

Select List of Jesuit Superiors, Provincials, and Presidents

Year	Superior General	English Assistant to the Superior General	Maryland–New York Provincial	President of Georgetown	President of Boston College	President of Holy Cross
1880						
1881						
1882			Robert Fulton 1882–89			
1883						
1884						
1885						
1886						
1887	Anton Anderledy 1887–92					
1888				J. Havens Richards 1888–98	Robert Fulton 1888–91	
1889			Thomas J. Campbell 1889–93			Michael O'Kane 1889–93
1890						
1891					Edward I. Devitt 1891–94	
1892	Luis Martín 1892–1906	Rudolph Meyer 1892–1906				

Edward A. McGurk
1893–95

John F. Lehy
1895–1901

William Pardow
1893–97

Timothy Brosnahan
1894–98

W.G. Read Mullan
1898–1903

Joseph Hanselman
1901–06

Edward Purbrick
1897–1901

John D. Whitney
1898–1901

Jerome Daugherty
1901–05

William F. Gannon
1903–07

Thomas E. Murphy
1906–11

Thomas J. Gannon
1901–06

Joseph Hanselman
1906–12

Franz Wernz
1906–14

1893
1894
1895
1896
1897
1898
1899
1900
1901
1902
1903
1904
1905
1906
1907

NOTES

Abbreviations

PERSONS

CWE	Charles W. Eliot
JBA	James Barr Ames
JHR	Rev. J. Havens Richards, S.J.
JJK	Bishop John J. Keane
LM	Rev. Luis Martín, S.J.
TB	Rev. Timothy Brosnahan, S.J.
TJC	Msgr. Thomas J. Conaty
WGRM	Rev. W. G. Read Mullan, S.J.

ASSOCIATIONS

ACCUS	Association of Catholic Colleges of the United States
BCAA	Boston College Alumni Association
CEA	Catholic Educational Association

PRINTED MATERIAL

BC alum.	Photocopies, Boston College alumni reminiscences
BCC	*Catalogue of the Officers and Students of Boston College*
BCS	*Boston College Stylus*
HCC	*Catalogue of the College of the Holy Cross*
HCP	*Holy Cross Purple*
SHR	*Sacred Heart Review*
WL	*Woodstock Letters*

ARCHIVES

ACUA	Catholic University of America, Department of Archives and Manuscripts
ACHC	Archives of the College of the Holy Cross
ARSI	Archivum Romanum Societatus Iesu (Roman archives of the Society of Jesus)
AUND	Archives of the University of Notre Dame
BCA	University Archives, Burns Library, Boston College
GUA	Georgetown University Archives and Special Collections
HUA	Harvard University Archives

Introduction

Epigraph: In the preface to *World's Columbian Catholic Congresses*, 4.

1. Sloan, *Faith and Knowledge*, 1 and throughout. Mead, *Nation with the Soul of a Church;* Tuveson, *Redeemer Nation;* Handy, *Christian America;* Marty, *Righteous Empire;* Hatch, *Democratization of American Christianity;* Gaustad, *Religious History of America*, esp. 113–63; Ahlstrom, *Religious History of the American People*, esp. pts. 4 and 7. On educational institutions, see Cremin's 3-vol. *American Education*, and Kaestle, *Pillars*, among others.

2. Gleason, *Contending with Modernity;* Leahy, *Adapting to America;* Gallin, *Negotiating Identity. Contending with Modernity* provides an excellent account of Catholic educators' efforts to respond to the rise of the modern academic order. Until its publication in 1995, those interested in the history of Catholic higher education relied heavily on two books by Edward J. Power: *History of Catholic Higher Education in the United States* (1958) and *Catholic Higher Education in America: A History* (1972). It is not surprising, therefore, that in a seminal 1962 historiographic essay on higher education, Frederick Rudolph described the literature on Catholic higher education as "small" and "disappointing," consisting primarily of filiopietistic institutional histories. Rudolph, *American College and University*, 514.

3. Rudolph, *American College and University;* Geiger, *American College.*

4. Veysey, *Emergence;* Shils, "Order of Learning."

5. Geiger, "Era," 56. Low quoted ibid., 83. Also see Shils, "Order of Learning"; Bass, "Ministry on the Margins," 43–57; Veysey, *Emergence*, 339.

6. Nineteenth-century colleges, particularly antebellum colleges, were often por-

trayed by historians as fossilized relics. See Hofstadter and Metzger, *Development of Academic Freedom,* and Veysey, *Emergence.* More recently, historians have cast the colleges in a more flattering light. See Rudolph, *American College and University;* Potts, "'Enthusiasm!'" and idem, "American Colleges in the Nineteenth Century"; McLaughlan, "American College in the Nineteenth Century"; Herbst, "American College History Re-Examination"; Axtell, "Death of the Liberal Arts College"; Smith, "Apologia pro Alma Matre"; Naylor, "Antebellum College Movement"; Burke, *American Collegiate Populations;* Geiger, *American College;* Allmendinger, *Paupers and Scholars;* Le Duc, *Piety and Intellect at Amherst;* Leslie, *Gentlemen and Scholars.*

7. Daniel Coit Gilman quoted in Flexner, *Gilman,* 18.

8. Winterer, *Culture of Classicism.*

9. Veysey, *Emergence,* chap. 2.

10. Rudolph, *American College and University,* 245.

11. Marsden, *Soul;* Reuben, *Making of the Modern University.*

12. Harper quoted in Storr, *Harper's University,* 24; Harper, "Trend," and idem, *Prospects.* Also see Hawkins, "University-Builders," 356, and idem, *Banding Together.*

13. Geiger, "Era"; Burke, *American Collegiate Populations.*

14. Horowitz, *Campus Life;* Rudolph, *American College and University.*

15. Wiebe, *Search for Order,* 118 and throughout.

16. Hawkins, *Banding Together;* Geiger, "Era"; Peterson, *New England College.*

17. For differing portraits of faculties from this era, see Palmieri, *Adamless Eden,* and Leslie, *Gentlemen and Scholars,* esp. chap. 3, "When Professors Had Servants."

18. Varga, "Rejoining," 70.

19. Rudolph, *American College and University;* Findlay, "SPCTEW and Western Colleges."

20. Power, *Catholic Higher Education in America,* 48.

21. Marsden, *Soul;* Reuben, *Making of the Modern University;* Hart, *University Gets Religion;* Roberts and Turner, *Sacred and the Secular;* Kemeny, *Princeton;* Cherry, *Hurrying toward Zion;* Marsden and Longfield, *Secularization.*

22. For a useful description of liberal Protestantism and modernism and their relationship, see Hutchison, *Modernist Impulse,* 1–4.

23. Marsden, *Soul,* esp. chap. 9; Turner, *Without God.*

24. Appleby, *"Church and Age Unite!";* McAvoy, *Great Crisis.*

25. Gleason, *Contending with Modernity,* 6–12; Nuesse, *Catholic University of America;* Ellis, *Formative Years.*

26. Marsden, introduction to Marsden and Longfield, *Secularization,* 5.

27. Appleby, *"Church and Age Unite!";* Gannon, "Before and After"; Reher, *Catholic Intellectual Life.*

28. Although some women's religious orders were influenced by Jesuit educational ideals and practices, strong gender boundaries in Catholic culture rendered Catholic women's higher education quite distinctive, both in terms of its development in the United States and in its practice: Schier and Russett, *Catholic Women's Colleges in America;* Oates, *Higher Education.*

29. O'Malley, *First Jesuits,* 16.

30. Boston College, Canisius College, College of the Holy Cross, Creighton Univer-

sity, Fairfield University, Fordham University, Georgetown University, Gonzaga University, John Carroll University, LeMoyne College, Loyola College in Maryland, Loyola Marymount University, Loyola University Chicago, Loyola University New Orleans, Marquette University, Regis University, Rockhurst University, Saint Joseph's University, Saint Louis University, Saint Peter's College, Santa Clara University, Seattle University, Spring Hill College, University of Detroit–Mercy, University of San Francisco, University of Scranton, Wheeling Jesuit University, Xavier University.

31. The section dealing with education in the *Constitutions* is reprinted in Ganss, *Ignatius' Idea;* the directive to adapt is at 333. Farrell, *Jesuit Code;* Donnelly, *Principles of Jesuit Education;* Fitzpatrick, *St. Ignatius and the Ratio Studiorum;* McGucken, *Jesuits and Education;* Duminuco, *Jesuit* Ratio Studiorum. The text of the *Ratio Studiorum* is available at www.bc.edu/bcflorg/avp/ulib/digi/ratio/ratiohome.html.

32. O'Malley, *First Jesuits;* O'Malley et al., *Jesuits.*

33. Bonney, "Address of Welcome," 2.

34. Hawkins, *Between Harvard and America.*

35. CWE, "Recent Changes in Secondary Education."

36. Brief accounts of the Jesuits' troubles with Harvard can be found in Kuzniewski, *Thy Honored Name,* 175–84; Power, *Catholic Higher Education in America,* 260–65; Durkin, *Georgetown University,* 191–92, 255–60; Dunigan, *History of Boston College,* 168–77; Donovan, Dunigan, and Fitzgerald, *History of Boston College,* 107–9; Hawkins, *Between Harvard and America,* 187–89.

37. On the complexities and importance of the "outsider" experience, see Moore, "Insiders and Outsiders," and *Religious Outsiders.* See also Lears, "Concept of Cultural Hegemony," and Fass, *Outside In.*

38. Thomas Bender quoted in Lears, "Concept of Cultural Hegemony," 586.

39. Sullivan, "Histories and Rituals," 3.

Chapter 1. The Descendants of Luther and the Sons of Loyola

Epigraphs: 1. Porter, *Educational Systems,* 70.; 2. "President Eliot Called a Bigot," unidentified clipping, ca. 23 Jan. 1900 (GUA, Brosnahan, box 8, folder 155).

1. John Paul II, *Constitutio Apostolica de Universitatibus Catholicis* (commonly referred to as *Ex Corde Ecclesiae*); Cobban, *Medieval Universities;* Knowles, *Evolution of Medieval Thought;* Rashdall, *Universities of Europe.*

2. Harbison, *Christian Scholar,* 121; Bruce, *Luther as an Educator;* Strauss, *Luther's House of Learning;* Spitz, "Importance of the Reformation."

3. Porter, *Educational Systems.*

4. Billington, *Protestant Crusade.*

5. Stevenson, *Scholarly Means;* Marsden, *Soul,* 123–33; Hall, "Noah Porter Writ Large?"; *Biographical Dictionary of American Educators,* s.v. "Porter, Noah."

6. Winterer, *Culture of Classicism.*

7. Veysey, *Emergence;* Roberts and Turner, *Sacred and the Secular.*

8. CWE, "New Education."

9. Thwing, "Twenty-Five Years," 356; James Forbes Rhodes quoted in Bledstein, *Culture of Professionalism,* 132. Roosevelt's accolade and others are found in Smith, *Harvard Century,* 27, 28. Also see Hawkins, *Between Harvard and America.*

10. Marty, *Righteous Empire;* Handy, *Christian America.*

11. Marsden, *Soul,* esp. chaps. 10 and 11.

12. Knox, "Problems for Educated Minds," 206.

13. "Bishop Keane and Harvard," and "Harvard and Catholic Colleges," *Pilot* (Boston), 1 July 1893. Walsh, "Boston Pilot"; O'Connor, *Boston Catholics,* 141–45; Kane, *Separatism and Subculture,* 65, 276–77.

14. Ahern, *Catholic University of America,* and *Life of John J. Keane;* Ellis, *Formative Years;* Nuesse, *Catholic University of America;* Gleason, *Contending with Modernity,* 6–12.

15. "Bishop Keane at Harvard," *Irish Catholic* (Dublin), 5 July 1890 (ACUA, clippings file); *L'Universe* (Paris), 29 Nov. 1890, quoted in Ahern, *Catholic University of America,* 63.

16. Eliot's invitation and directives regarding the Dudleian Lectures in CWE to JJK, 17 June 1890 (ACUA, JJK papers, box 5, folder 18). For Keane's response, see JJK to CWE, 19 July 1890 (HUA, UAI.1.150, box 78). Also see CWE to JJK, 9 Oct. 1890 (ACUA, JJK papers, box 5, folder 18); JJK to CWE, 11 Oct. 1890 and 24 Oct. 1890 (HUA, UAI.1.150, box 79); and CWE to JJK, 4 Nov. 1890 (ACUA, JJK papers, box 5, folder 18).

17. "Wisdom of the Ages," *Boston Herald,* 11 Feb. 1893 (HUA, 893.2 clippings file, 1893). Also see "Bishop Keane at Cambridge," *Boston Transcript,* 11 Feb. 1893 (HUA, ibid.). According to a note penned by D. S. Lamson, Father Robert Fulton, S.J., the third president of Boston College (1870–80), was invited by Richard H. Dana to deliver a Dudleian Lecture sometime during the 1870s. It was an invitation "foolishly" declined since it would have been the first delivered by a "Catholic Priest and what would have been particularly interesting by a priest of the Society of Jesus—which would have caused old Dudley to turn over in his coffin." D. S. Lamson, 1890 (BCA, David R. Dunigan papers, box 3, folder 7).

18. Hawkins, *Between Harvard and America,* 4; DiMaggio, "Cultural Entrepreneurship."

19. Saunderson, *Charles W. Eliot;* James, *Charles W. Eliot;* Cotton, *Life of Charles W. Eliot;* Hawkins, *Between Harvard and America;* DeWolfe, "Harvard Figure of Eliot." Eliot is discussed at length in Solomon, *Ancestors and Immigrants,* and Baltzell, *Protestant Establishment.* On his Harvard connections, see Morison, *Three Centuries,* 225.

20. Saunderson, *Charles W. Eliot,* xxiii, 1; Samuel Eliot quoted in Sexton, "Charles W. Eliot," 51 n. 13.

21. Morison, *Three Centuries,* 358; CWE to George H. Palmer, 19 May 1894, quoted in Saunderson, *Charles W. Eliot,* 10–11. On Eliot's religiosity, also see Thwing, "Twenty-Five Years"; Shepard, *God's People,* 51–53.

22. Hawkins, *Pioneer,* 18; Hart, "Faith and Learning."

23. White, *History of the Warfare;* idem, *Autobiography,* 2:573. Altschuler, *Andrew Dickson White;* Bishop, *History of Cornell,* 46–47.

24. Wind, *Bible and the University;* Shepard, *God's People,* 42–51; Cherry, *Hurrying toward Zion,* 1–13.

25. Wilson quoted in Kemeny, *Princeton,* 145; Craig, *Woodrow Wilson at Prince-*

ton, 9–10; also Wilbee, "Religious Dimensions." Other information is from *Dictionary of American Biography* and other encyclopedic sources.

26. CWE, "Inaugural," 31; Gilman, "Johns Hopkins University," 37. White quoted in Bishop, *History of Cornell,* 190–91; Patton quoted in Kemeny, *Princeton,* 89. Hart, *University Gets Religion,* 30–38.

27. CWE, "What Place Should Religion Have in a College?" Feb. 1886, typescript (HUA, UAI.5.150, box 334, folder 36), 10–11.

28. CWE, "Aims," 237, 235. The state universities were the first to face the issue of sectarianism. Given diverse state constituencies, they declared themselves nonsectarian, although nonsectarian meant broadly Protestant; see, for example, Curti and Carstensen, *University of Wisconsin,* 1:87–90; the chapter on the University of Michigan in Marsden, *Soul,* 167–80; and Skerpan, "Place for God." On Princeton's increasingly national aspirations, see Leslie, *Gentlemen and Scholars,* and Kemeny, *Princeton.*

29. CWE, "What Place Should Religion Have?" 11, 3.

30. CWE, "Aims," 238. Nineteenth-century denominational rivalries are discussed in Handy, *Christian America,* 61 and throughout; Finke and Stark, *Churching of America;* Butler, *Awash;* Hatch, *Democratization of American Christianity.*

31. Ellis, *John Lancaster Spalding;* Ahern, *Life of John J. Keane,* and idem, *Catholic University of America;* O'Connell, *John Ireland;* Colman, *Catholic University of America;* Ellis, *Cardinal Gibbons.*

32. Keane quoted in "Bishop Keane at Cambridge," *Boston Transcript,* and "Wisdom of the Ages"; "Commencement—Alumni Dinner," 103.

33. Choate quoted in "Commencement—Alumni Dinner," 68.

34. "Harvard and Catholic Colleges."

35. Ibid. Also see Gallivan, "Catholic Sons of Harvard," 499, where the author writes that Harvard's decision to award Keane an honorary doctorate "marked a wonderful progress in the breadth of view and universality of aim of the oldest and most famous institution of learning in America."

36. Minutes, 18 Apr. 1893 meeting of the Harvard Law School faculty (microfilm copy at Harvard Law School library). The Law School faculty included Christopher Columbus Langdell (dean of the Law School, 1870–95), James Barr Ames (dean of the Law School, 1895–1910), Jeremiah Smith, John Chipman Gray, Eugene Wambaugh, Joseph Henry Beale, Samuel Williston, and James Bradley Thayer. Thayer was absent from the meeting. On Eliot's attendance record, see Warren, *History of Harvard Law School,* 2:363.

37. Chase, "Modern Law School"; Johnson, *Schooled Lawyers;* Seligman, *High Citadel;* Sutherland, *Law at Harvard;* Stevens, *Law School.*

38. CWE, "New Education"; Fiske quoted in Hawkins, *Between Harvard and America,* 49.

39. CWE to Edward Everett Hale, 4 Feb. 1909, quoted in Sexton, "Charles W. Eliot," 47–48.

40. Changes in Harvard's admissions policies are chronicled in Harvard Law School Association, *Centennial History of Harvard Law School,* 47–52; Warren, *History of Harvard Law School,* 2:450–51, 461, 468; Sutherland, *Law at Harvard,* 167–

71. Eliot and Langdell bore affinities. They had both been students at Harvard. As a scientist (Eliot studied chemistry), Eliot's appointment as president was an anomaly: most college presidents were clergymen. As a practitioner of the law, Langdell's appointment was also an anomaly. Eliot's decision to hire Langdell lay, in part, in the fact that Langdell was scientifically disposed.

41. Minutes, 18 Apr. 1893. *Harvard Law Review* 7 (1893–94): 113. The special student category persisted for several more years before it disappeared.

42. *Dictionary of American Biography,* s.v. "Roche, James Jeffrey"; Lane, "James Jeffrey Roche"; Walsh, "Boston Pilot," v; Mann, *Yankee Reformers,* 45; Kane, *Separatism and Subculture,* 254, 261.

43. Roche to CWE, 19 June 1893 (HUA, UAI.5.150, box 83). Because the Catholic University of America admitted only graduate students, its status on the Law School's list was never an issue.

44. CWE to Roche, 20 June 1893, reprinted in the *Pilot,* 1 July 1893.

45. Morison, *Three Centuries,* 358; Thwing, "Twenty-Five Years," 356; Perry, "Charles William Eliot," 10. Also see Briggs, "As Seen by a Disciple," 599–601; Hawkins, *Between Harvard and America,* 17.

46. CWE to Roche, 20 June 1893.

47. Samson, "Jesuit Collegiate Instruction," 130.

48. Potts's quotation and Brownson's rejoinder are in Brownson, "Dangers of Jesuit Instruction," 86.

49. CWE to Roche, 20 June 1893.

50. Roche to CWE, 22 June 1893 (HUA, UAI.5.150, box 83); JHR to CWE, 3 Aug. 1893 (GUA, JHR papers, box 5, folder 7).

51. "Father Joseph Havens Richards, S.J.," *WL* 53 (1924): 248–71.

52. JHR to CWE, 3 Aug. 1893.

53. JHR to CWE, 16 July 1893 (HUA, UAI.5.150, box 137, folder 1224).

54. CWE to JHR, 4 Aug. 1893 (GUA, Brosnahan, box 8, folder 155). Eliot was extremely consistent in his statements about Catholic higher education. In 1901 he responded to a query regarding the Law School's list from a priest from Saint Francis Xavier College in Antigonish, Nova Scotia: "I am very sensible, however, that the experience of the Protestant colleges in America cannot have direct application to the colleges which are conducted by Catholic religious orders. The discipline of these orders is so very different from that of any Protestant college faculty, and the objects they have in view are so different, that the experience of one sort can hardly be of value to the other, although both are teaching bodies": CWE to Rev. Alexander Thompson, 22 Aug. 1901 (HUA, UAI.5.150, CWE ltr. bk. 92).

55. Thomas J. Campbell to JHR, 28 Aug. 1893 (GUA, Brosnahan, box 8, folder 155); Campbell to JHR, 29 Aug. 1893 (ibid.); JHR to CWE, 21 Sept. 1893 (HUA, UAI.5.150, box 137, folder 1224). Harvard University *Catalogue* (1893): 352–53 and (1894): 375–76.

56. "The Jesuits"—article in *Southern Quarterly Review,* 14.

57. O'Malley, *First Jesuits;* Ganss, *Ignatius of Loyola;* Meissner, *Ignatius of Loyola;* Ravier, *Ignatius of Loyola;* Brodrick, *Saint Ignatius Loyola.*

58. Ganss, *Ignatius' Idea,* 9–17; O'Malley, *First Jesuits,* 27–32.

59. On the early ministry of the Jesuits, see O'Malley, *First Jesuits*, esp. chap. 2. For a detailed account tracing the Jesuit expansion by region and country, see Campbell, *Jesuits;* Gagliano and Ronan, *Jesuit Encounters.*

60. De Polanco quoted in O'Malley, *First Jesuits*, 200; Ganss, *Ignatius' Idea*, 18–29; O'Malley, "The Jesuits, St. Ignatius, and the Counter Reformation," 12.

61. Nadal quoted in Feldhay, "Knowledge and Salvation," 200. Also see Martin, *Jesuit Mind*, on early activity in France.

62. O'Malley, *First Jesuits*, 210, 244–64; O'Malley, "How the Jesuits Became Involved"; Feldhay, "Knowledge and Salvation," 201; Ganss, *Ignatius' Idea*, 131.

63. The section on education in the *Constitutions* is reprinted in Canss, *Ignatius' Idea;* quote at 291.

64. O'Reilly, "Ignatius of Loyola," 439, 441–42 ff.; O'Malley, "Attitudes of the Early Jesuits," and "How the Jesuits Became Involved," 65–66.

65. O'Malley, "Historiography," 5; O'Malley, *First Jesuits*, 207, 272–83; Martin, *Jesuit Mind*, 84–104.

66. Ganss, *Ignatius' Idea;* Padberg, "Development"; Hughes, *Loyola;* McGucken, *Jesuits and Education;* Farrell, *Jesuit Code.*

67. In addition to Ganss, *Ignatius' Idea*, see Bernad, "Faculty of Arts"; McGucken, *Jesuits and Education*, 32–42; Donnelly, *Principles of Jesuit Education.*

68. O'Malley, *First Jesuits*, 201.

69. Ganss, *Ignatius' Idea*, 24, 209; Padberg, "Development," 80; O'Malley, *First Jesuits*, 16.

70. See, for example, Axtell, *Invasion Within.* For a remarkable record of the Jesuit experience, see Thwaites's 73-vol. *Jesuit Relations.*

71. Miller, *Errand*, 11; Marsden, *Soul*, 41. Also see Bremer, *Shaping New Englands;* Morgan, *Visible Saints;* Miller, *New England Mind.*

72. Cremin, *American Education*, 1:181, 182; "Education of a Saint," in Morgan, *Puritan Family.*

73. *New England's First Fruits*, reprinted in Morison, *Founding of Harvard College*, 420–47, quote at 432.

74. Ibid.

75. John Eliot quoted in Bailyn, "Foundations," 8. Also see Morison, *Founding of Harvard College*, 247 f.; Morgan, *Godly Learning*, 259n, Kimball, *"True Professional Ideal,"* table A2.6, n.p.

76. On the English sectaries arguing against advanced education for ministers, see Greaves, *Puritan Revolution*, esp. chaps. 1 and 6. The sectaries who criticized other Protestants, both Anglican and Puritan, found fault with academic degrees, robes, and other matters, often connecting them with pride and claiming that they were the accretions of popery; see, for example, Greaves, *Puritan Revolution*, 133; Kearney, *Scholars and Gentlemen*, 71–76.

77. On the learned clergy, Marsden, *Soul*, 37–38; Morgan, *Godly Learning*, 95–120; Greaves, *Puritan Revolution*, 7–9, 15 f., 125–32. In Massachusetts, Puritans burned at least one book arguing against university education for the clergy and banished one woman, Anne Hutchison, for expounding on the Scriptures without benefit of the appropriate gender or university training: Morison, *Founding of Harvard College*, 172–77; Greaves, *Puritan Revolution*, 122–23.

78. On Emmanuel graduates, see Bailyn, "Foundations," 9. In establishing a college, the Puritans of New England drew heavily upon the example of Sir Walter Mildmay's Puritan Emmanuel College at Cambridge in England. By Morison's careful count, by 1646 at least 130 university men had migrated to New England, and at least thirty-five of these, considerably more than one-quarter, had studied at Emmanuel: Morison, *Founding of Harvard College*, 92 f. These alumni left their mark, so much so that Cotton Mather wrote that "if *New-England* hath been in some Respects *Immanuel's Land*, it is well; but this I am sure of, *Immanuel-College* contributed more than a little to make it so": Mather, quoted at 92 n. 1.

79. Quoted in Morison, *Founding of Harvard College*, 251.

80. Marsden, *Soul*, 37; Cairns, "Puritan Educational Philosophy."

81. Marsden, *Soul*, 38–44; Morgan, *Godly Learning*, 258–63; Morison, *Founding of Harvard College*, 247–51; Morison, *Harvard in the Seventeenth Century*, 1:305–19.

82. Bercovitch, *Puritan Origins*, 62, 90; Miller, *Errand*.

83. Axtell, *Invasion Within;* Miller, *Errand*, and idem, *New England Mind*.

84. Morison, *Harvard in the Seventeenth Century*, 1:340–60; Axtell, *Invasion Within*, esp. 131–217.

85. See, among others, Demos, *Unredeemed Captive*.

86. *Records of the Governor and Company, Massachusetts Bay*, 3:112; *Acts and Resolves*, 1:423–24; *Protestant's Resolution;* Axtell, *Invasion Within*, 300.

87. Morison, *Harvard in the Seventeenth Century*, 2:630, 634.

88. Rogers, "Commencement Address," 396 (and also 389); Morison, *Founding of Harvard College*, 226–40.

89. Martin, "Jesuit Mystique," 31; *Oxford English Dictionary*, s.v. "Jesuit" and "Jesuitical." For the roots of general anticlericalism, see Barnett, *Idol Temples*.

90. Dunn, Savage, and Yeandle, *Journal of John Winthrop*, 1:305. Morison, *Founding of Harvard College*, 230–40.

91. Axtell, *Invasion Within*, 5; Miller, *Errand*, 15.

92. Rush quoted in Cremin, *American Education*, 1:564. Finke and Stark, *Churching of America*, 27; Ahlstrom, *Religious History of the American People*, 360–80.

93. Finke and Stark, *Churching of America*, 16.

94. Simpson quoted in Handy, *Christian America*, 70; Butler, *Awash;* Marty, *Righteous Empire*.

95. Marty, *Righteous Empire*, 44; "Editor's Table," 697; "Nation's Right to Worship," 689. Wayland quoted in Marty, *Righteous Empire*, 89. Also see Hutchison, "Protestantism as Establishment."

96. Rudolph, *Essays on Education;* Kaestle, *Pillars*, 75–79; Cremin, *American Education*, vol. 2, chaps. 2 and 3.

97. Boorstin, *Americans*, 153.

98. Findlay, "SPCTEW and Western Colleges"; Cremin, *American Education*, 2:386, 408; Tewskbury, *Founding of American Colleges and Universities*, 9–15.

99. Geiger, "Era," 55; Burke, *American Collegiate Populations*.

100. Boorstin reporting on Columbia President Frederick A. P. Barnard's concerns in *Americans*, 155.

101. Absalom Peters, "Discourse before the Society for the Promotion of Collegiate

and Theological Education at the West" (1851), quoted in Tewksbury, *Founding of American Colleges and Universities*, 3–4.

102. Beecher, *Plea for the West*, 12.

103. Hofstadter, *Paranoid Style*, 21; Franchot, *Roads to Rome*.

104. Titles taken from Billington's extensive bibliography in *Protestant Crusade*, 445–98.

105. Ibid. O'Malley, "Historiography," 11; Curran, "Tentative Bibliography"; Rockwell, "Jesuits as Portrayed by Non-Catholic Historians." On anti-Jesuitism in Europe, see Lacouture, *Jesuits*.

106. Billington, *Protestant Crusade*, 445–98. A sample of articles about the Jesuits includes Wells, "Soldiers of the Church Militant"; "Historical Sketch of the Jesuits"; De Pressensé, "Society of Jesus"; C.D. "The Jesuits," article in *Journal of Sacred Literature*; "The Jesuits," article in *Southern Quarterly Review*.

107. Webster, *American Dictionary of the English Language*, 1850 and 1864; Richardson, *New Dictionary of the English Language*.

108. Jenkins, "By the Great Waters," 547.

109. Parkman, *Jesuits in North America*, xix.

110. "The Jesuits"—article in *Southern Quarterly Review*, 23.

111. De Pressensé, "Society of Jesus," 426; Floy, "Jesuits," 44.

112. See, for example, Browning, *Aspects of Education*, 137–42 f.

113. "Historical Sketch of the Jesuits," 161, 162.

114. C.D., "Jesuits," 39, 40; Floy, "Jesuits," 42. The juxtaposition of Luther and Loyola can also be found in de Pressensé, "Society of Jesus," 409; Birdsey, "Dark Record," 252; Stonex, "Loyola and His Followers," 609.

115. Stonex, "Loyola and His Followers," 611; Barnard, "Jesuits and Their Schools," 252.

116. Wells, "Soldiers of the Church Militant," 32.

117. Beecher, "Plea for Western Colleges," 2:49.

118. Comments of Edward Beecher and "Dr. B" as recorded in *Proceedings of a Public Meeting*, 5 and 10, respectively.

119. Beecher, "Plea for Western Colleges," 2:50.

120. E. N. Kirk, *Church and College* (1845), quoted in Billington, *Protestant Crusade*, 278.

121. Porter, *Educational Systems*, 43, 50–51, 73, 81.

122. George W. Burnap, "Errors and Superstitions of Rome," 11 May 1853 (HUA, HUC 5340.153).

123. G.E.E., "Massachusetts Legislature," 51, 61.

124. CWE to John Duff, 8 Feb. 1907 (HUA, UAI.5.150, CWE ltr. bk. 97).

125. "Historical Sketch of the Jesuits," 173.

Chapter 2. Time: The Harvard Law School Controversy and the Modern Imperative

Epigraphs. 1: Luther, "An Appeal to the Ruling Class," 470. 2: Slosson, *Great American Universities*, 1.

1. Adams, *Education of Henry Adams*, 342, 343. On other reactions to the fair, see Badger, *Great American Fair;* Burg, *Chicago's White City.*

2. Bury, *Idea of Progress;* Bowler, *Invention of Progress;* Nisbet, *History of the Idea of Progress;* Pollard, *Idea of Progress;* Moorhead, *World without End;* Trautmann, "Revolution in Ethnological Time."

3. Fleming, "Picturesque History"; Lears, *No Place of Grace.*

4. Bence Jones quoted in Hamlin, "Attitude of the Christian Teacher," 3.

5. Melville, *White Jacket,* 144, 143.

6. Reuben, *Making of the Modern University,* esp. chap. 2; Hutchison, *Modernist Impulse,* 1–11; Marty, *Irony of It All,* pts. 1 and 2.

7. George W. Burnap, "Errors and Superstitions of Rome," 11 May 1853 (HUA, HUC 5340.153).

8. Marsden, introduction to Marsden and Longfield, *Secularization,* 5. Also see Marsden, *Soul,* 186; Bass, "Ministry on the Margins"; Cherry, *Hurrying toward Zion,* ix.

9. Butler quoted in Evans, *Newman Movement,* 4. Hollinger, "Inquiry and Uplift" and idem, "Justification by Verification"; Cutler, "Cathedral of Culture."

10. Le Conte, "Essential Characteristics," 177.

11. Brooks, "How Shall We Educate Our Boys?" 200.

12. CWE quoted in Jordan, *Days of a Man,* 2:2.

13. On early Jesuit education in Maryland, see Daley, *Georgetown University,* 1–8; Gleason, "Main Sheet Anchor"; Burns, "Early Jesuit Schools"; Power, *Catholic Higher Education in America,* 10–11. On Maryland Catholicism, see Hennesey, *American Catholics,* 36–45; Dolan, *American Catholic Experience,* 77–88.

14. Cassidy, "Catholic College Foundations," 3–72; Erbacher, "Catholic Higher Education for Men," 8–9.

15. Bangert, *History of the Society of Jesus,* 363–430; Campbell, *Jesuits,* 685–715.

16. Guilday, *Life and Times of John Carroll;* Dolan, *American Catholic Experience,* 101–24; Hennesey, *American Catholics,* chaps. 7 and 8.

17. John Carroll, writing in 1787, quoted in Curran, *Bicentennial History,* 15.

18. Daley, *Georgetown University,* 26, 47; final quote from Gleason, "Main Sheet Anchor," 583. Power, *Catholic Higher Education in America,* 15–21.

19. Broadside proposing the establishment of Georgetown, reprinted in Curran, *Bicentennial History,* xviii.

20. Carroll quoted in Gleason, "Main Sheet Anchor," 599.

21. Curran, *Bicentennial History,* 34, and chap. 3; Daley, *Georgetown University,* chaps. 4 and 6; Campbell, *Jesuits,* 705.

22. Campbell, "Century of Disaster," in *Jesuits,* 734–64.

23. McKevitt, "Jesuit Higher Education," 212–13; Campbell, *Jesuits,* 828; Bangert, *History of the Society of Jesus,* 478–85; McGucken, *Jesuits and Education,* 129.

24. Fenwick briefly served as Georgetown's president in 1817 and in 1825: Curran, *Bicentennial History,* 404.

25. Meagher and Grattan, *Spires of Fenwick,* 1–46; Lord, Sexton, and Harrington, *History of the Archdiocese of Boston,* 2:326–29; Kuzniewski, *Thy Honored Name,* 1–33.

26. Roothaan quoted in Kuzniewski, *Thy Honored Name,* 27.

27. Potts, "American Colleges in the Nineteenth Century."

28. Fenwick quoted in Kuzniewski, *Thy Honored Name*, 21, 22.

29. Francis Dzierozynski to Roothaan, 22 Aug. 1843, quoted in Kuzniewski, *Thy Honored Name*, 33. On Holy Cross's difficulties, see Kuzniewski, *Thy Honored Name*, e.g. 44–50, 78, 80, 81, 100–101; Lord, Sexton, and Harrington, *History of the Archdiocese of Boston*, 2:574–82; Meagher and Grattan, *Spires of Fenwick*, 85–99; G.E.E., "Massachusetts Legislature."

30. Meagher and Grattan, *Spires of Fenwick*, 60; Kuzniewski, *Thy Honored Name*, 55–56, 137–39.

31. Meagher and Gratton, *Spires of Fenwick*, 149. Also see *Holy Cross Alumni Directory, 1843–1967*.

32. Donovan, Dunigan, and FitzGerald, *History of Boston College*, 7–15; Garraghan, "Origins," 628; Lord, Sexton, and Harrington, *History of the Archdiocese of Boston*, 2:608–10. Boston College's first president, Father John Bapst, S.J. (1863–69) survived Know-Nothing violence. While tending to the pastoral needs of Catholics in Maine, Bapst was tarred and feathered by a mob in 1854. Donovan, Dunigan, and FitzGerald, *History of Boston College*, 33–34; Bangert, *History of the Society of Jesus*, 478.

33. *Pilot*, 27 Aug. 1864, reprinted in Donovan, Dunigan, and FitzGerald, *History of Boston College*, 41. AMDG is an abbreviation for the Jesuit motto *ad majorem Dei gloriam* (for the greater glory of God).

34. Donovan, Dunigan, and FitzGerald, *History of Boston College*, 41. On early Boston College, see Lord, Sexton, and Harrington, *History of the Archdiocese of Boston*, 3:349–56.

35. *HCC* (1897–98): 17.

36. *BCC* (1898–99): 31, 33.

37. "Father Timothy Brosnahan," *WL* 45 (1916): 99–117.

38. *BCC* (1898–99): 31–32.

39. Ibid., 32, 33.

40. *HCC* (1897–98): 17.

41. Geiger, "Era," 58. In 1890 the number of Jesuit colleges roughly matched or outnumbered those under the auspices of the Congregationalists (22), Episcopalians (6), Disciples of Christ (20), Lutherans (19), and the United Brethren (10). They were outnumbered by the main churches and branches of the colleges sponsored by the Presbyterians (35/14), Methodists (52/22), and Baptists (36/8).

42. "Law School," *Harvard Law Review* 7 (1893–94): 113; "Law School," *Harvard Law Review* 8 (1894–95): 220; "Law School," *Harvard Law Review* 17 (1903–4): 119. Enrollment data was published yearly in the *Harvard Law Review*.

43. Data is based on catalogs of Boston College and Harvard University for the years in question.

44. E. A. Gilmore to J. Francis Quinlan, 29 May and 3 June 1897 (HUA, Committee on Admission from Other Colleges, HUA, III.10.40.145.6).

45. "James Barr Ames"; Sutherland, *Law at Harvard*, ch. 7; Harvard Law School Association, *Centennial History of the Harvard Law School*, 175–89.

46. JBA to Quinlan (copy), 10 Aug. 1897 (GUA, Harvard folder 2).

47. Records of the Committee on Admission from Other Colleges (HUA, III.10.40.145.6); *BCC* (1908).

48. JBA to Quinlan, 10 Aug. 1897 (GUA, Harvard folder 2). The University of Notre Dame was added to the list in 1894; no records in the archives of Harvard or the University of Notre Dame regarding its inclusion have been located. Given the emphasis the university builders placed on science, it is possible that Notre Dame's reputation in the area may have worked in its favor. Manhattan College (est. 1853), run by the De La Salle Christian Brothers, was added to the Law School's list in 1900. J. D. Whitney, S.J., president of Georgetown (1898–1901), wrote the recently retired Richards about an encounter with Ames:

> I met Professor Ames the other day at Philadelphia, and he immediately spoke of the Eliot-Brosnahan controversy, and said that Dr. Eliot had made a mistake; "but," he added, "with regard to the Law School list, that is our doing, not his. We are responsible, not he. But believe me," he continued, "there is no thought of sectarian feeling or bigotry in the matter at all, and, as a proof of this, you will be glad to know that we have just put Manhattan on the list." I concealed my surprise at this last bit of information, and retired after some bit of commonplace. I had hoped to be able to talk with Professor Ames later on privately, but no opportunity [was] offered.

J. D. Whitney to JHR, 26 Feb. 1900 (GUA, JHR papers, box 7, folder 4).

49. JHR to JBA, 31 Aug. 1897 (GUA, JHR papers, box 6, folder 6) (copy dated 5 Nov. 1897 is in BCA, TB papers).

50. JBA to JHR, 10 Sept. 1897 (GUA, Harvard folder 2) (copy dated 5 Nov. 1897 is in BCA, TB papers).

51. TB to JHR, 8 Mar. 1898, and TB to JHR, 7 Nov. 1897 (BCA, Dunigan papers, box 1/3A, folder 11).

52. TB to JHR, 8 Mar. 1898.

53. William G. MacDonald to JHR, 1 Nov. 1896 (GUA, JHR papers, box 2, folder 1); TB to JHR, 10 Nov. and 12 Nov. 1896 (BCA, Dunigan papers, box 1/3A, folder 11); "Georgetown College," *WL* 26 (1897): 184.

54. JBA to TB, 11 Mar. 1898 (BCA, TB papers). For evidence of the change in policy, see JBA to John E. Swift (26 Aug. 1899), where Ames denies a Boston College student regular admission to the Law School (BCA, WGRM papers, folder 1).

55. JHR to TB, 16 Mar. 1898 (BCA, TB papers).

56. Ibid.; Kuzniewski, *Thy Honored Name*, 155 f.

57. Pubrick to LM, Feb. 1899 (ARSI, MD 13.I.35); "Father William George Read Mullan," *WL* 39 (1910): 392.

58. Hogan, *Catholic University of America.* Msgr. Conaty was raised to the rank of bishop in 1901.

59. CWE to TJC, 24 Oct. 1898 (HUA, UAI.5.150, CWE ltr. bk. 92); CWE to Lehy, 24 Oct. 1898 (BCA, WGRM papers, folder 1).

60. BCAA, 20 July 1899 (GUA, MPA, box 96, folder 520); Purbrick to LM, 20 Feb. 1900 (ARSI, MD 13.I.50).

61. WGRM to CWE, 1 Sept. 1899 (BCA, WGRM papers, folder 1); CWE to WGRM,

21 Oct. 1899 (BCA, WGRM papers, folder 2), and WGRM to CWE, 8 Nov. 1899 (HUA, UAI.5.150, box 140, folder 1469). Also see Richard Cobb, Harvard correspondence secretary, to WGRM, 4 and 15 Sept. 1899 (BCA, WGRM papers, folder 1), and H. C. G. von Jagemann to WGRM, 27 Oct. 1899 (BCA, WGRM papers, folder 2).

62. Von Jagemann to CWE, 6 Nov. 1899 (HUA, UAI.5.150, box 114, folder 196).

63. WGRM to CWE, 8 Nov. 1899.

64. JBA to CWE, 18 Nov. 1899 (HUA, UAI.5.150, box 140, folder 1469); WGRM to CWE, 1 Dec. 1899 (HUA, UAI.5.150, box 140, folder 1469); CWE to WGRM, 8 Dec. 1899 (BCA, WGRM papers, folder 2).

65. WGRM to CWE, 11 Jan. 1900 (HUA, UAI.5.150, box 140, folder 1469).

66. Ibid.; E. A. Gilmore to JBA, 25 July 1899 (HUA, UAI.1.150 box 124, folder 462).

67. CWE to WGRM, 17 Jan. 1900 (BCA, WGRM papers, folder 3).

68. WGRM to CWE, 23 Jan. 1900 (HUA, UAI.5.150, box 140, folder 1469); CWE to WGRM, 24 Jan. 1900 (BCA, WGRM papers, folder 3).

69. WGRM to CWE, 31 Jan. 1900 (HUA, UAI.5.150, box 140, folder 1469).

70. CWE to WGRM, 1 Feb. 1900 (BCA, WGRM papers, folder 3); CWE to WGRM, 6 Feb. 1900 (BCA, WGRM papers, folder 3).

71. "It Won't Hurt Me," unidentified clipping (BCA, TB papers).

72. "Protestantism," 6.

73. CWE, "Inaugural," 30–31; idem, "What Is a Liberal Education?" 208.

74. White quoted in Brill, "Religion and the Rise of the University," 152.

75. CWE, "New Education," 366; CWE, "Education of Ministers," 71, 67, 72; CWE to Roche, 20 June 1893, reprinted in the *Pilot*, 1 July 1893. For additional insight into CWE's views on the clergy, see Briggs, "As Seen by a Disciple," 599–601. Also see Turner, *Without God*, 217–21.

76. Kimball, *"True Professional Ideal,"* 11–12, 198–212; Rosenberg, *No Other Gods;* Marsden, *Soul*, chaps. 6 and 9; Hollinger, "Inquiry and Uplift," and idem, "Justification by Verification"; Turner, *Without God*, 123 f.

77. Barrows, *World's Parliament of Religions*, 1:4. Burg, *Chicago's White City*, 113; Badger, *Great America Fair*, 96.

78. Burnap, "Errors and Superstitions of Rome." Also see Buck, *Social Sciences at Harvard;* Trautmann, "Revolution in Ethnological Time"; Turner, *Without God*, 150–57; Roberts and Turner, *Sacred and the Secular*, esp. chap. 1.

79. Gilman, "Johns Hopkins University," 18. Numerous works examine the relationship between science and religion in the nineteenth century: Hovenkamp, *Science and Religion;* Bozeman, *Protestants in an Age of Science;* Dillenberger, *Protestant Thought;* Buck, *Social Sciences at Harvard;* Howe, "Reason and Revelation." For a historiographic analysis of the relationship between religion and science, see Kimball, *"True Professional Ideal,"* 200–212.

80. CWE, *Religion of the Future*, 20.

81. CWE quoted in Hawkins, *Between Harvard and America*, 129; CWE, "Education of Ministers," 71.

82. CWE, "What Place Should Religion Have?" 14–15. Eliot's faith in science is discussed in Sloan, *Faith and Knowledge*, 2–4, and Shepard, *God's People*, 51–59.

83. Meyer, "American Intellectuals," 599; Turner, *Without God;* Hutchison, *Modernist Impulse.*

84. CWE, "Inaugural," 8; Harper, "Some Present Tendencies," 51; CWE, "Education of Ministers" 70; Langdell, "Harvard Celebration Speeches," 124. Langdell's scientific approach to law is also discussed in Sutherland, *Law at Harvard,* 174–80.

85. Buck, *Social Sciences at Harvard,* 9; CWE, "Three Results," 238. Philosopher George Santayana wrote that the "most notable" characteristics of Harvard were "scientific enthusiasm and liberty of thought": Santayana, "Spirit and Ideals," 314. Hollinger, "Justification by Verification," 118; Reuben, *Making of the Modern University,* 36–60; Shils, "Order of Learning," 37 f.

86. Harper, "Scientific Study of the Student," 320.

87. CWE, "Inaugural," 1.

88. Morison, *Three Centuries,* 344, 348–58, 383; Moore, "Elective System at Harvard," 530–34.

89. CWE, untitled speech on electivism, 1895 (HUA, EPA, UAI.5.150, box 335, #62); CWE, "Liberty in Education," 127, 125.

90. Morison, *Three Centuries,* 343–44. For an extended examination of Eliot's views on electivism, see Hawkins, *Between Harvard and America,* chap. 3.

91. Saunderson, *Charles W. Eliot,* 3; CWE, untitled speech on electivism; CWE, "Liberty in Education." 129.

92. Babbitt, "President Eliot," 1; CWE, "Liberty in Education," 133, and "New Education," 218. Harper also espoused an individualistic approach: "Every opportunity should be given the student for the freest play of individual choice": "Waste in Higher Education," 95.

93. Carpenter, "Emerson, Eliot, and the Elective System," with CWE quoted on 30, Emerson on 17 and 22; Saunderson, *Charles W. Eliot,* 139–50.

94. CWE, "Inaugural," 11, 12, and "Liberty in Education," 132–33.

95. Seniors were free to elect all their courses by 1872, juniors by 1879, and sophomores by 1884: Hawkins, *Between Harvard and America,* 96.

96. CWE, "Recent Changes," 443.

97. Purbrick to LM, 19 Feb. 1900 (ARSI, MD 13.I.50); the editors to TB, 9 Dec. 1899, reprinted in "Father Timothy Brosnahan," *WL* 16 (1915): 109; West, "Is There a Democracy of Studies?"

98. "A Princeton Professor on Harvard's President," *SHR,* 13 Jan. 1900, 22; the *Casket* editorialist is quoted in "The 'Atlantic Monthly's' Ineffectual Heroism," *SHR,* 27 Jan. 1900, 56; *Bookman* 11 (Apr. 1900): 111. Soon after Brosnahan published "President Eliot and Jesuit Colleges" in the *Sacred Heart Review, Atlantic Monthly* editor Bliss Perry explained to Eliot that he had asked Andrew West to write a piece in August 1899. When West submitted it, Perry asked him to

strike out those sentences referring to your paper, upon the ground of our general policy of discouraging controversial contributions. I found . . . that Professor West . . . regarded those passages as germane to his argument. . . . Our Jesuit friends are now accusing me of disingenuousness, and though I cannot say that their anger troubles me very deeply, I am sorry now that I did not write you weeks ago and tell you what I have just written about the history of Professor West's article.

Perry to CWE, 17 Jan. 1900 (HUA, UAI.5.150, box 128, folder 608). Thirty-five years later, Perry recounted the incident in his memoirs:

> A more justifiable cause for wrath was soon found in an unlucky—and, I imagine, ill-informed—sentence by President Eliot in the October number. . . . [T]he editor promptly received about sixty letters from officials in Jesuit colleges, many of them to the tune of "Why is your contemptible publication anti-Catholic?" and all of them demanding space in the *Atlantic* for a reply. . . . It had long been the policy of the magazine not to print controversial replies to its articles. I now think this policy was wrong, but in 1899 I felt bound to conform to it. Fortunately my stenographer was a Catholic young lady with a sense of humor and a deep loyalty to the accepted policy of the magazine, and between us we concocted sixty soft answers which may or may not have assuaged the wrath of the educators.

Perry, *And Gladly Teach*, 170–71.

99. TB, "President Eliot and Jesuit Colleges," 11–12, 13–15, 14. Historian Frederick Rudolph, whose sympathies were not with the Jesuits of Boston College, asserted that "low academic standards seemed a more appropriate policy than the abandonment of *four centuries* of curricular certainty" (my italics). Rudolph repeated Eliot's mistake, demonstrating a lack of familiarity with the controversy: *American College and University*, 296.

100. TB, "President Eliot and Jesuit Colleges," 19.

101. Ibid., 16–25, quotes at 21, 21–22, 24.

102. Purbrick to LM, 19 Feb. 1900; W. T. Harris to John Whitney, 31 Mar. 1900 (GUA, Brosnahan, box 8, folder 155); E. Winchester Donald to TB, 15 Feb. 1900 (GUA, Brosnahan, box 8, folder 155). Also John D. Whitney to J. J. Wynne, 6 Feb. 1900 (GUA, JHR papers, box 7, folder 4). The extent of press coverage received by Brosnahan's essay is suggested in a regular feature in the *Sacred Heart Review* entitled *What Catholic Editors Say*, which excerpted editorials from the Catholic press nationwide.

103. *Bookman* 11 (Apr. 1900): 111; editorial in the *Pittsburg Observer*, quoted in *What Catholic Editors Say*, SHR, 3 Feb. 1900, 72.

104. "Eloquent about Trusts," *Worcester Telegram*, 23 Jan. 1900 (ACHC); "President Eliot Called A Bigot," unidentified clipping, ca. 23 Jan. 1900 (GUA, Brosnahan, box 8, folder 155). Also see "Rt. Rev. Rector of the Catholic University," *Pilot*, 27 Jan. 1900.

105. "All Against Harvard," *Boston Herald*, 6 Feb. 1900 (ACHC, 14.13–1).

106. "Earnest Protest," *Boston Globe*, 6 Feb. 1900 (BCA, WGRM papers, folder 7). Also see "Agitation Against Harvard," unidentified clipping, 6 Feb. 1900 (BCA, TB papers).

107. CWE to WGRM, 6 Feb. 1900.

108. "President Eliot Makes No Reply," unidentified clipping (GUA, Brosnahan, box 8, folder 155); "President Eliot Called a Bigot."

109. John O'Brien to CWE, 12 Feb. 1900, and CWE to John O'Brien, 14 Feb. 1900 (HUA, UAI.5.150, CWE ltr. bk.). Also see "Harvard's Stand," *Boston Globe*, 7 Feb. 1900.

110. TJC to TB, 20 Dec. 1899 (ACUA, TJC papers, box 1, folder 10); TB, "Relative Merit," 42, 45, 23. Hogan, *Catholic University of America*, 73–74.

111. "Jesuits to Meet in Chicago" *New York Times*, 11 Apr. 1900, 1; "Catholic Condemns Harvard," *New York Times*, 19 Apr. 1900. Audience comments following TB's "Relative Merit," at 44–47. For mixed reactions of Catholic educators, see Plough, "Catholic Colleges and the Catholic Educational Association," 94 ff.

112. "Course of Study at Harvard," *Saturday Review*, 21 Apr. 1900; *Bookman* 11 (June 1900): 294. Also see "Value of Courses," *Boston Globe*, 28 Apr. 1900; "Father Brosnahan's Second Paper," *SHR*, 28 Apr. 1900, 266–67; "President Eliot and Jesuit Colleges," *New York Sun*, 18 Apr. 1900.

113. WGRM to CWE, 25 May 1900 (HUA, UAI.5.150, box 140, folder 1469); "Alumni Pleased," *Boston Globe*, 29 June 1900; "Educators Argue," *Boston Globe*, 25 May 1900; "Harvard and Catholics," *Pilot*, 30 June 1900; "Harvard and the Jesuit Colleges," *Pilot*, 30 June 1900. Boston College Alumni Association requested that Mullan make documents related to the controversy available to them several days prior to its publication in the *Globe*: alumni representatives to WGRM, 21 May 1900, and WGRM to the alumni, with copies of his correspondence with CWE, 7 June 1900 (BCA, WGRM papers, folder 4).

114. CWE to WGRM, 2 June 1900 (BCA, WGRM papers, folder 3).

115. *Harvard University Catalogue* (1904–5): 592–93; quotes from Macksey to JBA, 12 Nov. 1906. Also see JBA to Macksey, 7 Nov. 1906, JBA to Macksey, 13 Nov. 1906, Macksey to JBA, 22 Nov. 1906, Macksey to J. G. Hart, chair, Committee on Admission, 23 Nov. 1906 (GUA, Harvard folder 2).

116. Donovan, Dunigan, and FitzGerald, *History of Boston College*, 109, and the author's conversations with long-time Boston College faculty.

117. Cafeu(?) to TB, 15 Mar. 1905 (GUA, Brosnahan, box 8, folder 155); Woods, "Catholic College—Its Chief Danger," 63.

118. Dwight to TB, 1 May 1900 (GUA, Brosnahan, box 8, folder 155); E. Winchester Donald quoted in LaFarge, *Manner Is Ordinary*, 67–68; Hawkins, *Between Harvard and America*, 189, 190.

119. Purbrick to LM, 20 Feb. 1900.

120. Wheeler to CWE, 14 Oct. and 9 Nov. 1903 (HUA, UAI.5.150, box 257, folder "Wheeler, Benjamin I."). A history of Santa Clara University reports that new entrance requirements for Berkeley's law and medical schools created consternation among the Jesuit faculty, who feared it was an attempt to standardize the curriculum throughout California: McKevitt, *University of Santa Clara*, 50–51.

121. Everett, "Jesuit Educators and Modern Colleges," 649.

122. Fagan, "What the Parish School Can Do," 48.

Chapter 3. Persons: The Bonds of Religion and the Claims of Class

Epigraph. Comment of the chair, following Guldner, "Moral Training," 43.

1. Shils, "Order of Learning"; Veysey, *Emergence;* Bledstein, *Culture of Professionalism.*

2. Thomas Bender quoted in Lears, "Concept of Cultural Hegemony," 586.

3. Graham, "Expansion and Exclusion," 761; Geiger, "Era," 51.

4. Berger, "Structure and Choice in the Sociology of Culture," 17. Berger's methodological advice warrants lengthy quotation:

> Cast a jaded eye on the celebration of loyalty or fidelity *as* abstractions and *to* abstractions; ask instead loyalty to what? fidelity to whom? Cultivate those odd social niches whose resources enable you to claim the voice of a "member" but that also provide alternative resources for effective dissent and resistance. Every community exacts some degree of conformity or compliance as its price of membership, and this is not necessarily felt as constraint, particularly if the community's norms are one's own and especially if one has never even consciously thought about it. Plural and diverse memberships create conditions that increase the prospect of one's *having to* think about it and to interact with diverse significant others regarding what to do about it. Plural and diverse memberships create conditions that increase the prospect of being reflexive about one's own socialization.

5. Philip Gleason discusses the large number of Catholics in non-Catholic settings in "American Catholic Higher Education," 27–28, and *Contending with Modernity,* 23–28. Catholic patronage of non-Catholic institutions and its significance has not received sufficient scholarly attention. Others have erroneously concluded that Catholics did not attend non-Catholic colleges; see, for example, a claim that "not many Irish attended Harvard, Yale, or Princeton, or, for that matter, any university": McCaffrey, *Textures of Irish America,* 26. Jencks and Riesman also fail to recognize the significant presence of Catholics at Harvard, claiming that "Boston College was founded to provide a local alternative" to Harvard which the Irish considered part of the "enemy Yankee camp." They further explain that "few . . . wanted to break radically with their background by choosing Harvard and typing themselves as Yankees": Jencks and Riesman, "Viability of the American College," 148, 150.

6. Kemeny, *Princeton;* Leslie, *Gentlemen and Scholars.*

7. Finkelstein, "Education Historians," 265. A number of recent studies have turned to the sociological literature on social capital and cultural capital to examine the purposes and efficacy of schools and education; see, for example, Labaree, *Making of an American High School.*

8. Wiebe, *Search for Order.*

9. Ryan, *Cradle of the Middle Class;* McDannell, *Christian Home in Victorian America;* Stevenson, *Victorian Homefront;* Warner, *Streetcar Suburbs;* Blumin, *Emergence of the Middle Class.* Gilman is quoted in Bledstein, *Culture of Professionalism,* 293.

10. Labaree, *Making of an American High School,* 6; Bledstein, *Culture of Professionalism;* Haskell, *Authority of Experts.*

11. Horowitz, *Campus Life*, 12; Townsend, *Manhood at Harvard*, esp. chap. 2. The image of "real college" and its role in higher education is developed in Brint and Karabel, *Diverted Dream;* "real school" is discussed in Tyack and Cuban, *Tinkering toward Utopia.*

12. McDannell, "'True Men as We Need Them,'" esp. 31; Kane, *Separatism and Subculture,* chap. 3.

13. Shannon, *American Irish*, 183.

14. Ibid., chap. 11; Clark, *Hibernia America*, chap. 4. Also see Moore, "Insiders and Outsiders," and *Religious Outsiders.*

15. TB to JHR, 8 Mar. 1898 (BCA, David R. Dunigan papers, box 1/3A, folder 11).

16. "President Eliot Called a Bigot," unidentified clipping, ca. 23 Jan. 1900 (GUA, Brosnhan, box 8, folder 155); "Harvard's Discrimination Denounced at Holy Cross Banquet," *Worcester Telegram*, 23 Jan. 1900 (ACHC, loc. 9, bk. 4); "President Eliot's Discrimination Against Catholic Colleges," ca. 6 Feb. 1900 (BCA, WGRM papers).

17. Barnes delivered similar addresses before the alumni of Boston College and Holy Cross; the quotes are from "President Eliot Called a Bigot" and "Earnest Protest," *Boston Globe*, 6 Feb. 1900.

18. "Eloquent about Trusts," *Worcester Telegram*, 23 Jan. 1900 (ACHC, loc. 8, bk. 4).

19. Ibid.

20. In 1950, Rev. Charles F. Donovan, S.J., of Boston College, asked his students to interview alumni from the 1890s. Nineteen alumni granted interviews to students or responded in writing. Fr. Donovan provided photocopies of the alumni recollections to the author [those records are henceforth cited as BC alum]. On the alumni of the period, including Splaine, see Donovan's essay, published as one of his occasional papers on the history of Boston College, "Boston College Remembered, 1891–1900."

21. Quote from Dolan, *American Catholic Experience*, 195; Smith, "Religion and Ethnicity"; Orsi, *Madonna of 115th Street.*

22. Finke and Stark, *Churching of America*, 55, 114.

23. McGreevy discusses the parish as locus of social organization in *Parish Boundaries*. Kauffman, *Ministry and Meaning;* Oates, *Catholic Philanthropic Tradition;* Walton, *To Preserve the Faith;* Dolan, *American Catholic Experience*, esp. chaps. 6, 9, and 10.

24. Perlmann, *Ethnic Differences*, 64; Kruszka quoted in Dolan, *American Catholic Experience*, 279; Walch, *Parish School.*

25. Carl Wittke quotes Disraeli to the effect that the potato was the "single root changing the history of the world": *Irish in America*, 7.

26. Laxton, *Famine Ships;* Fallows, *Irish Americans*, 48; McCaffrey, *Irish Diaspora;* Miller, *Emigrants and Exiles.*

27. Handlin, *Boston Immigrants*, 243.

28. In *Boston Immigrants*, Handlin provides a still useful description of the famine Irish in Boston. Also see Thernstrom, *Other Bostonians.*

29. Shannon, *American Irish*, 132; Kane, *Separatism and Subculture,* 4; Ryan, *Be-*

yond the Ballot Box, chap. 4; Thernstrom, *Other Bostonians;* Clark, *Hibernia America;* McCaffrey, *Textures of Irish America,* chap. 2.

30. Kane, *Separatism and Subculture.*

31. Haynes, "Amusements," 199.

32. McGinley, "Catholic Life," 22.

33. Lord, Sexton, and Harrington, *History of the Archdiocese of Boston,* esp. vol. 2, chap. 11; O'Connor, *Boston Catholics,* esp. chap. 4.

34. Quote from Walton, *To Preserve the Faith,* 99; Clark, *Hibernia America,* 39; Schneider, *In the Web of Class;* Kane, *Separatism and Subculture,* esp. chaps. 3 and 6.

35. Editorial in the *Pilot,* 27 Aug. 1864, quoted in Donovan, Dunigan, and Fitz-Gerald, *History of Boston College,* 41, 42.

36. *BCC* (1893–94): 29–30; *HCC* (1893–94): 23.

37. *Children of Immigrants,* 5:721. Also see Gleason, "Immigration and American Catholic Higher Education."

38. I.H.S. stands for "in hoc signo," which translates "in this sign" and is associated with Constantine, whose conversion is linked to a vision of a cross and the phrase *"In this sign thou shalt conquer."* Donovan, Dunigan, and FitzGerald, *History of Boston College,* 79; Daniel Gallagher, class of 1892, recalled that "Irish High School" was used in a "derisive manner." I.H.S. appeared on "hats for compulsory military drill which was discontinued in 1885." BC alum.

39. Warner, preface to Woods and Kennedy, *Zone of Emergence,* 21–22.

40. Woods and Kennedy, *Zone of Emergence,* 36; O'Connor, *Boston Catholics,* 121–22.

41. *BCC* (1894–95); BC alum.; Ryan, *Beyond the Ballot Box,* 73–74.

42. *Children of Immigrants,* 5:717, 719, 720, 723, 726, 730, 731. Duquesne University (known in its early days as the Pittsburg College of the Holy Ghost) was established by the Congregation of the Holy Ghost in 1878. The Jesuit colleges in the study included Boston College, Canisius College in Buffalo, the College of Saint Francis Xavier in New York, Saint John's in New York, Loyola College in Baltimore, Saint Ignatius College in Chicago, Saint Ignatius College in Cleveland, and Saint Xavier College in Cincinnati.

43. Rury, "Urban Catholic University," 9; Contosta, *Villanova University,* 39; Greeley, *American Catholic,* 46. Also see Gleason, "Immigration and American Catholic Higher Education"; Weiss, "Duquesne University."

44. TB to LM, 10 Nov. 1894 (ARSI, MD 1012.IV.9); BC alum.

45. BC alum.

46. Winterer, *Culture of Classicism.*

47. Alumnus Timothy Ahearn claimed that students who did poorly in Latin often struggled or flunked out: BC alum.

48. Ong, "Language Study"; BC alum; Donovan, "Classical Curriculum" in *Boston College: Glimpses of the Past.*

49. Kimball, *Orators and Philosophers.*

50. *BCC* (1899–1900): 32.

51. Untitled article, *BCS* 1 (1883): 1.

52. O'Malley, *First Jesuits,* 222; "Woodstock Academy," *WL* 25 (1896): 58–66.

53. Donovan, Dunigan, and FitzGerald, *History of Boston College,* 85.

54. In Jesuit education, according to O'Malley, theater was "cultivated . . . to an especially high degree over a long period of time in a vast network of schools almost around the globe"; the "significance of theater in all its aspects . . . can hardly be overestimated": O'Malley, *First Jesuits,* 223. Also see a number of essays in O'Malley et al., *Jesuits.*

55. Donovan, "Debate at Boston College" in *Boston College: Glimpses of the Past;* "Worcester, Holy Cross College," *WL* 29 (1900): 543–44; "Harvard Debate," *HCP* 11 (1900): 19–20.

56. Schwickerath, *Jesuit Education,* 574.

57. *BCC* (1899–1900): 32, 40–55.

58. BC alum.

59. Azarius, "Lessons of a Century," 148.

60. Delurey, "Teaching of History," 73, 80; comments by Tracy following Ryan, "Teaching of English," 105.

61. *BCC* (1899–1900): 42, 43, 44.

62. Morison, *Three Centuries,* 366–67; Hawkins, *Between Harvard and America,* 133–36.

63. BC alum. For religious life at Holy Cross, see Kuzniewski, *Thy Honored Name,* 161–62.

64. *BCC* (1891–92): 5; Boston College, consultors' minutes, 8 Feb. 1897 (BCA, Jesuit Community, Jesuit Consultors [RG 42]).

65. BC alum.

66. Horowitz, *Campus Life.*

67. *BCC* (1891–92): 5–6. Donovan, "Rules of Gentlemanly Conduct," in *Boston College: Glimpses of the Past.*

68. "For the Study of the *Ratio,*" 23 (1894): 317.

69. Klein, "Jesuits and Boyhood"; Kuzniewski, *Thy Honored Name,* 162–64, 173–74.

70. Donovan, "Nineteenth-Century Boston College."

71. Donovan, Dunigan, and FitzGerald, *History of Boston College,* 69–72.

72. Ibid., 123; Ryan, *Beyond the Ballot Box,* 74.

73. Donovan, Dunigan, and FitzGerald, *History of Boston College,* 85–86; BC alum. In spring 1900, a Boston College editorial writer noted that it was "not so many years ago that the base-ball club of our college was regarded as not a very formidable team." Yet change was at hand: the Boston College nine stood ready, according to this student, to face "the most formidable teams that ever battled for victory on the diamond." The "opening game with Harvard" was "worthy of notice," for the "splendid work of our nine was the subject of favorable comment, not only among our supporters, but also among those to whom the maroon and old gold signifies little": editorial, *BCS* 14 (1900): 220. Also see Kuzniewski, *Thy Honored Name,* 166–72.

74. BC alum.

75. "Boston College," 73.

76. Analysis based on Boston College catalogs, 1891 to 1900. On the English course, see Donovan, Dunigan, and FitzGerald, *History of Boston College,* 92–93. Ac-

cording to Klein, fewer than 10 percent of students at Fordham and Xavier (both in New York City) finished the full course of studies: "Jesuits and Boyhood," 382.

77. Data based on alumni records, including "Graduates of Boston College," 1908 (BCA).

78. "Boston College," 74; Merwick, *Boston Priests*, 229 n. 32. According to Ryan, "of 352 graduates before 1898, 156 entered the priesthood": *Beyond the Ballot Box*, 74.

79. JBA to CWE, 10 Oct. 1898 (HUA, UAI.5.150, box 100, folder 4); JBA to TB, n.d. (BCA, TB papers).

80. On Dolan: "Alumni," *BCS* 16 (1902): 317–18 and "Alumni," *BCS* 16 (1903): 571–72; Warren, *History of Harvard Law School*, 3:276. On Carney: ibid., 3:286; "Francis Joseph Carney," *Boston College Alumni News* 4 (1940–41): 3, 5; Harvard alumni records (HUA, HUG 300). On Coyne: Warren, *History of Harvard Law School*, 3:287; "Alumni News," 10 Feb. 1938, 18; Harvard alumni records (HUA, HUG 300). In 1902 *Woodstock Letters* reported that the "success" of the last Boston College men to enter Harvard Law School was "interesting and instructive." According to the report, when a "prominent New York law firm" asked the dean of the Law School for recommendations, he provided the names of two Boston College graduates. The report also noted that the "Board of Regents in New York has admitted our college to be ranked in the same standing as that of other colleges, without any restriction or qualification": "Boston College," *WL* 31 (1902): 141.

81. On Aylward, *BCS* (1902): 315; Harvard alumni records (HUA, HUG 300). Also see *Boston Herald*, 7 June 1940.

82. "Boston College," 73; "Francis Joseph Carney," 3.

83. Eugene A. McCarthy, ed., "President Eliot and Boston College: The Record of a Famous Educational Controversy," typescript, ca. 1936 (BCA), foreword.

84. BC alum.

85. "To the editor," *Alumni News* (10 Feb. 1938): 18.

86. "Boston College Alumni Protest," *SHR*, 7 July 1900, 435; "'Candor' Continues the College Controversy," *SHR*, 21 July 1900, 41.

87. "Boston College," *WL* 29 (1900): 354.

88. Geiger, "Era," 77. Data on Jesuit colleges derived from annual reports in *Woodstock Letters*. On the Law School controversy and enrollments in this period, see Devitt, "History of Maryland–New York Province," 415–17.

89. Fagan to LM, 8 Sept. 1902 (ARSI, MD 1013.III.9).

90. Illustrative of a new spirit of research at Harvard, the university's motto was changed from *Christo et Ecclesiae* to *Veritas* on the occasion of its 250th anniversary. Reuben, *Making of the Modern University*, 1–2; Morison, *Three Centuries*, 362.

91. Candor, "'Candor' Continues the College Controversy"; Veritas, "Criticizes Catholic Colleges," *SHR*, 4 Aug. 1900, 73.

92. "Catholic Colleges for Catholic Youth," *SHR*, 11 Aug. 1900, 89.

93. Quoted in Thernstrom, *Other Bostonians*, 45.

94. Baritz, *Good Life;* Blumin, *Emergence of the Middle Class;* Hilkey, *Character is Capital;* Bledstein, *Culture of Professionalism*, chap. 1; Dubbert, "Progressivism and the Masculinity Crisis"; Rotundo, "Body and Soul."

95. Carnegie quoted in Sheldon, "College-Bred Men in the Business World," 191.

On the following page, Sheldon quoted banker Henry Clewes: "I do not employ college men in my banking office. None need apply. I don't want them, for I think they have been spoiled for business life." See also Veysey, *Emergence*, 266–67, and Jones, "Is the College Graduate Impracticable?"

96. Baritz, *Good Life*, 56. A wry note: we find the following in Amory, *Proper Bostonians*, 11:

> There is a story in Boston that in the palmy days of the twenties a Chicago banking house asked the Boston investment firm of Lee, Higginson, & Co. for a letter of recommendation about a young Bostonian they were considering employing. Lee, Higginson could not say enough for the young man. His father, they wrote, was a Cabot, his mother a Lowell; farther back his background was a happy blend of Saltonstalls, Appletons, Peabodys, and others of Boston's First Families. The recommendation was given without hesitation.
>
> Several days later came a curt acknowledgement from Chicago. Lee, Higginson was thanked for its trouble. Unfortunately, however, the material supplied on the young man was not exactly of the type the Chicago firm was seeking. "We were not," their letter declared, "contemplating using Mr. ——— for breeding purposes."

97. Adams, *Education of Henry Adams*, 305–6; Handlin, "A Small Community," 99; Levine, *Culture of Aspiration*, 1 f.; Bledstein, *Culture of Professionalism*.

98. Auerbach, *Unequal Justice*, 22.

99. Johnson, *Schooled Lawyers*, 120.

100. Bledstein, *Culture of Professionalism*, 297; Geiger, "Era," 53, 77.

101. Morison, *Three Centuries*, 492. Also see Slosson, *Great American Universities*, 33.

102. CWE, "Inaugural," 21; Wagoner, "Charles W. Eliot"; Solomon, *Ancestors and Immigrants*, 180–86; Baltzell, *Protestant Establishment*, 144–53.

103. Story, "Harvard and the Boston Brahmins" and *Forging of an Aristocracy*.

104. Slosson, *Great American Universities*, 104. Also see Baltzell, *Protestant Establishment*, 145–47.

105. Townsend, *Manhood at Harvard*, 93; Thernstrom, "'Poor but Hopefull Scholars,'" 123.

106. Slosson, *Great American Universities*, 8; Morison, *Three Centuries*, 492.

107. Brown, *Harvard Yard*, 14. As to whether such students felt their cohort to be in decline, there is little evidence, but some of their elders thought themselves so. Henry Adams, for instance, felt the world had grown weary of his kind: Adams, *Education of Henry Adams*.

108. Santayana quoted in Veysey, *Emergence*, 265; Brown, *Harvard Yard*, 15.

109. Santayana, "Spirit and Ideals," 321; Slosson, *Great American Universities*, 10.

110. Geiger, "Era," 56.

111. Quest, "Fast Set," 551.

112. Morison, *Three Centuries*, 492; Santayana, "Spirit and Ideals," 323. Also see Townsend, *Manhood at Harvard*, 80–81; Handlin, "Making Men of Boys," 59; Fleming, "Harvard's Golden Age?" 77.

113. CWE quoted in Townsend, *Manhood at Harvard*, 22; Briggs, "Transition from School to College," 358; Shaler, "Discipline," 10, 14. Also Handlin, "Making Men of Boys"; Fleming, "Eliot's New Broom," 74–76.

114. Readers of the *North American Review* learned that "the Faculty may frown, but they will rarely do more than frown or admonish": Quest, "Fast Set," 548.

115. *BCC* (1898–99): 42; A. B. Hart quoted in Townsend, *Manhood at Harvard*, 83.

116. Horowitz *Campus Life*, 12.

117. Morison, *Three Centuries*, 422. Although Morison's depiction of Harvard in the 1890s (penned in the 1930s) grates on contemporary sensibilities, Morison's commitment to a racially inclusive Harvard is confirmed by his signature on a 1922 petition protesting a university decision to disallow African Americans from living in Harvard's dormitories: "To the President and Fellows of Harvard College" (HUA, UAI.5.160 1922–25, folder 42). On the experiences of African Americans, see Sollors et al., *Blacks at Harvard;* Wechsler, "Academic Gresham's Law," 579–80; Wagoner, "American Compromise"; Du Bois, "That Outer Whiter World at Harvard."

118. Quest, "Fast Set," 548.

119. CWE quoted in Townsend, *Manhood at Harvard*, 95.

120. Thernstrom, "'Poor but Hopefull Scholars,'" 125.

121. Fleming, "Harvard's Golden Age?"

122. Reed, "College Is Like the World," 284–85.

123. A persnickety Charles Kendell Adams complained that the college student was "neither a boy nor a man." The collegian "refuses to be treated as a child, and, on the other, he finds it impossible to conduct himself like a human being that has passed the period of infancy": Adams, "Discipline in American Colleges," 15.

124. Wilson quoted in Horowitz, *Campus Life*, 102; Rudolph, *American College and University*, chap. 7; Fleming, "Harvard's Golden Age?"; Solomon, *Ancestors and Immigrants*, 89; Morison, *Three Centuries*, 420.

125. Rudolph, *American College and University*, 375; Fleming, "Harvard's Golden Age?" 86.

126. Townsend, *Manhood at Harvard*, 108.

127. Rudolph, *American College and University*, chap. 18; Smith, *Sports and Freedom*.

128. Lyons, *College Novel*, 7.

129. Post, *Harvard Episodes*, 2, 5.

130. Slosson, *Great American Universities*, 506.

131. Horowitz, *Campus Life*, 12, 39 f.

132. Veysey, *Emergence*, 281 n. 55; Thernstrom, "'Poor but Hopefull Scholars,'" 126, 127.

133. Wechsler, "An Academic Gresham's Law," 567; Synnott, *Half-Opened Door;* Wechsler, *Qualified Student;* Oren, *Joining the Club;* Rosovsky et al., *Jewish Experience at Harvard and Radcliffe;* Solomon, *In the Company of Educated Women;* Gordon, *Gender and Higher Education;* Sollors et al., *Blacks at Harvard*.

134. Lodge quoted in Ryan, *Beyond the Ballot Box*, 75; Shaler, "Scotch Element," 516.

135. According to Thernstrom, "integration of a substantial Catholic minority provoked very little unease and tension": "'Poor but Hopefull Scholars,'" 127. Marsden similarly argues, "Even at prestigious schools of the East there was little evidence of overt discrimination against Catholics, although there was always strong discrimination based on social class": *Soul,* 357.

136. O'Callaghan, "Catholics at Harvard," 74–75; LaFarge, "Report on the Condition of Catholic Students at H.U.," 1904 (GUA Special Collections, John LaFarge papers); CWE to WGRM, 2 June 1900 (BCA, WGRM papers, folder 3).

137. Wills, "University Community," 57–59, 73–74.

138. Lord, Sexton, and Harrington, *History of the Archdiocese of Boston,* 2:355.

139. Wills, "University Community," 68–69. For Dwight, also see Walton, *To Preserve the Faith,* 110. On notable converts, see Lord, Sexton, and Harrington, *History of the Archdiocese of Boston,* 2:722–25.

140. LaFarge, *Manner Is Ordinary.*

141. Wills, "University Community," 62–63, 71–72, 76; Gallivan, "Catholic Sons of Harvard," 500.

142. Ryan, *Beyond the Ballot Box,* 104–5.

143. Morison, *Three Centuries,* 199; Wills, "University Community," 70, 77; LaFarge, *Manner Is Ordinary,* 62; quote from New Haven *Register,* 6 Aug. 1905 (HUA, HUG 300).

144. Quoted in Ryan, "St. Paul's Catholic Club," 264–65.

145. Wills, "University Community," 75–78; Evans, *Newman Movement;* Gray, "Development of the Newman Club Movement." Also see "St. Paul's Catholic Club," and Ryan, "St. Paul's Catholic Club" (HUA, HUD 3762.5000).

146. Ryan, "St. Paul's Catholic Club," 266–67; Wills, "University Community," 75–78.

147. Kennedy, "East Boston," 200.

148. Gallivan, "Catholic Sons of Harvard," 500.

149. Shannon, *American Irish,* 42; Adams, "Men and Things," 102.

150. "Harvard and Jesuit Colleges," *New York Sun,* June 1900 (GUA, Brosnahan, box 8, folder 155).

151. Ryan, "St. Paul's Catholic Club," 265.

152. As recorded in Victor Henderson to G. Stanley Hall, 6 Feb. 1900 (ACUA, TJCRF A-D 8A): "President Harper, President Low, President Eliot, and President Gilman all unite with President Wheeler in believing that it is eminently proper that the Catholic University of America should be invited to participate."

153. Francis Peabody to TJC, 30 June 1898 (ACUA, TJC papers, box 3, folder 7); Gibson Bell to TJC, 20 Oct. 1900; TJC to Bell, 27 Oct. 1900, and Bell to TJC, 31 Oct. 1900 (ACUA, TJCRF, A-D 8a).

154. WGRM to TJC, 25 May 1900 (ACUA, TJC papers, box 3, folder 4); "Boston College," *WL* 29 (1900): 354.

155. BCAA to TJC, 6 May 1901 (ACUA, TJC papers, box 1, folder 11) and 25 May 1901 (ACUA, TJC papers, box 2, folder 12); Francis Peabody to TJC, 5 May 1901 and TJC to Peabody, 12 May 1901 (ACUA, TJCRF, box 2, folder 12).

156. LaFarge, "Report on the Condition," 4–5; Purbrick to LM, Feb. 1899 (ARSI, MD 1012.I.35); minutes of the consultors, 2 Oct. 1899 (BCA, Jesuit Community: Jesuit Consultors [RG42]); LaFarge, *Manner Is Ordinary*, 59, 64.

157. Kernan, "Catholic Colleges," *New York Freemans Journal*, 27 Aug. 1898, and "Our Catholic Colleges," ibid., 8 Oct. 1898; Bugg, *People of Our Parish*, 196.

158. WGRM, "Drift," 160, 161–62.

159. TB to LM, 10 Nov. 1894 (ARSI, MD 1012.IV.9); Pardow to LM, 24 Nov. 1895 (ARSI, MD 1011.II.48); Fagan to LM, 8 Sept. 1902.

Chapter 4. Place: Americanism and the Higher Education of Catholics

Epigraph: "'Candor' Protests," *SHR*, 11 Aug. 1900, 86.

1. LM to WGRM, 7 Apr. 1900 (ARSI, MD prov. ltr. bk. 3). Martín sent similar advice to John Lehy, president of Holy Cross. Kuzniewski, *Thy Honored Name*, 184.

2. De Pressensé, "Society of Jesus," 410.

3. O'Malley, "Mission," 8.

4. Nadal quoted in O'Malley, "To Travel to Any Part of the World," 6. Also see Daley, "In Ten Thousand Places," and O'Malley, *First Jesuits*, 67–68.

5. "Histoire de la Chute de Jèsuites," 251–52; TB, "President Eliot and Jesuit Colleges," 7. For a comparison of the Jesuits to other religious orders in North America, see Axtell, *Invasion Within*, esp. chaps. 5 and 6.

6. McAvoy, *Great Crisis*; Dolan, *American Catholic Experience*, 296–317; Hennesey, *American Catholics*, chaps. 14 and 15. For a review of the literature on the Americanism controversy, see Gleason, "New Americanism in Catholic Historiography."

7. Gleason, *Conservative Reformers*; idem, "Immigrant Assimilation"; Curran, *Michael Augustine Corrigan*; Zwierlein, *Life and Letters of Bishop McQuaid*.

8. Halsey, *Survival of American Innocence*.

9. Jonas, *Divided Mind*; Cross, *Emergence of Liberal Catholicism*. Biographies of liberals include Ahern, *Life of John J. Keane*; Ellis, *Cardinal Gibbons*; O'Connell, *John Ireland*. Also see Fogarty, *Vatican and the Americanist Crisis*. On efforts to extend Catholic influence, see Portier, "Catholic Theology in the United States," 324–28, and Wangler, "American Catholic Expansionism: 1886–1894."

10. Cross, *Emergence of Liberal Catholicism*, 195; *Longinqua Oceani*, in *Papal Encyclicals*, 2:364.

11. *Testem Benevolentiae*, reprinted in McAvoy, *Great Crisis*, 379–91; quotes from 390.

12. Ibid., 380, 390.

13. O'Malley, *First Jesuits*. 210.

14. "'Candor' Protests," *SHR*, 11 Aug. 1900, 86.

15. Bugg, *People of Our Parish*, 187–190, 195.

16. *National Cyclopaedia*, s.v. "O'Malley, Austin."

17. O'Malley, "Catholic Collegiate Education"; Cassilly, "Catholic Students at State Universities," 114; JHR to Dr. John R. Slattery, 3 Aug. 1893 (GUA, JHR papers, box 5, folder 7, ltr. bk., 440); Delurey, "Drift," 164. Also see Plough, "Catholic Colleges."

18. O'Malley, "Catholic Collegiate Education," 292–93, 294. On enrollments for this period, also see Gleason, "American Catholic Higher Education," 19.

19. O'Malley, "Catholic Collegiate Education," 291–92.

20. Dr. O'Malley's correspondence and completed surveys are located in AUND.

21. Kelsey, "State Universities and Church Colleges," 827; Cassilly, "Catholic Students at State Universities."

22. Mahoney, "One Hundred Years," 10.

23. Farrell, "Catholic Chaplain"; Mercier, "Report on Statistics of the Catholic Colleges of the United States" (ACUA, NCEA box 3, folder "Secret Vatican Archives" [105/1]); John A. Conway to Francis Howard, 15 Mar. 1908 (AUND, CBUR, Msgr. Howard).

24. Ireland, Church and Modern Society, 7.

25. Review of "The Church and Modern Society," 217.

26. Cross, Emergence of Liberal Catholicism, 36.

27. De Meaux, "Catholic Centennial," 374, 375.

28. Cross, Liberal Catholicism, 38; O'Connell, John Ireland.

29. Ireland, "Mission of Catholics," 55, 58.

30. Jonas, Divided Mind.

31. Elliott, "Human Environments," 466; Ireland, "Mission of Catholics," 56.

32. Elliott, "Human Environments," 469; also Cross, Liberal Catholicism, 62.

33. O'Brien, Isaac Hecker.

34. Elliott, "Missionary Work," 2:56, 55, 58. On evangelical Catholicism, see Jonas, Divided Mind, and Dolan, Catholic Revivalism.

35. Ireland, "Mission of Catholics," 81; "A Layman Succeeds," 109; Lentz, "Conversion of the American People."

36. Gleason, Contending with Modernity, 6–12.

37. Spalding quoted in Nuesse, Catholic University of America, 15–16, 17.

38. Zwierlein, Life and Letters of Bishop McQuaid, 3:391–96; Curran, Michael Augustine Corrigan, 120–24, 157–67; Nuesse; Catholic University of America, 38–48; Fagan to LM, 8 Sept. 1902 (ARSI, MD 1013.III.9). Also see Ellis, Formative Years.

39. Conde B. Pallen quoted in Marty, Irony of It All, 181; unidentified bishop quoted in Cleary, "Catholic Participation," 591.

40. Cleary, "Catholic Participation," 590; Keane quoted in Barrows, World's Parliament of Religions, 1:182; Downey, "Tradition and Acceptance"; Seager, "Pluralism"; Ziolkowski, Museum of Faith.

41. Andrew Dickson White to JJK, 21 Nov. 1891 (ACUA, JJK papers, box 5, folder 12); JJK to CWE, 24 Oct. 1890 (HUA, UAI.1.150).

42. William A. McQuaid to JJK, 11 Nov. 1891 (ACUA, JJK papers, box 5, folder 34).

43. Unidentified speaker quoted in Ahern, Life of John J. Keane, 109 n. 75.

44. Ludlow Lapham to JJK, 5 Nov. 1889, and Bernard McQuaid to JJK, 25 Feb. 1890; also Lapham to JJK, 10 Feb. 1890; Rev. A. G. Evans to JJK, 21 Feb. 1890; and Lapham to JJK, 3 Mar. 1890 (ACUA, JJK papers, box 5, folder 12). Zwierlein, Life and Letters of Bishop McQuaid, 3:396.

45. "Catholic Young Men," 722, 721; Robinson, "Attitude of the Educated Protestant," 644.

46. J. M. Naughton to O'Malley, 9 Nov. 1897; Martin Centner to O'Malley, 9 Nov. 1897; Charles B. Lenahan to O'Malley, 25 Oct. 1897 (AUND, Austin O'Malley papers).

47. Centner to O'Malley, 9 Nov. 1897; McWilliams, "Presence of Catholic Students," 197.

48. Kramer, "Catholics in Non-Catholic Colleges," 178, 180.

49. "Nature Not All," *Boston Globe*, 2 Apr. 1894 (HUA, HUG 300). According to Francis G. Peabody, the Plummer Professor of Christian Morals, Harvard had intended for some time to have a Catholic lead the service, in order to demonstrate that Harvard's "services are purely unsectarian, and that any earnest disciple of any faith is welcome in Appleton chapel." "A Catholic Priest," *Advertiser*, 16 Mar. 1894.

50. Gallivan, "Catholic Sons of Harvard," 499, 510.

51. O'Callaghan, "Puritan Catholicized," 112; O'Callaghan, "Catholics at Harvard," 79.

52. O'Callaghan, "Catholics at Harvard," 79–80.

53. TJC, "Catholic College," 15.

54. O'Malley, "Catholic Collegiate Education," 299, 301.

55. Kramer, "Catholics in Non-Catholic Colleges," 177; Charles G. Herbermann to Austin O'Malley, 8 Nov. 1897 (AUND, O'Malley papers); Farrell, "Catholic Chaplain," 161; "Catholic Young Men," 723.

56. Meyer, *Science of the Saints*, 2:354.

57. O'Malley, "Catholic Collegiate Education," 300, 302; Delurey, "Teaching of History," 75, 76.

58. O'Malley, "Catholic Collegiate Education," 296; Bugg, *People of Our Parish*, 191.

59. Meyer, *Science of the Saints*, 2:360.

60. Delurey, "Drift," 166; Michael Corrigan quoted in *BCS* 13 (1899): 511.

61. Kernan, "Catholic Layman in Higher Education," 381.

62. "Pastoral Letter of 1866," in Guilday, *National Pastorals*, 215–16.

63. "Pastoral Letter of 1884," ibid., 249, 252; Messbarger, *Fiction With a Parochial Purpose*, 56, 57–58. Also see McDannell, *Christian Home in Victorian America*, esp. chap. 3.

64. O'Reilly, *True Men as We Need Them*, 253–54; McDannell, "'True Men as We Need Them.'"

65. Sadlier, *Blakes and Flanagans*, 11, 66.

66. Ibid., 305, 378.

67. Ibid., 390.

68. Smith, "One of Many," 66, 63, 55.

69. WGRM, "Drift" (1899); Delurey, "Drift" (1899); Burns, "Elective System" (1900); TJC, "Catholic College" (1901); Poland, "Some Thoughts on Pedagogics" (1902); Guldner, "Moral Training" (1903); Neill, "Statistics of Attendance" (1904); Mercier, "Catholic Higher Education" (1905); "Attendance of Catholic Students at Non-Catholic Colleges" (1905); Cassilly, "Catholic Students at State Universities"

(1906); Farrell, "Catholic Chaplain" (1907); Mercier, "Catholic Higher Education" (1908).

70. "Pastoral Letter of 1884," in Guilday, *National Pastorals*, 244, 246–47; Gleason, "Baltimore III and Education," 274–76.

71. "Roman Catholic Students," 764; Zwierlein, *Life and Letters of Bishop Bernard McQuaid*, 3:403; Mahoney, "Catholic Colleges for Women."

72. Zwierlein, *Life and Letters of Bishop McQuaid*, 3:403; *Acerbo Nimis* quoted in Evans, *Newman Movement*, 27.

73. Murphy, "Cornell Plan of Bishop Bernard J. McQuaid"; Evans, *Newman Movement*, 27–32; Zwierlein, *Life and Letters of Bishop McQuaid*, 3:404–5.

74. At one point, three hundred Catholic students at Wisconsin petitioned Messmer for "pastoral care" and assistance in the "advancement in religious knowledge and the practice of Christian virtue commensurate with their advancement in worldly arts and sciences": Evans, *Newman Movement*, 29.

75. Farrell, "Catholic Chaplain," 150, 161; Brosnahan following Farrell's talk, 175, 176.

76. Yorke, following Farrell, "Catholic Chaplain," 177.

77. Denis O'Connell to Francis Howard, 26 Jan. 1907 (ACUA, DORF, box 2, folder O'Connell).

78. "Memorial on Catholic College Education Presented by the Standing Committee of the Catholic Colleges of the United States to the Archbishops of the United States, Apr. 11, 1907" (ACUA, NCEA, box 3, "Secret Vatican Archives," folder 105/1); Walch, *Parish School*, 30–32.

79. Gibbons quoted in Evans, *Newman Movement*, 36; "Archbishop Wants Better Colleges," *New York Times*, 12 July 1905 (ACUA, NCEA, box 75); Gleason, *Contending with Modernity*, 24–25; Mahoney, "One Hundred Years," 11–12.

80. Editorial, *BCS* 13 (Apr. 1899): 264.

81. "Alumni," *HCP* 10 (Mar. 1900): 469.

82. BCAA to "Reverend Dear Sir," 27 June 1900 (ACUA, TJCRF, box 1, folder 10).

83. Ibid.

84. Clerical advice worked in at least one case. Walter Drum, an 1890 graduate of Boston College, sensed a vocation to the Society of Jesus; it was not, however, a religious call welcomed with enthusiasm. Procrastinating, Drum decided to pursue a Ph.D. at Harvard; it would be, he thought, a "great honor to the Society to enter from Harvard." Drum later realized that the "devil was hoodwinking" him. Earning a degree from Harvard was less about bringing honor to the Society than affording himself the opportunity to "have two more years of life, to drink life to the dregs, and then leave the dregs." Provincial Thomas Campbell set him straight, telling Drum that he was "old enough to make your decision now. . . . If you are going to be a Jesuit, enter the Society now, and don't waste two years at Harvard." Gorayeb, *Life and Letters of Walter Drum, S.J.*, 33–34.

85. WGRM, "Drift," 160.

86. Editorial, *BCS* 12 (1898): 366; "Judge McDonough's Discourse," *HCP* 10 (June 1900): 26.

87. "College World," *HCP* 10 (Mar. 1900): 477–78.

88. Editorial, *BCS* 12 (June 1898): 366.

89. John Conway to Denis O'Connell, 19 Jan. 1907 (ACUA, DORF, box 1, folder 14).

90. O'Malley, "Catholic Collegiate Education," 302.

91. "Catholic Education," *BCS* 14 (1900): 206.

92. McAvoy, *Great Crisis*, 365.

93. "Alumni," *BCS* 14 (1900): 116.

94. Editorial, *BCS* 14 (1900): 222; "Alumni," *BCS* 14 (1900): 115.

95. "Non-Sectarian?" *HCP* 12 (1901): 285–86; "Alumni," *HCP* 10 (1900): 465.

96. "Catholic Education," *BCS* 14 (1900): 211, 212; editorial, *BCS* 13 (1899): 47. Also see Briggs, "Fathers, Mothers, and Freshmen."

97. "Catholic College," *BCS* 16 (1903): 531–32.

98. Ibid., 531, 532.

99. On the nineteenth-century feminization of religion, see Douglas, *Feminization of American Culture.*

100. Editorial, *BCS* 13 (1899): 47; "Worcester County Alumni Association," *HCP* 10 (1900): 360.

101. Levine, *American College and the Culture of Aspiration.*

102. "Catholic College," *BCS* 16 (1903): 534, 535.

103. Elliott quoted in McAvoy, *Great Crisis*, 261; Cross, *Emergence of Liberal Catholicism*, 27.

104. Buetow, *Of Singular Benefit*, 171–76; Walch, *Parish School*, 92–94; Holaind, "The Parent First." On the Jesuits as conservatives, see throughout Appleby, *"Church and Age Unite!"*; Schultenover, *View from Rome*; Cross, *Emergence of Liberal Catholicism*; and McAvoy, *Great Crisis.*

105. Poland, "Some Thoughts on Pedagogics," 33–34.

106. Ahern, *Catholic University of America*, 263–97; Nuesse, *Catholic University of America*, 71, 77–78, 84–85; McAvoy, *Great Crisis*, 139–41; Gleason, *Contending with Modernity*, 7–11.

107. "Oil and Water in Religion," *Rochester Union and Advertiser*, 26 June 1899, 7.

108. O'Malley, *First Jesuits*, 21.

109. Conway quoted in Denis O'Connell to Francis Howard, 4 Mar. 1907 (ACUA, DORF, box 2); Conway to James Burns, 27 Apr. 1907 (ACUA, NCEA, Howard papers, box 1).

Chapter 5. *Novus Ordo Academicus* and the Travails of Adapting

Epigraph: Schwickerath, Jesuit Education, 15.

1. McDonough, *Men Astutely Trained*, 481 n. 34.

2. Veysey, *Emergence*, 339; Fagan, "Educational Legislation," 22.

3. "College," *WL* 34 (1905): 429.

4. McGuckin describes the period between 1895 and 1905 as a period of "storm and stress" for the Jesuits: *Jesuits and Education*, 142.

5. Marty, "Is There a *Mentalité?*" 19; Gleason, *Contending with Modernity.*

6. "Colleges of the Society," *WL* 19 (1890): 440; "Students in Our Colleges," *WL* 20 (1891): 483.

7. "About Teaching," 161, 162, 170.

8. JHR to Father Provincial, 12 Oct. 1890 (GUA, JHR papers, box 7, folder 1, ltr. bk., 314).

9. "Father Rudolph J. Meyer," *WL* 42 (1913): 92–96. Meyer is discussed at length in Schultenover, *View from Rome.*

10. JHR to Rudolph Meyer, Oct. 1893 (GUA, JHR papers, box 7, folder 2, 170–71).

11. JHR to TJC, 5 Aug. 1897 (ACUA, TJCRF, box 3, folder 9).

12. Purbrick to LM, 19 Feb. 1900 (ARSI, MD 13.I.49).

13. Purbrick to LM, 19 Feb. 1900. Almost two years earlier, Purbrick wrote to Martín that he felt Harvard's admissions policy was a form of "Puritanic religious prejudice" and a response to the "wonderful growth in Boston of Catholic influence in municipal affairs"; Purbrick to LM, 22 Nov. 1898 (ARSI, MD 1013.I.32).

14. Purbrick to LM, 19 Feb. 1900 and 22 Nov. 1898. On student drinking at Holy Cross, see Kuzniewski, *Thy Honored Name,* 173.

15. Purbrick to LM, 19 Feb. 1900.

16. Hawkins, *Banding Together;* Veysey, *Emergence,* 313; Rudolph, *American College and University,* 436–38; Gleason, *Contending with Modernity,* 32–38. Efforts to rationalize education accord with the analysis advanced in Wiebe, *Search for Order.* Also see Varga, "Rejoining," 69.

17. Fagan to LM, 8 Sept. 1902 (ARSI, MD 1013.III.9).

18. TJC, "Catholic College."

19. "President Eliot Called a Bigot," unidentified clipping, ca. 23 Jan. 1900 (GUA, Brosnahan, box 8, folder 155).

20. Gannon to Rudolph Meyer, Aug. 1903 (ARSI, MD 1013.II.19); Fagan, "What the Parish School Can Do," 47. The Jesuits' troubles in Europe during the nineteenth century are discussed in Campbell, *Jesuits;* for France, see Kurtz, *Politics of Heresy,* 30–32; Padberg, *Colleges in Controversy;* Moody, *French Education,* 64, 68, 94–95, 107.

21. For a summary of the troubles with the New York regents, see Bernad, "Faculty of Arts," 297–308; Richards, "Regents"; Gleason, *Contending with Modernity,* 30–31; Varga, "Rejoining," 71.

22. Mullaney, "Regents," 638, 639.

23. Richards, "Regents," 133, 134. In 1896, when Richards was writing, the initial tussle over the Law School's selective admissions policy was not widely known and the three Jesuit colleges were still on the Law School's list.

24. Litt. ann., Boston College 1898–99 (ARSI, MD Prov., litt. ann. 1502).

25. Richards, "Regents," 133.

26. TJC, "On the Teacher," 70.

27. "Preliminary Report of the Committee on Studies to V. Rev. Father Provincial," Missouri Province, July 1900 (ARSI, MD 1013.III.7).

28. Purbrick to LM, 22 Nov. 1898; Poland, "Some Thoughts on Pedagogics," 33.

29. Poland, "Some Thoughts on Pedagogics," 36; Fagan to LM, 8 Sept. 1902.

30. Fagan, "Educational Legislation," 19.

31. Schultenover, *View from Rome*, 188–92. The relationship between Pius and Martín is described in Campbell, *Jesuits*, 905.

32. Pius IX, *Syllabus of Errors*, in Corrigan, *Church and the Nineteenth Century*, 295.

33. Leo XIII, *Aeternis Patris* (or "On the Restoration of Christian Philosophy according to the Mind of St. Thomas Aquinas, the Angelic Doctor"), xvi.

34. Pius X, *Pascendi Dominici Gregis*, 89, 72<TH>f.

35. Ibid., 90.

36. Kurtz, *Politics of Heresy*, chap. 1 and throughout.

37. Pius X, *Pascendi Dominici Gregis*, 71, 72, 91.

38. Ibid., 93–97.

39. Kurtz, *Politics of Heresy*, 38, 43.

40. The Jesuits' role in the promulgation of "The Church and Liberal Catholicism" is discussed at length in Schultenover, *View from Rome*, chaps. 3 and 4.

41. McAvoy, *Great Crisis*, 154–55; Ahern, *Catholic University of America*, 172, 180; Kurtz, *Politics of Heresy*, 15–16, 39, 145; Fogarty, *Vatican and American Hierarchy*, 142, 157–59, 176, 185; O'Connell, *John Ireland*, 280, 334–35.

42. Schultenover, *View from Rome*, esp. chaps. 3 and 4.

43. On George Tyrell, see O'Connell, *Critics on Trial*, 105–13, 169–76, 187–92, 274–85; Schultenover, *View from Rome*, 79–80, 203–4.

44. Schultenover, *View from Rome*, 203. Denis O'Connell saw in America's victory vindication of the Americanists' platform: the "meanness & narrowness of old Europe goes with it [Spain], to be replaced by the freedom & openness of America. This is God's way of developing the world": quoted in Fogarty, *Vatican and American Hierarchy*, 163. Also see Schultenover, *View from Rome*, 50–54; O'Connell, *John Ireland*, 454–55.

45. Schultenover, *View from Rome*, 199–203, quotes at 200.

46. Ibid., 68.

47. Martín, "On Some Dangers," 503, 506–7.

48. Ibid., 507, 540.

49. Ibid., 508, 511, 512.

50. Ibid., 509, 510.

51. Gleason, *Contending with Modernity*, 12–17, quote at 12; Gannon, "Before and After"; Appleby, *"Church and Age Unite!"*; Reher, *Catholic Intellectual Life*.

52. This argument follows the contours of Gleason's argument in *Contending with Modernity* that American Catholic higher education's response to modernity was initially institutional and later ideological. It extends and complements Gleason's work (which is almost entirely American in focus) by showing how the antimodern mindset of the European-based leadership of the Society of Jesus affected the American-based Jesuits' ability to respond to the exigencies of a new academic order wherein their most pressing issues tended to be institutional and practical.

53. Curran, *Bicentennial History*, 139–45; "Varia," *WL* 22 (1893): 535–57.

54. Gannon to Meyer, Aug. 1903.

55. WGRM, "Drift," 161; JHR to Meyer, 5 Feb. 1896 (GUA, JHR papers, box 7, folder 3).

56. Poland, "Some Thoughts on Pedagogics," 42.

57. Macksey, "Ethical Influence"; Schwickerath, *Jesuit Education*, 569–71.

58. JHR to Meyer, 11 Feb. 1895 (GUA, JHR papers, box 7, folder 2, ltr. bk., 400), and 5 Feb. 1896.

59. JHR to Meyer, 5 Feb. 1896. Also see JHR to LM, 11 Feb. 1895 (ARSI, MD 1012.X.40).

60. TB to LM, 9 Aug. 1895 (ARSI, MD 1012.IV.11).

61. The proverb in Latin and English is found in Lucas, *Landmarking*, 1.

62. Schwickerath, *Jesuit Education*, 540–41.

63. Purbrick to LM, 1 July 1897 (ARSI, MD 1013.I.7), and 10 Feb. 1898 (ARSI, MD 1013.I.18).

64. JHR to Meyer, 5 Feb. 1896; Gannon to LM, 10 Dec. 1905 (ARSI, MD 1013.II.48).

65. Gannon to LM, 20 Mar. 1903 (ARSI, MD 1013.II.15); WGRM, "Drift," 161, 163. For modernizing efforts in student discipline at the University of Notre Dame during this period, see Egan, "New Departure in Catholic College Discipline."

66. LM to TB, 16 Oct. 1895 (ARSI, MD prov. ltr. bk. 3:302–3).

67. LM to JHR, 12 Mar. 1895 (ARSI, MD prov. ltr. bk. 3:265–67); LM to Gannon, 15 June 1903 (ARSI, MD prov. ltr. bk. 4:70).

68. Virtual duplicates from LM to Pardow, 7 Mar. 1895 (ARSI, MD prov. ltr. bk. 3:252–55), and to JHR, 12 Mar. 1895.

69. LM to Pardow, 24 Feb. 1896 (ARSI, MD prov. ltr. bk. 3:17–19); LM to JHR, 12 Mar. 1895.

70. Gannon to LM, 17 Apr. 1896 (ARSI, MD 1012.VIII.27).

71. LM to Purbrick, 27 Nov. 1899 (ARSI, MD prov. ltr. bk. 3:447–50).

72. LM to JHR, 12 Mar. 1895; LM to Gannon, 29 Sept. 1904 (ARSI, MD prov. ltr. bk. 4:117).

73. LM to Pardow, 24 Feb. 1896.

74. TB, "President Eliot and Jesuit Colleges," 6–7; LM quoted in McGucken, *Jesuits and Education*, 135. For Martín's full text in Latin, see "Adhortatio de Studendi Ratione."

75. Roothaan to the members of the Society, 1832, quoted in Hughes, *Loyola*, 289.

76. Roothaan quoted in Farrell, *Jesuit Code*, 390.

77. Kuzniewski, *Thy Honored Name*, 55. Also see Meagher and Grattan, *Spires of Fenwick*, 60.

78. JHR to Anton Anderledy, 1 Sept. 1888 (ARSI, MD 1012.X.1).

79. Fagan to LM, 8 Sept. 1902.

80. Stonestreet quoted in Bernad, "Faculty of Arts," 259.

81. JHR to Father Provincial [Robert Fulton], 6 May 1889 (GUA, JHR papers, box 7, folder 1, ltr. bk. 83).

82. Hanselman to LM, 24 Nov. 1903 (ARSI, MD 1013.XXV.13).

83. Meyer to rectors, 2 June 1887 (GUA, Woodstock College, box 13, folder 225); Gleason, *Contending with Modernity*, 52–53.

84. LM to Pardow, 24 Feb. 1896, and 22 Mar. 1896 (ARSI, MD prov. ltr. bk. 3:331).

85. "Woodstock Academy for the Study of the Ratio," *WL* 23 (1894): 91; "Woodstock Academy for the Study of the Ratio," *WL* 25 (1896): 256. The proceedings are published under the same title, *WL*, 23 (1894): 91–107, 296–336; 24 (1895): 109–23, 207–24; and 25 (1896): 52–72, 233–56.

86. Fagan, "Meeting of the N.E.A.," *WL* 29 (1900): 128.

87. Nuesse, *Catholic University of America*, 121–22.

88. Hawkins, *Banding Together*, 1; Mahoney, "One Hundred Years."

89. JHR to Fr. Frisbee, 3 Sept. 1896 (GUA, JHR papers, box 6, folder 4); also "Conference on Studies," *WL* 25 (1896): 542.

90. Bernad, "Faculty of Arts," 280–84; Veysey, *Emergence*, 311–14; Gleason, *Contending with Modernity*, 33–38.

91. JHR to Frisbee, 3 Sept. 1896; JHR to Rev. C. W. Doherty, 24 Aug. 1896 (GUA, JHR papers, box 6, folder 4); Mahoney, "One Hundred Years," 19–20; Gleason, *Contending with Modernity*, 46–51.

92. JHR to Meyer, late 1893 (GUA, JHR papers, box 7, folder 2).

93. "System of Education," *BCC* (1899–1900): 28.

94. Fagan to LM, 8 Sept. 1902; TB to JHR, 24 Sept. 1896 (BCA, Dunigan papers, box 1/3A, folder 16).

95. Fagan to LM, 8 Sept. 1902.

96. Ibid.

97. LM to Purbrick, 25 Aug. 1900 (ARSI, MD prov. ltr. bk. 3:468); LM to Gannon, 27 Sept. 1903 (ARSI, MD prov. ltr. bk. 4:75).

98. Gannon to LM, 4 Oct. 1905 (ARSI, MD 1013.II.44).

99. Joseph F. Hanselman to "Rev. and dear Father," 2 July 1906 (BCA, Dunigan papers, box 1/3A, folder 16).

100. Donovan, Dunigan, and FitzGerald, *History of Boston College*, 92–93; Kuzniewski, *Thy Honored Name*, 184–85.

101. "College Course, Revised Schedule [1906]" (GUA, MPA, box 97, folder 20D).

102. "Schedule of Studies for the Colleges of the Maryland New York Province, 1910" (ARSI, MD 1014.IV.24).

103. CWE to WGRM, 17 Jan. and 1 Feb. 1900 (BCA, WGRM papers, folder 3).

104. TB to Pardow, 14 July 1906 (ARSI, MD 1014.I.3).

105. "Last Days of Our Father General," *WL* 35 (1906): 100–109.

106. Padberg, O'Keefe, and McCarthy, *For Matters of Greater Moment*, 496–97; McGucken, *Jesuits and Education*, 135–36.

107. Cassilly to O'Connell, 23 Feb. 1906 (ACUA, DORF, box 4, folder 10); Denis O'Connell to John Conway, 18 Jan. 1907 (ACUA, DORF, box 1, folder 14).

108. Circular letter, 1 Jan. 1908 (GUA, MPA, box 97, folder 520 D2).

109. "Explanatory Remarks on the Schedule of Studies for the Colleges of the Maryland New York Province, 1910," 16 (GUA, MPA, box 86, 520D1–520:D).

110. "Proceedings of the General Committee on Studies," [1908] (GUA, MPA, box 97, folder 520 D2).

111. Bernad, "Faculty of Arts," 370–86; Gleason, *Contending with Modernity,* 55–56, 59.

112. At the ACCUS meeting, James Burns, C.S.C., of the University of Notre Dame, emerged as a powerful spokesman for adaptation to American education. On his leadership at Notre Dame, see Burns, *Being Catholic, Being American,* chap. 3. Another figure active in the ACCUS, Lawrence Delurey, O.S.A., of Villanova, railed against modern education at ACCUS meetings, yet Villanova expanded and substantially revised its curriculum during his presidency (1895–1910): Contosta, *Villanova University,* 55–76.

113. Gleason, *Contending with Modernity,* 51–61.

114. Quoted ibid., 59.

115. Symptomatically, in 1918 the College Department of the Catholic Educational Association (formerly, ACCUS) became the Department of Colleges and Secondary Schools; eleven years later, the college and high school representatives split into separate divisions and the earlier name, College Department, was readopted: Mahoney, "One Hundred Years," 19–20.

116. Quoted in Bernad, "Faculty of Arts," 387; Gleason, *Contending with Modernity,* 59–61.

117. Unidentified Jesuit quoted in McGucken, *Jesuits and Education,* 143.

118. Reuben, *Making of the Modern University;* Marsden, *Soul;* Sloan, *Faith and Knowledge;* Mahoney, "Rise of the University."

Conclusion

Epigraph: F. Heiermann to Francis Howard, 27 Mar. 1906 (ACUA, NCEA, F. W. Howard papers, box 1, "Heiermann").

1. Marty, *Irony of It All,* 8.

2. Bangert, *History of the Society of Jesus,* 497; O'Malley, "From the 1599 *Ratio Studiorum* to the Present," 140.

3. "Students in Our Colleges," *WL* 29 (1900): 550; American Council on Education, *American Universities and Colleges,* vol. 2.

4. Gleason, *Contending with Modernity,* 170–88, 197–206; Leahy, *Adapting to America,* 36–37, 42, 44–50; Mahoney, "One Hundred Years," 20–24; Varga, "Rejoining," 77 f.; Goodchild, "Turning Point." Goodchild's account of Midwestern Jesuits' troubles with accreditation is definitive.

5. During the twentieth century, neo-Thomism is sometimes called Thomism, sometimes neoscholasticism.

6. Mahoney, "Rise of the University," 126; Sloan, *Faith and Knowledge.*

7. Reuben, *Making of the Modern University;* Gleason, *Contending with Modernity,* 154–63.

8. Mark Sullivan, "BC Observes 400th Anniversary of Jesuits' *Ratio Studiorum,*" *Boston College Chronicle* 8 (28 Oct. 1999).

9. O'Malley, "From the 1599 *Ratio Studiorum* to the Present," 144. Also see McFarland, "Studia Humanitatis, Pietas, and Christianitas."

10. The phrase "men and women for others" derives from a speech given in 1973

by Pedro Arupe, S.J., the general superior, in which he articulated a profile of an ideal Jesuit college graduate.

11. O'Malley, "From the 1599 *Ratio Studiorum* to the Present," 141.

12. Gallin, *Negotiating Identity*, xi.

13. Marsden, *Soul*, 275.

14. Roberts and Turner, *Sacred and the Secular*, 75.

15. John Cogley quoted in Gleason, *Contending with Modernity*, 317.

16. Gallin, *American Catholic Higher Education*, 5–6, 7–12; Gleason, *Contending with Modernity*, 314–17. The Jesuit representatives included Gerard J. Campbell (president, Georgetown University); Charles F. Donovan (academic vice-president, Boston College); Thomas R. Fitzgerald (academic vice-president, Georgetown University); Robert J. Henle (academic vice-president, Saint Louis University); Neil G. McCluskey (University of Notre Dame); Leo McLaughlin (president, Fordham University); Vincent T. O'Keefe (assistant general, Society of Jesus); Paul C. Reinert (president, Saint Louis University); Michael P. Walsh (president, Boston College).

17. Gallin, *American Catholic Higher Education*, 5–6, 37–57, quote at 43; 137–39; Gleason, *Contending with Modernity*, 317.

18. Gallin, *Independence and a New Partnership*, 36–52 and throughout; Gallin, *Negotiating Identity*, 118–20; Gleason, *Contending with Modernity*, 314–16.

19. Quoted in Gleason, *Contending with Modernity*, 315.

20. Ibid., 297–304, 319–20.

21. Holtschneider and Morey, "Relationship Revisited," 6.

22. Leahy, *Adapting to America*, ix; Gleason, *Contending with Modernity*, 322; Gallin, *Negotiating Identity*, xi xiii; Lutz, "Can Notre Dame Be Saved?"; Burtchaell, *Dying of the Light*, 563; Dougherty et al., "Secularization of Western Culture"; Woodward, "Catholic Higher Education: What Happened?"

23. Currie, "Where We Are and Where We Are Going."

24. Mahoney, Schmalzbauer, and Youniss, "Religion: A Comeback on Campus."

25. On faculty members' efforts to connect faith and work, see Schmalzbauer, *People of Faith*.

26. Roof, *Generation of Seekers*.

27. A recent study of a Jesuit university finds strong evidence of religious vitality: Cherry et al., *Religion on Campus. Conversations*, a quarterly devoted to Jesuit higher education, also documents religious activity.

BIBLIOGRAPHY

Archival materials, newspaper articles, and brief articles and notices from journals are cited in the notes but not listed in the bibliography.

"About Teaching." *Woodstock Letters* 21 (1892): 161–70.

Acts and Resolves of the Province of the Massachusetts Bay, 1692–1714. Vol. 1. Boston: Commonwealth of Massachusetts, 1869.

Adams, Charles Kendell. "Discipline in American Colleges." *North American Review* 149 (1889): 15–17.

Adams, Henry. *The Education of Henry Adams: An Autobiography.* Boston, Mass.: Houghton, Mifflin, 1918.

Adams, Henry Austin. "Men and Things." *Donahoe's Magazine* 40 (1898): 101–2.

Ahern, Patrick Henry. *The Catholic University of America, 1887–1896: The Rectorship of John J. Keane.* Washington, D.C.: Catholic University of America Press, 1948.

———. *The Life of John J. Keane: Educator and Archbishop, 1839–1918.* Milwaukee, Wis.: Bruce, 1954.

Ahlstrom, Sydney E. *A Religious History of the American People.* New Haven, Conn.: Yale University Press, 1972.

Allmendinger, David F. *Paupers and Scholars: The Transformation of Student Life in Nineteenth Century New England*. New York: St. Martin's Press, 1975.

Altschuler, Glenn C. *Andrew Dickson White—Educator, Historian, Diplomat*. Ithaca, N.Y.: Cornell University Press, 1979.

American Council on Education. *American Universities and Colleges*. 16th ed. New York: Walter de Gruyter, 2001.

Amory, Cleveland. *The Proper Bostonians*. New York: E. P. Dutton, 1947.

Appleby, R. Scott. *"Church and Age Unite!": The Modernist Impulse in American Catholicism*. Notre Dame, Ind.: University of Notre Dame Press, 1992.

"Attendance of Catholic Students at Non-Catholic Colleges." *Catholic Educational Association: Proceedings and Addresses of the Second Annual Meeting*. Columbus, Ohio: Published by the Association, 1905.

Auerbach, Jerold S. *Unequal Justice: Lawyers and Social Change in Modern America*. New York: Oxford University Press, 1976.

Axtell, James. "The Death of the Liberal Arts College." *History of Education Quarterly* 11 (1971): 339–52.

———. *The Invasion Within: The Contest of Cultures in Colonial North America*. New York: Oxford University Press, 1985.

Azarius, Brother. "Lessons of a Century of Catholic Education." *Catholic World* 50 (1889): 143–54.

Babbitt, Irving. "President Eliot and American Education." *Forum* 81 (1929): 1–10.

Badger, Reid. *The Great American Fair: The World's Columbian Exposition and American Culture*. Chicago, Ill.: Nelson Hall, 1979.

Bailyn, Bernard. "Foundations." In Bailyn et al. *Glimpses of the Harvard Past*.

Bailyn, Bernard et al. *Glimpses of the Harvard Past*. Cambridge, Mass.: Harvard University Press, 1986.

Baltzell, E. Digby. *The Protestant Establishment: Aristocracy and Caste in America*. New York: Random House, 1964.

Bangert, William V. *A History of the Society of Jesus*. St. Louis, Mo.: Institute of Jesuit Sources, 1972.

Baritz, Loren. *The Good Life: The Meaning of Success for the American Middle Class*. New York: Alfred A. Knopf, 1989.

Barnard, Henry. "The Jesuits and Their Schools." In *Memoirs of Eminent Teachers and Educators with Contributions to the History of Education in Germany*. Rev. ed. Hartford, Conn.: Brown & Gross, 1878.

Barnett, S. J. *Idol Temples and Crafty Priests*. New York: St. Martin's Press, 1999.

Barrows, John Henry, ed. *The World's Parliament of Religions*. 2 vols. Chicago, Ill.: Parliament Publishing, 1893.

Bass, Dorothy. "Ministry on the Margins: Protestants and Education." In *Between the Times: The Travail of the Protestant Establishment in America, 1900–1960*, edited by William R. Hutchison. New York: Cambridge University Press, 1989.

Beecher, Lyman. *Plea for the West*. Cincinnati: Truman & Smith, 1835.

———. "A Plea for Western Colleges." Reprinted in H. Shelton Smith, Robert T. Handy, and Lefferts A. Loetscher, eds., *American Christianity: An Historical Interpretation*. 2 vols. New York: Charles Scribner's Sons, 1960–63.

Bercovitch, Sacvan. *The Puritan Origins of the American Self.* New Haven, Conn.: Yale University Press, 1975.

Berger, Bennett M. "Structure and Choice in the Sociology of Culture." *Theory and Society* 20 (1991): 1–19.

Bernad, Miguel Anselmo. "The Faculty of Arts in the Jesuit Colleges in the Eastern Part of the United States: Theory and Practice (1782–1923)." Ph.D. diss., Yale University, 1951.

Billington, Ray Allen. *The Protestant Crusade, 1800–1860.* New York: Macmillan, 1938.

Birdsey, Emer. "A Dark Record." *Ladies' Repository* 10 (1872): 249–55.

Bishop, Morris. *A History of Cornell.* Ithaca, N.Y.: Cornell University Press, 1962.

Bledstein, Burton J. *The Culture of Professionalism: The Middle Class and the Development of Higher Education in America.* New York: W. W. Norton, 1976.

Blumin, Stuart M. *The Emergence of the Middle Class: Social Experience in the American City, 1760–1980.* Cambridge: Cambridge University Press, 1989.

Bonney, Charles G. "Address of Welcome." In *Proceedings of the International Congress of Education of the World's Columbian Exposition.* 2d ed. New York: National Educational Association, 1895.

Boorstin, Daniel J. *The Americans: The National Experience.* New York: Vintage Books, 1965.

"Boston College—Its History and Influence." *Donahoe's Magazine* 29 (1893): 67–77.

Bowler, Peter J. *The Invention of Progress: Victorians and the Past.* Cambridge, Mass.: Basil Blackwell, 1989.

Bozeman, Theodore Dwight. *Protestants in an Age of Science: The Baconian Ideal and Antebellum American Religious Thought.* Chapel Hill: University of North Carolina Press, 1977.

Bremer, Francis J. *Shaping New Englands: Puritan Clergymen in Seventeenth-Century England and New England.* New York: Twayne, 1994.

Briggs, LeBaron Russell. "Fathers, Mothers, and Freshmen." *Atlantic Monthly* 83 (1899): 29–37.

———. "The Transition from School to College." *Atlantic Monthly* 85 (1900): 354–59.

———. "As Seen by a Disciple: President Eliot." *Atlantic Monthly* 144 (1929): 588–604.

Brill, Earl Hubert. "Religion and the Rise of the University: A Study of the Secularization of American Higher Education." Ph.D. diss., American University, 1969.

Brint, Steven, and Jerome Karabel. *The Diverted Dream: Community Colleges and the Promise of Educational Opportunity in America, 1900–1985.* New York: Oxford University Press, 1989.

Brodrick, James. *Saint Ignatius Loyola: The Pilgrim Years.* San Francisco, Calif.: Ignatius Press, 1998.

Brooks, Henry S. "How Shall We Educate Our Boys?" *Overland Monthly* 5 (1885): 200–205.

Brosnahan, Timothy. "The Relative Merit of Courses in Catholic and Non-Catholic Colleges for the Baccalaureate." In *Report of the Second Annual Conference of the*

Association of Catholic Colleges of the United States. Washington, D.C.: Catholic University of America Press, 1900.

———. "President Eliot and Jesuit Colleges." Boston, Mass.: Sacred Heart Review, 1900.

Brown, Rollo Walter. *Harvard Yard in the Golden Age.* New York: Current Books, 1948.

Browning, Oscar. *Aspects of Education: A Study in the History of Pedagogy.* New York: Industrial Education Association, 1888.

Brownson, Orestes. Review of "Dangers of Jesuit Instruction," a sermon by William S. Potts preached at Second Presbyterian Church, St. Louis, 25 September 1845. *Brownson's Quarterly Review* 3 (1846): 62–89.

Bruce, Gustav Marius. *Luther as an Educator.* 1928. Reprint. Westport, Conn.: Greenwood Press, 1979.

Buck, Paul, ed. *Social Sciences at Harvard, 1860–1920: From Inculcation to the Open Mind.* Cambridge, Mass.: Harvard University Press, 1965.

Buetow, Harold A. *Of Singular Benefit: The Story of Catholic Education in the United States.* London: Macmillan, 1970.

Bugg, Lelia Hardin. *The People of Our Parish: Being Chronicle and Comment of Katharine Fitzgerald, Pew-Holder in the Church of St. Paul the Apostle.* Boston, Mass.: Marlier, Callanan, 1901.

Burg, David F. *Chicago's White City of 1893.* Lexington: University of Kentucky Press, 1976.

Burke, Colin B. *American Collegiate Populations: A Test of the Traditional View.* New York: New York University Press, 1982.

Burns, James A. "Early Jesuit Schools in Maryland." *Catholic University Bulletin* 13 (1907): 361–81.

———. "The Elective System of Studies." In *Report of the Second Annual Conference of the Association of Catholic Colleges of the United States.* Washington, D.C.: Catholic University of America Press, 1900.

Burns, Robert E. *Being Catholic, Being American: The Notre Dame Story, 1842–1934.* Notre Dame, Ind.: University of Notre Dame Press, 1999.

Burtchaell, James Tunstead. *The Dying of the Light: The Disengagement of Colleges and Universities from Their Christian Churches.* Grand Rapids, Mich.: William B. Eerdmans, 1998.

Bury, J. B. *The Idea of Progress: An Inquiry into its Origin and Growth.* New York: Dover, 1932.

Butler, Jon. *Awash in a Sea of Faith: Christianizing the American People.* Cambridge, Mass.: Harvard University Press, 1990.

Cairns, Earle E. "The Puritan Educational Philosophy of Education." *Bibliotheca Sacra* 104 (1947): 326–36.

Campbell, Thomas J. *The Jesuits, 1534–1921.* New York: Encyclopedia Press, 1921.

Carpenter, Hazen C. "Emerson, Eliot, and the Elective System." *New England Quarterly* 24 (1951): 13–34.

Cassidy, Francis P. "Catholic College Foundations and Development in the United States (1677–1850)." Ph.D. diss., Catholic University of America, 1924.

Cassilly, Francis B. "Catholic Students at State Universities." *Ecclesiastical Review* 4 (1906): 113–20.

―――. "Catholic Students at State Universities." In *Catholic Educational Association: Report of the Proceedings and Addresses of the Third Annual Meeting.* Columbus, Ohio: Published by the Association, 1906.

"Catholic Young Men and State Universities." *Ave Maria* 58 (1904): 721–23.

C.D. "The Jesuits." *Journal of Sacred Literature* 30 (1851): 38–70.

Chase, Anthony. "The Birth of the Modern Law School." *American Journal of Legal History* 23 (1979): 329–48.

Cherry, Conrad. *Hurrying toward Zion: Universities, Divinity Schools, and American Protestantism.* Bloomington: Indiana University Press, 1995.

Cherry, Conrad, Betty A. DeBerg, and Amanda Porterfield. *Religion on Campus.* Chapel Hill: University of North Carolina Press, 2001.

The Children of Immigrants, vol. 5. In *Reports of the Immigration Commission,* vol. 33. Washington, D.C.: Government Printing Office, 1911.

"Church and Modern Society." Review in *Catholic World* 65 (1897): 214–22.

Clark, Dennis. *Hibernia America: The Irish and Regional Cultures.* New York: Greenwood Press, 1986.

Cleary, John F. "Catholic Participation in the World's Parliament of Religions." *Catholic Historical Review* 65 (1970): 585–609.

Cobban, A. B. *The Medieval Universities: Their Development and Organization.* London: Methuen, 1975.

Colman, J. Barry. *The Catholic University of America, 1903–1909: The Rectorship of Denis J. O'Connell.* Washington, D.C.: Catholic University of America Press, 1950.

"Commencement—The Alumni Dinner." *Harvard Graduates Magazine* 2 (1893–94): 98–104, and 3 (1894–95): 62–77.

Conaty, Thomas J. "The Catholic College of the Twentieth Century." In *Report of the Third Annual Conference of the Association of Catholic Colleges of the United States.* Washington, D.C.: Catholic University of America Press, 1901. Reprinted in *Catholic University Bulletin* 7 (1901): 304–19.

―――. "On the Teacher." In *Report of the Second Annual Conference of the Association of Catholic Colleges of the United States.* Washington, D.C.: Catholic University of America Press, 1900.

Contosta, David R. *Villanova University: American—Catholic—Augustinian, 1842–1992.* University Park: Pennsylvania State University Press, 1995.

Corrigan, Raymond. *The Church and the Nineteenth Century.* Milwaukee, Wis.: Bruce, 1938.

Cotton, Edward H. *The Life of Charles W. Eliot.* Boston, Mass.: Small, Maynard, 1926.

Craig, Hardin. *Woodrow Wilson at Princeton.* Norman: University of Oklahoma Press, 1960.

Cremin, Lawrence A. *American Education.* 3 vols. New York: Harper & Row, 1970–88. Vol. 1, *The Colonial Experience, 1607–1783* (1970). Vol. 2, *The National Experience, 1783–1876* (1980). Vol. 3, *The Metropolitan Experience, 1876–1980* (1988).

Cross, Robert D. *The Emergence of Liberal Catholicism.* Cambridge, Mass.: Harvard University Press, 1958.

Curran, Francis X. "Tentative Bibliography of American Anti-Jesuitiana." *Woodstock Letters* 81 (1952): 293–304.

Curran, Robert Emmett. *The Bicentennial History of Georgetown University: From Academy to University.* Washington, D.C.: Georgetown University Press, 1993.

———. *Michael Augustine Corrigan and the Shaping of Conservative Catholicism in America, 1878–1895.* New York: Arno Press, 1978.

Currie, Charles L. "Where We Are and Where We Are Going in Jesuit Higher Education: Sunset or Sunrise?" *America* 182 (20 May 2000): 7–11.

Curti, Merle, and Vernon Carstensen. *The University of Wisconsin: A History, 1848–1925.* Madison: University of Wisconsin Press, 1949.

Cutler, William W. "Cathedral of Culture: The Schoolhouse in American Educational Thought since 1820." *History of Education Quarterly* 29 (1989): 1–40.

Daley, Brian E. "'In Ten Thousand Places': Christian Universality and the Jesuit Mission." *Studies in the Spirituality of Jesuits* 17 (1985): 1–33.

Daley, John M. *Georgetown University: Origin and Early Years.* Washington, D.C.: Georgetown University Press, 1957.

Delurey, Lawrence A. "The Drift toward Non-Catholic Colleges and Universities." In *Report of the First Annual Conference of the Association of Catholic Colleges of the United States.* Washington, D.C.: Catholic University of America Press, 1899.

———. "The Teaching of History in College." In *Report of the Third Annual Conference of the Association of Catholic Colleges of the United States.* Washington, D.C.: Catholic University of America Press, 1901.

De Meaux, Vicomte C. "Catholic Centennial in the United States." *Catholic World* 51 (1890): 373–94.

Demos, John. *The Unredeemed Captive: A Family Story from Early America.* New York: Random House, 1994.

De Pressensé, Edmond. "The Society of Jesus." *American Church Review* 27 (1875): 408–27.

Devitt, Edward I. "History of the Maryland–New York Province XVI: Boston College and the Church of the Immaculate Conception." *Woodstock Letters* 64 (1935): 399–421.

DeWolfe, M. W. "The Harvard Figure of Eliot." In *Classic Shades: Five Leaders of Learning and Their Colleges.* Boston, Mass.: Little, Brown, 1928.

Dillenberger, John. *Protestant Thought and Natural Science.* Westport, Conn.: Greenwood Press, 1977.

DiMaggio, Paul. "Cultural Entrepreneurship in Nineteenth-Century Boston: The Creation of an Organizational Base for High Culture in America." In *Rethinking Popular Culture: Contemporary Perspectives in Cultural Studies,* edited by Chandra Mukerji and Michael Schudson. Berkeley: University of California Press, 1991.

Dolan, Jay P. *The American Catholic Experience: A History from Colonial Times to the Present.* Notre Dame, Ind.: University of Notre Dame Press, 1992.

———. *The Immigrant Church: New York's Irish and German Catholics, 1815–1865.* Baltimore, Md.: Johns Hopkins University Press, 1975.

———. *Catholic Revivalism: The American Experience, 1830–1900.* Notre Dame, Ind.: University of Notre Dame Press, 1978.

Donnelly, Francis P. *Principles of Jesuit Education in Practice.* New York: P. J. Kenedy & Sons, 1934.

Donovan, Charles F. *Boston College: Glimpses of the Past.* Chestnut Hill, Mass.: University Press of Boston College, 1994.

———. "Boston College Remembered: 1891–1900." Chestnut Hill, Mass.: Boston College, 1991.

———. "Nineteenth-Century Boston College: Irish or American?" Chestnut Hill, Mass.: Boston College, 1982.

Donovan, Charles F., David R. Dunigan, and Paul A. FitzGerald. *History of Boston College: From the Beginnings to 1990.* Chestnut Hill, Mass.: University Press of Boston College, 1990.

Dougherty, Jude P., et al. "The Secularization of Western Culture and the Catholic College and University." Washington, D.C.: Association of Catholic Colleges and Universities, 1981.

Douglas, Ann. *The Feminization of American Culture.* New York: Knopf, 1977.

Downey, Dennis B. "Tradition and Acceptance: American Catholics and the Columbian Exposition." *Mid-America* 63 (1981): 79–92.

Dubbert, Joe. "Progressivism and the Masculinity Crisis." In *The American Man,* edited by Elizabeth H. Pleck and Joseph H. Pleck. Englewood Cliffs, N.J.: Prentice-Hall, 1980.

Du Bois, W. E. Burghardt. "That Outer Whiter World at Harvard." In *The Harvard Book: Selections from Three Centuries,* edited by William Bentinck-Smith. Rev. ed. Cambridge, Mass.: Harvard University Press, 1982.

Duminuco, Vincent J., ed. *The Jesuit* Ratio Studiorum: *400th Anniversary Perspectives.* New York: Fordham University Press, 2000.

Dunigan, David R. *A History of Boston College.* Milwaukee, Wis.: Bruce, 1947.

Dunn, Richard S., James Savage, and Laetitia Yeandle, eds. *The Journal of John Winthrop, 1630–1649.* Cambridge, Mass.: Harvard University Press, 1996.

Durkin, Joseph T. *Georgetown University: The Middle Years.* Washington, D.C.: Georgetown University Press, 1963.

"Editor's Table." *Harper's New Monthly Magazine* 17 (October 1858): 694–700.

Egan, Maurice Francis. "A New Departure in Catholic College Discipline." *Catholic World* 50 (1890): 569–73.

Eliot, Charles W. "The Aims of the Higher Education." [1891]. In *Educational Reform.*

———. *Educational Reform: Essays and Addresses.* New York: Century, 1898.

———. "Inaugural Address." [1869]. In *Educational Reform.*

———. "Liberty in Education." [1885]. In *Educational Reform.*

———. "The New Education: Its Organization." *Atlantic Monthly* 33 (1869): 203–30, 359–67.

———. "On the Education of Ministers." [1883]. In *Educational Reform.*

———. "Recent Changes in Secondary Education." *Atlantic Monthly* 84 (1899): 433–44.

———. *The Religion of the Future.* Boston, Mass.: J. W. Luce, 1909.

———. "Three Results of the Scientific Study of Nature." In *American Contributions to Civilization and Other Essays and Addresses.* New York: Century, 1897.

————. "What Is a Liberal Education?" *Century* 28 (1884): 203–12.

Elliott, Walter. "Human Environments of the Catholic Faith." *Catholic World* 43 (1886): 463–70.

————. "Missionary Work of the Church in the United States." In *Progress of the Catholic Church in America and the Great Columbian Catholic Congress of 1893.* 2 vols. in 1. 6th ed. Chicago, Ill.: J. S. Hyland, 1897.

Ellis, John Tracy. *The Formative Years of the Catholic University of America.* Washington, D.C.: American Catholic Historical Association, 1946.

————. *John Lancaster Spalding, First Bishop of Peoria, American Educator.* Milwaukee, Wis.: Bruce, 1962.

————. *The Life of Cardinal Gibbons, Archbishop of Baltimore, 1834–1921.* Milwaukee, Wis.: Bruce, 1952.

Erbacher, Sebastian Anthony. "Catholic Higher Education for Men in the United States, 1850–1866." Ph.D. diss., Catholic University of America, 1931.

Evans, John Whitney. *The Newman Movement: Roman Catholics in American Higher Education, 1883–1971.* Notre Dame, Ind.: University of Notre Dame Press, 1980.

Everett, Ruth. "Jesuit Educators and Modern Colleges." *Arena* 23 (1900): 647–53.

Fagan, James P. "Educational Legislation." [1901]. *National Catholic Educational Association Bulletin* 4 (1908): 8–40.

————. "Meeting of the N.E.A. at Chicago." *Woodstock Letters* 29 (1900): 123–36.

————. "What the Parish School Can Do for the College." In *Catholic Educational Association: Report of the Proceedings and Addresses of the Second Annual Meeting.* Columbus, Ohio: Published by the Association, 1905.

Fallows, Marjorie R. *Irish Americans: Identity and Assimilation.* Englewood Cliffs, N.J.: Prentice-Hall, 1979.

Farrell, Allan P. *The Jesuit Code of Liberal Education: Development and Scope of the Ratio Studiorum.* Milwaukee, Wis.: Bruce, 1938.

Farrell, John J. "The Catholic Chaplain at the Secular University." In *Catholic Educational Association: Report of the Proceedings and Addresses of the Fourth Annual Meeting.* Columbus, Ohio: Published by the Association, 1907.

Fass, Paula S. *Outside In: Minorities and the Transformation of American Education.* New York: Oxford University Press, 1989.

"Father Joseph Havens Richards, S.J." *Woodstock Letters* 53 (1924): 248–71.

"Father Rudolph Meyer." *Woodstock Letters* 42 (1913): 922–96.

"Father Timothy Brosnahan." *Woodstock Letters* 45 (1916): 99–117.

"Father William George Read Mullan." *Woodstock Letters* 39 (1910): 389–94.

Feldhay, Rivka. "Knowledge and Salvation in Jesuit Culture." *Science in Context* 1 (1987): 193–215.

Findlay, James. "The SPCTEW and Western Colleges: Religion and Higher Education in Mid-Nineteenth Century America." *History of Education Quarterly* 11 (1971): 31–62.

Finke, Roger, and Rodney Stark. *The Churching of America, 1776–1990: Winners and Losers in Our Religious Economy.* New Brunswick, N.J.: Rutgers University Press, 1992.

Finkelstein, Barbara. "Education Historians as Mythmakers." *Review of Research in Education* 18 (1992): 255–97.

Fitzpatrick, Edward A., ed. *St. Ignatius and the Ratio Studiorum.* New York: McGraw-Hill, 1933.

Fleming, Donald. "Eliot's New Broom." In Bailyn et al., *Glimpses of the Harvard Past.*

———. "Harvard's Golden Age?" In Bailyn et al., *Glimpses of the Harvard Past.*

Fleming, Robin. "Picturesque History and the Medieval in Nineteenth-Century America." *American Historical Review* 100 (1995): 1061–94.

Flexner, Abraham. *Daniel Coit Gilman: Creator of the American Type of University.* New York: Harcourt, Brace, 1946.

Floy, J. "The Jesuits." *Ladies' Repository* 10 (1850): 41–45.

Fogarty, Gerald P. *The Vatican and the Americanist Crisis: Denis J. O'Connell, American Agent in Rome, 1885–1903.* Rome: Universitía Gregoriana, 1974.

———. *The Vatican and the American Hierarchy from 1870 to 1965.* Stuttgart: Hiersemann, 1872.

Franchot, Jenny. *Roads to Rome: The Antebellum Protestant Encounter with Catholicism.* Berkeley: University of California Press, 1994.

Friedman, Lawrence A. *A History of American Law.* New York: Simon & Schuster, 1973, 1985.

Gagliano, Joseph A., and Charles E. Ronan, eds. *Jesuit Encounters in the New World: Jesuit Chroniclers, Geographers, Educators, and Missionaries in the Americas, 1549–1767.* Rome: Institutum Historicum S.I., 1997.

Gallivan, James A. "Catholic Sons of Harvard." *Donahoe's* 32 (1894): 499–510.

Gallin, Alice, ed. *American Catholic Higher Education: Essential Documents, 1967–1990.* Notre Dame, Ind.: University of Notre Dame Press, 1992.

———. *Independence and a New Partnership in Catholic Higher Education.* Notre Dame, Ind.: University of Notre Dame Press, 1996.

———. *Negotiating Identity: Catholic Higher Education since 1960.* Notre Dame, Ind.: University of Notre Dame Press, 2000.

Gannon, Michael V. "Before and After Modernism: The Intellectual Isolation of the American Priest." In *The Catholic Priest in the United States: Historical Investigations,* edited by John Tracy Ellis. Collegeville, Minn.: St. John's University Press, 1971.

Ganss, George E., ed. *Ignatius of Loyola: The Spiritual Exercises and Selected Works.* New York: Paulist Press, 1991.

———. *Saint Ignatius' Idea of a Jesuit University.* Milwaukee, Wis.: Marquette University Press, 1956.

Garraghan, Gilbert J. "Origins of Boston College." *Thought* 18 (1942): 627–56.

Gaustad, Edwin Scott. *A Religious History of America.* Rev. ed. San Francisco, Calif.: HarperCollins, 1990.

G.E.E. "The Massachusetts Legislature, and The 'College of the Holy Cross.'" *Christian Examiners and Religious Miscellany,* fourth series, 21 (1849): 51–61.

Geiger, Roger L. "The Era of Multipurpose Colleges in American Higher Education, 1850 to 1890." *History of Higher Education Annual* 15 (1995): 51–92.

———, ed. *The American College in the Nineteenth Century*. Nashville, Tenn.: Vanderbilt University Press, 2000.

"The General Assembly." *Princeton Review* 36 (July 1864): 506–74.

Gilman, Daniel C. "Higher Education in the United States." In *University Problems in the United States*.

———. "The Johns Hopkins University: In Its Beginning." In *University Problems in the United States*.

———. "The University of California in Its Infancy." In *University Problems in the United States*.

———. *University Problems in the United States*. New York: Century, 1898.

Gleason, Philip. "American Catholic Higher Education: A Historical Perspective." In *The Shape of Catholic Higher Education*, edited by Robert Hassenger. Chicago, Ill.: University of Chicago Press, 1967.

———. "Baltimore III and Education." *U.S. Catholic Historian* 4 (1985): 273–311.

———. *The Conservative Reformers: German-American Catholics and the Social Order*. Notre Dame, Ind.: University of Notre Dame Press, 1968.

———. *Contending with Modernity: Catholic Higher Education in the Twentieth Century*. New York: Oxford University Press, 1995.

———. "Immigrant Assimilation and the Crisis of Americanization." In *Keeping the Faith: American Catholicism Past and Present*. Notre Dame, Ind.: University of Notre Dame Press, 1987.

———. "Immigration and American Catholic Higher Education." In *American Education and the European Immigrant*, edited by Bernard J. Weiss. Urbana: University of Illinois Press, 1982.

———. "The Main Sheet Anchor: John Carroll and Catholic Higher Education." *Review of Politics* 38 (1976): 576–613.

———. "The New Americanism in Catholic Historiography." *U.S. Catholic Historian* 11 (1993): 1–18.

Goodchild, Lester F. "The Turning Point in American Jesuit Higher Education: The Standardization Controversy between the Jesuits and the North Central Association, 1915–1940." *History of Higher Education Annual* 6 (1986): 81–116.

Gorayeb, Joseph. *The Life and Letters of Walter Drum. S.J.* New York: America Press, 1928.

Gordon, Lynn D. *Gender and Higher Education in the Progressive Era*. New Haven, Conn.: Yale University Press, 1990.

Graham, Patricia Albjerg. "Expansion and Exclusion: A History of Women in American Higher Education." *Signs* 3 (1978): 759–73.

Gray, M. Alexander. "Development of the Newman Club Movement, 1893–1961." *Records of the American Historical Society of Philadelphia* 74 (1963): 70–128.

Greaves, Richard L. *The Puritan Revolution and Educational Thought: Background for Reform*. New Brunswick, N.J.: Rutgers University Press, 1969.

Greeley, Andrew M. *American Catholic: A Social Portrait*. New York: Basic Books, 1977.

———. *From Backwater to Mainstream: A Profile of Catholic Higher Education*. New York: McGraw-Hill, 1969.

Guilday, Peter Keenan. *The Life and Times of John Carroll, Archbishop of Baltimore, 1735–1815*. New York: Encyclopedia Press, 1922.

———, ed. *The National Pastorals of the American Hierarchy, 1792–1919*. Westminster, Md.: Newman Press, 1923, 1954.

Guldner, G. "Moral Training without Religion." In *Report of the Fifth Annual Conference of the Association of Catholic Colleges of the United States*. Baltimore, Md.: Sun Printing, 1903.

Hall, Peter Dobkin. "Noah Porter Writ Large? Reflections on the Modernization of American Higher Education and Its Critics, 1866–1916." In Geiger, ed., *The American College in the Nineteenth Century*.

Halsey, William M. *The Survival of American Innocence: Catholicism in an Era of Disillusionment*. Notre Dame, Ind.: University of Notre Dame Press, 1980.

Hamlin, Charles E. "The Attitude of the Christian Teacher in Respect to Science." *Baptist Quarterly* 6 (1872): 1–29.

Handlin, Oscar. *Boston's Immigrants, 1790–1880: A Study in Acculturation*. Rev. and enlarged ed. Cambridge, Mass.: Harvard University Press, 1991.

———. "A Small Community." In Bailyn et al., *Glimpses of the Harvard Past*.

———. "Making Men of Boys." In Bailyn et al., *Glimpses of the Harvard Past*.

Handy, Robert T. *A Christian America: Protestant Hopes and Historical Realities*. 2d ed. New York: Oxford University Press, 1984.

Harbison, E. Harris. *The Christian Scholar in the Age of the Reformation*. New York: Scribner, 1956.

Harper, William Rainey. *The Prospects of the Small College*. Chicago, Ill.: University of Chicago Press, 1900.

———. "The Scientific Study of the Student." In *The Trend in Higher Education*.

———. "Some Present Tendencies of Popular Education." In *The Trend in Higher Education*.

——— *The Trend in Higher Education*. Chicago, Ill.: University of Chicago Press, 1905.

———. "The Trend of University and College Education in the United States." *North American Review* 174 (1902): 457–65.

———. "Waste in Higher Education." In *The Trend in Higher Education*.

Hart, D. G. "Faith and Learning in the Age of the University: The Academic Ministry of Daniel Coit Gilman." In Marsden and Longfield, *Secularization*.

———. *The University Gets Religion*. Baltimore, Md.: Johns Hopkins University Press, 1999.

"The Harvard Debate." *Holy Cross Purple* 11 (1900): 219–20.

Harvard Law School Association. *The Centennial History of the Harvard Law School, 1817–1917*. Boston, Mass.: Harvard Law School Association, 1918.

Haskell, Thomas L., ed. *The Authority of Experts: Studies in History and Theory*. Bloomington: Indiana University Press, 1984.

Hatch, Nathan O. *The Democratization of American Christianity*. New Haven, Conn.: Yale University Press, 1989.

Hawkins, Hugh. *Banding Together: The Rise of National Associations in American*

Higher Education, 1887–1950. Baltimore, Md.: Johns Hopkins University Press, 1992.

———. *Between Harvard and America: The Educational Leadership of Charles W. Eliot.* New York: Oxford University Press, 1972.

———. "Charles W. Eliot, University Reform, and Religious Faith in America, 1869–1909." *Journal of American History* 51 (1964): 191–213.

———. *Pioneer: A History of the Johns Hopkins University, 1874–1889.* Ithaca, N.Y.: Cornell University Press, 1960.

———. "The University-Builders Observe the Colleges." *History of Education Quarterly* 11 (1971): 353–62.

Haynes, Fred E. "Amusements." In *City Wilderness: A Settlement House Study,* edited by Robert A. Woods. Boston, Mass.: Houghton, Mifflin, 1898.

Hennesey, James. *American Catholics: A History of the Roman Catholic Community in the United States.* New York: Oxford University Press, 1981.

Herbst, Jurgen. "American College History Re-Examination Underway." *History of Education Quarterly* 15 (1975): 259–66.

Hilkey, Judy. *Character is Capital: Success Manuals and Manhood in Gilded Age America.* Chapel Hill: University of North Carolina Press, 1997.

"Histoire de la Chute de Jèsuites." *Princeton Review* 17 (April 1845): 239–52.

"A Historical Sketch of the Jesuits." *Christian Review* 7 (1843): 161–85.

Hofstadter, Richard. *The Paranoid Style of American Politics.* New York: Alfred A. Knopf, 1965.

Hofstadter, Richard, and Walter Metzger. *The Development of Academic Freedom in the United States.* New York: Columbia University Press, 1955.

Hogan, Peter. *The Catholic University of America, 1896–1903: The Rectorship of Thomas J. Conaty.* Washington, D.C.: Catholic University of America Press, 1949.

Holaind, René. "The Parent First." New York: Benziger Brothers, 1891.

Hollinger, David A. "Inquiry and Uplift: Late Nineteenth-Century Academics and the Moral Efficacy of Scientific Practice." In Haskell, ed., *The Authority of Experts.*

———. "Justification by Verification: The Scientific Challenge to the Moral Authority of Christianity in Modern America." In *Religion and Twentieth-Century American Intellectual Life,* edited by Michael J. Lacey. New York: Cambridge University Press, 1989.

Holtschneider, Dennis H., and Melanie Morey. "Relationship Revisited: Catholic Institutions and Their Founding Congregations." Occasional paper no. 47. Washington, D.C.: Association of Governing Boards, 2000.

Holy Cross Alumni Directory, 1843–1967. Worcester, Mass.: Holy Cross College, 1967.

Horowitz, Helen Lefkowitz. *Campus Life: Undergraduate Cultures from the End of the Eighteenth Century to the Present.* Chicago, Ill.: University of Chicago Press, 1987.

Hovenkamp, Herbert. *Science and Religion in America, 1800–1860.* Philadelphia: University of Pennsylvania Press, 1978.

Howe, Daniel Walker. "Reason and Revelation." In *The Unitarian Conscience: Harvard Moral Philosophy, 1805–1861,* with a new introduction, 1970. Middletown, Conn.: Wesleyan University Press, 1988.

Hughes, Thomas. *Loyola and the Educational System of the Jesuits.* New York: Charles Scribner's Sons, 1892.

Hutchison, William R. *The Modernist Impulse in American Protestantism.* Durham, N.C.: Duke University Press, 1992.

———. "Protestantism as Establishment." In *Between the Times: The Travail of the Protestant Establishment in America, 1900–1960,* edited by William R. Hutchison. Cambridge: Cambridge University Press, 1989.

Ireland, John. *The Church and Modern Society: Lectures and Address.* 2 vols. Chicago, Ill.: D. H. McBride, 1896.

———. "The Mission of Catholics in America." In *The Church and Modern Society.*

Jaher, Frederic Cople. "The Education of American Lawyers." *History of Education Quarterly* 21 (1981): 105–13.

"James Barr Ames." *Harvard Law Review* 23 (1910): 321–38.

James, Henry. *Charles W. Eliot, President of Harvard University, 1869–1909.* 2 vols. Boston, Mass.: Houghton, Mifflin, 1930.

Jencks, Christopher, and David Riesman. "The Viability of the American College." In *The American College: A Psychological and Social Interpretation of Higher Learning,* edited by Nevitt Sanford. New York: Wiley, 1962.

Jennings, Francis. "Francis Parkman: A Brahmin Among Untouchables." *William and Mary Quarterly* 42 (1985): 305–28.

Jenkins, Thomas Jefferson. "By the Great Waters of the Ojibway." *Catholic World* 61 (1895): 546–59.

"The Jesuits." *Southern Quarterly Review* 12 (1855): 14–36.

John Paul II. *Constitutio Apostolica de Universitatibus Catholicis [Ex Corde Ecclesiae].* Rome: Libreria Editrice Vaticana, 1990. Reprinted in English in *Origins* 20 (4 October 1990): 265–76.

Johnson, William R. *Schooled Lawyers: A Study in the Clash of Professional Cultures.* New York: New York University Press, 1978.

Jonas, Thomas J. *The Divided Mind: American Catholic Evangelists in the 1890s.* New York: Garland, 1988.

Jones, Robert Ellis. "Is the College Graduate Impracticable?" *Forum* 30 (1901): 583–94.

Jordan, David Starr. *The Days of a Man: Being Memories of a Naturalist, Teacher, and Minor Prophet of Democracy.* 2 vols. Yonkers-on-Hudson, N.Y.: World Book, 1922.

Kaestle, Carl F. *Pillars of the Republic: Common Schools and American Society, 1780–1860.* New York: Hill & Wang, 1983.

Kane, Paula M. *Separatism and Subculture: Boston Catholicism, 1900–1920.* Chapel Hill: University of North Carolina Press, 1994.

Kauffman, Christopher J. *Ministry and Meaning: A Religious History of Catholic Health Care in the United States.* New York: Crossroad, 1995.

Kearney, Hugh F. *Scholars and Gentlemen: Universities and Society in Pre-Industrial Britain.* London: Faber, 1970.

Kelsey, Francis W. "State Universities and Church Colleges." *Atlantic Monthly* 80 (1897): 826–32.

Kemeny, P. C. *Princeton in the Nation's Service: Religious Ideals and Educational Practice, 1868–1928.* New York: Oxford University Press, 1998.

Kennedy, Albert J. "East Boston." In Woods and Kennedy, *The Zone of Emergence.*

Kernan, Thomas F. "The Catholic Layman in Higher Education." *Catholic World* 71 (1900): 361–65.

Kimball, Bruce A. *Orators and Philosophers: A History of the Idea of Liberal Education.* Expanded ed. New York: College Entrance Examination Board, 1995.

———. *The "True Professional Ideal" in America: A History.* Cambridge, U.K.: Blackwell, 1992.

Klein, Christa Ressmeyer. "Jesuits and Boyhood in Victorian New York." *U.S. Catholic Historian* 7 (1988): 375–91.

Knox, Charles E. "Problems for Educated Minds in America in the New Century." *Princeton Review* 6 (1877): 197–220.

Knowles, David. *The Evolution of Medieval Thought.* Baltimore, Md.: Helicon Press, 1962.

Kramer, F. J. "Catholics in Non-Catholic Colleges." *Globe* 13 (1903): 174–80.

Kurtz, Lester R. *The Politics of Heresy: The Modernist Crisis in Roman Catholicism.* Berkeley: University of California Press, 1986.

Kuzniewski, Anthony J. *Thy Honored Name: A History of the College of the Holy Cross, 1843–1994.* Washington, D.C.: Catholic University of America Press, 1999.

Labaree, David F. *The Making of an American High School: The Credentials Market and Central High of Philadelphia, 1838–1939.* New Haven, Conn.: Yale University Press, 1988.

Lacouture, Jean. *Jesuits: A Multibiography,* translated by Jeremy Leggatt. 1991; Washington, D.C.: Counterpoint, 1995.

LaFarge, John. *The Manner Is Ordinary.* New York: Harcourt, Brace, 1954.

Lane, Roger. "James Jeffrey Roche and the Boston Pilot." *New England Quarterly* 3 (1960): 341–36.

Langdell, Christopher C. "Harvard Celebration Speeches." *Law Quarterly Review* 3 (1887).

"The Last Days of Our Father General." *Woodstock Letters* 35 (1906): 100–109.

"The Law School." *Harvard Law Review* 7 (1893–94): 113–15; 8 (1894–95): 220–22; 17 (1903–4): 119–21.

Laxton, Edward. *The Famine Ships: The Irish Exodus to America.* New York: Henry Holt, 1997.

"A Layman Succeeds Where a Priest Fails." *Missionary* 7 (1903): 109–10.

Leahy, William P. *Adapting to America: Catholics, Jesuits, and Higher Education in the Twentieth Century.* Washington, D.C.: Georgetown University Press, 1991.

Le Conte, Joseph. "The Essential Characteristics and Mutual Relations of School, the College, and the University." *Princeton Review* 1 (1880): 177–204.

Le Duc, Thomas. *Piety and Intellect at Amherst College, 1865–1912.* New York: Columbia University Press, 1946.

Lears, T. J. Jackson. "The Concept of Cultural Hegemony: Problems and Possibilities." *American Historical Review* 90 (1985): 567–93.

————. *No Place of Grace: Antimodernism and the Transformation of American Culture, 1880–1920.* Chicago, Ill.: University of Chicago Press, 1981.

Lentz, F. G. "The Conversion of the American People." *Catholic World* 55 (1892): 884–87.

Leo XIII. *Aeternis Patris.* Reprinted in *The Papal Encyclicals, 1878–1903,* edited by Claudia Carlen. Wilmington, N.C.: McGrath, 1981.

————. *Longinqua Oceani.* Reprinted in *The Papal Encyclicals, 1878–1903,* edited by Claudia Carlen. Wilmington, N.C.: McGrath, 1981.

————. *Testem Benevolentia.* Reprinted in McAvoy, *The Great Crisis, 1895–1900.*

Leslie, W. Bruce. *Gentlemen and Scholars: College and Community in the "Age of the University," 1865–1917.* University Park: Pennsylvania State University Press, 1992.

Levine, David O. *The American College and the Culture of Aspiration, 1915–1940.* Ithaca, N.Y.: Cornell University Press, 1986.

Lord, Robert H., John E. Sexton, and Edward T. Harrington. *History of the Archdiocese of Boston.* 3 vols. New York: Sheed & Ward, 1944.

Lucas, Thomas M. *Landmarking: City, Church, and Jesuit Urban Strategy.* Chicago, Ill.: Loyola University Press, 1997.

Luther, Martin. "An Appeal to the Ruling Class." In *Martin Luther: Selections from His Writing,* edited with introduction by John Dillenberger. Garden City: N.Y.: Anchor, 1961.

Lutz, David W. "Can Notre Dame Be Saved?" *First Things* 19 (January 1992): 35–40.

Lyons, John O. *The College Novel in America.* Carbondale: Southern Illinois University Press, 1962.

Macksey, Charles. "The Ethical Influence of College Athletics." In *Catholic Educational Association: Report of the Proceedings and Addresses of the Third Annual Meeting.* Columbus, Ohio: Published by the Association, 1906.

Mahoney, Kathleen A. "Catholic Colleges for Women: Historical Origins." In Schier and Russett, *Catholic Women's Colleges in America.*

————. "One Hundred Years: The Association of Catholic Colleges and Universities." *Current Issues in Catholic Higher Education* 19 (1999): 3–47.

————. "The Rise of the University and the Secularization of the Academy: The Role of Liberal Protestantism." *History of Higher Education Annual* 16 (1996): 117–31.

Mahoney, Kathleen A., John Schmalzbauer, and James Youniss. "Religion: A Comeback on Campus." *Liberal Education* 87 (fall 2001): 36–41.

Mann, Arthur. *Yankee Reformers in the Urban Age: Social Reform in Boston, 1880–1900.* New York: Harper & Row, 1954.

Marsden, George M. "The Soul of the American University: A Historical Overview." In Marsden and Longfield, *Secularization.*

————. *The Soul of the American University: From Protestant Establishment to Established Nonbelief.* New York: Oxford University Press, 1994.

Marsden, George M., and Bradley J. Longfield, eds., *The Secularization of the Academy.* New York: Oxford University Press, 1992.

Martin, A. Lynn. *The Jesuit Mind: The Mentality of an Elite in Early Modern France.* Ithaca, N.Y.: Cornell University Press, 1988.

———. "The Jesuit Mystique." *Sixteenth-Century Journal* 4 (1973): 31–40.

Martín, Luis. "Adhortatio de Studendi Ratione." *Woodstock Letters* 22 (1893): 102–6.

———. "On Some Dangers of Our Times." In *Select Letters of Our Very Reverend Fathers General to the Fathers and Brothers of the Society of Jesus.* Woodstock, Md.: Woodstock College, 1900.

Marty, Martin E. *The Irony of It All, 1893–1919.* Vol. 1 of *Modern American Religion.* Chicago, Ill.: University of Chicago Press, 1986.

———. "Is There a *Mentalité* in the American Catholic House?" *U.S. Catholic Historian* 6 (1987): 13–23.

———. *Righteous Empire: The Protestant Experience in America.* New York: Dial Press, 1970.

McAvoy, Thomas. *The Great Crisis in American Church History, 1895–1900.* Chicago, Ill.: Henry Regnery, 1957.

McCaffrey, Lawrence J. *The Irish Diaspora in America.* Washington, D.C.: Catholic University of America Press, 1976, 1984.

———. *Textures of Irish America.* Syracuse, N.Y.: Syracuse University Press, 1992.

McDannell, Colleen. *The Christian Home in Victorian America, 1840–1900.* Bloomington: Indiana University Press, 1986.

———. "'True Men as We Need Them': Catholicism and the Irish-American Male." *American Studies* 27 (1986): 19–36.

McDonough, Peter. *Men Astutely Trained: A History of the Jesuits in the American Century.* New York: Free Press, 1992.

McFarland, Michael C. "Studia Humanitatis, Pietas, and Christianitas: The Jesuit Tradition in the Liberal Arts." The Rodino Lecture, 23 January 2001. www.holycross.edu/departments/president/website/rodino.htm.

McGinley, A. A. "The Catholic Life in Boston." *Catholic World* 67 (1898): 20–36.

McGreevy, John T. *Parish Boundaries: The Catholic Encounter with Race in the Twentieth-Century Urban North.* Chicago, Ill.: University of Chicago Press, 1996.

McGucken, William J. *The Jesuits and Education: The Society's Teaching Principles and Practice, especially in Secondary Education in the United States.* Milwaukee, Wis.: Bruce, 1932.

McKevitt, Gerald. "Jesuit Higher Education in the United States." *Mid-America: A Historical Review* 73 (1991): 209–26.

———. *The University of Santa Clara: A History, 1851–1977.* Stanford, Calif.: Stanford University Press, 1979.

McLaughlin, James. "The American College in the Nineteenth Century: Toward a Reappraisal." *Teachers College Record* 80 (1978): 287–306.

McWilliams, R. L. "The Presence of Catholic Students at Our State Universities." *American Ecclesiastical Review* 35 (1906): 197–200.

Mead, Sidney E. *The Nation with the Soul of a Church.* New York: Harper & Row, 1975.

Meagher, Walter J., and William J. Grattan. *The Spires of Fenwick: A History of the College of the Holy Cross, 1843–1963.* New York: Vantage Press, 1966.

Meissner, W. W. *Ignatius of Loyola: The Psychology of a Saint.* New Haven, Conn.: Yale University Press, 1992.

Melville, Herman. *White Jacket; Or, The World in a Man-of-War.* Boston, Mass.: L. C. Page, 1892.

Mercier, Louis. "Report on Statistics of the Catholic Colleges of the United States." In *Catholic Educational Association: Report of the Proceedings and Addresses of the Fifth Annual Meeting.* Columbus, Ohio: Catholic Educational Association, 1908.

Merwick, Donna. *Boston Priests, 1848–1910: A Study of Social and Intellectual Change.* Cambridge, Mass.: Harvard University Press, 1973.

Messbarger, Paul R. *Fiction with a Parochial Purpose: Social Uses of American Catholic Literature, 1884–1900.* Boston, Mass.: Boston University Press, 1971.

Meyer, D. H. "American Intellectuals and the Victorian Crisis of Faith." *American Quarterly* 27 (December 1975): 585–603.

Meyer, R. J. *The Science of the Saints.* 2 vols. St. Louis, Mo.: B. Herder, 1902.

Miller, Kerby A. *Emigrants and Exiles: Ireland and the Irish Exodus to North America.* New York: Oxford University Press, 1985.

Miller, Perry. *Errand into the Wilderness.* 1956; Cambridge, Mass.: Harvard University Press, 1984.

———. *The New England Mind: The Seventeenth Century.* New York: Macmillan, 1939.

Moody, Joseph N. *French Education since Napolean.* Syracuse, N.Y.: Syracuse University Press, 1978.

Moore, Charles S. "The Elective System at Harvard." *Harvard Graduates Magazine* 11 (1903): 530–34.

Moore, R. Laurence. "Insiders and Outsiders in American Historical Narrative and American History." *American Historical Review* 87 (1982): 390–423.

———. *Religious Outsiders and the Making of Americans.* New York: Oxford University Press, 1986.

Moorhead, James H. *World without End: Mainstream American Protestant Visions of the Last Things, 1880–1925.* Bloomington: Indiana University Press, 1999.

Morgan, Edmund S. *The Puritan Family: Religion and Domestic Relations in Seventeenth-Century New England.* New York: Harper & Row, 1944, 1966.

———. *Visible Saints: The History of a Puritan Idea.* New York: New York University Press, 1963.

Morgan, John. *Godly Learning: Puritan Attitudes Towards Reasoning, Learning, and Education, 1560–1640.* New York: Cambridge University Press, 1986.

Morison, Samuel Eliot, ed. *The Development of Harvard University since the Inaugural of President Eliot, 1869–1929.* Cambridge, Mass.: Harvard University Press, 1930.

———. *The Founding of Harvard College.* Cambridge, Mass.: Harvard University Press, 1935.

———. *Harvard in the Seventeenth Century.* 2 vols. Cambridge, Mass.: Harvard University Press, 1936.

———. *Three Centuries of Harvard.* Cambridge, Mass.: Harvard University Press, 1936.

Mullan, W. G. Read. "The Drift toward Non-Catholic Colleges and Universities." In

Report of the First Annual Conference of the Association of Catholic Colleges in the United States. Washington, D.C.: Catholic University of America Press, 1899.

Mullaney, J. F. "The Regents of the State of New York and Catholic Schools." *American Catholic Quarterly Review* 17 (1892): 634–43.

Murphy, Michael J. "The Cornell Plan of Bishop Bernard J. McQuaid." *St. Meinrad Essays* 12 (1959): 76–87.

"A Nation's Right to Worship." *Princeton Review* 31 (1859): 664–97.

Naylor, Natalie A. "The Antebellum College Movement: A Reappraisal of Tewksbury's Founding of American Colleges and Universities." *History of Education Quarterly* 13 (1973): 261–74.

Neill, Charles P. "Statistics of Attendance of Catholic College Students at Non-Catholic Colleges and Universities, and Cause Thereof." In *Catholic Educational Association: Report of the Proceedings and Addresses of the First Annual Meeting.* Columbus, Ohio: Published by the Association, 1904.

New England's First Fruits. Reprinted in *The Founding of Harvard College*, by Samuel Eliot Morison. Cambridge, Mass.: Harvard University Press, 1935.

Nisbet, Robert. *A History of the Idea of Progress.* New York: Basic Books, 1980.

Nuesse, C. Joseph. *The Catholic University of America: A Centennial History.* Washington, D.C.: Catholic University of America Press, 1990.

Oates, Mary J. *The Catholic Philanthropic Tradition in America.* Bloomington: Indiana University Press, 1995.

———, ed. *Higher Education for Catholic Women: An Historical Anthology.* New York: Garland, 1987.

O'Brien, David J. *Isaac Hecker: An American Catholic.* New York: Paulist Press, 1992.

O'Callaghan, Peter J. "Catholics at Harvard." *Catholic Family Annual* (1895): 74–80.

———. "The Puritan Catholicized." *Catholic World* 65 (1897): 111–14.

O'Connell, Marvin R. *Critics on Trial: An Introduction to the Catholic Modernist Crisis.* Washington, D.C.: Catholic University of America Press, 1994.

———. *John Ireland and the American Catholic Church.* St. Paul: Minnesota Historical Society Press, 1988.

O'Connor, Thomas H. *Boston Catholics: A History of the Church and Its People.* Boston, Mass.: Northeastern University Press, 1998.

O'Malley, Austin. "Catholic Collegiate Education in the United States." *Catholic World* 67 (1898): 289–304.

O'Malley, John W. "Attitudes of the Early Jesuits Towards Misbelievers." *The Way Supplement* 68 (1990): 62–73.

———. *The First Jesuits.* Cambridge, Mass.: Harvard University Press, 1993.

———. "From the 1599 *Ratio Studiorum* to the Present." In Duminuco, *The Jesuit Ratio Studiorum.*

———. "The Historiography of the Society of Jesus: Where Does It Stand Today?" In O'Malley et al., eds., *The Jesuits: Cultures, Sciences, and the Arts.*

———. "How the First Jesuits Became Involved in Education." In Duminuco, *The Jesuit Ratio Studiorum.*

———. "The Jesuits, St. Ignatius, and the Counter Reformation: Some Recent

Studies and Their Implications for Today." *Studies in the Spirituality of Jesuits* 16 (1982): 1–28.

———. "Mission and the Early Jesuits." *The Way Supplement* 79 (1994): 3–10.

———. "To Travel to Any Part of the World: Jerónimo Nadal and the Jesuit Vocation." *Studies in the Spirituality of Jesuits* 16 (1984): 1–20.

O'Malley, John W., et al., eds. *The Jesuits: Cultures, Sciences, and the Arts, 1540–1773*. Toronto: University of Toronto Press, 1999.

Ong, Walter J. "Latin Language Study as a Renaissance Puberty Rite." *Studies in Philology* 56 (1959): 103–24.

O'Reilly, Bernard. *True Men as We Need Them; A Book of Instruction for Men in the World*. [1878]. New York: P. J. Kenedy, 1899.

O'Reilly, Terence. "Ignatius of Loyola and the Counter-Reformation: The Hagiographic Tradition." *Heythrop Journal* 31 (1990): 439–70.

Oren, Dan A. *Joining the Club: A History of Jews and Yale*. New Haven, Conn.: Yale University Press, 1985.

Orsi, Robert Anthony. *The Madonna of 115th Street: Faith and Community in Italian Harlem, 1880–1950*. New Haven, Conn.: Yale University Press, 1985.

Padberg, John W. *Colleges in Controversy: The Jesuit Schools in France from Revival to Suppression, 1815–1880*. Cambridge, Mass.: Harvard University Press, 1969.

———. "Development of the *Ratio Studiorum*." In Duminuco, *The Jesuit* Ratio Studiorum.

Padberg, John W., Martin D. O"Keefe, and John L. McCarthy, eds. *For Matters of Greater Moment: The First Thirty Jesuit General Congregations*. St. Louis, Mo.: Institute of Jesuit Sources, 1994.

Palmieri, Patricia. *In Adamless Eden: The Community of Women Faculty at Wellesley*. New Haven, Conn.: Yale University Press, 1995.

Parkman, Francis. *The Jesuits in North America in the Seventeenth Century*. Introduction by Conrad E. Heidenreich and José Brandão. Lincoln: University of Nebraska Press, 1997.

Perlmann, Joel. *Ethnic Differences: Schooling and Social Structure among the Irish, Italians, Jews, and Blacks in an American City, 1880–1935*. New York: Cambridge University Press, 1988.

Perry, Bliss. *And Gladly Teach*. Boston, Mass.: Houghton, Mifflin, 1935.

Perry, Ralph Barton. "Charles William Eliot: His Personal Traits and Essential Creed." *New England Quarterly* 1 (1931): 5–29.

Peterson, George E. *The New England College in the Age of the University*. Amherst, Mass.: Amherst University Press, 1964.

Pius IX. *The Syllabus of Errors*. Reprinted in Corrigan, *The Church and the Nineteenth Century*. Milwaukee, Wis.: Bruce, 1938.

Pius X. *Pascendi Dominici Gregis*. Reprinted in *The Papal Encyclicals, 1903–1939*, edited by Claudia Carlen. Wilmington, N.C.: McGrath, 1981.

Plough, James Howard. "Catholic Colleges and the Catholic Educational Association: The Foundation and Early Years of the C.E.A., 1899–1919." Ph.D. diss., University of Notre Dame, 1967.

Poland, John W. "Some Thoughts on Pedagogics." In *Report of the Fourth Annual Conference of the Association of Catholic Colleges of the United States*. Washington, D.C.: Catholic University of America Press, 1902.

Pollard, Sidney. *The Idea of Progress: History and Society*. New York: Basic Books, 1968.

Porter, Noah. *The Educational Systems of the Puritans and Jesuits Compared*. New York: M. W. Dodd, 1851.

Portier, William L. "Catholic Theology in the United States: 1840–1907." *Horizons* 10 (1983): 317–33.

Post, Waldron Kintzing. *Harvard Episodes*. New York: G. P. Putnam's Sons, 1903.

Potts, David. "American Colleges in the Nineteenth Century: From Localism to Denominationalism." *History of Education Quarterly* 11 (1971): 363–80.

———. "'College Enthusiasm!' as Public Response." *Harvard Educational Review* 47 (1977): 28–42.

Power, Edward J. *Catholic Higher Education in America: A History*. New York: Appleton-Century-Crofts, 1972.

———. *A History of Catholic Higher Education in the United States*. Milwaukee, Wis.: Bruce, 1958.

"Proceedings of a Public Meeting in Behalf of the Society for the Promotion of Collegiate and Theological Education at the West held in Park Street Church, Boston, May 28, 1845." New York: J. F. Trow, 1845.

"Protestantism." *Princeton Review* 9 (January 1837): 1–29.

A Protestant's Resolution Shewing his Reason Why He will not be a PAPIST. 28th ed. London: Thomas Field, 1761.

Quest, Aleck. "The Fast Set at Harvard University." *North American Review* 147 (1888): 524–53.

Rashdall, Hastings. *The Universities of Europe in the Middle Ages*. Oxford, U.K.: Clarendon Press, 1895.

Ravier, André. *Ignatius of Loyola and the Founding of the Society of Jesus*. Translated by Maura Daly, Joan Daly, and Carson Daly, 1973; San Francisco, Calif.: Ignatius Press, 1987.

The Records of the Governor and Company of the Massachusetts Bay in New England. Vol 3, 1644–57. Edited by Nathaniel Shurtleff. Boston, Mass.: By order of the Legislature, 1854.

Reed, John. "College Is Like the World." Reprinted in *The Harvard Book: Selections from Three Centuries*, rev. ed., edited by William Bentinck-Smith. Cambridge, Mass.: Harvard University Press, 1982.

Reher, Margaret Mary. *Catholic Intellectual Life in America: A Historical Study of Persons and Movements*. New York: Macmillan, 1989.

Reuben, Julie A. *The Making of the Modern University: Intellectual Transformation and the Marginalization of Morality*. Chicago, Ill.: University of Chicago Press, 1996.

Rice, Louise. "Jesuit Thesis Prints and the Festive Academic Defence at the Collegio Romano." In O'Malley et al., *The Jesuits: Cultures, Sciences, and the Arts*.

Richards, J. Havens. "The Regents of the University and Our Colleges." *Woodstock Letters* 25 (1896): 124–34.

Richardson, Charles. *A New Dictionary of the English Language.* New York: William Jackson, 1839.

Roberts, Jon H., and James Turner. *The Sacred and Secular University.* Introduction by John F. Wilson. Princeton, N.J.: Princeton University Press, 2000.

Robinson, W. C. "The Attitude of the Educated Protestant Mind toward Catholic Truth." *Catholic World* 54 (1893): 644–51.

Rockwell, William Walker. "The Jesuits as Portrayed by Non-Catholic Historians." *Harvard Theological Review* 7 (1914): 358–77.

Rogers, Nathaniel. "Commencement Address." [1652]. In *Publications of the Colonial Society of Massachusetts,* vol. 31. Boston, Mass.: Published by the Society, 1935.

Roof, Wade Clark. *A Generation of Seekers: The Spiritual Journeys of the Baby Boom Generation.* San Francisco, Calif.: Harper, 1993.

"Roman Catholic Students at Non-Catholic Universities." *Outlook* 75 (1903): 764–65.

Rosenberg, Charles E. *No Other Gods: On Science and American Social Thought.* Baltimore, Md.: Johns Hopkins University Press, 1976.

Rosovsky, Nitza, Pearl K. Bell, and Ronald Steel. *The Jewish Experience at Harvard and Radcliffe: An Introduction to an Exhibition Presented by the Harvard Semitic Museum on the Occasion of Harvard's 350th Anniversary.* Cambridge, Mass.: The Museum, 1986.

Rotundo, E. Anthony. "Body and Soul: Changing Ideals of American Middle-Class Manhood." *Journal of Social History* 16 (1982–83): 23–38.

Rudolph, Frederick. *The American College and University: A History.* Introductory essay and supplemental bibliography by John R. Thelin. 2d ed. Athens: University of Georgia Press, 1990.

———, ed. *Essays on Education in the Early Republic.* Cambridge, Mass.: Harvard University Press, 1965.

Rudy, Willis. "Eliot and Gilman: The History of an Academic Friendship." *Teachers College Record* 54 (1953): 307–18.

Rury, John L. "The Urban Catholic University in the Early Twentieth Century: A Social Profile of DePaul, 1898–1940." *History of Higher Education Annual* 17 (1997): 5–32.

Ryan, Edmund J. "The Teaching of English in College." In *Report of the Third Annual Conference of the Association of Catholic Colleges of the United States.* Washington, D.C.: Catholic University Press of America, 1901.

Ryan, Dennis P. *Beyond the Ballot Box: A Social History of the Boston Irish, 1845–1917.* London: Associated University Presses, 1983.

Ryan, John J. "The St. Paul's Catholic Club." *Harvard Alumni Bulletin* 17 (13 January 1915): 264–65.

Ryan, Mary P. *Cradle of the Middle Class: The Family in Oneida County, New York, 1790–1865.* Cambridge: Cambridge University Press, 1981.

Sadlier, Mrs. J. [Mary Ann]. *The Blakes and Flanagans: A Tale Illustrative of Irish Life in the United States.* New York: D. and J. Sadlier, 1879.

Samson, G. W. "Jesuit Collegiate Instruction, as Affecting Present Questions of Education and Society." In *Proceedings: National Baptist Educational Convention.* New York: W. I. Pooley, 1870.

Santayana, George. *Character and Opinion in the United States.* New York: W. W. Norton, 1921.

———. "The Spirit and Ideals of Harvard University." *Educational Review* 17 (1894): 313–25.

Saunderson, Henry Hallan. *Charles W. Eliot: Puritan Liberal.* New York: Harper & Brothers, 1928.

Schier, Tracy, and Cynthia Russett, eds. *Catholic Women's Colleges in America.* Baltimore, Md.: Johns Hopkins University Press, 2002.

Schmalzbauer, John. *People of Faith: Religious Conviction in American Journalism and Higher Education.* Ithaca, N.Y.: Cornell University Press, 2003.

Schneider, Eric C. *In the Web of Class: Delinquents and Reformers in Boston, 1820s–1930s.* New York: New York University Press, 1992.

Schultenover, David G. *A View from Rome: On the Eve of the Modernist Crisis.* New York: Fordham University Press, 1993.

Schwickerath, Robert. *Jesuit Education: Its History and Principles Viewed in the Light of Modern Educational Problems.* St. Louis, Mo.: B. Herder, 1903.

Seager, Richard Hughes. "Pluralism and the American Mainstream: The View from the World's Parliament of Religions." *Harvard Theological Review* 82 (1989): 301–24.

Seligman, Joel. *The High Citadel: The Influence of Harvard Law School.* Boston, Mass: Houghton, Mifflin, 1978.

Sexton, John Edward. "Charles W. Eliot, Unitarian Exponent of the Doctrine of Toleration in Religion." Ph.D. diss., Fordham University, 1978.

Shaler, Nathaniel. "Discipline in American Colleges." *North American Review* 149 (July 1889): 10–15.

———. "The Scotch Element in the American People." *Atlantic Monthly* 77 (1896): 508–17.

Shannon, William V. *The American Irish: A Political and Social Portrait.* New York: Macmillan, 1963.

Sheldon, Winthrop D. "College-Bred Men in the Business World." *New Englander and Yale Review* 56 (1892): 189–210.

Shepard, Robert S. *God's People in the Ivory Tower: Religion in the Early American University.* Brooklyn, N.Y.: Carlson, 1991.

Shils, Edward. "The Order of Learning in the United States from 1865 to 1920: The Ascendancy of the Universities." In *The Order of Learning: Essays on the Contemporary University,* with an introduction by Philip G. Altbach. New Brunswick, N.J.: Transaction, 1997.

Skerpan, Alfred Lindsay. "A Place for God: Religion, State Universities, and American Society, 1865–1920." Ph.D. diss., University of Wisconsin–Madison, 1998.

Sloan, Douglas. *Faith and Knowledge: Mainline Protestantism and American Higher Education.* Louisville, Ky.: Westminster John Knox Press, 1994.

Slosson, Edwin E. *Great American Universities.* New York: Arno Press, 1977.

Smith, John Talbot. "One of Many." In *His Mayor, The Mayor: And Other Tales.* New York: Vatican Library, 1891.

Smith, Richard Norton. *The Harvard Century: The Making of a University to a Nation.* New York: Simon & Schuster, 1986.

Smith, Ronald A. *Sports and Freedom: The Rise of Big-Time College Athletics.* New York: Oxford University Press, 1988.

Smith, Timothy. "Religion and Ethnicity in America." *American Historical Review* 83 (1978): 1155–85.

Smith, Wilson. "Apologia pro Alma Matre: The College as Community in Ante-Bellum America." In *The Hofstadter Aegis: A Memorial,* edited by Stanley Elkins and Erick McKilrick. New York: Knopf, 1974.

Sollors, Werner, Caldwell Titcomb, and Thomas A. Underwood, eds. *Blacks at Harvard: A Documentary History of African-American Experience at Harvard and Radcliffe.* New York: New York University Press, 1993.

Solomon, Barbara Miller. *Ancestors and Immigrants: A Changing New England Tradition.* Cambridge, Mass.: Harvard University Press, 1956.

——. *In the Company of Educated Women.* New Haven, Conn.: Yale University Press, 1985.

Spalding, J. L. *Education and the Higher Life.* Chicago, Ill.: A. C. McClurg, 1897.

——. *Means and Ends of Education.* Chicago, Ill.: A. C. McClurg, 1895.

——. *Opportunity, and Other Essays and Addresses.* Chicago, Ill.: A. C. McClurg, 1900.

Spitz, Lewis W. "The Importance of the Reformation for the Universities: Culture and Confessions in the Critical Years." In *Rebirth, Reform, and Resilience: Universities in Transition, 1300–1700,* edited by James M. Kittelson and Pamela J. Transue. Columbus: Ohio University Press, 1984.

Stevens, Robert. *Law School: Legal Education in America from the 1850s to the 1980s.* Studies in Legal History, edited by G. Edward White. Chapel Hill: University of North Carolina Press, 1983.

Stevenson, Louise L. *Scholarly Means to Evangelical Ends: The New Haven Scholars and the Transformation of Higher Learning in America, 1830–1890.* Baltimore, Md.: Johns Hopkins University Press, 1986.

——. *The Victorian Homefront: American Thought and Culture, 1860–1880.* Boston: Twayne, 1991.

Stonex, W. G. "Ignatius Loyola and His Followers." *Ladies' Repository* 20 (1860): 609–11.

Storr, Richard J. *Harper's University: The Beginnings.* Chicago, Ill.: University of Chicago Press, 1966.

Story, Ronald. *The Forging of an Aristocracy: Harvard and the Boston Upper Class, 1800–1870.* Middletown, Conn.: Wesleyan University Press, 1980.

——. "Harvard and the Boston Brahmins: A Study in Institutional and Class Development, 1800–1865." *Journal of Social History* 8 (1974–75): 94–121.

Strauss, Gerald. *Luther's House of Learning: Indoctrination of the Young in the German Reformation.* Baltimore, Md.: Johns Hopkins University Press, 1978.

Sullivan, Lawrence E. "Histories and Rituals: A Case of a National Rite of Mourning." Tempe: Department of Religious Studies, Arizona State University, 1991.

Sutherland, Arthur E. *The Law at Harvard: A History of Men and Ideas, 1817–1967.* Cambridge, Mass.: Harvard University Press, 1967.

Synnott, Marcia Graham. *The Half-Opened Door: Discrimination and Admissions at Harvard, Yale, and Princeton, 1900–1970.* Westport, Conn.: Greenwood Press, 1979.

"System of Education." In *Catalogue of the Officers and Students of Boston College, 1898–1899.* N.p. Published for Boston College.

Tewksbury, Donald G. *The Founding of American Colleges and Universities before the Civil War.* 1932; New York: Arno Press, 1969.

Thernstrom, Stephan. *The Other Bostonians: Poverty and Progress in the American Metropolis, 1880–1970.* Cambridge, Mass.: Harvard University Press, 1973.

———. "'Poor but Hopefull Scholars.'" In Bailyn et al., *Glimpses of the Harvard Past.*

Thwaites, Reuben Gold, ed. *The Jesuit Relations and Allied Documents: Travels and Explorations of the Jesuit Missionaries in New France, 1610–1701; The Original French, Latin, and Italian Texts, with English Translations and Notes.* 73 vols. Cleveland, Ohio: Burrows Bros., 1896–1901.

Thwing, Charles F. "President Eliot's Twenty-five Years of Service." *Forum* 17 (1894): 355–71.

Townsend, Kim. *Manhood at Harvard: William James and Others.* New York: W. W. Norton, 1996.

Trautmann, Thomas R. "The Revolution in Ethnological Time," *Man,* n.s. 27 (1992): 379–97.

Turner, James. *Without God, Without Creed: The Origins of Unbelief in America.* Baltimore, Md.: Johns Hopkins University, 1985.

Tuveson, Ernest L. *Redeemer Nation: The Idea of America's Millennial Role.* Chicago, Ill.: University of Chicago, 1968, 1980.

Tyack, David, and Larry Cuban. *Tinkering toward Utopia: A Century of Public School Reform.* Cambridge, Mass.: Harvard University Press, 1995.

Varga, Nicholas. "Rejoining the American Educational Mainstream: Loyola College, 1890–1931 as a Case Study." *Records of the American Catholic Historical Society* 96 (1986): 67–82.

Veysey, Laurence R. *The Emergence of the American University.* Chicago, Ill.: University of Chicago Press, 1965.

Wagoner, Jennings L. "An American Compromise: Charles W. Eliot, Black Education, and the New South." In *Education and the Rise of the New South,* edited by Ronald K. Goodenow and Arthur O. White. Boston, Mass.: G. K. Hall, 1981.

———. "Charles W. Eliot, Immigrants, and the Decline of American Idealism." *Biography* 8 (1985): 25–36.

Walch, Timothy. *Parish School: American Catholic Parochial Education from Colonial Times to the Present.* New York: Crossroad, 1996.

Walsh, Francis Robert. "The Boston Pilot: A Newspaper for the Irish Immigrant, 1829–1908." Ph.D. diss., Boston University, 1968.

Walton, Susan S. *To Preserve the Faith: Catholic Charities in Boston, 1870–1930.* New York: Garland, 1993.

Wangler, Thomas E. "American Catholic Expansionism: 1886–1894." *Harvard Theological Review* 75 (1982): 269–93.

Warner, Sam Bass, Jr. *Streetcar Suburbs: The Process of Growth in Boston (1870–1900).* Cambridge, Mass.: Harvard University Press, 1962.

Warren, Charles. *History of the Harvard Law School and of Early Legal Conditions in America.* 3 vols. New York: Lewis, 1908.

Webster, Noah. *An American Dictionary of the English Language.* Springfield, Mass.: George and Charles Merriam, 1850.

———. *An American Dictionary of the English Language.* Springfield, Mass.: G. & C. Merriam, 1864.

Wechsler, Harold S. "An Academic Gresham's Law: Group Repulsion as a Theme in American Higher Education." *Teachers College Record* 82 (1981): 567–88.

———. *The Qualified Student: A History of Selective College Admission in America.* New York: Wiley, 1977.

Weiss, Bernard J. "Duquesne University: A Case Study of the Catholic University and the Urban Ethnic, 1878–1928." In *American Education and the European Immigrant, 1840–1940,* edited by Bernard J. Weiss. Urbana: University of Illinois Press, 1982.

Wells, William. "The Soldiers of the Church Militant." *Ladies' Repository* 34 (1874): 27–32.

West, Andrew F. "Is There a Democracy of Studies?" *Atlantic Monthly* 84 (1899): 821–27.

White, Andrew Dickson. *Autobiography of Andrew Dickson White.* 2 vols. New York: Century, 1907.

———. *A History of the Warfare of Science with Theology in Christendom.* New York: D. Appleton, 1896.

Wiebe, Robert H. *The Search for Order, 1877–1920.* New York: Hill & Wang, 1967.

Wilbee, Victor Roy. "The Religious Dimensions of Three Presidencies in a State University: Presidents Tappan, Haven, and Angell at the University of Michigan." Ph.D. diss., University of Michigan, 1967.

Wills, Jeffrey. "University Community." In *The Catholics of Harvard Square,* edited by Jeffrey Wills. Petersham, Mass.: Saint Bede's Publications, 1993.

Wind, James P. *The Bible and the University: The Messianic Vision of William Rainey Harper.* Atlanta, Ga.: Scholars Press, 1987.

Winterer, Caroline. *The Culture of Classicism: Ancient Greece, Rome, and American Intellectual Life, 1780–1910.* Baltimore, Md.: Johns Hopkins University Press, 2002.

Wittke, Carl. *The Irish in America.* Baton Rouge: Louisiana State University Press, 1956.

Woods, Henry, "The Catholic College—Its Chief Danger." *National Catholic Educational Association Bulletin* 31 (1934): 58–72.

Woods, Robert A., and Albert J. Kennedy. *The Zone of Emergence: Observations of the Lower, Middle, and Upper Working Class Communities of Boston, 1905–14,* edited with preface by Sam B. Warner. Cambridge, Mass.: Harvard University Press, 1962.

Woodward, Kenneth. "Catholic Higher Education: What Happened?" *Commonweal* (4 April 1993): 15–18.

Worcester, Joseph E. *Dictionary of the English Language.* Boston, Mass.: Hickling, Swan, & Brewer, 1860.

The World's Columbian Catholic Congresses and Educational Exhibit. Chicago, Ill.: J. S. Hyland, 1893.

Ziolkowski, Eric J., ed. *A Museum of Faiths: Histories and Legacies of the 1893 World's Parliament of Religion.* Atlanta, Ga.: Scholars Press, 1993.

Zwierlein, Frederick J. *The Life and Letters of Bishop McQuaid.* 3 vols. Rochester, N.Y.: Art Print Shop, 1925–27.